Medieval Slavery and Liberation

Medieval Slavery and Liberation

Pierre Dockès

Translated by
Arthur Goldhammer

The University of Chicago Press

Pierre Dockès is professor of political economy at the University of Lyons. He is the author of *L'Espace dans la pensée économique; L'Internationale du capital;* and, with J. Michel Servet, *Sauvages et ensauvagés.*

Frontispiece
Servant offering wine to his master; eleventh-century historiated initial (Bibliothèque municipale, Reims; photo Giraudon)

Originally published in France as *La Libération médiévale,* © 1979, Flammarion.

The University of Chicago Press, Chicago 60637
The University of Chicago Press, Ltd., London
© 1982 by The University of Chicago
All rights reserved. Published 1982
Printed in the United States of America
88 87 86 85 84 83 82   5 4 3 2 1

Library of Congress Cataloging in Publication Data

Dockès, Pierre.
  Medieval slavery and liberation.

  Translation of: La libération médiévale.
  Bibliography: p.
  Includes index.
  1. Slavery—History.   2. Slavery—Emancipation—
History.   I. Title.
HT865.D613   305.5'6   81-11594
ISBN: 0-226-15482-3   AACR2

Contents

Acknowledgments

I should like to thank Philippe Didier, Nicole Dockès, Stephen Marglin, Jean-Pierre Poly, Christian Schnakenbourg, the A.E.H. research group at the University of Lyons II and particularly Maurice Comte, Daniel Dufourt, Hubert Houdoy, Gerard Klotz, Paul Rousset, and Jean-Michel Servet, and the economists of the Institut Vizioz of Guadeloupe, especially Eryc Edinval and Claude Deglas, for all our discussions and for their criticisms of my various writings. I should also like to point out that this work, which relates to research carried out over a number of years in conjunction with Bernard Rosier, has profited from innumerable discussions with him and from a series of working papers of which he was the author.[1]

The pride of man makes him love to domineer, and nothing mortifies him so much as to be obliged to condescend to persuade his inferiors. Wherever the law allows it, and the nature of the work can afford, therefore, he will generally prefer the service of slaves to that of freemen.

Adam Smith, *An Inquiry into the Nature and Causes of the Wealth of Nations,* bk. 3, chap. 2

Why, Clinias, the human animal is a kittle beast and so, clearly, is not likely to be, or become, readily amenable to the indispensable distinction between real slave and real free man and master, and so this form of property presents a difficulty. . . . When we face all this evidence we may well feel perplexed to know how to treat the whole problem.

Plato, *Laws* 6. 777b-c

Introduction

Slavery? A bad memory a chapter of history now definitively behind us? Legitimate historical curiosity apart, why study this ancient form of social relation? Why try to understand what caused ancient slavery to come to an end?

Because to understand how and why slavery came to an end in the early Middle Ages is not a matter of indifference to anyone who believes in the possibility of an end to wage labor. Present fashion favors conceptions of history according to which all social revolutions, past and future, are doomed to failure, and all social struggle is inane, because when all is said and done, the only result is the replacement of one master by another. There is no denying that after centuries of struggle, exploitation does indeed continue to exist. Only its form has changed. The surplus labor extracted here and there by the masters of today's world is not smaller in proportion to the total amount of labor than the surplus extracted long ago.[1] But the change in the conditions of exploitation is not, in my view, negligible: the factory is (as Fourier was the first to write, and as Marx repeated after him) the prison palliated, the roman *villa* was a prison pure and simple. What is important is the history, the striving for liberation. Even if an end to alienation is a utopian goal, it is nevertheless a concrete goal: utopia in a concrete form has always loomed on the horizon of social struggle, giving direction to the battle. The danger of social regression, however, is far from negligible.

Slavery is not one type of domination and exploitation among others, not merely an aspect of one bygone phase of history. Slavery is the primary and primordial relation of exploitation, that form of exploitation out of which serfdom and wage labor arise, and that form toward which the master always strives: only force can compel the master to forgo the use of slaves.[2] Whence the many "ends" of slavery, and its many rebirths.

For the nineteenth-century positivist, who took from the *philosophes* of the Enlightenment his belief in the progress of mankind and forged from that belief a certainty of steady advance toward a radiant future, impelled by science and technology, slavery was something that belonged in the museum of horrors, and freedom the destination of mankind's journey. To be frank, Michelet's *Histoire de France* is not a book that one can read with impunity, but if one "dives in," let it be with eyes open.

For the mechanistic "Marxist," the practitioner of that "general historico-philosophical theory" that Marx explicitly rejected after he and Engels had produced it,[3] slavery, in itself a considerable improvement over cannibalism or the practice of massacring prisoners of war,[4] gave way to serfdom in the first stage of progress, and then serfdom itself gave way to wage labor, which was but a formal emancipation. Finally and inevitably the social revolution to come will make a real emancipation possible. This unidirectional march of history, never reversed in any important respect, is a consequence of the determination of the course of history by the economic base, "in the last instance." The end of history will come in the form of a "revival"—a word Marx at first wrote down, then repented of, in the first draft of a letter to Vera Zasulich[5]—of the primitive communist social relations characteristic of early societies, but only after prodigious development of the productive forces of social labor.

On this view, at a certain level of development of the productive forces, slavery was necessary, but later, after further development, it inevitably gave way to the feudal mode of production, which embodied social relations of a new type corresponding to the enhanced productive powers of society. Thus, as Marx observed in a well-known remark—or was it a joke?—different types of mills give you different types of social relations. Furthermore, it is held that the underlying trend was progressive, despite the various "revivals" of slavery that took place between the sixteenth and the nineteenth century. Slavery, as Marx tells us, was indeed necessary to American capitalism, and therefore to the capitalist world, but its scope remained limited. The future, so far as it could be foretold, seemed to be one from which slavery had vanished.

Then came Nazism, the labor camps, the death camps, and the use of millions of slave-laborers in the factories of Germany to further the German war effort.[6] Was German victory unthinkable? What if the "thousand-year Reich," the empire based on slavery promised by the Führer, had turned out to be more than a bad dream? What protected us from a "revival" of this sort: was it the development of the productive forces that protected us then, and protects us even now?

> So was hätt einmal fast die Welt regiert!
> Die Völker wurden seinen Herr, jedoch
> Dass keiner uns zu früh da triumphiert—
> Der Schoss ist fruchtbar noch, aus dem das kroch.[7]

> [Such a thing once almost ruled the world! The peoples of the world mastered it in the end, but don't let anyone sing too soon of victory: the womb from which it crawled can still bear fruit.—Trans.]

If this form of slavery could emerge from the capitalist mode of production, if slavery could be reborn in our own day, perhaps the reason is that the present level of development of the productive forces is compatible with this type of social relation. The "revival" of primitive communism at quite another level of development need not be the only possible revival! The truth about the concentration camps of the U.S.S.R. under Stalin is just now coming to light, and it is far more heinous than anything that the "specialists in anti-Communism" of the fifties had to say. Solzhenitsyn makes J'ai choisi la liberté look like a novel for spinsters! So capitalism is not the only belly full of horrors, and not the only system to exhibit if not slavery then at least a kind of forced labor that closely resembles it.[8]

Hence I believe that the present analysis of ancient slavery may be of some use. For slavery, too, "the peoples of the world mastered it in the end." Once again we raise the question that Marc Bloch asked himself on the eve of his murder by the Nazis: "How and why did ancient slavery come to an end?"

It bears emphasizing that when we use the term "slavery" to characterize contemporary phenomena, the word is not being used vaguely or imprecisely. In order to give a precise definition of what we mean by slavery, though, we must look to antiquity, the period during which slavery was the chief form of exploitation and oppression. Only then can we pin down what the word might mean, and how slavery is to be distinguished from other types of social relation that existed alongside it in the ancient world and afterward.

I. Definition of Slavery

To the question What is slavery? we may first give an answer based on law, on the right of property in another human being, comprising three elements: *usus, fructus, abusus.* Consequent upon the legal definition of the property right is the purchase or sale of the slave commodity.[9] Only as a first approximation can this answer be regarded as satisfactory, and then only if we trace it back to the social relation of which the legal relation is generally, but not always, the reflection.

De facto forms of slavery exist in which property rights over the body of the slave are not recognized, but in which to all intents and purposes the master enjoys uninfringed liberty to use the slave's body as he wishes (to extract from it surplus labor, services, or pleasure), along with rights over any children born to the slave, and the right, either absolute or subject to legal limitation, to kill the slave if he so chooses. Here, too, trade in slaves follows as a consequence, though slave trade need not be systematized or legalized.[10]

A) Slavery and Death

Let us begin by citing a standard definition of slavery: "The slave is a person, male or female, subject to the absolute dominion of a master in virtue of purchase, inheritance, or war."[11] The relation envisaged by this definition would seem to be based on power over life and death, i.e., on the freedom to make use of another human being's life and to inflict his death. Yet such a power over life and death belongs also to the *paterfamilias* in regard to his children, to the sovereign in regard to all, to the magistrate in regard to prisoners at law, and to the warrior, who assumes it over his prisoners of war. These are all different situations: Can they be grouped together?

Such a grouping has three focal points: he who has given life can take it back (the case of the father in regard to his child); he who has committed a grave misdeed must be punished by death; he who has been vanquished on the field of battle must die. Slavery follows as a consequence: the slave is one who should have been killed and who survives by the grace of the master; he is one of the "living dead" (*mort-vivant*).

The word *servus*, "slave," in Roman law originally referred to a person whose life had been spared (*servatus*[12]) by grace. Jurists have come up with some fine phrases to characterize this condition. D'Olive (du Mesnil), for instance, writes that "servitude is the image of death," and Boutaric observes that the slave, who has presumably made his last will and testament prior to his capture, is "held to be dead from that moment . . . *he is in a state of suspense, as it were.*"[13] The point is one of the utmost importance for the comprehension of slavery and the struggles of slaves throughout history.

To be reprieved, to be living dead is the fate of the prisoner of war, who would traditionally have been killed by his captor. If the captor *allows his prisoner to live,*[14] the latter recognizes the former as his master, and in fact cannot but so recognize him. It is also the fate of the debtor whose creditor forgoes his right to exact his due in blood (Shylock was not a figment of Shakespeare's imagination). The *paterfamilias* can kill because he has given life; and it is because he can kill his children that he can also sell them: historically, this has been one of the most deeply rooted sources of slavery.

Leaving aside the case of the father, who has indeed given life and can lay claim to the life that he has given, we may say that slavery comes into being when the master, who not only might have but legitimately ought to have killed another human being forbears to do so. Thus it is easy to see the difference between the master's power of life and death over his slave and the sovereign's power of life and death over his subjects. An absolute ruler can always deprive one of his subjects of life, whereas the master should already have killed the person who has become his slave. In other words, a person who lives at all times in peril of his life under an absolute ruler or a totalitarian regime is not (not yet!) one of the "living dead," not living in "suspended" nonexistence, as does the slave, who has already been "condemned" to death.[15]

Not only is the slave one whose life has been spared by the grace of his master; according to the traditions of antiquity and philosophical teaching down to Hegel,[16] he is also one who is afraid of death. The slave is aware of his servitude not only because he is cognizant of the existence of his master, but also because he has tasted death, the experience essential to his condition, and been afraid of it: This consciousness, [i.e., the slave] is none other than a consciousness that has endured not merely some slight anxiety over this or that thing or at a particular instant, but rather a consciousness that has been affected by anxiety through and through, because it has experienced the fear of death, the absolute master."[17]

The experience of death precedes servitude: the slave is one who has preferred life to liberty, one who, of two masters, has chosen the master who "allows him to live," rather than "death, the absolute master." Inevitably, then, an end to servitude implies acceptance of death, the experience by which servitude came into being. No emancipation is possible until the slave dares hazard death, which accounts for the terror of an uprising that constantly haunts the masters, as well as for the terror by which they rule. And this also accounts for the violence of slave revolts, and for their infrequent occurrence, since those who venture to rebel know that truly they are asking to be given liberty or given death, and that the latter wish is almost always granted. Echoes of these rebel slaves have reverberated through the centuries, from the comrades of Spartacus to the maroons of the Antilles, from the Jews of Treblinka to the *zeks* of Kengir.[18]

It would be a mistake to regard the connection between slavery and death exclusively as a consequence of the (private) master's recognized power of life and death over his slaves. In many circumstances, in fact, this power is limited by law, so that the master can administer punishment only in certain cases, for certain crimes; the state retains the right to mutilate or kill the slave, the master being liable to punishment if he should flout the law. This is an interesting development: the state emerges as the administrator of the collective interest of the master class and the sole agency authorized to exercise the supreme power of that class, the right to put the slave to death.

It should be noted that in this situation the right to execute (or mutilate) the slave is taken from the masters only to be given in turn to *their* state, that is, to themselves, but in a socialized form, to the masters collectively. The master-slave relationship is still dominated by death as the final recourse, but administered by the state, by the masters collectively.

That the state rather than the masters individually now exercises the power to inflict death is a change of some moment, however. Collectively, the interests of the masters are not the same as their individual interests. The state, in other words, has a certain autonomy. It may happen, for example, that an individual master will be reluctant to put a criminal slave to death for fear of suffering a considerable financial loss (or even to mutilate the slave, for fear of losing a part of his productivity). Crime by slaves must be put down ruthlessly, however, for it is always damaging to the interests of the masters as a group, to the slave system, and hence to the state. In the Antilles in the eighteenth century, for example,[19] masters were reluctant to put fugitive slaves to death when they were captured. The state, however, did the job and reimbursed the master for his loss.[20]

Finally, in the case of the African slave shipped to America or the barbarian led away in chains by the Roman armies, the slave was a "living dead man" not only because he had been physically reprieved but also, and perhaps primarily, because his ties to his native soil, his family, and his community had been broken. Deprived of all rights to land, he was a man without a country, a stranger to every community, and dead because he was cut off from the cults of family worship: when he died, no one would offer up a sacrifice.[21] Henceforth the slave could no longer conceive of himself as having a human existence, i.e., as a citizen attached to some part of the earth, as a member of a family. He was the stranger par excellence. Stranger by origin as one who came from another part of the world, he was also a stranger to himself, since he was part of no community.[22] He was, in a word, *apolis*. This accounts for the dream of Spartacus' return, the dream of reestablishing ties with one's native community, or, failing that, of reconstructing a community along the same lines as the community of origin: in other words, that anomalous vision, the city of slaves. It also explains why slave cults always attempt to dig up the cults of old, though invariably with an excruciating awareness that the course of history cannot be turned back, that the severed "roots" cannot be knitted back together.

It is likely that this severing of roots also explains why slaves have been able to find refuge in the bosom of the master's family and religion, being assimilated in a sense as children of the master. Cults of the master's family, ties with his name and lineage, stand in contradiction to slave cults and a servile "class consciousness" (a current example of which may be seen in the coexistence of voodoo cults with Christianity), a contradiction that is necessary, given the social and moral death attendant upon the cutting of the slave's roots: the rootless slave goes through life as both the "child" and the enemy of his master.

Accordingly, when we come to examine social practice, we find this same contradiction in the form of ambivalent attitudes. Destructiveness and rebellion are always smoldering, ready to flare up into open revolt, but resignation is undeniably also a fact of life. To be one of the living dead is not to choose between resignation and revolt (whether the question is one of slaves or of concentration camp prisoners), but rather to be resigned and rebellious at the same time.[23] It is thus easy to understand why the masters are perpetually astonished when their "good" slaves fall back into savage ways and rebellion breaks out.

Reprieved from death, set apart, isolated from every community, hence dead, alien to citizenship, homeless, a stranger to himself, the slave is no longer a man, but a member of a subhuman species located somewhere between women and animals: we have only to recall Aristotle's well-known classification, in which the slave was an animate instrument, like an animal, but more efficient than an animal, being endowed with speech.[24] It is perhaps less well known that, during the Middle Ages, for example, slaves were generally classed with the live-stock. This is the case with the Salic law. Burgundian law sets up a hierarchy of animality: a slave is worth five and a half oxen or five hogs. Salic law lays it down that the male slave is the equivalent of a stallion, the female slave of a mare.[25]

P. Bonnassié adds that proscriptions of sexual relations between free women and male slaves generally appear in the texts together with proscriptions against bestiality; the barbarian penitentials, such as that of the Visigoths, took great interest in both these monstrous crimes. The only case in which the slave is not classed with the animals is that of sexual relations between the master and a female slave.[26]

Most important of all was the identification of the slave with the beast of burden as an instrument of labor. For Aristotle (who held that the day that slavery would end because shuttles would do their own weaving lay as far in the future as the day that hens would have teeth!) it is above all because slavery is and always will be economically indispensable that it is almost natural, resting on a hierarchy of specializations that nature has imposed on men, in mind and body. Because of this hierarchy, transmitted from generation to generation by heredity, some, the "virtuous" victors in battle, are predestined to be masters, while others, the vanquished, are no less predestined to be slaves (where the judgment rendered by combat reveals the inborn inequality).[27]

B) The Slave System: Relations of Production and the Economic Formation of Society

Why does the master, public or private, spare the life of his slave? Because he intends to "profit" from the slave's labor, use his services, or enjoy him for pleasure.

Let us first consider the case where utilization of the slave's labor power gives rise to surplus labor, extracted in the form of a surplus product (material goods).

Taken collectively, the slaves of a Roman *villa* (the collective slave) work a certain number of hours in order to produce their food and clothing, and the rest of the time in order to produce goods that will *either* be consumed directly "at the table" of the master (a "precocious" instance of this use of slaves was the familial slavery that existed in Rome prior to the great conquests, and a late instance is to be found in the autarchic *villae* of the late empire) *or* be sold on the market as commodities. In the latter case, the slaves are productive laborers: *their uti-*

lization enriches their master. When surplus labor is not sold but, in its material form, is used to provide the master with the necessities of life and, in some cases, accumulated (for instance, in such construction projects as barns, canals, castles, and so forth), the situation is similar. When the services rendered by the slave are intangible and not destined for sale,[28] hence consumed on the spot by the master, the question is still more complex.

If the services are rendered within the confines of the *villa*, it is possible to reckon in terms of the total number of slaves associated with the operation, or, in other words, in terms of the "collective slave," the producer of surplus labor. In many cases, however, slaves are used outside the *villa* proper and are not associated with the attempt to extract a surplus product: they are expenses to be deducted from income, rather than the means of earning it.[29] In Rome in particular, there were large numbers of urban slaves, symbols of wealth and power, who served their master in his quest for a variety of pleasures, tangible and intangible, and enabled him to display the preeminence of his family, to make his "greatness" conspicuous. There is nothing to prevent one from extending the notion of the collective slave to society as a whole, taking the view that slaves of all kinds, whether productive or not, are servile creatures and hence elements of the collective slave, which is productive as such. We would rather leave the nonproductive urban slaves out of account (in the context of the present study, which in no way pretends to be exhaustive, this will most likely mean forgetting about them altogether!), and we shall "more or less" exclude them (see below) from the slave class.

It is most important to bear in mind that there exist societies in which slaves do mainly household service, rarely productive labor. Slaves may be luxury goods, sexual objects, ornaments, symbols of wealth; they may even be stockpiled for future sacrifice (as in certain precolonial African slave societies). In cases such as these, there is slavery but no *slave system* [*esclavage, mais pas esclavagisme*].

If there is to be a slave system, then, slavery must constitute a relation of production. The collective slave must be a productive worker, a source of income for the master. Originally the criminal or prisoner of war who is spared may be put to work in the service of the master. This quickly leads to a state of affairs in which the slave is produced (by means of sexual reproduction or razzia) in order to be put to productive use generally mediated by sale on the market: the slave has become a commodity. The master-slave relation thus becomes a relation of production.

In consequence, there is a sharp distinction between the slave system and such similar systems as prisons and concentration camps. In the latter the individual is not enslaved *in order to* become a productive worker giving rise to surplus labor; it is rather because the individual is politically hostile to the regime or a criminal that society "profits" from his incarceration by extracting from him a surplus product.[30]

In the societies of ancient Rome and of the early medieval West slavery was (became) a relation of production, like serfdom and wage labor, at least in regard to the slaves of the villas.

In order to speak of a slave system, however, a second condition must also be met: slavery must be the predominant relation of production. This, as we shall see, was the case in Rome during a relatively brief period, stretching at most from the first century B.C. to the early third century A.D.

It is possible, however, to characterize certain situations as preceding or succeeding a slave system. We may say that conditions preceding the erection of a slave system obtain when slaves are found performing productive labor domestically, and are neither mere ornaments nor symbols but producers of food and clothing, of a surplus product from which the master draws the necessities of life and which may even be accumulated. Even if this relation is not the predominant one in a given society, it may tend, as we shall see, to become so.

When the relative importance of slavery as a relation of production declines, the situation is that which succeeds the existence of a slave system. This was the case between the third and the tenth century: collectively, the slaves in the Carolingian villas were still productive. In the end the ebb of slave relations left practically no slave in western Europe by the tenth century. If we look, however, at the Mediterranean world in its entirety, matters stand quite differently: while the number of productive slaves declined in relation to the number of slaves who rendered services only, still no break is evident until the renaissance of (regional) slave systems in modern times (sixteenth to nineteenth centuries).[31]

C) Serfdom

When a slave system declines we may ask what the connection is between the social relations of slavery and the subsequent relations of production, which, for the sake of simplicity, we shall call serfdom. When we say "subsequent," we do not mean to imply that serfdom always arises out of slavery. There are cases in which the peasantry was subjugated directly in the wake of conquest, and other cases in which the subjugation of the collectivity bears a close resemblance to the mode of production often described as "Asiatic." In the eastern provinces of the Roman Empire the peasantry as a whole was subjugated in this way by overlords, and yet this was by no means the consequence of the degeneration of a slave system.

In western Europe, particularly Gaul, almost the entire peasantry was reduced to serfdom in about the tenth century.[32] This came about for two reasons. First, the status of the free rural population declined. This was a trend that began in the late empire with the rise of the colonate (when the freeholder became a *colonus*, rather similar in many respects to the medieval serf) and resumed in the early Middle Ages.[33] Second, the status of slaves rose. As we shall see, this twofold process can be understood only as the twin aspects of a more general trend; it precludes our viewing serfdom simply as a degenerate form of slavery and suggests rather that we ought to think of serfdom as the result of a long and intricate process of homogenization.

Still, the Roman slave (*servus*) was granted individual lodging and a plot of land (in the cultivation of which he enjoyed relative autonomy). This process was known as domiciling or "hutting" (*casement*, *chasement* in French), and the domiciled slave, or *servus casatus*, was the forerunner of the serf (for which the Latin word *servus* was again used). The persistence of the term—even if its use was far from universal—makes it clear that the serf was seen as a logical successor to the slave and that serfdom was at least in part a post–slave system.

The problem is to distinguish clearly between the situations of slave and serf. Legally, the *servus casatus* still had the status of a slave. But in actuality, supposing that he enjoyed relative autonomy at home and at work, his situation was quite different. This objective difference is indicative of a "shift" toward serfdom, which was all the more significant in that there was hardly any difference at all between the tenant of an ingenuous (i.e., freeborn) tenure and the *servus casatus*, or domiciled slave so far as their real situation was concerned. Hence the formal liberty of the freeholder and the formal subjection of the domiciled slave tended more and more to merge in the single status of the man of a master. It is known that personal status (slave/freeman) rubbed off on the status of the tenure (servile/ingenuous) to such an extent that the freeman who took up a servile tenure became subject to the conditions of servitude attaching to the land, and vice versa. Owing to such "mixed" occupations, marriages, and the influence of the lord's power—an inescapable reality—homogenization went on steadily throughout the early Middle Ages.

If it is relatively easy to see how the serf came to be a serf, it is sometimes more difficult to distinguish between the serf and the (as yet) free man,[35] owing to local, regional, and historical differences, as well as to the confusion between personal status and the status of the land

and between de jure and de facto situations. Legally, serfdom was frequently defined by special prohibitions: mortmain (prohibition or limitation of the right to transfer property at the time of death), prohibition
of *formariage* (marriage out of rank or condition) without special authorization (which could be purchased), prohibition or limitation of
choice of domicile and change of location. Two points need to be made,
however. First, these restrictions may be proof not so much of the existence of a legal status of serf as of a situation of dependence.[36] Hardly
ever are all of them found to be in force simultaenously, moreover, and
no one alone is sufficient to prove the existence of a serf status. Second,
while it is true that the serf, or the servile tenure, was frequently taxed
more heavily and arbitrarily, particularly in regard to *corvées*, we find no
general law applicable to this case, either.

To simplify matters, one might choose to focus on a perhaps typical
situation (though it may have occurred no more frequently than others),
in which the serf, a former *servus casatus* or *colonus*, had been or was
just now being (1) deprived of the right to leave the domain, to marry,
or to transfer property without authorization from the master, (2) obliged
to perform extensive labor on the demesne, and (3) forced to pay taxes
(generally in kind) on his tenure. What made the serf a serf, as distinct
from a slave, was autonomy in his family life and working conditions
on the one hand and the inescapable fact of power over life and limb
on the other. As to the question of economic and domestic autonomy,
the problem is that we find situations running the gamut from the gang
laborer to the serf. If we regard the "pure" slave system as one based
on labor gangs, in which the slaves lived crowded together in ergastula[37]
or barns and were fed at the master's expense, candor obliges us to
acknowledge that there were also many "impure" forms, in which the
slave might have the benefit of a small hut in which he lived together
with something like a family group, or even a tiny enclosed plot, such
as the Negro slaves in the Antilles possess, and yet remain a slave who
worked chiefly in a labor gang on the demesne. Such a situation bears
a strong resemblance to that of the servus casatus. The only distinction
between the two lies in the presence of some real autonomy in domestic
life (a home in which the man is "king in his castle") and in working
conditions (the serf being free to "manage" his plot in accordance with
rules laid down by the collectivity); neither situation being precisely
delineated, this distinction is not always clear-cut.

In view of his relative autonomy, the serf has hardly anything in
common with that figure of living death, the slave. Throughout the early
Middle Ages the slave continued to be punishable at will by imprisonment, shackling, mutilation in a variety of ways, crucifixion, and so

forth. This very likely continued to be the lot of the domiciled slave, at least initially. But his domestic, physical, and economic independence—inextricably bound up with the shift in the balance of power between the *servi* as a group and the master—led to an evolution in the direction of "serfdom." Legal remnants of the old status (like mortmain) persisted in the new, but with the relative homogenization of the peasantry, now more or less generally brought into line with the condition of the serf in both legal status and real circumstances, those who obtained exemptions from those legal restrictions came to be regarded as privileged. *Freedom thus became a privilege* (and throughout the ancien régime, the expression "our liberties" signified "our privileges"). In Rome men had in principle been free, and slaves were dead men who had been reprieved. In the tenth century the general law for the peasant masses was servitude (even if the texts still made reference to Rome), and the struggle for emancipation was a fight for a *renaissance*.

A further problem stems from the fact that slavery persisted in western Europe until the tenth century, and well after that in the Mediterranean world (not to mention its avatars in the modern world). What is more, there was no slave system in the eastern provinces of the Roman Empire, where the entire peasantry was subjugated. In addition, the late empire witnessed the rise of the colonate, an event of importance sufficient to allow us to speak of a first "end" to slavery. Slavery, finally, was different in each locality. In order to take account of social relations of so many diverse forms (spatially and temporally), it is convenient to introduce the notion of an "economic formation of society."[38]

In this work we are going to study particular social formations. On the one hand we shall be looking at the social formation usually referred to as the western portion of the Roman Empire (Italy, Gaul chiefly, Spain, Britain). On the other hand, we shall also be focusing on the early medieval social formation in the same geographical area.

The diversity to be found on every level of the analysis is the source of much difficulty.

To begin with, the economic formation of society (abbreviated hereafter as EFS; see below for a discussion of the term—Trans.) associated with the western empire can be studied only in relation to other EFS's, e.g., those associated with the eastern portion of the empire, the rest of the world, or the barbarian peoples. Culture, history, language, social relations, family relations, religion (just to cite a few noteworthy elements of these EFS's) are all items of difference not only between the empire and the barbarians, but also between the two major sections of the empire itself.

Still more delicate is the question of diversity within the western imperial EFS itself. This diversity is so great that it is not a priori evident that one can speak of a single EFS: Rome and Italy, Italy and Gaul or Spain, Britain—each of these might be taken to constitute a distinct social formation. And what prodigious diversity we find from locality to locality! We can scarcely imagine it at present, so far have we come toward worldwide homogenization under capitalism. There was indeed the Roman "cement" that held the empire together, some of which is still visible even today in great public works and a far-flung urban civilization,[39] but in the countryside there were a great many local particularities, especially in regard to social relations.

At a specific time and place, let us say in the early days of the late empire in southern Gaul, we find urban domestic slaves, urban slaves working as craftsmen in workshops, other slaves living together under a single roof, slaves practicing the liberal professions, freed slaves working as independent artisans, freed slaves and freemen working for wages (not only in households—this was seldom the case because of domestic slavery—but in the pay of businessmen, chiefly merchants, of course, hence paid by commercial capital) and, in the countryside, gang laborers on a vast scale, but even at this early date also *coloni* (pre-serfdom), peasant freeholders (still), and new or ongoing peasant communities: What variety!

If we now look at individual localities, we find this impression of variety strengthened even further. In particular, the relative importance of these various types of social relations varied widely from place to place, and the whole structure was subject to a complex process of evolution, the tempo and tendency of which were again different from one area to the next, and even divergent. Thus it is clear that any historical analysis of this period must be based on local history.

It is not enough, however, to gather factual data about this wealth of local history, because to gather data, and to make sense of the facts, one must have a theory, and to have a theory one needs to know what were the most important relations of production, hence to identify the significant discontinuities in space and time.

Let us begin, then, by saying that one economic formation of society existed in the western part of the empire, another in the east and in North Africa: in the western provinces the main social relation was slavery in the form of gang labor, while in the "protected" provinces or kingdoms of the east we find a subjugated peasantry. By the same token, this "preponderance" of one or the other type of relation accounts for temporal discontinuities: the great imperial slave system, the generalization of serfdom. Specifically, our problem is this: How is one type of principal social relation transformed into another? In other words, how was feudal society formed? Can we understand, as Marx puts it, the *economic* formation of society? The term "economic," as it occurs in the German phrase *Ökonomische Gesellschaftsformation*, was intended by Marx to focus attention on a theory of history: historical materialism. This emerges with particular clarity from the fact that the complete phrase occurs for the first time in 1859 in the Preface to the *Critique of Political Economy*, following the exposition of that theory. We shall attempt to show that the theory which is summed up in the phrase "economic formation of society" can be regarded as Marxist, i.e., consistent with Marx's work as a whole and not merely with the famous opening sentences of the Preface to the *Critique of Political Economy*, only if it is looked at in dialectical relation to the phrase "social formation of the economy."

In this dense "underbrush" of social relations, we shall try to identify the dominant relation of production—gang slavery, serfdom—and to study, first, the relationship between this relation of production and the level of development of the productive forces, and second, the relationship between this complex structure, or mode of production, and the superstructure; this, we hope, will enable us to make our way through the maze of material without losing sight of the "red line."

D) The Slave Class and the Class Struggle

In view of the wide variety of types of slavery found in the Roman Empire, is it illegitimate to speak of a slave class? Definitely not. Whenever there are relations of production, whenever there is exploitation, then antagonistic classes also exist. In what follows we shall regard the major conflict as that between the masters, the landowning class, the owners of slaves and means of production on the one hand, and the slave class on the other. We should like to demonstrate that this conflict played the determining role in the birth of feudal society. These two were not the only classes in the imperial EFS, because other relations of production did in fact exist. The urban slaves, moreover, excepting those who worked as craftsmen, cannot be regarded as part of the slave class, as we have mentioned previously, in view of their productive role; neither can they be regarded, however, as entirely excluded from that class, not only because it is possible in principle to subsume them under the head of the collective slave (looking at production from the standpoint not of the *villa* but of society as a whole), but chiefly because the property relation of slave to master was the same as in the case of other slaves, urban slaves, too, being regarded as dead men who had been granted a reprieve. More than that, the ideology of the urban slaves was in some instances quite similar to that of other slaves, and urban slaves did (though rarely!) take part in the struggle with the masters. Accordingly, we shall regard urban slaves as standing outside the slave class in the strict sense, while emphasizing the complex relationship between the urban slaves and the slave class proper, the latter being taken to consist of slaves who worked in labor gangs in the *villae* (including slaves who performed services within the *villa* confines).

It is thus in virtue of the relations of production that the (two) classes are pitted against one another. Given that these relations involve conflict, the class and the class struggle are inseparable.[40]

But *what kind* of class struggle? In Marxist analysis, a distinction is often made between economic struggles (chiefly aimed at reducing the amount of surplus labor) and ideological and political struggles (for power, and, more than that, for the suppression of relations of production and even, with the end of capitalism, for the elimination of all exploitation). Some would argue that the relations of production are inextricably intertwined with the *economic* struggle between the classes, where both the class and its essential, primary, "basic" struggle are defined in one stroke, it being taken for granted that ideological struggles are built on this basic foundation.[41] To reason along these lines, however, is to hew closely to the distinction (first made by Marx[42] and later taken up and further developed by Lukács[43]) between a class "in itself" (objectively determined by the process of production) and a class "for itself" (i.e., possessing a class consciousness and engaged in struggle in behalf of its class interests), which has the disadvantage of assuming that classes exist prior to their engagement in class struggle. The difficulty (which is far from negligible) is that, if the notion of the class "in itself" now contains the economic struggle, the ideological and political struggles remain distinct and secondary: one has a class that exists a priori and therefore engages in class struggle *at the economic level* and then goes on to engage in class struggle at the ideological and political levels. This view represented a theoretical advance over earlier formulations but is still inadequate.

The fact is that class consciousness and the class struggle can be grasped only *dynamically* and in their *unity*. Wherever we find relations of production, i.e., class conflict, we must also find not only economic class struggle but also an embryonic class consciousness, that is, *the* class struggle, in its three inextricably intertwined "components." If it is true that we cannot conceive of class without economic conflict, an inevitable concomitant of every class-bound mode of production, it is also true that the other two aspects of *the* class struggle are present as well, though their presence may well manifest itself in a form apt to be found disconcerting when viewed a priori.

Let us consider the case of the slave class. It is generally agreed that an embryonic class consciousness (a "class instinct") is present from the beginning, and that some slaves are aware of standing apart from other men, of existing outside any city of men, of being different from freemen, and of being regarded by their masters as "talking tools" (*instrumentum vocale*). And it is further agreed that slaves developed this "class instinct" in *the* class struggle, in which they became aware of their fundamental (and not merely short-term, economic) class interests, i.e., of interests extending as far as the abolition of *their* slavery. It seems to us that this class consciousness is an inherent part of relations of production in the slave system.

Now let us turn to the class struggle. Open mass struggles of major proportions are found in the very earliest days of the slave system but disappear from view for several centuries thereafter. Were these struggles political? Spartacus did not want to "seize power," but the slaves who followed him wanted, as a group, to abolish their own slavery. The struggles that smoldered constantly in the *villae* were not simply economic: slaves attempted to set fire to the master's house and harvest, to murder or mutilate him, to flee their captivity, and so forth: the struggle was pervasive, complex, well developed. When, in the latter years of the late empire, great mass movements stirred once more and slaves rebelled and fled into brush and woodland, it was only the long-smoldering class struggle once again coming to a head: a new eruption of *the* class struggle in its three aspects, economic, ideological, and political.

While the idea of slaves struggling to seize power, even with Spartacus, is a naive one, no less than the idea of a class struggle to smash the state, slaves did fight to bring down the state wherever it proved possible to do so: the state was the power that subjugated them, and to hope for its destruction can only have been to hope for the destruction of the political power of the masters. The slaves even tried to substitute an organization of their own for the state when they could in the Sicilian uprising at the end of the republic, for example, or in Gaul with the Bacaudae in the third century.[44]

In the same vein, we shall see that, while slaves did not go so far as to formulate in abstract terms the idea of a battle to eliminate slavery for all time in all places,[45] or even, without a good deal of difficulty, throughout Italy, to say nothing of the whole empire, their struggle was not to "reverse" the master-slave relationship, to make free men of slaves and slaves of free men (as is often said), but rather to change the relations of production. And yet J.-P. Vernant, to name one, has written that "the slave class bore within it no new society. The political victory of the slaves, if such an hypothesis ever so much as made sense, would not have represented a threat to the relations of production or modified the forms of property. All historians are agreed that even where slave revolts took on the character of an organized political or military conflict . . . they remained limited in their vision and could not have led to a transformation of the social system of production."[46] We hope to show, on the contrary, that slave struggles, even at their most utopian (the city of slaves), were pregnant with a new society, conceived as a return (often in a geographical sense, as for the comrades of Spartacus) to a community, hence also as a fight for rights to a plot of land. We further hope to show that in the end, particularly through domiciling, these struggles did in fact bring about a change in the relations of production and forms of property. Thus class conflict was necessarily ideological as well as economic. Slave ideology is profoundly contradictory, hard to grasp, and as yet little studied. What is known[47] is that there were agrarian cults, religions specific to slave groups,[48] fairly loose but constantly sought ties with the religious sects of the slaves' native communities, and hostility to the official religions and to the religion of the masters, but at the same time integration into the family cults; there were egalitarian desires or demands but also acceptance of the hierarchy of classes implicit in the slave system (whence the ambivalent love-hate attitude toward slaves of higher status).

Opposition to the official ideology may be seen in periods during which the slaves, enjoying for a short while the fruits of ephemeral victory, organized themselves[49] and attempted to found communities (dreaming of those from which they had been cut off by their capture) and to renew their ties to the land, to their families, or to a city (whereupon we come to the core of the contradiction). In these "revolutionary moments" we can more readily grasp the continuity of the day-to-day ideological struggle, inseparable from the economic and political struggles, and the *totality* comprising all three types of struggle,[50] along with such other forms of conflict as battles to reduce the level of exploitation, to ameliorate conditions, to resist repression or take vengeance against it, as well as open mass uprisings by slaves aimed at eliminating, if not slavery as such, then at least their own slavery.

Does this mean that we are to think in terms of perpetual class conflict, of smoldering resistance or massive and violent revolt? Clearly, the answer is No.

The functions of the notion of class struggle in historical discourse are many. It may be invoked as a myth, frequently redemptive, sometimes alienating, and sometimes even as a kind of intellectual terrorism, designed to provoke guilt. It may also serve as a mechanical or vulgar-

Marxist explanation of changes in the relations of production. One can fall into this mythological way of thinking only if:

1. One forgets that social conflicts are sustained by an economic environment, which they modify, using as levers the existing ambient productive forces, together with such new technologies as may be brought into play;

2. One imagines that the only form of social practice is one of "class against class" (where the classes are precisely defined and clearly delineated static entities) and neglects instances of voluntary servitude in the sense of La Boétie: not happiness in slavery, but integration in a hierarchy, in which submission to the power of superiors bestows power over subordinates;

3. One abstracts, finally, from other types of conflict, particularly wars and political struggles between different cities, empires, or ethnic groups, which interact in a highly complex way with class struggles and cannot be considered, a priori, as logically subordinate to them.

During the empire, for example, the masters ultimately learned how to establish a hierarchy of slaves, how to divide the slaves along ethnic lines, how to subjugate them ideologically, and how to induce them to collaborate with the masters in order to make their way up through the various and sundry ranks of the hierarchy. Slavery is violent in its essence, but "voluntary servitude" is always (or nearly always) found to coexist with coercive force. We hope to show that subjugation by consent is only one aspect of the strategy used by the masters in their struggle with the slaves.

It may happen that a contradiction will arise between the notion of "voluntary servitude" and the consciousness of belonging to a "class" engaged in struggle with another class: the coexistence of the two, in dynamic conflict, accounts for the complexity of slave ideology and its evolution in relation to the balance of power between masters and slaves. For example, all seems to have been calm in the imperial *villa* during the second century; "good" slaves vied with one another in docility and even efficiency, and conflicts between slaves in the *villa* even required the arbitration of the master for settlement; civil conflict at that time seemed to eclipse slave struggles in importance. But this means only that the balance of power was favorable to the masters, not that the class struggle had ceased to be present at the root of things.

What, then, was the role of conflict between masters and slaves in destroying the old mode of production? In other words, as Marc Bloch asked in the title of a 1947 article in *Annales*, "How and why did ancient slavery come to an end" during the early Middle Ages? Was slavery a social relation strictly associated with a certain level of development of the productive forces and destined to disappear with the introduction of the water mill or the shoulder harness or the hinged stern rudder so exhaustively studied by Lefebvre-Des-Nöettes?[51] Were there other causes that can be reduced to a desire on the part of the master to increase the productivity of the laborers he was exploiting (both in children born and surplus labor extracted)?

Let us pause to clarify our position:

—There is no question here of denying the extreme importance of technological progress and development of man's productive powers in the evolution of society; rather, we maintain that precisely because technology is so important, it must be viewed as a product of man in society, a social product, and not as neutral with respect to social and legal-political relations. Indeed, the timing, scale, and form of technological developments are conditioned by these relations. If laws of history do exist, they are to be looked for not in society as a frozen structure but in society *as the site of the class struggle* and of contradiction, technological advance being just one mode of setting such struggles in motion.

—The role of the state is fundamental, because, as a coalition of segments of the dominant class, the state is the determining factor at the level of interclass relations, and because the class struggle is the locomotive of history. Until we have explained the causes of the collapse of the Roman imperial state (as well as the prior causes of its inception and growth), we shall have explained nothing. In trying to locate the object of struggle, it is today commonplace (cf. the work of Roland Barthes and Michel Foucault, for example) to stress the multiplicity of power rather than its singularity. Power is said to be multifarious, ubiquitous, hydra-headed, many-tentacled: the power of fathers over their children, of men over women, of professors over students, of doctors over patients, of priests over the faithful—we are all fascists! It is true that these many forms of oppression will not automatically disappear with the end of economic exploitation, of capitalism. But we must not let this blind us to the connection between power and the relations of production, between the state and slavery.

II. The Role of the Class Struggle

That the slaves constituted a class pitted against the master class is a fact known to every Marxist historian. We have thought it necessary to point out explicitly that the class struggle between masters and slaves was *inherent* in the social relation itself.[52] We have also argued that class analysis should not blind the historian to the existence of other relations of production within the economic formations of imperial and early medieval society and that the interaction of these other social relations with slavery must be studied dynamically (in particular, in order to determine how the relative importance of the different types of relations varied with time). We noted, moreover, that not all slaves were productive workers in the same way or to the same degree, so that the slaves as a group may not have constituted a single class; in any case the slave class was fragmented into groups occupying very diverse social and economic positions and was unified only in that all slaves shared the condition of "living death."

But what role did this class struggle play in the economic and social formation of medieval society? The well-known opening words of the Communist Manifesto, according to which "the history of all hitherto existing society is the history of class struggles," are insufficient, no matter how indefatigably one goes on repeating them, as is evident from the fact that *all* Marxists accept them, in spite of the deep divisions among Marxists today as in the past over the precise place to be accorded the class struggle. The point is really to relate the class struggle to the development of the productive forces.

Let us first examine the answer given by vulgar materialism.[53] To take an extreme case, Lefebvre-Des-Nöettes saw the end of slavery as due to the spread of the shoulder harness, and, in the case of the galley slaves, of the hinged rudder. Let us not be too quick to reject this hypothesis merely because of its audacity. The truth is that we find more subtle and consequently more convincing expressions of the same view, based on an exclusively economic (or demographic) causality, in the work of a good many historians of Antiquity and the Middle Ages. We shall therefore direct our criticisms of the materialist argument at these more subtle expressions.

Some critics have been at pains to class this vulgar materialism together with the analyses put forward by Marx or by certain Marxists. Their animadversions on Marx are based on his all too well-known witticism according to which "the handmill gives you society with the feudal lord; the steam-mill society with the industrial capitalist."[54] Further grist for the critical mill is provided by Stalin's writings: "Why did capitalism win out over feudalism? Because it set up a higher standard of productivity and provided society with the possibility of acquiring a vastly greater quantity of goods than did feudalism. Capitalism won out because it made society wealthier."[55] But to be fair, Marx's witticism cannot be used to demonstrate the nonsensicality of historical materialism, because it stands in complete contrast to the *totality* of Marx's work. Even Stalin never denied the importance of the class struggle in history (except in isolated passages of his work, which it is artificial to single out for criticism).

While non-Marxist historians frequently accord no role whatever to class struggle in bringing about the transition from slavery to serfdom, the Marxists, for their part, often assign it no more that a "derivative and secondary explanatory role," in keeping with the general line of argument followed by Kautsky or Plekhanov, the Mensheviks or Stalin. Was the class struggle of secondary importance? Was it no more than a mediation? The question is worth examining in some detail. When the class struggle finally came to a head in social revolution and victoriously swept away the old economic order of society, was this merely (or chiefly) a result of the development of the productive forces? If we answer this question in the affirmative, our materialism will be of the mechanistic or economistic variety. It is our contention that this mechanistic materialism was in fact elaborated by Marx himself, and that it can therefore draw upon certain passages in his work for support:[56] accordingly, we have chosen to look closely at what is no doubt the clearest synthesis of this position, the often cited passages of the Preface to the *Critique of Political Economy* of 1859.[57] Furthermore, when Engels answered critics by spelling out what he and Marx meant to say, he only scaled down the mechanism and continued to uphold the economistic argument as valid "in the last instance."[58] In our view, Althusser follows the same line of argument, though he covers his tracks by having recourse to "structuralo-Marxism."

A critical analysis of mechanistic materialism is indispensable, we think, if our own work is to be seen in proper perspective. So as not to weigh down the Introduction unduly, however, we have placed our comments in an Appendix.[59] In the chapters that follow we hope to strike further blows against the mechanistic position, notwithstanding the fact that it undeniably stems from *certain* of Marx's own writings.[60] We believe, however, that in showing that the class struggle was the cause of the transition to serfdom and that the development of the productive forces was a by-product of the battle between master and slave (and later between lord and serf), we have remained faithful to what is essential in Marx's theory of history.

One of our goals is to contribute to the attempt to set forth a new interpretation of history and to criticize today's "official" history. The official view accepts mechanistic materialism as one of its chief explanatory paradigms and maintains that the water mill was the cause of feudalism, that the stirrup or the shoulder harness introduced a discontinuity into the economy and society of the Middle Ages, and that the steam engine was the cause of capitalism. When projected into the future, this same official history is used to buttress the view that the development of the productive forces within capitalism will be determining for the transition to socialism. But where does innovation come from? From a force that is supposed always to increase the productivity of labor! And where do changes in social and legal-political relations come from? Always, it is said, from the formation of groups within society receptive to technological changes that make for increased productivity, or, as is sometimes argued, directly from the possibility of enhancing productivity through a change in social organization, from slavery to serfdom, from serfdom to the free peasant, and so forth! Mechanistic materialism puts all its chips on the development of the productive forces, the determining factor, "in the last instance," of all history, but it does not explain how that development takes place. What a gaping hole in the argument! To indulge in argument by caricature a moment longer, let us suppose that banal seigniory was, if only "in the last instance," the result of the water mill;[61] is the water mill, then, supposed to have fallen full-blown from heaven, not merely into the mind of Vitruvius, but into the material reality of the Middle Ages?[62]

When one looks closely at the matter, what one finds, frequently relegated to footnotes, is quite another history, the history of social struggles, of class confrontation, of conflict that has made development of the productive forces imperative. Marglin, for instance, cites Marc Bloch to the effect that the water mill was forcibly introduced by the lords: it was the lords of the ban who gave us the water mill, rather than the reverse[63] By the same token, it was the lords who forced the peasants to stop fulling cloth by foot and bring their cloth to the castle's fulling mill instead.[64]

Although it is beyond doubt that water mills and fulling mills were important instances of technological progress, they were introduced into the medieval economy not because they were more productive, but rather because the balance of power between the classes enabled lords to force peasants to eschew hand-milling and foot-fulling—technologies compatible with the autonomy of the peasant family—in favor of the *banalités*, or seigniorial monopolies, by means of which the lords were able to extract from their peasants a greater surplus than before.[65] The master's interest has always been in the relation of exploitation itself, and consequently in its origin and reproduction, which explains why the portion of exploited labor that the master was able to appropriate was of paramount importance, and the productivity of that labor only of indirect importance: indirect, that is, in that productivity increases were important only to the extent that they increased the amount of surplus. By the same token, Marglin shows that the end of the putting-out system and its replacement by centralized production in factories, as well as the major technological innovations of the nineteenth century, can be explained by the desire of the employers to enhance their power and increase their share of the product, and not at all by the intention to increase productivity, even if increased productivity did result indirectly from the changes. In theory, moreover, increasing the productivity of labor should have made possible a reduction of its intensity. But the *opposite* actually occurred: increased productivity was accompanied by increased intensity of labor.

To the question, What caused technological progress such as we find actually occurred in history? Marglin provides an answer. Technological progress was a by-product of the exploitation of men by other men. It was frequently a way of seeking new means to extract a surplus or to increase the rate of exploitation, frequently a response to class struggle by the workers aimed at reducing the amount of the surplus. And this is what technology still is and must remain, until mankind has taken control of its own collective destiny. As Marglin points out, the most important lesson to be drawn from the battle over the mills described by Marc Bloch is this: it is not technological superiority that necessitates replacement of the hand mill by the water mill, but rather the nature of power under feudalism and the necessity to strengthen its hand. "It is not the water mill that gives you the feudal lord, but the feudal lord that gives you the water mill." This explains why it is imperative to construct models illustrating how "technology" is determined by class conflict, models that should be both dynamic and dialectical.[66]

To hold that there is a correspondence between the productive forces and the relations of production, to accept, in other words, the concept of a mode of production, is not the same thing as to accept that the productive forces determine the relations of production, since the reverse determination has been shown to have been true historically. In the ancient world the slaves waged a victorious and progressive class struggle: the feudal mode of production emerged as a result of slave revolts, both directly and as a result of the attempts by the masters to respond to rebellion by changing the *form*, but not the nature, of exploitation. Rebellion changed social relations by forcing masters to grant plots of land to their slaves (which was the rebels' purpose). Similarly, peasant revolts throughout the Middle Ages destroyed the initial form of feudal serfdom, necessitated the substitution of rent in kind for labor dues, and forced the lords to look for new forms of exploitation: the *banalité*, or lord's monopoly of the water mill and other services, was one answer to these changes. Ultimately the productive forces had to adapt to the new situation. In some cases the outcome of such struggles was to make the peasant a landowner. Social conflict also forced the economy as a whole to evolve (in such ways as increased urbanization and the spread of commodities and the use of money), as did the class struggles of the bourgeoisie (though it is impossible to say which of the two was more important).

Marglin's analysis calls for the same question that Engels put to Dühring: How did it come about that Robinson was the master and Friday the slave? Are we not once again faced with an instance of "direct political force," in which social relations and the relative power of the classes are left unexplained? If we imagine a triangle in which each vertex is labeled with one of the possible determining factors, matter (or economics), ideas (or consciousness) and relations of production (or class struggle), then we may say that in the Preface to the *Critique of Political Economy* Marx makes the first paramount (as against Hegel, who gave pride of place to the second) and mediatizes the third, whereas Marglin rightly gives precedence to the third factor. But if the dialectic hobbles along on one leg in the formulations put forth by Marx and Engels, on which we have focused attention until now, does it not hobble along on the other leg in Marglin's analysis (even when he warns against such lopsidedness)? The shock value of Marglin's inversion of Marx is eye-opening, particularly when he says the the water mill was a product of the lord, the steam mill of the capitalist (although neither Marx nor any present-day Marxist would seriously advance as true the propositions thereby confuted). Of course, for Marglin, the force that figures in the relations between the classes is not to be confused with pure violence, "direct political force."

It should be clear that a given level of development of the productive forces is not compatible with every type of social relation. Social relations never exist "in the air": the slaves of antiquity were not fighting for socialism as such, nor were the slaves of Haiti or the serfs and peasants of the Middle Ages, even though we know the latter did fight for certain "collectivist" objectives. Taking any sort of adialectical approach to history ultimately involves a danger greater than merely getting causes and effects mixed up; rather, the danger is one of missing the connection between the productive forces and the relations of production, thereby undermining the very notion of a mode of production.

Marx started out by saying that "in the social production of their existence, men inevitably enter into definite relations, which are independent of their will, namely, relations of production appropriate to a given stage in the development of their material forces of production."[68] Hence we must reject the idea that a given level of development of the productive forces corresponds in a unique way to a particular social relation, while retaining the essential idea, that "not everything is possible."

When we speak of a mode of production, i.e., of a certain correspondence between productive forces and relations of production, we most emphatically do not mean that a certain level of development of the productive forces cannot correspond to more than one type of social relation. Is it not the case, for example, that the present level of development of the productive forces is compatible with a slave system (as Nazi Germany had begun to prove)? And also with socialism, for that matter? The answer is yes, though it is undeniable that, depending on which type of social relations actually does correspond to the existing level of development, society must reinterpret, modify, and adapt the productive forces in appropriate ways, and, above all, must create radically different means of production as needed. Furthermore, Marx admits that communist social relations will be a "revival" of the communist relations of ancient classless societies, but at a quite different level of development of the productive forces. To put it in somewhat different terms, the association between relations of production and productive forces admits of *several* solutions, and not of one *unique* solution. Each type of social relation gives rise to its own peculiar dynamic, and therefore leads to diverging evolutionary paths.

It is clear, moreover, that because the development of the productive forces and of certain so-called superstructrual elements is *cumulative* in character (machinery, science, etc.), it is impossible to conceive of a situation in which the stone axe or the spinning wheel would coexist with the theory of relativity, or in which the swing plow would coexist with atheism (in its present form, at any rate). But despotic state structures, fundamentally quite similar to one another, are found at quite disparate levels of development of man's productive powers. And if we focus on forms of property, it is interesting to note that under feudalism there was virtually no interest in Roman property law, because the feudal system had broken away from the Roman concept of property; we must await the first stirrings of capitalism in the Middle Ages for Roman property law to be rediscovered.

Etienne Balibar has given an analysis similar to Marglin's, but clearly Marxist in conception. In Balibar's words, "*This* [the type of social relations embodied in the structure of a particular social formation] explains *that* [economic phenomena such as accumulation, growth, etc.], and not the reverse." Marglin would have no difficulty accepting this proposition.

Balibar reminds us that the essential thesis of historical materialism asserts the "primacy" of the fundamental relation of production within the historical complex of relations of production and productive forces. Every mode of production is characterized "first and foremost by the nature of the fundamental relation of production (and exploitation), and then, derivatively, by the nature of the productive forces and their tendency to undergo certain kinds of transformation."[69] Thus the class struggle appears within the mode of production, where it plays the determining role.

Furthermore, the class struggle involves more than just resistance to oppression by the exploited class (and does not begin with such resistance), being reflected in the very forms of exploitation: "First of all, there is always a prior class struggle systematically waged by capital against the proletariat."[70] The class struggle waged by the exploiting class is "at all times the motor that drives the development of capitalist relations of production and also, in the absence of capitalist relations and as a precondition of their development, the motor that drives the development of the productive forces, hence also of the most advanced forms of organization and equipment."[71]

The exploiting class determines the development of the productive forces, because it engages in class struggle in order to impose and to reproduce the exploitative relations on which it depends for its existence; furthermore, when the exploited class fights back and succeeds in reducing the rate of exploitation or undermining an existing form of exploitation, the exploiting class reacts by trying to find new forms of organization, means of production, and so forth, either to attain a higher rate of exploitation or to bring forth new forms of exploitation.

Balibar goes on to set forth three "self-evident" propositions:

—Relations of production cannot exist without the productive forces as base ("hence . . . without production").

—The emergence of a particular type of relation of production (capitalist, for example) is impossible at certain stages of development of the productive forces. In other words, the notion that "anything is possible" is rejected.

—The (capitalist) relations of production must foster development of the productive forces in order to continue their own existence.

The important thing to notice is that, in contrast to the Preface to the *Critique of Political Economy* and similar passages in the works of Marx, *Capital* is the place where Marx shows himself to have been the first to overcome the dilemma that so many Marxists have persisted in setting themselves, namely, the argument that *either* the productive forces must have primacy in a mechanistic argument of some sort, *or* we must accept the subjective idealist, voluntarist position, according to which the relations of production can develop independently of their material realization.[72] Instead, Marx takes a characteristic line of approach. Rather than begin by giving a description of the productive forces and then describing the "consequences" for the development of capitalist relations of production, Marx starts out with a discussion of commodities, i.e., of value, exchange, and circulation. He then goes on to study that particular form of exchange in virtue of which money capital and the capitalist relation of exploitation acquire fundamental importance, and, finally, he analyzes the forms of absolute and relative surplus value, "which control and account for the development of the productive forces."[73]

By way of illustration, let us turn now to part 4 of volume I of *Capital* (concerned with the production of relative surplus value). Marx argues that technical progress, or enhancement of the forces of production, is always aimed at increasing exploitation (or at preventing a decrease in the rate of exploitation due to a workers' success in the class struggle). Marx cites John Stuart Mill's statement that "it is questionable if all the mechanical inventions yet made have lightened the day's toil of any human being." Marx provides the following gloss: "That is, however, by no means the aim of the capitalistic application of machinery. Like every increase in the productiveness of labor, machinery is intended to cheapen commodities, and, by shortening that portion of the working-day, in which the laborer works for himself, to lengthen the other portion that he gives, without an equivalent, to the capitalist. In short, it is a means for producing surplus value."[74] In what follows he substantiates this contention at great length. Earlier he had described the division of labor in manufacture as "a refined and civilized method of exploitation."[75] Marx stresses that "since handicraft skill is the foundation of manufacture, and since the mechanism of manufacture as a whole possesses no framework, apart from the laborers themselves, capital is constantly compelled to wrestle with the insubordination of the workmen."[76] The introduction of machinery was also a way of enforcing order, as Marx notes when he asks, "Is Fourier wrong when he calls factories 'tempered bagnos'?"[77]

A very necessary part of this whole approach is the section devoted to primitive accumulation (vol. I, part 8). There Marx studies the means used by the nascent (hence at first essentially parasitic) bourgeois class, within the feudal social formation and by virtue of its feudal relations, to develop the then embryonic capitalist relations, or, in other words, to produce capital, as a social relation. These means included the use of force and violence, made possible not only by the new (in terms of magnitude) power of money accumulated in parasitic activities (such as trade, particularly with colonies, and finance), but also (as is sometimes insufficiently emphasized) by virtue of the wide variety of bonds forged between the new class and the old order. The bourgeois class struggle begins with this nascent class and is the foundation of the bourgeoisie qua class. Out of this class struggle the new type of social relation arises: the class struggle *produces* the proletariat. By dint of either "plain" violence, whether public or private, or the violence of money, the bonds between the producers and the means of production, including the land, are broken, and the two antagonistic classes of the capitalist mode of production are brought into being.

To cap his argument Marx contends that the historical tendency of production is just this, that "capitalist production begets, with the inexorability of a law of Nature, its own negation."[78] Unquestionably the words "inexorability of a law of Nature" still have a "mechanistic" ring, but the important thing to note is that, when Marx says "production," he is thinking of social relations within the mode of production: what else could he mean by "negation" of production?

As further evidence we may adduce the letters from Marx to Mikhailovsky and Vera Zasulich.[79] Is the Russian rural commune destined to disappear? On a mechanistic materialist view of the matter, the answer would have to be yes: with the development of the productive forces in Russia, these ancient forms of social and property relations must inevitably vanish. Marx tells us that *if* the socialist revolution is victorious in Russia, then it will be possible to reestablish the commune on its old basis. The commune might even become the cornerstone of a socialist agriculture: the relations of production and property relations bequeathed by the ancient rural commune provide the "natural basis for collective appropriation."[81] The existence of these archaic social and legal relations could serve as underpinnings for the new socialist relations, thus giving Russia "the finest chance ever offered by history to a people."[82]

It is not our purpose, however, to search for passages in the writings of Marx on the basis of which we might depict him as the critic of the interpretation of historical materialism according to which the determining role is played by the productive forces, an interpretation set forth by Marx himself. Indeed, Marx's whole approach is incompatible with a Marxian positivism of this kind, which was so quickly to win acceptance among non-Marxist historians.[83] Marx sums up his basic approach in the following terms: "It is always the direct relationship of the owners of the conditions of production to the direct producers—a relation always naturally corresponding to a definite stage in the development of the methods of labor and thereby its social productivity—which reveals the innermost secret, the hidden basis of the entire social structure."[84] Natural *correspondence*, then, but let us place the accent on the idea that the development of man's productive power is determined by the antagonistic relations of production, i.e., by the class struggle, the converse being false: in other words, the productive forces provide the means for class struggle, and their development is the effect of class struggle.[85]

Is the upshot of our argument merely to reverse the direction of determination? Yes, but this does not mean that we end up with another mechanism! This being the case, why not say that the antagonistic relations between the classes of society determine, "in the last instance," the level of development (or lack thereof) of the productive forces?

"In the last instance": "If this modest little phrase, seemingly so unimportant," as Althusser is pleased to call it, makes it possible "to adopt a dialectical position"[86] in regard to the economy, why can't it do as much for the treatment of social relations? It will be objected that "this is not materialism," but the objection will not do: to repeat ourselves, the relation between the master and the slave is as material as the master's whip. "In the last instance" is a way of hedging one's bets, of avoiding social determinism and mechanism; if it is good enough to avoid the pitfall of economic determinism, is it not also good enough to avoid the danger of mechanism on the other side, social determinism? No: in fact, it works in neither case, as our critique will make clear; historical materialism cannot be made dialectical merely by introducing the phrase "in the last instance."[87] It is our hope that the critical analysis given in the appendix to this Introduction will help to clarify the approach we have taken.

III. The Class Struggle and the State

Consider the case of the serfs: producers, they are at the same time "possessors" of the means of production and labor needed to produce their means of subsistence. "Under such conditions the surplus-labor for the nominal owner of the land can only be extorted from them by other than economic pressure, whatever the form assumed may be."[88] In some instances the serf's obedience to and dependence on his master was based on *religious alienation* of some kind. This was common in cases where the master was a priest or associated with the clergy: the relation of production masked itself as a relation to God. In such cases the "serf" was obliged to work for the priest—or for the priest's "brother," the lord or sanctified king—and to relinquish a portion of his time or surplus product. He was compelled to do so not by temporal power, but by spiritual power.

It seems to me that spiritual power has rarely "operated" alone in history. Whether religion played a leading or merely a supporting role, was armed might *ever* entirely absent?

The reproduction of the social relation of dependence between serf and lord was no doubt accomplished through the *political* structure of society: the serf was forcibly compelled to obey the lord and work his land. Indeed, it may be said that, in the feudal mode of production, the "regional political structure" played the "leading role."[89] As Marx says, it is always to the relations of production that one must look for the "innermost secret, the hidden basis of the entire social structure,"[90] but the lords must have recourse to "other than economic pressure, whatever the form assumed may be," including brute force (and religious ideology), to establish those relations in the first place.

Is the situation just described peculiar to precapitalist modes of production? It is of course true that, once a radical separation has been introduced (by force) between the producer and his means of production, the producer is obliged to sell his labor power; no policeman is needed to drag the worker from his bed each morning. Hence there is no need to reproduce the social relations of production from one day to the next; the same, however, cannot be said of *the* relation of production, i.e., the separation of the producer from his tools. In other words, without the state and its appurtenances, the police, the courts, the army, and so on, it would be impossible to reproduce the capitalist relations of production.

What accounts, then, for the superior power of the slave masters, the feudal overlords, and the capitalist bourgeoisie? As Engels forcefully argued against Dürhing and the theory of "direct political force": "Crusoe enslaved Friday 'sword in hand.' Where did he get the sword from?"[91] A superficial answer to this question would emphasize material means, economic power: by developing the productive forces, the bourgeoisie multiplied its own power many times over. There is a more fundamental answer, however: *the ruling class derives its power from the relations of production, by virtue of which it is able to confiscate the surplus labor or surplus product and turn it back against the direct producers.* Where else do the lord's swords, suits of armor, and horses come from, if not from the labor of the peasant?[92] To be sure, the newly born bourgeoisie drew its power within the feudal regime from its parasitic role and not, at least not initially, from exploitation, but ultimately it comes to the same thing whether the surplus product is swallowed up in trade or directly extracted in the form of rent or forced labor. The bourgeoisie used the power obtained in this way to produce the bourgeois social relation, i.e., capital and the class of wage laborers (one has only to think of the confiscation or purchase of peasant lands, which produced vagabonds by the thousands, who were then forcibly incarcerated in prison-factories, asylum-factories, and hospital-factories); eventually the bourgeois class used this social relation to appropriate surplus value, the source of its economic, ideological, and political power.

Even this more fundamental explanation is insufficient, however. If, in view of their confiscation of the surplus product via the relations of production, the masters always had the upper hand, and consequently the ability to reproduce and deepen the conditions of exploitation, where would the exploited class find the strength to throw off this yoke? Yet history, which is the history of class struggle, is also the history of the victories of the exploited.

The power of the exploited class resides in its concentrated mass, its organization, and its consciousness of its own class interest. It is the class struggle itself that makes organization and class consciousness possible. There are, however, certain objective situations, certain relations of production, in which the exploited are more readily *serialized*,[93] to borrow a term from Sartre, by their masters. This is the case with serfdom. On the other hand, there are objective situations in which the masses are necessarily concentrated and tend more readily to form a social group. This is the case with slave labor gangs. Situations of the latter kind require the ruling class to coordinate its interests and centralize its power to combat the concentrated masses of the exploited (in the *villae* in the case of slave labor). Whence the necessity of a centralized state. Some class-based societies can do without a state to exercise central coordination of the forces of repression. In particular, there are situations in which the masters have succeeded in obtaining a relatively high level of serialization of the workers, which makes possible a relatively less cumbersome form of association. This is the case with feudalism, in which the delegation of authority through vassalage is generally sufficient to insure control of the peasants. By contrast, the *villa* with its gangs of slaves, and the factory, or "tempered bagnos," require the existence of a state, coordinating the interests of the masters and centralizing their power, in order to confront the masses of slaves or wage laborers, whose concentration gives them power in the smoldering class conflict, which may at any moment flare into open conflagration.

If it is true that social relations in both the slave system and in advanced capitalism (i.e., *latifundia*, factories) require the existence of such a centralized state for their reproduction, then we believe it can be shown that:[94]

—the existence of such a state is not always within the realm of possibility;

—the logic of the development of the relation of production itself leads to the decay of the state;

—and, therefore, the development of a relation of production necessarily produces its own negation.[95]

The point to be made here is that the domiciling of slaves became necessary because of the decay of the state (a product of the logic of the slave system); hence it was not the decline of slavery that brought about the end of the Roman state, as Max Weber believed, but rather the decline of the state that put an end to the slave system and gave rise to serfdom, by tipping the balance of power in the class struggle.[96]

This was a point made forcefully long ago by Plato, and our ambition is merely to provide a gloss on his remarks. The situation examined by Plato is that of "individual wealthy private citizens in our states who possess many slaves." We find the following exchange between Socrates and Glaucon in *The Republic:*

> "You are aware," says Socrates "that they [the masters] are unafraid and do not fear their slaves?"
>
> "What should they fear?"
>
> "Nothing, but do you perceive the reason why?"
>
> "Yes, because the entire state is ready to defend each citizen."
>
> "You are right. But now suppose some god should catch up a man who has fifty or more slaves and waft him with his wife and children away from the city and set him down with his other possessions and his slaves in a solitude where no free man could come to his rescue. What and how great would be his fear, do you suppose, lest he and his wife and children be destroyed by the slaves?"
>
> "The greatest in the world, if you ask me."
>
> "And would he not forthwith find it necessary to fawn upon some of the slaves and make them many promises and emancipate them, though nothing would be further from his wish? And so he would turn out to be the flatterer of his own servants."
>
> "He would certainly have to, or else perish."[97]

Appendix: Note on the Determinism of the Productive Forces in History

Many are the historians who, implicitly or explicitly, look upon economic or even demographic or natural causes as the determining factors in history. The purpose of the following pages is not to analyze what Marx characterized as vulgar materialism, typified for us by Lefebvre-Des-Nöettes, but rather to criticize mechanistic economic determinism, the source of which may undoubtedly be traced to *some* of the writings of

Marx and Engels, although in our view it is wholly incompatible with the essentials of Marx's theory.

A) Historical Materialism or Economic Determinism

In the Preface to the *Critique of Political Economy*,[98] Marx explicitly spells out the "guiding principle," or, as one says nowadays, the "problematic," that he and Engels adopted in their work. "In the social production of their existence," he writes, "men inevitably enter into definite relations, which are independent of their will, namely, relations of production appropriate to a given stage in the development of their material forces of production. The totality of these relations of production constitutes the economic structure of society, the real foundation, on which arises a legal and political superstructure and to which correspond definite forms of social consciousness." (We shall subsequently have occasion to cite the rest of this passage.)

Here we find the definition of the "mode of production of material life," the relation between the productive forces and the relations of production. The productive forces enable man to appropriate nature in a certain way. The relations of production are relations between men, which necesarily emerge as a result of the relations between men and nature (the relations of production are social relations, but not all social relations are relations of production, even if they are based on the relations of production).

1. Correspondence

From the passage cited above one point emerges clearly: corresponding to a given stage in the development of the productive forces are certain relations of production, termed [by Marx's English translators—Trans.] "appropriate" to that stage of development. On this basis there then arises a definite superstructure, consisting of legal and political relations and forms of social consciousness. Thus corresponding to a certain stage in the development not only of the division of labor,[99] but also of the means of production, the forms of organization, scientific knowledge, and so on, we find certain social classes and forms of class conflict, and corresponding to this whole structure we find certain forms of property, political power, and ideas, which men "make for themselves," i.e., produce out of themselves, their relations to nature and to one another, and their beliefs.

2. Historical Determination of the "Superstructure"

Marx then goes on to say that "the mode of production of material life conditions the general process of social, political, and intellectual life. It is not the consciousness of men that determines their existence, but their social existence that determines their consciousness." In this last sentence Marx is arguing for a one-sided determination. Marx undoubtedly regarded this argument as crucial to his battle against the "Hegelians." A sharp distinction must be made between this causal determination[100] and the process that leads to the determination, within the "material base," of the relations of production.

3. The Process of Determination of the Relations of Production

Marx further states that "at a certain stage of development, the material productive forces of society come into conflict with the existing relations of production or—this merely expresses the same thing in legal terms—with the property relations within the framework of which they have operated hitherto. From forms of development of the productive forces these relations turn into their fetters. Then begins an era of social revolution. The changes in the economic foundation lead sooner or later to the transformation of the whole immense superstructure."

Starting from a given state of correspondence (a mode of production), limits to the development of the productive forces are set by the framework of given property and production relations. During the initial phase, the property relations are "forms of development of the productive forces." Beyond a certain limit, however, "these relations turn into their fetters." When this happens, the relations of production, as well as their "legal expression," the property relations, must change. But how is it possible for the relations of production to adapt to the productive forces? Social revolution makes such a change possible.

This oft-cited passage raises two questions. First, in what sense does the economy play a leading or determining role.

There is naturally no point in taxing Marx with an objection that he himself refuted: "material interests" may rule the modern world, but, it is objected, they did not rule the ancient world, which was dominated by politics, or the Middle Ages which were dominated by Catholicism. After making fun of the fact that such "old and worn-out trivialities" could have been raised against him, Marx goes on to point out that if Catholicism or politics played the *leading role*, the economic conditions of the period in question explain why this was so.[101] Economics is still the determining factor even in societies in which it is not "dominant," in which it does not play the "leading role." Hence economic determination must be effected by other agencies. No doubt it was because surplus labor could only be extorted by "other than economic pressure, whatever the form assumed may be,"[102] that economics could not play the leading role, as in the Middle Ages, for example, and yet, as always, the development of the productive forces determined the social transformations that took place.

Second, at what level or stage of development of the productive forces do the relations of production and the legal and political relations that express those forces in other terms "turn into fetters" and cease to be "forms of development" of the productive forces?

The question is an important one, because Marx and Engels judged that capitalist property relations in the nineteenth century had become fetters, whereas it is beyond all doubt that between 1860 and the present capitalism has been at the root of a prodigious development of the productive forces.[103]

Two further questions follow from this one; one of them will turn out to be secondary, while the other is crucial.

What kinds of transition from lower to higher stages of development of the productive forces are possible? (Of course, the transition reveals how the former property relations were fetters on development.) Is continuous change—merely quantitative in nature—the only possible kind? Or do we find discontinuities, major innovations? The old relations of production do not become fetters merely because an ever greater number of water mills accumulates. A breakthrough to the steam mill, a qualitative jump, is needed. Often, however, quantitative development beyond a certain point can by itself bring on a qualitative discontinuity.[104]

Is it possible to "measure" the degree of development of the productive forces independently of the social relations? Is the productive power of a slave gang identical to that of a group of free men? The answer is no, as Marx was aware, and though he "forgets" to say so here, this ultimately became an essential aspect of his theory.

The productive forces also "embody" the division of labor (a point given prominence in *The German Ideology*), the forms of labor organization, and scientific knowledge. How is the division of labor in the shop to be defined independently of social relations? Once again we encounter the correspondence between the productive forces and the relations of production, but now the two are so inextricably intertwined that it is impossible to "measure" the degree of development of the productive forces, or even to define them, to know what they are, apart from the human relations associated with them. Moreover, scientific knowledge, and, more generally, knowledge of any sort, is both superstructural and at the same time part and parcel of the productive forces. The conceptual labor of the architect is as material as the labor of the mason. Concepts issued from the mind of Einstein are no less real than the atomic reactors that are their logical product. Both are productive forces.

In no way are the productive forces to be regarded as a mere assemblage of machinery. Even if they were no more than that, however, how would we evaluate their level of development? We have no intention of treating this question here. Let us say merely that the problems it raises are not radically different from those associated with the notion of capital and its measurement in neoclassical economics. Observe only that the productive power of a given physical stock of machinery depends on the social relations that obtain among the men who run the machines.

4. Dialectical Materialism and Historical Materialism

Did Marx, in laying the foundations of historical materialism and breaking away from the conceptions of vulgar materialism, continue to bear the imprint of the philosophy he was destroying?

As we have seen, of course, the material base determines the superstructure in a unique way. As for the process that leads by way of social revolution from the development of the productive forces to the change in the relations of production, however, matters are more complex. The essential "law" of dialectical materialism, as enunciated by Mao, in the wake of Lenin, is the following: "The fundamental cause of the development of things and phenomena is not external, but internal."[105] Applied to the "thing" or "phenomenon" that is history, this "law" means that every mode of production develops by virtue of its internal contradictions, and that this development leads to the negation and disappearance of the mode of production, which negates itself in the process of asserting itself. Dialectical reasoning is not like the "teaser" according to which the chicken is the cause of the egg, and the egg the cause of the chicken! Nor is the dialectic to be confused with a feedback mechanism of the type studied in cybernetics.

Accordingly, it is clear that the process described in the Preface, by which new relations of production are formed, can in some sense be called dialectical: the very development of the productive forces within the ancient mode of production (slave system) gives rise to (or accentuates) contradictions with the relations of production, and hence causes the mode of production to vanish. But what if this very development of the productive forces were itself the effect of the internal contradictions? It is clear that when the relations of production are not appropriate to the level of development of the productive forces, the productive forces will be fettered, but it is not enough to say that, when these relations are appropriate, they are just "forms of development of the productive forces." *If there is no contradiction between the productive forces and the relations of production, there is nothing to explain the development of the productive forces!* To posit the existence of *correspondence* (why not *harmony!*) between the productive forces and the relations of production as the "cause" of the development of the productive forces is out of the question. The development simply remains unexplained.

In other words, to say there is a correspondence between the productive forces and the relations of production cannot explain why the productive forces develop, unless we assume that they are always developing, that they somehow have a natural tendency to forge ahead in the absence of fetters on their development! This amounts to the assumption of a sort of growth "drive" in the productive powers themselves: thus what is explained is not the development of the productive forces, but the absence of development (when there are "fetters"). Still, this "phenomenon" should be studied as a consequence of internal contradictions. Not internal to the material base, vulgarly defined as an accumulation of "things," but internal to the antagonistic relations of production, to the class struggle, which is the real material base: the exploiting class develops the productive powers only because it can thereby reproduce and expand its ability to exploit other classes, or because it needs to reestablish that ability after an historical victory by the exploited classes.

5. Place of the Class Struggle

In the passage from Marx cited above, the class struggle figures thus: "Then begins an era of social revolution." The social revolution would thus seem to be a mechanical consequence of the development of the productive forces. It is not made clear that revolution is only the culminating moment of a continuous class struggle, the moment when the balance of power is tipped in favor of a dominated class. One or more classes then violently smash the old social relations and establish new ones. Only by understanding this shift in the balance of power can we understand how "the changes in the economic foundation lead sooner or later to the transformation of the whole immense superstructure."

When does the dominated class or classes[106] emerge victorious from the struggle? Does victory always come only after the productive forces have developed to an adequate degree, i.e., only when legal and political relations have become fetters on that development? If so, how can we tell when these relations have become impediments to further development? What about capitalist relations in France between 1860 and 1960, for example? In the end, is it not the victory of the revolution that gives the clue?

On this view of the matter, the victorious violent rising of the dominated class or classes plays the role of a midwife in bringing forth from the womb of the old society the new society that is growing in embryo within it. While the history of society is the history of class struggle, the class struggle is not the locomotive of history. It is always the development of the productive forces that topples the inappropriate superstructure, but mediated through the class struggle. Violence is the lever with which the old order can be overthrown, but violence can succeed only because the economic base has changed. The nascent bourgeoisie, for example, grew rich by expanding trade and industry under feudalism. It grew powerful as a result, and thus laid the groundwork for its future victory. Similarly, capitalism allows the productive forces to develop, but as a result growing segments of society necessarily sink into poverty and proletarian status, so that the balance of power tips more and more in favor of the broad mass of the people.

If this argument were correct, it would follow that the shifting balance of power between the classes and the course of the class struggle are determined mechanically by the material base alone. The class struggle would then be only a mediation, and the material base the unique determining factor.

B) "In the Last Instance":
Materialism Scaled Down

Engels preserves economic determinism, but attempts to place the accent on the multiplicity of "conditions" that impinge on the causality of economics: Engels gives the same answer as before to the question "Why?" but his answer to the question "How?" turns out to be less simple than a reading of the Preface to the *Critique* alone would lead one to believe.

1. Various passages from Engels's writings are frequently cited, in particular two letters, one to Borgius, the other to Joseph Bloch.

In his letter to Borgius (dated January 25, 1894), Engels wrote:

> The economic situation therefore does not produce an automatic effect as people try here and there conveniently to imagine, but men make their history themselves; they do so however in a given environment, which conditions them, and on the basis of actual, already existing relations among which the economic relations— however much they may be influenced by other, political and ideological, relations—are still ultimately ["in the last instance"— Trans.] the decisive ones, forming the keynote which alone leads to understanding.[107]

In an earlier letter (dated September 21, 1890) to Joseph Bloch, Engels had written: "According to the materialist conception of history, the *ultimately* ["in the last instance"—Trans.] determining element in history is the production and reproduction of real life. More than this neither Marx nor I have ever asserted. Hence if somebody twists this into saying that the economic element is the *only* determining one, he transforms that proposition into a meaningless, abstract, senseless phrase."[108] Engels further states that "we make our history ourselves, but, in the first place, under very definite assumptions and conditions. Among these the economic ones are ultimately decisive. But the political ones, etc., and indeed even the traditions which haunt human minds also play a part, although not the decisive one."

2. These texts are quite similar. The same key words occur in both: "make our own history," "conditions," "determines in the last instance." Thus:

a) "Men make their own history"[109]

b) But they are *conditioned* by a given milieu,[110] i.e., they make their own history on the basis of "actual, already existing" conditions, hence conditions they can do nothing to alter.

c) Among these "actual, already existing" conditions economic conditions are, "in the last instance," determining, although legal, political, and ideological conditions may exert some influence.[111]

Hence the analysis is carried out on three levels: economic determination applies only to the "actual, already existing" base, which conditions the struggles between men, and these struggles make history. Note that, in his letter to Bloch, Engels does not write "the determining element *of* history" but "the determining element *in* history."[112] It is indeed men who *make* history, as B. Rosier has pointed out:[113] "To call for class struggle ('Workers of the world, unite') would make no sense if a strict economic determinism operated."

There are two problems, however. First, the word "conditions" leaves a good deal of room for interpretation. To what extent is the class struggle autonomous in regard to the already existing milieu?

Granted that the question is no longer one of direct determination *of* history by economics, that men make history, it may then be asked to what extent the introduction of the class struggle into the argument serves only as a mediation between the economic determination of the milieu and the conditioning of the class struggle by that milieu? Is the effect not merely to add an additional link to the chain of determinations (namely, the class struggle)?

The second problem has to do with the meaning of the phrase "in the last instance," if we regard the milieu as determined by economics. The loosest possible interpretation, namely, that economics plays an essential role, is not merely undialectical, but also so broad as to be acceptable to virtually all historians today. The naïve interpretation—that the relations between economic base and superstructure are reciprocal but are blocked off at a certain moment in time—is scarcely admissible: to take this view would be to liken the dialectic to a game of tennis, in which the economic base always managed to put in a forehand smash to end the match. This leaves the interpretation in terms of different levels; the double determination, in other words, operates on two different levels. The economic base determines social relations and the conditions of the class struggle, whereas change in legal and political relations and ideology affect only the *form* of development of the productive forces. This is the interpretation accepted by a good many contemporary Marxist writers (for example, the authors of the *Traité marxiste d'économie politique* and Charles Bettelheim). The essence-form distinction is dialectical, however, only if the bridges between these two levels are not burned: when social relations or legal and political relations change, technological progress may take various forms, and these have an impact on the development of the productive forces themselves. Hence it must be accepted that men produce their economic base and that the balance of power between the classes determines the development of the base, and not merely the form of development. If men make their own history, they also make their own economic history; that is, they produce the division of labor and machinery, and establish the form and fix the importance of technological progress: in short, they produce the *new* real basis of society. Furthermore, the prior social and legal-political relations condition this new real basis.

3. If a breakthrough occurs on the level of social relations and the legal-political superstructure, leading to transformation on the level of the productive forces, can we not say that the material base, hitherto fettered, has made up for lost time? We hope to show that such a conception is mistaken, and hence that the theory according to which the relations of production and the entire superstructure are ultimately determined by the economy is false.

We shall begin with the text in which Engels criticizes Dühring and his naive concept of "direct political force," and reaffirms that the economy is the basis of society.

Violence without arms, explains Engels, is impossible. "Force, nowadays, is the army and navy, and both, as we all know to our cost, are 'devilishly expensive.' . . . Force is conditioned by the economic order, which furnishes the resources for the equipment and maintenance of the instruments of force."[114]

When Engels considers the army, he of course studies its weaponry, but he also looks at the "human material." "The whole organization and method of fighting of armies, and along with these victory or defeat, proves to be dependent on material, that is, economic conditions; on the human material, and the armaments material, and therefore on the quality and quantity of the population and on technical development."[115] For a specific example he takes the major material innovation introduced by the armies of revolutionary France, the organization in a column rather than a line formation. In a magisterial analysis, Engels explains that this innovation did not spring full-blown from the brow of some captain of genius: "Only a revolution such as the French, which brought about the economic emancipation of the burghers and especially the peasantry, could find the method of the mass army and at the same time the free form of movement which shattered the old rigid lines—the military counterparts of the absolutism against which they were fighting."[116] But it follows from this that it was the revolutionary overthrow of the old legal and political relations that caused the development of the material forces, i.e., of the army, which in this particular case happens to be a destructive rather than a productive force.

This analysis is unexceptionable, and in itself not in the least heterodox.[117] Were the old relations not fetters on the material powers, the forces of destruction? Furthermore, since the legal and political forms of the ancien régime were destroyed by the development of the productive forces, Engels is able to pull "his" version of the productive forces out of a hat, land back on his feet as a mechanistic materialist, and hold on to the notion of ultimate determination by the material base conceived (vulgarly) as the mere accumulation of means of production.

But was the development of the productive forces under feudalism a "gift from on high"? Who was responsible for this development, and why? What about the class struggles of the bourgeoisie against the lords for emancipation of the towns, followed closely by further struggles against the "poor," the peasants, and the vagabonds—did they not count for something? We agree with Engels when he points out that the French Revolution, by emancipating the bourgeoisie and the peasantry (or by completing the process of emancipation), led to a development of the productive forces of mankind—not only in the case he studies, the army, where the force is in fact destructive, but in other areas as well. But we cannot follow him in viewing this social and legal-political revolution as having been determined by a prior development of the economic base, not even "in the last instance," *because we believe that this development was itself a product of class struggles.*

What we have seen thus far of the argument for determination "in the last instance" by economics may be summed up as follows:

—Either the argument comes down to a truism: economics is one essential element among many determinants of the actual milieu by which men are conditioned.

—Or the whole argument rests on a blocking off of one side of the dialectic, as is implicit in Engels's contention that "the economic conditions are ultimately decisive." On this view of the matter, the reciprocal relations between the economic base and the superstructure are seen as a "feedback loop," which at a certain moment becomes blocked, cutting off the effects of legal and political relations on the economic base.

—Or the argument relies on a revival of the scholastic distinction between essence and form, since it is hard to understand why the superstructure should not have an effect on the essence through the form, unless it is argued that, in principle, "development in itself" cannot be affected by the "form of development."

4. Althusser flatly rejects the idea that the relations of production merely superimpose themselves on the productive forces as their form. He rightly stresses the unity of the productive forces and relations of production, and attacks the distinction between them as a technocratic and economistic error.[118]

As a structuralist Marxist, Althusser explains that the contradiction must not be viewed as unequivocally "determined once and for all, fixed in its role and essence; it turns out to be determined by the structured complexity by which its role is assigned, that is—if the reader will pardon me for resorting to this frightful word—complexly-structurally-unequally-determined. . . . Frankly, I should have preferred a shorter word, namely, overdetermined."[119] Althusser claims that working with a complex totality in which many different determinations operate does not land him in a situation in which determination is "equivocal,"[120] for he incorporates the notion of the dominant determination. Hence he arrives at the determination "in the last instance" by the economic factor,[121] and he lays great stress on the theoretical importance of this category of "determination in the last instance,"[122] which, he says, enables him to distinguish between Marxism and idealism, to adopt a materialist position, and at the same time to distinguish his position from that of mechanistic determinism. The image used by Marx, that of a building with a foundation and several stories, is, writes Althusser, an interesting one: "The notion of 'determination in the last instance' here plays the role of shattering the tranquil image of the circle or sphere."[123]

And the class struggle? As Althusser has written, there is a unity of the productive forces and the relations of production: "The productive forces are at once the material base [or technological basis, in Marx's terms] and the historical form of existence of the relations of production, i.e., the relations of exploitation."[124] The sentence is a noteworthy one: the existence of antagonistic classes is inscribed within the production process itself, "at the very heart of production; within the relations of production."[125] In consequence, to speak of ultimate determination by the economy is to raise the *economic* class struggle to the position of the dominant determination: "What is determining in the last instance, then, is the economy, hence the economic class struggle, extended by the political class struggle for state power, and thus we see how the class struggle at the base interacts (or fails to interact) with the class struggle in the superstructure."[126]

Since what is required is that there be, on the one hand, a factor that is determining in the last instance, and, on the other hand, a certain number of factors that are determined, and since Althusser, out of concern to avoid the error of mechanism, i.e., the view that the relations of production and the class struggle are determined by the level of development of the productive forces, asserts the unity of the productive forces and relations of production, he is forced to rely on the opposition between the "economy" as a whole, including the economic class struggle, and the superstructure as a whole, including the political class struggle, which is seen as an extension of the economic struggle. The discontinuity (necessitated by the requirement that the economy be ultimately determining) is introduced between a class struggle at the base and a class struggle in the superstructure, the latter either interacting or not interacting with the former. This is the mistake. The class struggle, at once economic and political, is a unified whole, its various aspects inextricably bound up with one another. Althusser hopes to avoid economism by incorporating a segment of the class struggle into the economy. But this leads him straight into an argument of an economistic type.

Nevertheless, Althusser did at least contribute to a new departure with his insistence on the unity of the productive force and the relations of production, which made it easier to understand, as against the interpretation of Marxism that is unfortunately widely current today, that the relations of production are just as material as hand mills, water mills, or steam mills. Having said this, a major problem remains: if the relations of production are inconceivable without class struggle—both economic and political—how are the relations between the productive forces and the relations of production to be understood, especially if it is true that the productive forces cannot be defined independently of the relations of production and vice versa? There would seem to be just three possibilities, each with drawbacks. Either one accepts the separation of the economic class struggle from the political class struggle, where the latter is determined and the former is, along with the productive forces, part of the economic element of the social structure. We have already said that we regard this answer as unacceptable. Or else one looks upon the mode of production as a "black box," a sort of economic catch-all containing the productive forces, the relations of production, and the class struggle, with no thought of the internal interrelations among them; the "black box" is then held to determine, in the last instance, everything else. If we choose this alternative, historical materialism loses half its explanatory power. Or—yet a third alternative—one assumes at the relations of production are determined by the productive forces, whether "in the last instance" or not: this is nothing more than economism.

5. There is no doubt that Althusser's thought was influenced by Mao Tse Tung, chiefly through one of Mao's essays, the celebrated *On Contradiction* (1937).[127] Hence we must go back to the source in the writings of Mao to see if we can find there a rigorous critique of the economistic orthodoxy. What we shall find is that the "critical" aspect of Mao's writings is clear, but the rigor more doubtful.

After drawing a distinction between the principal contradiction and the secondary contradictions,[128] Mao explains what the principal aspect of a contradiction is: "The principal aspect is the one playing the leading role in the contradiction."[129] He adds that "this situation is not static; the principal and the non-principal aspects of a contradiction transform themselves into each other."[130] Furthermore, "some people think that this is not true of certain contradictions. For instance, in the contradiction between the productive forces and the relations of production, the productive forces are the principal aspect; in the contradiction between theory and practice, practice is the principal aspect; in the contradiction between the economic base and the superstructure, the economic base is the principal aspect; and there is no change in their respective positions. This is the mechanical materialist conception, not the dialectical materialist conception."[131] Mao maintains instead that "in certain conditions, such aspects as the relations of production, theory, and the superstructure in turn manifest themselves in the principal and decisive role." But he also holds that "the productive forces, practice, and the economic base generally play the principal and decisive role; whoever denies this is not a materialist." This "generally" would seem to impose rather severe limitations on the scope of Mao's previous statement, playing the same role here as the phrase "in the last instance" played in Engels; but Mao's proviso is a vague one, designed to show that he is sticking close to materialism. In our view, it would seem that the three contradictions cited are not all to be placed on the same plane: while it is true that one is no longer a materialist if one tries to go beyond the view that the superstructure "reacts" on the economic base and to maintain instead that the superstructure plays the leading role in the contradiction, the same cannot be said of the relations of production. To say that the relations of production play the leading role in the contradiction with the productive forces is not to abandon materialism in the slightest; nor is there any need to cling to the idea that "generally" the productive forces play the decisive role. By the same token, it would seem that Mao Tse-Tung has no need to reduce the influence of the relations of production on the productive forces to one of mere "reaction," a step away from his much stronger statement that the relations of production can constitute the main aspect of the contradiction.

In this work we shall try to preserve what seems to us Mao's key idea: the decisive, leading role of the relations of production, and hence of the class struggle. At the same time we shall try to avoid both the facile vagueness of the notion that the foregoing statement is true only exceptionally, the productive forces "generally" being dominant, and the interpretation of society in mechanistic terms. We hope to use the "case study" of the collapse of the ancient slave system to show the inadequacy of any attempt to interpret historical materialism in economistic or mechanistic terms, even in Engels's "scaled-down" version, or Althusser's "structuralist" version.

1

If those are the fat cats, I pity the people! And if those are the peasants, I pity the country! I can see from here the anarchy of millet and sweet potatoes in those tiny plots.

Aimé Césaire, *La Tragédie du Roi Christophe*

The Villa, Society, and the State

The nature of slavery changes from one period of history to another, and, within a given period, it varies from one region to the next. Even in one particular spot at one moment in time, quite different kinds of slaves are found: the social division of labor and internal hierarchy of society have always been particularly marked among the servile masses, being intimately bound up with slavery itself. In antiquity we find a great number of slave types, varying with the time and place. The Greek slave differs from the Roman, the Roman slave of the late republic from the Roman slave of the late empire, and the rural slave of, say, the first century A.D. from the utterly dissimilar urban household slave—and so on. We shall be interested chiefly in the rural slave system based on labor gangs in the vast Roman estates (vast, anyway, in a relative sense for the period in question), this having been the predominant social relation in the Roman social formation of the late republic and the first two centuries of the empire; in other words, we shall be focusing on

what Marx called the *Gutsklavenwirtschaft* (agricultural economy based on the slave system).[1] We shall be looking neither at urban slavery (domestic slaves, craftsmen, teachers, etc.) nor at slaves owned by small-holders when this was the dominant form of property. Just as today it is possible to distinguish a working class proper within the salaried population as a whole, so it is possible to regard the slaves of the labor gangs as constituting a distinct social group within the larger group of all slaves.

Similarly, the notion of the feudal mode of production covers several different modes of exploitation. In western Europe, in France in particular, a long evolutionary process has been observed: there was a transition from the slave system to the feudal mode of production (FMP) with serfdom, followed by a change in the form of this mode of production, and finally by a transition to the capitalist mode of production (CMP).[2] The small, independent peasant, who in some cases even owned property and who paid rent in one or more forms, was quite different from the serf, the man of another man, whether the latter was a former *servus casatus*[3] or a descendant of the *coloni*, originally free men who had been granted a plot of land and given protection by a lord. The central problem of this work is to study the transition from the gang-labor slave to the serf by way of domiciling. This problem cannot, however, be studied independently of the transformation of the condition of the work force through the failure to reproduce the slave gang, as well as through the use of tenants; more generally, therefore, the problem is linked to that of the subjugation of free peasants. Serfdom has two origins: on the one hand slaves *rose* to serfdom, while on the other hand free and independent men, settled on small plots more or less integrated into a community governed by certain rules, *sank* into serfdom. While we are chiefly interested in the first of these, it can be studied only in conjunction with the second.

We shall proceed in the following order: genesis of the *villa*[4] slave system, "ends" of the slave system, forms of exploitation in the early Middle Ages and challenges to them, and elaboration of a "new" feudal mode of production.

I. Genesis of the *Villa* Slave System

There is reason to distinguish between the period of the republic and that of the empire in regard to the mode of exploitation of the slaves. It is not by chance that the transition in mode of exploitation parallels the superstructural transition from the republican state to the imperial state. The slave wars of the first period stand in stark contrast to the "lull" during the second, the era of repression, which continues until the "crisis" of the third and fourth centuries.

*A) From the Formation of the First Great Estates to
the Slave Wars*

In the fourth century B.C. clan society disappeared. The patriciate, the group of families that held the land and (through the Senate) the political power in early Rome after the expulsion of the Etruscans (at the beginning of the fifth century) had to make room during the fourth century for certain plebeians, chiefly those who had grown wealthy during the preceding century. These plebeians had access to the various magistracies, and the Senate, which was then composed of former and active magistrates, became the place where the new ruling class exercised its power. Ultimately the aristocracy came to consist of families that had given at least one magistrate to the republic, and there was a tendency to transform the aristocracy into a nobility, as closed to outsiders as the old patrician caste had been: the families of the senators had a hold on the magistracies.

During the fourth and third centuries B.C., however, landed property of small to medium size was still dominant both in Latium and throughout the rest of Italy; the bulk of the fortune of the typical Roman citizen was held in this form. The wars of conquest of the third and second centuries would change this situation radically. The *nobilitas*, which controlled the military, would not only keep for itself the bulk of the booty of conquest, particularly conquered lands, but would also seize the land of the smallholders.

What happened, in effect, was that the Roman citizen, a smallholder and soldier, saw the first of these two roles become incompatible with the second, as military service expanded until it filled virtually the whole of a man's active life. Upon returning from the wars, the Roman soldier was forced *either* to borrow in order to start farming again, even though he had no hope of paying back his loans and would soon have to sell off his land,[5] *or* to sell out right away. It was chiefly the senators who laid hands on the lion's share of the *ager publicus*, which expanded immeasurably in the wake of the conquests. They did this by making use of the right of "occupation," under which anyone who could demonstrate that he had sufficient means to exploit a given property could obtain exclusive rights to its enjoyment, as a precarium (in theory) and against the payment of a rent (in practice symbolic).

In short, we witness the passage, in the space of two centuries, from a situation that brings to mind the yeomen of "merrie olde England" or the peasants of nineteenth-century France (with this considerable dif-

ference: there was no individualistic spirit among these ancient farmers)
to a society dominated by vast domains held by the *nobilitas*.

Thus it is clear that the wars of conquest, the system of rapine and
tribute that was soon expanded to cover the entire Mediterranean world,
made possible the accumulation of enormous monetary capital, based
on violence sanctioned by the state and hence concentrated, to begin
with, in the hands of the "captains," the senators. The senators were
accordingly able to gobble up the land of the poorest members of the
society. Soon thereafter, however, a part of this wealth found its way
into the hands of a new class of merchants, usurers, speculators, and
publicans (tax farmers): this was the equestrian order, which controlled
the world of finance and would before long start raising crops on estates
of its own. Thus this two-headed ruling class bore the seeds of conflict
within it.

The economy was one based on plunder of goods and money, which
went hand in hand with an economy based on razzias, or man-hunting
raids, quite like other economic systems in which property is associated,
not as in our capitalist societies with labor or the exploitation of labor,
but with violence and military conquest: hence slavery was not at first
concerned with the buying and selling of labor on a market, but rather
with the captive who mortgaged his life to his conqueror or was obliged
to pay a ransom. Here lay the source of the slave's value, which was
transferred to the market only subsequently (in both the logical and the
historical sense). If at first the slave was a symbol of power, hence of
wealth, he nonetheless became a source of profit, very considerable
profit, when he went to work on the large estate. The wars of the third
and second centuries brought a great influx of slaves to Rome and to all
of Italy. The contemporary industry of piracy further swelled this current. These masses of slaves, by now quite cheap, contributed to the
ruin of the independent small peasant in Italy. The peasant who could
no longer sell what his small plot produced in the face of competition
in grains from the conquered countries and in such "new" products as
meat, olives, and garden produce from the large Italian estates, facing
ruin upon his return from the wars, sold his land and headed for Rome,
enticed there by distributions of corn (at first conducted through the
clientele system but before long taken over by the public authorities,
after the corn laws).

The great estates of Italy under the Roman Republic and after the
Punic wars were rarely held in single tenancy. Little grain was grown
for current consumption in Rome, the lands serving chiefly to support
large-scale livestock raising (with slaves tending the herds on the "occupied" portion of the *ager publicus*). The various forms of rapine sup-

ported one another and led to an increase in both the size and number of estates.

Did the agrarian reforms introduced by Tiberius and Caius Gracchus and the later distributions of land to veterans by Caesar and Augustus lead to a period, during the late republic and early empire, when the importance of large-scale property was in decline? Was the late imperial *latifundium* a revival of this form of property, under a quite different form of organization (in which large numbers of *coloni,* roughly comparable to sharecroppers and in one degree or another tied to the land, provided the labor)? The agrarian reform movement and the distribution of land to veterans (250,000 families in the last century of the republic) may not, it seems to us, have had the results that some writers have imagined. Once parcelled out, the land was in one way or another very strongly affected by the forces unleashed in the broad process of peasant expropriation and concentration of property and exploitation. In contrast to J.-P. Brisson,[6] who emphasizes an interim period during which there was a return to small or medium holdings, M. I. Finley describes a clear tendency toward larger holdings during the late republic (and the empire).[7] Already in 133 B.C., for example, Tiberius Gracchus succeeded in forcing through a law limiting the size of individual holdings on the *ager publicus* (which, though theoretically the property of the state, was in practice appropriated by the Roman elite) to 500 *jugera,* plus 250 per child, with a maxium of 1000 *jugera,*[8] or 250 hectares (leaving untouched "privately held" lands and tenements). Proof that the estates in the *ager publicus* were considerably larger than this is afforded by the senators' violent reaction to this law and by the increase in receipts in consequence of confiscations and redistributions. To our present way of thinking, these dimensions may seem rather small. At the time, however, they were considerable, as is attested by the fact that, when Caesar settled veterans on the land, he assigned a parcel of 10 *jugera* (2.4 hectares)— the *jugum* being the amount of land a man could plow in one day. Since Roman law provided for dividing the patrimony between the children in equal parts, the size of the individual plot after two or three generations was reduced to a few acres.[9]

Finley explains that the Second Punic War had ruined much of southern Italy, thus leading to a growth in the size of the *latifundia* through purchase of the lands of ruined peasants while simultaneously permitting rapid growth of the *ager publicus,* which led to an increase in the size of the great estates through usurpation of the public land. The period of civil war that intervened between Sulla and Augustus also favored the concentration of landholdings. To mention one interesting example (useful, obviously, only as an index): a piece of land was sold by a woman,

Cornelia, to Lucullus for 10 million sesterces. To get an idea of the magnitude of this figure, consider that the pay of a legionnaire in the late first century was 1200 sesterces per year.[10] To what extent this was an exceptional case is difficult to know. At the beginning of the empire we find examples of properties of medium size selling for 300,000 sesterces and of larger properties selling for around 1 million.

To give some idea of the order of magnitude of the very large Roman estates in the late republic, let us cite Ahenobarbus, who, in raising an army against Caesar, promised to each of his men (whether they numbered 4,000 or 15,000 is uncertain) ten hectares, to be taken from his estates in Etruria![11] During the empire, particularly the late empire, the process of concentration of lands and expropriation of peasants continued. Furthermore, while the large slave-worked estate was common during the late republic in Sicily and Italy, populated chiefly by pastoralists, it spread during the empire throughout the western provinces (in the remainder of the empire, on the other hand, large estates were not dependent on slave-labor gangs of the classical type; instead, virtually the entire local population was subjugated, which accounts for the fact that these regions (1) did not import slaves, and/or (2)were hunting grounds for pirates and slave traders supplying the west).

If there is reason to doubt the effectiveness of the agrarian reforms and land distributions, they do nevertheless reveal the "land hunger" of the expropriated peasants and indicate the kinds of demands we find raised by the populace throughout antiquity, as typified, for instance, by the clamoring of soldiers, before and after demobilization, for cancellation of their debts and for grants of land. These demands amounted to a revolutionary program directed against the senatorial class of great landowners, a program that the equestrian order, which controlled most of the liquid capital, was destined to support against the senatorial power, thus setting the stage for the civil wars of the late republic.

If Tiberius Gracchus spoke for the dispossessed peasants against the senate, however, he first waged a public campaign against the masses of slaves in the countryside. He attacked the slave system as dangerous, citing the slave war in Sicily (133 B.C.) that grew out of it. Of course Tiberius took no interest in the fate of the slaves as such. Was the purpose of his speech to urge the ruling class to reform itself and the latifundian mode of exploitation, or was it to persuade the senators to consent to agrarian reform, using the fears aroused by the slaves as a pretext? There is no way to tell, but the important point is to note that the question of slavery rose to a position of paramount importance at this time. This was the moment when Roman society tilted toward the slave system, when the trend toward concentration of estates and expropriation of small landowners was heightened by that system, and, in consequence, also the time when the political struggle between landless peasants (as well as peasants threatened with the loss of their land) and latifundists took shape.

The same causes may be adduced to explain the civil wars and slave wars of the first and second centuries (B.C.): namely, the victories of Roman imperialism and the razzias that brought new land and slaves to Rome and broke down, or, more precisely, began to shatter, the old social structure (the process would come temporarily to an end in the latter days of the late empire). A priori, it *seems* clear that the external cause (Roman imperialism) produced the slave system and that the extension of the social relations of slavery could not but eliminate the small landowners in the long run and exacerbate the civil war. Conversely, as we shall see, the crushing of the slave revolts presupposes a certain unity, a certain consensus of civil society, a "class front" on the part of the free men that was in part the result of the slave war itself. It was the reconstitution of a certain unity of civil society, a unity achieved through systematic social differentiation, that made possible first the Caesarean state and later the Augustan state and the Roman Empire. The state apparatus—the organized, centralized repression of the slave masses—made possible the extension of the slave system and gave rise to the belief that the question of slavery had been "solved" (a belief still shared by some historians today).

Can we be satisfied, however, to point to the external factor, the imperialist victories, as the cause of the evolution? What explains the conquests, the triumphs of the Roman armies? The conquering spirit was chiefly republican; the empire would ultimately not so much extend as consolidate what had been achieved earlier. Hence it is to the social relations of republican Rome that we must look for an explanation of the necessity of imperialism and its triumphs. Struggles internal to Roman civil society, we find, made the conquests necessary, first for the senatorial class and later for the class of traffickers. Why not accept the ancient explanation of the victories, which were said to have been achieved by the strength of citizen armies, armies composed of small landowners, knit together by communal bonds and practices into a solid unit? Republican society, with its internal contradictions and civil conflict, produced imperialism and hence the slave system, which led to the exacerbation of civil conflict, as well as the slave wars, which would lead to a (temporary) coalition of the whole body of free men around the great landowners, as well as to the concentration of estates, the disappearance of intermediate social strata and small landowners, and finally to the shattering of civil society.

The late republic (second and first centuries B.C.) was marked throughout by slave wars.[12] The first broke out in Sicily, where livestock was raised on immense estates, in 139 or 140 B.C. The 400 rebel slaves who took the town of Henna soon became the masters of a "kingdom," and by 135 B.C. the slave army numbered no fewer than 200,000 soldiers, an enormous figure that gives us some idea of the volume of slaves imported through war and piracy. This example proved contagious, for a revolt broke out at Delos, a center of the slave traffic, as well as in Greece, where bands of fugitive slaves, sometimes numbering upwards of a thousand men, engaged in fighting over a wide area, and also in Latium and Campania. Three successive consuls would be needed before the armies of Eunus and Cleon could be overcome (which did not happen until 134).

A second slave war took place in Sicily, this time between 104 and 100 B.C., again beginning with the revolt of a few hundred slaves, who were soon joined by tens of thousands of their fellows, and perhaps also by some free peasants.[13] The Roman armies were to suffer several defeats before finally crushing the slave forces.

Lastly, there was the revolt of Spartacus, which stemmed from the flight of a few gladiators in 73 B.C., soon joined by tens of thousands of slaves from the *latifundia*. Before long the army of Spartacus counted some 120,000 men in its ranks. Everyone knows of the victories won by these slaves, which ultimately left Rome cut off when rebel slaves marched triumphantly throughout Italy. This lasted until the senate gave the *imperium* to Crassus, one of the largest land-grabbers and traffickers in land and slaves, who recruited 50,000 men, armed 30,000 of them out of his own funds, restored a fierce discipline in the army (reviving the decimation), and finally shed the slave armies in 71 B.C., destroying its remnants in southern Italy, while Pompey did the same in the north.

B) The Imperial State

Crassus and Pompey, the massacrers of the rebellious slaves, became consuls (forcing themselves illegally on the state). From that time on the only question was who would reestablish an enduring order. This role finally fell to Caesar, the leader of the "popular party" (opposed to the *optimates*, the senatorial conservatives). The popular party was the successor of the Gracchi and their followers, but in the interim the makeup and leadership of the party had changed. The Gracchi, though allied with the equestrians, were chiefly Italian plebeians who had been dispossessed of their *microfundia*, thereby being reduced to *proletarii* in Rome.[14] In Caesar's popular party, it seems, the ranks of the equestrian faction were swelled by men of ambition and new wealth, men eager for conquest and the booty of victory. Caesar's victory, therefore, could only come in the form of a penetration of the old ruling class by these "parvenu" elements, leading to the establishment of a new order in which the political importance of the senators was downgraded, along with that of the equestrian order itself, a change that worked together with the distribution of land to veterans to stabilize the social structure. If not for this, why did the veterans, lordless plebeians, support Caesar in the first place? With their aid Caesar established a quasi-permanent salaried army (Marius had done this previously), an army which, at the time of Caesar's death, comprised thirty-nine legions (each, at that time, of 6,000 men)—quite a respectable force.

After the death of Caesar, the civil war resumed, and the triumph of Octavian represented the victory of the most conservative forces: what followed was the establishment of an imperial social order, intended to be immutable, in which the senatorial and equestrian families (the new equestrian order consisted of the *equites* of the old plus the publicans and new "bureaucrats")[15] dominated the rest of the citizenry, Roman citizens were systematically favored over provincials, and the slave was kept in his place as a "talking tool." Augustus was in fact very strict on the subject of slavery, hostile to emancipation and to freedmen, hesitant about broadening the *droit de cité*, and in favor of moral order and the family.

This political order and its attendant repression were, of course, possible and enduring only because a state apparatus was set up and made increasingly powerful. The empire was organized in a series of concentric circles around the person of the emperor himself. In the inner circle was a coalition made up of members of the exploiting class, owners of *villae*, wealthy merchants, speculators, traffickers in land and slaves, and high state officials. A second circle embraced all Roman citizens, all of whom, from the greatest latifundist to the lowliest of the *proletarii*, profited from imperialism and lived on the tribute in grain extracted from the provinces. The third circle comprised free men who were not Roman citizens but in many cases masters of slaves and sometimes latifundists and/or members of municipal bourgeoisies. Finally, the fourth circle included freedmen. (In this sketch we have neglected the many differences between one province and another.) These were concentric circles, but they overlapped, so that imperial society embodied a complex hierarchy of ethnic and social distinctions, which gave the impression of a near continuum.

This "modern" state was embodied primarily in a strong administration and a permanent professional army and was sustained by a fiscal system which, though still inadequate, was, all in all, quite remarkable for the time. This state apparatus, first adumbrated by Caesar and later systematized under Augustus, underwent further development during the early empire.

The imperial army no longer recruited by conscription; it had become a professional army, with a status, privileges and obligations (different for the legion and the auxiliaries), but was not yet a hereditary military "caste." It was relatively small (between 300,000 and 500,000 men) and stationed chiefly along the frontiers, in camps that tended to become permanently established (wherein lie the roots of a good many cities), or in garrisons near Rome, as well as in Lyons and Carthage. It is important to stress that it was not the function of the army to comb Italy and the provinces for potential sources of civil and social unrest. If this implies that armed force was not needed to bring slave rebellions to heel (just as the army today is not needed to maintain the social order from day to day), it nevertheless does not follow that the army and the police, integrated along with other components into the state apparatus, were not indispensable to the maintenance of social order.

It is interesting to note that the organization of the army rather accurately reflected the social and imperial order. The army was composed of different corps recruited from specific social or ethnic categories. The Praetorian cohorts, which made up the emperor's guard and were stationed first in Italy and later, for all practical purposes, in Rome itself, recruited exclusively among Italians.[17] The legions (which numbered fifty after the victory at Actium and subsequently between twenty-eight and thirty) were made up of Roman citizens (peregrines could ultimately become legionnaires and automatically became Roman citizens if they did). The auxiliaries were recruited among foreigners (approximately equalling the legions in numbers of men). The cohorts of watchmen, recruited among freedmen and the urban cohorts made up the police force of the city of Rome (there were also local police forces).

This army received regular pay, but wages were low, and the duration of enlistment varied from fifteen to twenty-five years, depending on the type of army. The bulk of a soldier's compensation consisted of land distributed to the veterans of the legions, a practice instituted from the very first and continued as long as it was practicable. Legionnaire veterans (around forty years of age) were also called upon to replenish the municipal reserves of Italian and provincial cities, generally their native *municipium*. In some cases, though, veterans settled in cities along the campaign route (this proved a very effective method for integrating the provincial cities into the empire and "transmitting" Roman discipline via the citizen-soldier and his prestige). The veteran of an auxiliary troop was granted Roman citizenship for himself and for the peregrine woman with whom he lived. These benefits, far from being honorific, were not always enough (in view of the low pay and long duration of service) to insure a healthy influx of recruits. This explains why the auxiliary troops, who lived and procreated in long-established army camps, were encouraged to pass on the profession of arms to their sons.

Within the army, we find that internal promotion was of great importance. The centurion rose out of the ranks after fifteen years' service and subsequently advanced from one cohort to another, the cohorts themselves forming a hierarchy (each was numbered, and the first centurion of the first cohort, or *primipile*, held an important post). Certain centurions ultimately gained access to the equestrian order, after passing through the Roman urban cohorts. Promotion could not, of course, take a man all the way to the top! Only senators were granted command of a legion (at least up to the time of Septimius Severus, after which some *equites* obtained commands): this professional army was not led by amateurs,[18] but by high civil servants who shuttled back and forth between military and civilian service.

This army, whose structure and chain of command were based on social and ethnic criteria but allowed a good deal of mobility in the ranks, was the cornerstone and image of the empire.

With Augustus and afterwards the imperial administration underwent further development. There was a central administration, the backbone of the government, made up of persons with direct ties to the emperor and connections to the imperial council and to the bureaus, the equivalent of our modern ministries. The Praetorian prefect (chief of the emperor's bodyguard, who in fact exercised very broad powers), was the second most powerful personage in the state. There were also local administrations of different sorts in Rome, in Italy, in the so-called senatorial provinces (in theory governed by the senate), in still other provinces, known as imperial provinces, and, finally, in the protected kingdoms. Everywhere this administration was on the whole rather efficient, strictly centralized and hierarchical, and usually completely controlled by the emperor, though in some cases enjoying a pseudo-autonomy (the protected kingdoms) or subject to the senate's power to nominate officials (in the senatorial provinces). In fact, however, these nominations were greatly influenced by the emperor.

The leading personnel of this administrative bureaucracy (to say nothing of the very highest positions, which for a long while were filled almost exclusively by senators) were recruited from the equestrian class, which became the bureaucratic class. From the equestrian order one could rise to the senatorial class, and access to the equestrian order from below was possible by favor of the emperor or with the aid of cash. For a long time, however, the (normally) lower ranks of the bureaucracy were filled largely by freedmen of the emperor. Indeed, until the crisis brought on by their extraordinary unpopularity at the end of the first century, these emancipated slaves played a very large role: owing everything to the emperor, generally capable and faithful, they took on an importance that was eventually deemed excessive.

Like the army, the administration provided much opportunity for advancement within its ranks. This was true not only at the bottom of the hierarchy, for the slaves and freed imperial slaves, but also at the top, from which one could gain access to the senatorial order. Above all, administrative careers seem to have been favored by the sons of bourgeois families. In the end, the municipal bourgeoisie of the Italian and provincial cities furnished the most substantial support of the imperial order, Rome's chief success having been its ability to organize the empire not only through its central administration but also through the reproduction in each city of a municipal organization similar to that of Rome, which welded the provincial ruling classes together around the city hub.

Thus the administration in no way constituted an autonomous caste: public office was fused with membership in the ruling classes, Roman and provincial, whose power and wealth were based on landed property and the slave system, as well as on liquid fortunes (the former, of course, made it possible to acquire the latter).

The army and bureaucracy required a substantial system of financing. As late as Augustus, to be sure, the finances of the state were backed by the emperor's personal fortune. But the two spheres gradually became more and more distinct, with the realization that the finances of the state must be established on a firm basis through an efficient system of taxation. The Augustan state was ordinarily financed by a direct tax on land, paid by the landowners, excepting those on Italian soil (or covered by Italian law); this was the *tributum*. Along with this went a tax on movable property (which in Egypt was a head tax), the *tributum capitis*. The system was completed by three long-standing indirect taxes—on emancipations, sales of slaves, and customs duties—along with an inheritance tax and a tax on commodity sales. Roman taxation was surely inadequate, given the burden of the army (for salaries and campaign expenses) and the bureaucracy. Yet it was remarkably stable, relatively equitable (in view of the land tax, the tax on movable property, the inheritance tax, etc.), and notable for the fiscal administration itself, which made it possible to collect direct taxes without a system of publicans. In a manner of speaking, this was the fiscal system that reformers were never able to establish in France under the ancien régime!

Since tax receipts were insufficient, it was necessary to resort to confiscation of property in many guises, ranging from (more or less) voluntary bequests to seizure of the property of political opponents, with appropriation of intestate estates falling in between. Monetary manipulations were also an unwelcome necessity. Bear in mind, however, that during this period "benefactions," i.e., financing of "public benefits" by the wealthy in the absence of any legal compulsion, played a considerable role. The great man or ruler not only owed it to himself to show his might through displays of magnificence, he also produced that might by means of prodigious expenditures of money (politics, moreover, was closely bound up with such expenditures: just as wealth "followed" political power, so money had to be spent to acquire power in the first place). That "public benefits" were privately financed explains why taxation could occupy a comparatively small place (if the luxuries of the cities had had to be financed out of the public treasury, the tax burden would have been far too light).

An adequate system of taxation, however, is only a technical necessity, made possible by certain social conditions. More generally, the existence of a state apparatus comprising the army, the police, the courts, the fiscal administration, a "prefectural" bureaucracy, and so forth is possible only because a certain social structure, the foundation of the state, is in place. If the state, under Augustus and throughout the early empire until the crisis of the third century, represented a coalition of the class of large landowners and monied wealth, a coalition achieved after two centuries of civil conflict that culminated in control of the upper levels of the civilian and military bureaucracy, its social base was far broader. This was due in large part to the existence of a systematic hierarchy of intermediary classes and ethnic groups, in which each class or group depended on the state to establish its superiority over the inferior groups in the hierarchy. This tended to reinforce the power of the state and to establish solidarity among the successive strata in the ethnic and social pyramid, all of which profited from imperialism and the slave system. If the social order was imposed despotically on the heavily exploited classes (slaves in the west and subjugated peasantry in the east) by means of the repressive apparatus of the state and of private landowners (who had their own "police" on large estates), it was ultimately accepted by the intermediary classes, all of which reaped benefits from the slave or quasi-slave system, as well as from imperialism in the case of the Italians. This was all the more true because of the *high level of social mobility*: the slave with *peculium* might acquire a fortune and buy or be granted his freedom, so that his descendants could live as truly free men. By the same token, the foreigner could become a peregrine, a quasi citizen. Finally, the imperial order was knitted together by collusion of the ruling classes in the outlying regions with the central state, that is, with the Roman and Italian ruling class.

The whole edifice was crowned by an effective ideology, that is, an ideology tailored in such a way as to line up both the intermediary social strata and the provinces behind the central ruling class and Rome. The social order was seen as a reflection of an immutable divine order (or anyway an order that ultimately settled into immutability), and the emperor, before long, as someone who, if not a god, tended more and more to be regarded as a divinity, or as the mortal image of one. We also note the importance of the *vox populi*, which "compelled" Augustus (and his successors down to the fourth century) to take on the burden of the empire, together with the idea that the monarch served others and did not own the empire personally. Power was said to be democratic and to insure *libertas*, "the corollary of a virtuous, rational, human power, as opposed to domination. *Libertas* also defended the empire against the barbarians, for *libertas* was essentially Roman."[20] Thus the Roman ideology was one of fear and contempt, from the top to the bottom of the social hierarchy and from the center of the empire to its periphery, capped by fear of and contempt for the slave and the barbarian: these were the people one oppressed and exploited, the people one owned and subjugated, the people one snatched away in razzias and kept as slaves, and the people one feared, this fear being the mortar that held the various strata of the society together. Finally, there was the remarkable "invention" that enabled the emperor and the "great" to bypass the ethnic and social hierarchies, the emperor being guarded by a corps of barbarians, the 500 *Germani corporis custodes*, and the inner circles of the imperial bureaucracy (or the private *villa* bureaucracy) being composed of privileged slaves and freedmen of the emperor (or wealthy landowners). In short, the motto everywhere was "divide and conquer, stratify and rule."

C) The Chained Slave in the Villa

The shepherd slaves who rebelled on the immense republican estates in Italy, and above all in Sicily, had, on the whole, great freedom of movement and were even left to themselves much of the time. During the late republic, a new type of large estate began to spread throughout Italy and the provinces: the classical *villa* system was born. Is there warrant to believe that during the first century B.C. authoritarian redistribution of land gave rise to a system based on property in the small to medium range? As we said earlier, we are skeptical of this supposed decline of the *latifundium*, which can in any case have been only temporary, since all historians are agreed on the importance of the *latifundia* in the first century A.D. (whether these large estates had been reconstituted or had merely grown in size). What changed was chiefly the organization of the estate. The bands of slaves that had once followed the flocks through the immense plains of the great Roman estates, as described by Appianus, were now a thing of the past. The *latifundium* consisted of one or more distinct *villae*, each of which constituted an agricultural unit, a coherent whole. Like the industrial plant today, the *villa* is the element of the system we should concentrate on in order to grasp the nature of exploitation concretely.

In the first centuries of the Christian era the *villa*[21] supported large numbers of slaves, who worked in small groups on varied and specialized tasks coordinated by a steward and overseers. Very closely supervised, the slaves ate in "refectories" and lived in "barracks." Centrally controlled in labor divided on technical lines and constantly under surveillance, these slaves worked in conditions not unlike those of chaingang laborers day. For three centuries there would be no mass revolts of slaves under this regime.

It is this new type of latifundian system, based on the slave-operated *villa*, that we must now pause to consider at some length. We may begin by asking what is known of the relative importance of the *villae* as a form of habitation, not only for the masters and their domestic servants, but also for the slaves of the *familia*, who were housed by the master and worked his lands. What portion of the total arable belonged to large estates? Aerial photography, most notably that of Roger Agache,[22] has led to a profound revision of opinion on these questions. As has been noted, for example, by Marcel Le Glay,[23] the northern portion of France was once thought to have contained few *villae*, and the Artois to have been completely forested, but aerial photography has shown that these northern plains harbored more than a thousand *villae*. The same is true for the Beauce region, which A. Dauzat (solely on the evidence of toponymics) had imagined to be unbroken forest and which Marc Bloch (despite his criticism of toponymics and emphasis on archaeological research) still viewed as a region of vast steppes punctuated here and there by farms. It turns out that the area was very heavily populated and had a high density of *villae*. The same is true for Armorica, which was once supposed to have been left largely untouched by the conquerors. Of course, the regions of long-standing colonization, such as the Narbonnaise, also contained many large *villae*. To sum up the results of recent research, it may be said that, little by little, a map of Roman Gaul is emerging on which the *villa* figures as the most typical mode of habitation and exploitation of both land and men, clearly predominant wherever conditions were sufficiently salubrious and the soil sufficiently fertile.[24] The drought of 1976 provided the opportunity to increase our knowledge still further, and once again the relative importance of the *villa* stood out before our very eyes. But, as Columella attests, and as we shall see shortly, the same holds true for Britain[25] and Spain as well.

Of course this does not mean that the population of the countryside and the *villa* were completely identical. For one thing, the *villa* system allowed groups of *coloni* and other tenants with one kind of contract or another to live together in hamlets or villages appertaining to the *latifundium* of which their lands were a part. For another, the *vici*, or villages independent of the *villa*, harbored more or less autonomous communities of peasants (the heirs of the ancient rural commune, with property in land on an individual basis, though subject to very strong collective rules[26] and endowed with abundant common lands), as well as craftsmen and merchants, thus constituting genuine country towns.

In the provinces colonized by Rome, the confiscated lands were divided up according to the centuriation, with the overwhelming majority of the population consisting of the oppressed (though this did not exclude collaboration by the upper class, the class of Gallo-Roman masters of *villae*, for example, a phenomenon we find duplicated in Spain, Britain, and North Africa). Apart from the forested, mountainous, or outlying areas "abandoned" to the "natives" and relatively untouched by colonization, everything fitted into a system, in which the major roads served to interconnect the cities, the administrative, military, and commercial centers in which the masters and their entourages lived, and the *villae* and their estates took in most of the land and the greater part of the populace. What we see is no longer western and Mediterranean Europe, made up of small villages subjugated politically and fiscally but more or less autonomous economically; rather, we are now looking upon the western empire, closer perhaps to what colonialism and the slave system would one day make of the Antilles and the southern United States prior to 1860, to the Portuguese Alentejo until very recently, or to what the word *latifundium* still signifies throughout large parts of South America today. It is for this reason that we must try to understand the *villa* system, as much from the archaeological logical record, insofar as building can inform us about the nature of the economic and social system, as from the written record. Among written documents we have looked especially at the writings of Columella, because of the period in which he wrote (first century) and the location of his estate (Spain), and also because of his intelligence and acumen.

To begin with, then, the estate (*fundus*) itself generally consisted of a cultivated portion, a portion of grasslands, and a third, wooded part, not to mention wasteland, brush land, and so on. The size of the estate varied widely and in some cases is difficult to determine. The famous estate of Chiragan[27] seems to have contained a thousand hectares under cultivation and some 7,000–8,000 hectares in all, but this was no doubt an unusually large estate; the typical great estate probably consisted of something like a thousand hectares.[28] The Montmaurin estate[29] in Haute-Garonne was of this size (during the first and second centuries). The estate of Saint-Ulrich in Moselle seems to have measured only 200 hectares, notwithstanding the presence of large buildings and the impression it gives of very great wealth.[30] An estate, moreover, could include more than one *villa* (at Gondrexange in Moselle, for example, thirteen farms totaled some 1,300 hectares).

The estate aspired to be self-sufficient, which does not mean that it did not sell a considerable portion of its product. Self-sufficiency implies merely that an effort was made—and sometimes carried to rather extreme lengths—to buy as little as possible, to feed and clothe the workers (and the master when he was in residence) out of what was produced locally, and even to make, and certainly to maintain and repair, needed tools on the estate itself. Such an aim presupposes the production of a variety of crops, foods, fertilizers, fuels, and handicrafts. Frequently, however, the *villa* produced only a limited number of commodities for sale on the marketplace of a nearby town, intended either to feed the armies in the vicinity or for export. The *villa* in some cases tended toward single-crop production (as far as market crops were concerned) in certain regions. *Villae* in central and northern Gaul, for example, tended to be grain producers or livestock-raisers. What were the relative proportions of labor expended in the *villa* for, respectively, commodity production and production of the means of subsistence? Everything depended on the productivity of labor, on the rate of exploitation, and on the level of self-sufficiency in the production of means of subsistence, raw materials, and implements.

The *villa* itself may be defined, in the strict sense, as "a group of buildings, generally enclosing one or two courtyards, a dwelling house, outbuildings, and workshops."[31] It was thus the center of the estate (or, since a *latifundium* could include several *villae*, of a portion of an estate). Le Glay has given us excellent descriptions of the different types of *villae* in Romanized Gaul, and useful knowledge is available of the nature of the different buildings and of their relations to one another and to the courtyards. Studying the plans of the *villae*, especially those that occur with a certain regularity (the *villae* of northern Gaul, for example, were a particular type) can help us to understand the social system and the system of production: the physical organization of a city, a Roman *villa*, a typical factory, a concentration camp, or an apartment reveals the bare bones of a system, whether in a still-vital society or a bygone civilization. We have rather good knowledge of these plans, thanks to aerial photography (particularly that of R. Agache again), and sometimes almost perfect information, thanks to the drought of 1976.[32] Consider the highly typical plan of the *villa* of Grivesne (a modest-sized Picardian *villa*), as described by Le Glay: facing forward and in general serving as the central axis of the whole complex was the main house (in which the master lived when he was in residence), behind which lay a first rectangular courtyard: this was the *pars urbana*. It was frequently bordered by buildings connected by a gallery. A wall separated this court from a second courtyard, much larger than the first, known as the *pars rustica*, around which stood a series of outbuildings, sometimes connected, sometimes not, and, on one side, a second dwelling, that of the steward, or *villicus*. Sometimes other buildings stood outside the courtyard, thought by Agache to have been the places where noisy or dangerous work was done.

It is often difficult to know what the different parts of a given building were used for. Besides the main building it is rather easy to identify the bakery and the threshing yard and, on the circumference of the rustic courtyard, the kitchen (identified by the broken pottery, traces of food, etc.), the workshops (revealed by the presence of millstones, slag, forge scraps, etc.), and the cellars. Le Glay tells us that the other buildings described by Columella [33] are more difficult to locate: the cattle sheds, stables, chicken house, repair shops for wagons and tools, granaries and silos, and the various barns.

If we pause for a moment at this point, we may notice, first, the strict separation of the master's dwelling place from the rest. It was not only set apart physically (as at Grivesne, for example, with a wall between the *pars urbana* and the *pars rustica*) but also by the different forms of construction (taking "form" in the broad sense, to cover all the physical aspects of the building), with luxurious construction on the one hand, a veritable "castle," sometimes extraordinarily sumptuous, and simple and efficient construction on the other hand, for the appurtenances and outbuildings. There is nothing surprising about this, of course: this disparity, the most visible and most important of all, corresponds to the division of the society into its *two principal classes* (though the body social was divided into a great many *social categories*).

A second remark that may be made at this point has to do with the location and relative size of the steward's dwelling: here we see the first sign of the social hierarchy, reflecting the importance of the role of the *villicus* in managing and overseeing the *villa*, and yet also indicating "his place," on the side of the *pars rustica*.

Finally, the specific uses assigned to the various buildings and courtyards show us that the *villa* relied on coordinated management on a rather large scale, including division of labor and specialized utilization of space.

But what were things like for human beings in the *villa*? On this point Le Glay is all but silent. He merely reminds us that there were two possible systems in use and that the estate was divided between them: on the one hand the reserved land was worked by slaves and agricultural laborers who lived within the buildings of the *villa*, while on the other hand there were farmers (*coloni, colones, possessores*) who lived either in isolated dwellings on their own plots of land or grouped together in hamlets. Was it not the case, however, that the *villa* was based chiefly on one of the two systems, even if it *may* have been true that in Gaul there were fewer slaves than in other provinces?[34] Without an idea of the slave system it would be impossible to understand the operation of these large properties, for it is clear from Agache's photographs of *villae* whose estates covered a considerable portion of Gaul that these were not consistent with a system based on more or less self-sufficient peasants dependent to one degree or another on a lord.[35] One has only to observe the size and layout of the *villae* to understand that they involved a system based on centralized exploitation of lands and men, even if a portion of the estate was also let to tenants (just as a glance at a modern factory is enough to convince us that industrial production is not a form of craft handiwork). There are Roman mosaics (like those of Tabarka in Tunisia[36] dating from the fourth century) showing the enormous detached buildings that housed the slaves; the plans of the *villae rusticae*, moreover, often indicate that their dormitories were integrated into the central buildings (Villa Boscoreale at Pompeii, for example). Slaves might also be housed in huts not far from the other buildings, inside stockades that surrounded the whole complex.

Le Glay, of course, is basing his descriptions on what is today visible of the *villa* architecture. But is there no extant material sign of slavery? When he describes the uses assigned to the various portions of the main structure, Le Glay relies, naturally, on Columella and his accurate descriptions. But virtually everything associated with slavery in *De re rustica* has disappeared from his account. Where did the slaves sleep? Where did they eat and—surely we must ask this—how did they work? For answers to these questions we have had to turn to the original sources, and chiefly to the major work of Columella.[37]

Caution is, of course, in order, because *De re rustica* is a theoretical and normative work and not a mere description of the estates managed by the author (himself a great landowner), even if we are told that the lessons the book contains were drawn from the concrete cases discussed. In picturing for us the organization of the estate and the physical inter-relation of different work-sites and tasks, as well as schedules and methods of cultivation and husbandry, Columella is setting forth a model, though to be sure it is a model obtained inductively from the study of one or more concrete cases, along with the inspiration provided by the earlier writings of Cato and Varro. Columella's book is a first-rate "management manual." Quite obviously it is a manual that assumes an aptitude for economic calculation, and, when it was written,[38] the disparity between Columella's model and actual practice in the *villae* was immense, comparable to the disparity that exists today between the theory of industrial management and everyday business practice.

It is sometimes said that Columella is treating medium-sized estates, reflecting a certain decline of the *latifundium* at the time of the transition from the republic to the empire. My own view is that the commentators who argue this point have mistaken the author's declarations of intention for the model he actually presents. At the beginning of book i, he does indeed praise reasonable moderation, explaining that one should not own more land than one has the means to cultivate (or to have cultivated), and above all he criticizes those immensely wealthy landowners who possess whole regions but abandon them to herds of livestock and wild animals, populating the lands with slaves in chains or men condemned for debt.[39] This, however, is merely criticism of the old-style *latifundium*[40] with its extensive husbandry and troops of slaves; the barbarous old methods come in for their share of blame (particularly the *nexum*, or debt bondage), and the customary reverence is shown for the small ancestral farm. The large-scale slave system is criticized only as tradition dictated (Cato is frequently cited), so as not to seem to be encouraging an unpopular system, which had ruined and was still ruining the owners of small property. But the system favored by Columella is clearly that of the *villa* on a *latifundium* of 200 to 1000 hectares, with slavery (including chained slaves, though he seems to commiserate with their lot). Throughout his discussion, Columella rather reminds us of present-day representatives of big business, who are fond of beginning their speeches with homages to "factories on a human scale" and expressions of pity for the assembly-line worker (a "necessary evil").

The *villa* (in the sense of the complex of central buildings) described by Columella closely resembles those we have been able to discover through aerial photography. We find the master's house and his winter and summer apartments, his bedrooms and his dining rooms, his baths and his promenades. Our interest, however, lies chiefly in the *pars rustica*, particularly in several points where we can add to Le Glay's description. We find the different places intended for particular uses, such as storage of tools, animals, raw materials, and food, as well as production areas (ovens, mills, workshops, etc.); their prodigious diversity and clear-cut specialization in particular functions reinforces the idea that we are looking at a large-scale, centralized operation. But we also find information pertaining to matters human, to the men of the *familia*, the slaves of the *villa*. The kitchen must have had high ceilings (so that the beams would be safe from the fire) and huge dimensions to accommodate the slaves in all seasons. Here was the master's table or hearth, where his men were fed with "their master's bread" (the slaves' food, prepared by slave cooks in this mass kitchen, was distributed to them here). We know where the unchained slaves slept: in the slave *cellae*, half barns, half hovels, or possibly in barracks divided into stalls. And we also know where the chained slaves slept (when they were not working): in the *ergastula*, or subterranean prisons which the "good" Columella describes thus: "As for the chained slaves, as healthy as possible an *ergastulum* should be provided, lighted by a large number of narrow windows high enough so that the slaves cannot reach them with their hands."[41]

Bringing together all the information that can be drawn from the various Latin agronomists and from Vitruvius, it is possible to draw up a typical plan[42] that corresponds rather well to what we surmise from aerial photographs the *villae rusticae* must have looked like. A broad entryway opened on to a large central courtyard (taking the place of the *atrium*), probably partially covered by four sections of roof sloping inward and forming galleries. The kitchen, which gave on to the courtyard (or was located in the courtyard) stood close by the refectory, the baths for the slaves (the water was heated in the kitchen), and the cowshed (the heat was good for the cows). The stables for the horses, on the other hand, stood far from the kitchen (so as not to frighten the horses with the fire). The *villicus* lived near the entryway so as to be in a position to watch everyone's comings and goings: he had to be able to see the whole of the inner and outer courtyard from his dwelling. The slaves responsible for tending the cows and sheep were housed with the animals, but the rest of the slaves were grouped together in the *cellae* (which Columella thought should face south) for easy surveillance. Off the inner courtyard we find the wine press and the cellars (on the north side) and the storeroom for oil (on the south side). The granaries were in the upper storey, facing north (to catch the north wind for better ventilation).[43] The whole group of buildings stood inside an enclosure (stockade), which formed an outer courtyard containing the threshing yard and the oven.

Thanks to Columella we also gain a clear sense of the social divisions in the *villa*. Let us first dispose of the tenants (the *coloni* in the sense the word had then), as Columella himself does in all cases in which the land was not barren or unhealthy. He explains that if the climate was healthy and the soil fertile an estate cultivated by tenants always returned less than one cultivated by a steward and slaves, provided that the master was able to take personal charge at regular intervals and appointed a good steward. The point is a crucial one: the slave system was more profitable if there was effective and efficient surveillance, less profitable if there was not (and where the soil was "bad," the master might as well let the tenants "muddle through," for any return was better than none at all). Add to this one further remark: Columella was in favor of permanent tenants drawn from the region, so that they would look upon the land as their own. This would also allow the master to deal good-naturedly with the *colonus*, especially where rent payments were concerned, unless it became necessary to show greater severity and take control of the operation himself (which reduces the autonomy of the tenant a good deal).

Inadequate surveillance ran the risk of making the slave system unworkable, Columella explains, because the slaves could do much damage to their master's property. How? Through negligence, fraud, and theft: they could rent the oxen outside the estate for their own benefit, for example, or cut down on what was fed to the animals, plow inaccurately, count out more seed than they actually used, sow carelessly, steal grain on the way to threshing or allow it to be stolen, and misrecord the amounts of grain stored away (opening the way to theft or spoilage). Not only the slaves, but also the *villicus*, might engage in such acts.

Thus if surveillance was possible and the land not sterile, the best system was to use a slave labor force. Columella explains that this force should be, not a homogeneous one, but one rather systematically differentiated by a hierarchical and functional division of labor. Apart from the *villicus* and his wife (whose role as second-in-command, in charge of interior affairs, was of great importance), we find the foremen, the turn keys, the skilled workers, the masses of *mediastini*, or slaves without any particular skill, and, at the very bottom of the heap, the chained slaves.

Since the master was often absent, the system had to run without him, that is, without the actual presence of a free man on the premises. This was a marvelous feat of self-organization, which the Nazi concentration camps would later imitate without attaining this degree of perfection.[44] This manner of organization explains why the choice of a steward was so important, along with his training and the rules that prescribed what he must do and what he was forbidden to do.

The qualities of the steward were those of the good manager in all periods, the qualities of a man placed between a master and the masses whom he must make work efficiently (for the master). Columella gives a precise description of these qualities: the steward must be a man in the prime of life (too young and he would lack natural authority, too old and he would be frail and easily fatigued), intelligent (though he need not know how to write—there being the ever-present danger of falsification to contend with—and he could get by with a good memory), robust and vigorous (as we shall see later on, he had to "get his hands dirty"), and, so as to be more closely connected with the estate, married to a woman chosen from among the family of slaves. Best of all was the steward born in the *villa* and trained on the premises. This raised a problem of some delicacy: his training required contact with quite a few different specialists, for he had to learn everything, and, as we shall see, each worker had his own specialized task. Thus trained as a "jack of all trades" and hence in a position to oversee them all, he would have responsibility for the management of the *villa*, take part directly in all the different projects, maintain discipline, and punish offenders. Naturally he had to be honest, a good worker, authoritative without being abusive, and so forth.

The master, however, was obliged for his own security to lay down a list of prohibitions on the activities of the *villicus* himself,[45] a list that at first sight seems rather curious but was in fact quite rational. First, the steward must endeavor to leave the estate as little as possible; of course his job sometimes required him to go into town or to the market, but he was not to frequent those places (his presence on the estate was necessary to oversee the slaves, and in town he would only fall into dissolute ways, spend money, and come into contact with strangers—all things dangerous for the property of the master). In the same vein, although the steward had to buy and even sell goods when necessary, in no case was he to become a merchant (for there was danger in this of outside contacts and fraud, as well as independence of the sort that comes from a knowledge of the markets and buyers, besides which the estate required his constant attention to the exigencies of production). He must receive only the friends of the master and not mingle either with the slaves of the family or above all with strangers (there was constant fear of sedition supported or fomented from outside, and then, too, such contacts facilitated fraud). The master forbade sacrifices not ordered by himself and contact with sorcerers (Columella explains that mysticism and slave religions were on the rise and deemed dangerous for the order of the *villa*, as well as for the public order in general, so that cults and practices likely to lead to crime must not be allowed to develop).

Since the master was frequently absent, he obviously had to rely to a great extent on the "honesty" of the *villicus*. Still, according to Columella, the master was well advised to gather information from his chained slaves as well as from the best of the unshackled. In this way he could hear the complaints of both groups and find out whether those in chains had been maltreated. As the ultimate authority, the master knew how to deal with justified grievances, but he must also deal severely with anyone who complained merely to slander his superior or to incite sedition.[46] Here we recognize the usual sort of "bypass" procedure, which allowed for direct access from the bottom of the hierarchy (the chained slave) to the very top (the master), whereby the lower echelons were able to appeal decisions taken by the intermediate echelons, thus effecting a surveillance of the overseers by the overseen.

Still, of all the ways for the master to secure the complicity of the *villicus*, the best was social position itself: if the *villicus* stood utterly apart from and above the other slaves (relating to them only as work required or to mete out rewards), his risk in acting against his master's interests would be enormous, however careless the master might be in watching over his property.

It is interesting to ask how the work that the steward was responsible for was organized. The slaves were divided into ten-man work teams; no worker was ever to be left alone or with a single other worker, for this would have complicated the task of surveillance. Too many men in the team, on the other hand, would lead to slacking, each man being able to rely on the others to get the work done. These *decuriae*, as the work teams were called, were scattered about the estate (size permitting). Each was supervised by a team captain, who thus constituted an intermediary stratum in slave society. Columella tells us that team organization stimulated the workers to follow one another's lead and facilitated the identification of slackers. Since the whole team was responsible for the accomplishment of a given task, punishment of slow workers would be approved by the other slaves on the team.

Men were carefully selected for fitness to each specialty, matching the man to the job. Columella describes the qualities required for ox-drivers and plowmen, two important specialties, as well as for team captains. Chained slaves were deemed fit for vineyard work, first of all because the work was always carried out in groups under the eyes of a guard, so that "natural" good behavior was of little importance, and, second, because the work required clever men, and the most intelligent slaves were often the most depraved and seditious, hence likely to be in chains. Thus far we have spoken only of the specialties of the "yard slaves." "House slaves" specialized either in crafts, in preparation of food for the family, or in production jobs associated with the processing of grains and other foods (ovens, mills, etc.) after harvest.

The jobs assigned to the different teams and men had to be worked out carefully. When a worker had no specific job, Columella tells us, he would be afraid that by doing his own work he would also be doing someone else's, and so would try to unload a part of his job onto the rest of the team. This remark also gives us some idea of how the team fostered competition among its members and set them to watch over one another.

Time seems to have been quite precious. The *villicus* was enjoined to see that the time spent in getting from the *villa* to the work site was as brief as possible and that there were no stragglers. The *villicus* was to be the first man up in the morning, at an early hour, and it was he who mustered the various teams for work in short order. He was to march "briskly" at their head and see to it that no one dawdled along, "like a general leading his troops gaily and courageously into battle." At night, "like the good shepherd," he must follow his flock home to see that none went astray in the fields.[47] Work was to go on uninterruptedly, with no daydreaming or idling. The team captains and the steward should constantly exhort their men to work. If one of them should flag, the steward himself should look to him, perhaps even taking up his tool for a moment to encourage him. In a similar vein, Columella tells us that the slaves should be provided good clothing to enable them to work in all seasons. Furthermore, there were to be twice as many tools available as were needed, so that no time need be wasted looking for tools outside the *villa*.[48] Even holidays could be used for various kinds of work, of which Columella provides a list.[49] Summing up, we may say that all these prescriptions were designed to insure that the labor force would be employed at full capacity. One intended purpose of using men to the full in this way was to leave them exhausted by nightfall, incapable of anything but sleep, without time to talk among themselves, much less to hatch fraudulent schemes or seditious plots.

To get a maximum return on slaves required maintaining the work force in good condition. Many injuries occurred in the course of farm labor, and there were also sicknesses to contend with. Every night, the *villicus*, again resembling "the good shepherd," was to check on the health of the slaves. There were infirmaries to care for the sick and injured, kept sanitary by the wife of the steward. In this connection, we may point to one of many often remarkably astute observations made by Columella. Every morning, he says, the wife of the steward was to check to see whether there were any slaves who had not gone out with the work teams, whether because they were genuinely ill or malingering. If a slacker turned up, she was to take him to the infirmary, "for it is better to let a slave worn out by work rest for a day or two than to force him to work and expose him to the danger of a real disease."[50] To attend in this way to serious cases of fatigue where no known disease was involved was a sign not of generosity but of good management.

It was also necessary to provide for the reproduction of the work force. The method adopted was that of encouraging repeated pregnancies by promising a diminution or even complete elimination of labor, and sometimes even freedom. Columella recommends the following system: after producing three boys a woman would be excused from all labor; more than three and she would be set free.[51] Of course, as Columella constantly reminds us, everything relied on surveillance. To begin with, there was the all-embracing surveillance of the master. On each visit, we are told, he had to inspect the lands, the vineyards, the orchards, and the live stock, look over the tools and movable property, count his slaves, check for negligence, and keep an eye out for anything that might disturb the established order.[52]

Next, there was the surveillance of the steward. In order to supervise the men of the estate, he had to be familiar with all the different jobs; he was to prevent the workers from leaving the estate, make a roll call of the chained slaves, check to see that they were securely shackled at the ankle, inspect men, clothing, and tools, and check each day to see that all the various jobs had been done. He was responsible for overseeing the preparation and distribution of the food and for checking on fraud by the cooks. He had to accustom the slaves to taking their meals "at the master's table," where he himself ate and set an example in regard to frugality and proper bearing (not reclining when he ate, but sitting up, except on holidays). For the sake of effective surveillance, Columella insists that there must be no "conviviality" between the slaves and the steward. The steward should have nothing to do with the slaves except in connection with work; he was their chief, the master's eye and hand, and he must respect the distinction and see to it that others respected it, never inviting any of them to his table except to mete out rewards, and then only on holidays. No one else must ever be allowed to take his place.

Finally, each team captain must exercise a strict and constant oversight within his own limited sphere. A system of this kind depends for its

operation on rewards and punishments. The steward himself was selected from the best of the slaves. Team captains, guards, and so on
were also promoted from the ranks. Columella is most emphatic in
urging the *villicus* to give encouragement to the best slaves and to note
carefully the qualities of each so as to match each man to one of the
variety of jobs and to select those suited for training in a more advanced
specialty. Furthermore, even with corrupt, devious, thieving, or worse,
seditious slaves, it was still best to show indulgence for the least hard-
working and to use prevention rather than punishment: "The most
effective surveillance that can be applied to the most perverse of men
is to require him to carry out his job under strict supervision, keeping
an eye on him at all times." In other words, "the steward should put
his effort into overseeing [the slaves] and keeping them from committing
an offense, rather than hastening to administer punishment when they
have gone wrong through his own negligence," i.e., because he was not
watching more closely.[54] Paternalism is omnipresent in Columella's book,
particularly the paternalism of the *paterfamilias*, i.e., the master of the
servile family: of great interest is the passage in which Columella depicts
himself in familiar conversation with the slaves whose conduct is irre-
proachable, jesting with them, allowing them to joke and laugh, even
going so far as to consult them in regard to one project or another, on
the theory that they would work especially diligently on a job on which
they believed their opinion had been sought.[55] The *villicus*, of course,
could not go this far, but he should nevertheless give the appearance
of moderation, indulgence, and justice.

Columella's model clearly emphasizes indulgence and prevention
rather than punishment. It is often taken as a paragon of the slave
system, a model of what Fourier (and later Marx) liked to call the "mitigated jail," referring to the factory. But are not such paragons always
described in terms of this sort? In the cruelest of forced-labor camps
there are always wardens willing to argue that the punishments, however severe, are mere "blemishes" that might have been avoided with
better supervision. One has only to think—to take an extreme case—of
what Olga Wormser-Migot called Goering's "humanity" in early Nazi
hagiography.[56] Or think of the ideology of slave-owners in the southern
United States or the Antilles, not unlike that of wardens and guards in
present-day prisons, of Soviet officials in Stalin's concentration camps,
and so on.

Punishment did exist, however, and it seems to have been terrible
indeed, to judge by Columella's description of the *ergastula*, by the need
to check the shackles of the slaves thus punished, by the pity that
Columella feels (or says he feels),[57] by the necessity to check to see

whether the slaves were properly clothed and fed, and to find out whether they had been treated unjustly, injustice being all the more frequent, Columella explains, because slaves were subject to the authority of several kinds of superior (*villicus*, chain-gang guard, work-team captain). The purpose of the master's checking was not to improve the circumstances of the man in shackles, for which the slave himself was held responsible, but because the slaves "are far more to be feared when the cruelty or greed of their superiors has reduced them to despair."[58] When slavery or other systematic forms of oppression hold sway everywhere, and only masters or their retainers wield the pen, it is difficult to know exactly what punishments were administered. All we know is that what has come to our notice—by way of a master's pen—must inevitably have been toned down in many respects.

The *villa* system described by Columella[59] has little in common with what might be called extermination through labor. Gang slavery was rather more like the factory system, the mitigated prison, inmate-run, strictly hierarchical, based on systematic social differentiation and constant surveillance from top to bottom, and on a careful organization of labor, with jobs divided up among men and work teams and each job spelled out in detail, the whole system being designed to use the work force to the full, as well as to provide internally for its maintenance and reproduction. This was indeed a model system, and not only for the Roman Empire!

A similar model underlies any system of exploitation based on formal submission, i.e., oppression, such as the "modern" *latifundium* with agricultural wage laborers or peons, the labor camp, the chain gang, the habitation of the Antilles, as well as the charity workshop, the Colbertian manufactory, and, in large measure, the factory from the nineteenth century down to the present day.

To confine ourselves to the Roman Empire, let us note the relatively large size of the great estates, which tended over the centuries to grow even larger.[60] Pliny the Elder spoke of six estates that together covered the plains of North Africa, and in the late first century A.D., Frontinus[61] described private estates larger than the territory of cities, with a labor force large enough to populate *vici* that surrounded the *villa* "like ramparts." And what are we to say about the fortune of the second-century Athenian, Herodes Atticus? He owned estates in Greece, Egypt, and Italy, and his fortune in land may have amounted to 100 million sesterces,[62] no doubt an exceptionally large figure. We also know the number of slave laborers employed in 404 by the future Saint Melania (24,000)—for her sainthood was connected to her relinquishing this wealth—on a large number of estates scattered throughout the Roman world (Italy, Spain, Brittany, Sicily), some of them immense: one of these estates alone incorporated sixty-two hamlets. What is more, not even the largest landed fortunes, like that of Melania, could compare with the estates of the emperor or, from the fourth century on, the estates of the Church,[63] which alone could rival the emperor in landholdings thanks to the property owned by the popes and the dioceses. The emperor and the Church, the two greatest expropriators, accumulated estates of such vast acreage as to "strain the imagination."[64]

Still, this growth of the great estates and their increasing importance relative to property of small and medium size does not mean that the *villa* slave system continued to operate as it had done between the first and third centuries. The crisis of the third century began profound modifications in the economy of the *villa*.

II. "Ends" of Slavery

We have put "ends" in the plural because slavery "ended" more than once. At least there was one "end" for the ancient historian, associated with the rise of the colonate system, and another for the medievalist, associated with the domiciling (*casement*) of slaves. It is obviously unproductive to periodize this history according to the day the political history of the western Roman Empire came to an end. What will be paramount for us is the process of the decline of the state and its causes and social consequences, just as the paramount phenomenon hitherto has been the rise of the centralized state with Augustus and the empire, of which we have also tried to examine the causes and social consequences.

The crisis of the Roman state, followed by a shift in its geographic center, the decline of the western portion of the empire, and, finally, the end in the west of any form of state whatever, was not an instantaneous phenomenon but a multisecular process punctuated by temporary reversals, stretching from the period of the great crisis of the third century (A.D.) to the failure of the Carolingian state. The forward march of this process was halted from time to time: order was restored in the late third and early fourth centuries, and later came Charlemagne's attempt to found an empire. It is precisely in these periods of public, hence social, order that we find a relatively abundant documentation, whence the tendency for the historian to accentuate these periods and to envision more turbulent periods in their image. As regards our problem, this is a particularly serious flaw, since we must study the decline of the state by examining periods during which that decline came temporarily to a halt, periods that seem to contradict the process itself.

It is no secret that for centuries now there has scarcely been a subject more frequently analyzed than the causes of "the decline and fall of the Roman empire." As we shall see, the question of the cause or causes of this long death-agony of the state is of the utmost importance; it was not chance that the most serious crisis of the state in the west occurred just as the slave system there was crumbling as the dominant relation of production; by contrast, the state was able to survive in the east, where the subjugated peasantry provided a different, and enduring, social basis for the economy.

A) The Crisis of the Third Century

The general crisis of Roman society that occurred in the third century has been studied extensively.[65] Here we can do no more than describe it succinctly, recalling a few of its more important aspects. In the final chapter we shall return to these facts in order to place them in context in the light of our central hypothesis.

Among the more visible manifestations of the crisis of the empire are the barbarian invasions in both the east and the west. Previously, during the second century, there had been a sort of prelude to these invasions. But now the penetration was deeper, and above all between 240 and 270 the empire was pressed in upon from all sides almost simultaneously. First there were the Goths, as early as 233-234, then the Vandals in about 248, then the Vandals again but this time in conjunction with the Burgundians in 268-270. Indeed, all the barbarian tribes seem to have pressed forward in 269-272: there was barbarian pressure on Gaul until 277, on northern Italy until 271, and on the Danube, in the provinces of Rhaetia, Noricum, and Pannonia. At the same time the powerful Persian kingdom made war on the empire and emerged victorious, with the emperor Valerian himself being captured in 260. What is more, Egypt was invaded (by the Palmyrans and Blemmyes) in 268-270. Around 260 we even find Frankish tribes encountering Moors in Africa after crossing Gaul and Spain. And Alemanni from Gaul and Switzerland joined others of the same tribe from Rhaetia in the Cisalpine.[66]

The crisis of the state was particularly striking. In our (brief) discussion of the rise of the imperial state, we placed the accent on the army, the administration, and the fiscal system: in each of these spheres, where there was not outright decomposition, there was increased local autonomy. Similar phenomena appeared in many places at once in a chain reaction that soon plunged all of Roman society into crisis.

By the first century the armies were recruiting less and less among Roman citizens and had become half peregrine (the auxiliaries), later going so far as to incorporate corps of *numeri* (in the time of Trajan and

Hadrian), which not only included barbarians (already present among the auxiliaries), but even preserved their methods of fighting, their weapons, and their leaders in the lower ranks. Although in the second century these troops of *numeri* were still under Roman command, they passed under barbarian command in the third. The "barbarization" of the army was not yet complete, however: the majority of the soldiers were still provincials from regions where the army was stationed (hence often scarcely "Romanized"). On the other hand, more and more soldiers and officers were recruited among the *ex castris* (soldiers born in army camps). The centurions themselves were no longer recruited among the Italians or the populations of the old Romanized provinces. Promotion through the ranks became more widespread, but if the son of a centurion was (from the time of Septimius Severus) very close[67] to the equestrian order, and the primipilate became a springboard to an equestrian career, the military itself became more and more a specialized profession: under Gallienus senators could no longer become officers of high rank, these positions being reserved to the equestrian class, whose members combined military with bureaucratic careers.

Once the army became autonomous, it tended more and more to become a distinct, hereditary caste, but this evolution was far from complete in the third century. The army became the source of political power for several reasons: in addition to its new-found autonomy, we may cite not only the general crisis, but also ambition on the part of the leaders of the military and the prefects of the praetorian guard, the fact that power in the provinces was held by soldiers of the equestrian order squeezing senators out of these positions, the need to turn back the barbarian advances, and, as always, the defeats. If, increasingly, the emperor was the sole official with political power, he was now no more than a military leader whose reign was likely to be brief and unstable and might even coincide with the reign of another emperor entirely controlled by the army. This, in any case, was the situation between the advent of Maximianus (in 235) and Diocletian (284).

The collapse of the state was marked not only by military anarchy, in which the army could make and break emperors, but also by an increasingly serious fragmentation of the bureaucracy: thanks to its remarkable solidity, the Roman bureaucracy survived the crisis but became more and more autonomous in its functioning. The bureaucracy operated on its own, ultimately, because the emperors, by eliminating all power but their own (the senate having lost what political power it had), created a situation in which virtual omnipotence amounted to absolute impotence: the emperors became mere cat's-paws of the legions. Above all, administration fell increasingly into the hands of distinct regional bureaucracies, in some cases legally, in others as a result of usurpation by local forces.

The problems of the state were clearly aggravated by the fiscal crisis. This increased the difficulty of paying a regular salary to the army, which consequently became discontent and looked to its own interests by seizing power, in the process moving still further in the direction of autonomy (recruiting was virtually impossible except among the *ex castris,* given the pay situation). The fiscal crisis also made it necessary to break up and regionalize the bureaucracy and led to despotism in certain areas. Life in the cities became more and more difficult for the wealthy (who were heavily taxed there), compelling them to take up residence on their estates. The fiscal crisis contributed, moreover, to a worsening of the economic crisis, of which it was one consequence. Unrest, invasions, the breakdown of public services and transportation were all connected with the production crisis and hyperinflation, which soon reached such proportions that money began to be supplanted by barter. Because of the monetary crisis taxes were levied in kind, thus widening and deepening the fiscal crisis, and so on.

It is impossible to spell out in detail the connections among the various "local" crises that fused together to produce this extraordinarily complex general crisis: the crisis of the state, the economic crisis, the monetary crisis, the fiscal crisis, and the urban crisis are all partially explicable in local terms (each surely having its own dynamic), but the most important point is that they all affected one another in ways apparently impossible to disentangle. So far was this true that the hardest thing to understand is not so much the web of cumulative effects and proliferating interactions as the causes of the remission of the empire's terminal disease, all in all a rather spectacular happenstance.

What is needed, therefore, is a set of conjectures concerning the dominant causal sequences. It will be seen that for us the strategic question is that of the multisecular process of concentration of estates, the increasing wealth and power of the great landowners, and the pauperization of the intermediary classes: these factors, in a certain sense responsible for the crisis, were subsequently reinforced by it.

In the third century, the great landowners grew wealthier, extended their estates, enhanced their power, and established the independence of their *villae*. As producers and monopolizers of the food supply and as speculators, they earned substantial profits, which were reinvested in land (increasingly so as money quickly lost its value). At the same time, small peasants were crushed by the weight of taxation; the poorest were the first to be forced to sell, but soon the urban middle classes and landowners among them had to yield. When the great landowners took refuge in their *villae*, the masses who depended on their subsidies and expenditures were forced to follow. In the countryside nothing stood between the great landowners and their dependents.

The general social crisis, by furthering the concentration of estates, fractured civil society (that is, the society of free men) into just two classes, the powerful and the poor, eliminating the intermediary strata.

The Augustan state had represented a coalition of the great landowners, financiers, and bureaucrats, but its social base was far broader, thanks to the system of social distinctions and social, political, and ethnic stratification and to the distribution to the intermediary strata of a portion of the profits of slavery and imperialism. But the logic of the slave mode of production entailed the extension of the great estate and the expropriation of the free peasants. The widespread unrest, the invasions, the independent armies, the economic crisis, the spreading brigandage, and the general disorganization could not but reinforce this process of concentration. The final crisis was yet to come, however. For the time being the latifundists and the state were able to respond with extreme despotism. An instrument of class repression, the state laid the groundwork for its demise by intensifying its true nature. The violence of the state was added to the violence of the great landowners in an attempt to bind the peasants to the soil of the masters' estates; the reasons for this had to do not only with finance but also—the point is an important one, and we shall have occasion to come back to it—with manpower, which, as historians delicately phrase it, the great landowners "lacked."

B) Reestablishment of Order and the Colonate: The First "End" of Slavery

The imperial order was reestablished at the end of the third century with Diocletian, and at the beginning of the fourth century with Constantine. In the face of a broad range of "aggressions," the ruling class reacted: an attempt was made to freeze the social structure and to make the social division of labor hereditary. Inevitably, as the wealth of the empire came into the hands of the "powerful," notably through increases in the size of their latifundia, as Roman citizenship was degraded to a mere bauble to be distributed to virtually the whole empire, and as the free status of the peasant lost its real significance, despotism became the only way the social edifice could be shored up for a time, i.e., the only way to insure that a few thousand great landowners could continue to exploit the vast masses of slaves and more or less subjugated free men. Augustan society had been a complex structure in which "differentials" of many kinds insured "social equilibrium," i.e., allayed the class struggle on the principle of "divide and conquer," providing for a certain social mobility even for slaves (whose fates in certain exceptional cases are known). But the antagonism of the classes was only alleviated or masked, and it was implicit in the developmental logic of the Augustan empire that eventually simplification of the social structure would destroy the very basis of the society. For the logic of the latifundists was monopolistic, and so inevitably the rest of the populace was relegated to the ranks of the "poor," who sank further and further into hopeless subjection.

No solution immediately offered itself to the "powerful" except coercion by the state but at that very moment the social basis of the state was growing narrower and narrower. Hence failure was inevitable.

In 332 a new law set in train a series of measures by which the state of the "powerful," the latifundists, tried—with some success, it seems—to bind the peasants to the soil.[68] In *practice*, however, the establishment of the colonate was not accomplished by mere bureaucratic action. The law, that is, legal violence, served to justify and consolidate the brutal fact of life, the violence of the landowners; initially the term *colonus* referred simply to someone who cultivated a plot of land on lease, and it is revealing that it came subsequently to mean a tenant bound to the soil.

The tendency of the body social to break down into two classes necessitated this transformation of the free tenant into the *colonus*. The "powerful," relying on the state apparatus they controlled (at least during this period of "restoration of order"), succeeded, very likely on a wide scale, in subjecting the peasant to his master by binding him to the soil. How could this have been enforced, if not by the power of the master?

The same circumstances also explain the increased importance of the *patronicium* (patronate), which first rose during the crisis and was consolidated in the subsequent period, when governmental authority reasserted itself. The powerful offered their protection in the manner of *mafiosi*, and it was quite difficult for a poor peasant to avoid being forced to "sell" his land without payment and become a tenant: thus alongside the free tenant who became a *colonus*, we also find the peasant landowner who became a tenant, in other words, a *colonus*. Sometimes whole villages passed under the protection of a master and became his property. The expropriation and (subsequently) subjection of the peasant were accomplished in a variety of ways: through pure violence, violence hidden behind the contract, indirect violence via the fiscal pressure of the state, and offers of protection against threats of violence.

Historians of the late empire emphasize the financial aspect.[69] Fiscal pressure in the cities did impel the "powerful" to abandon them, because the disappearance of the intermediate strata and the insolvency of the poor threatened to leave no one else to bear the brunt of taxation (and the Roman tax system only augmented this tendency by making it easy to evade taxes on the large estate revenues). Once landowners began leaving the cities, the whole process built up rapidly. Soon all the great proprietors had left for their *villae*. With them went the portion of the profits they had once spent in the cities, thereby ruining, or completing the ruin, of the urban economy, and of the money economy in general. Taxes became increasingly difficult to levy, which aggravated the problems faced by the state, and so on, all of this building up to the point where the economy itself was transformed, coming to be based on more or less self-sufficient estates.

The same problems of finance led the state to impose on villages of free peasants the *consortium,* or collective responsibility of the residents, which had the effect of binding them to the soil. Since the peasant who was unable to pay his taxes became an outlaw, his only recourse was to take refuge in the patronage of one of the powerful.

This is the context in which historians have determined that slavery diminished in the fourth century (and to some degree even earlier, in the third century). Why did the great landowners in some, perhaps even most, cases "abandon"[70] their slaves in favor of tenants bound to the soil and consequently subjects, yet owners for themselves and their children of title to their tenement, which they worked individually? This is one aspect of our problem. To bring out the other aspect, let us observe that beginning in the third and fourth centuries we find, alongside the *coloni,* who enjoyed the status of free men, the domiciled slave (*servus casatus*) to whom had been given a hut (*casa*) and a plot of land to work during a portion of his working hours, the other portion still being given over to the master's land (though in some cases the slave might be totally exempt from work of this latter kind). How is this domiciling to be explained? This is the second aspect of our problem. The transition to the early forms of serfdom took place in one of two ways: either by "upgrading" slaves to the status of domiciled slaves or by "downgrading" free peasants to *coloni* following expropriation.

How significant was the phenomenon of domiciling in the late empire? Marc Bloch deems it to have been of great significance,[71] but many contemporary historians belittle its importance. Is this perhaps because "medievalists" generally hold that gang slavery was still important in the early Middle Ages? But were there not perhaps major "revivals" of slavery in certain periods? And particularly during the new empire created by Charlemagne—which would be an interesting sign?

However that may be, we know that toward the end of the late empire the main lineaments of what is generally called landed seigniory (or the manorial system) were in place. The master lived, as lord of the domain, with his peasant tenants, bound to the soil, his chained slaves, and his domiciled slaves. The *villa*, which in all periods had striven for self-sufficiency,[72] purchasing as little as possible outside, now sold almost nothing on markets that had been drastically curtailed.

C) Collapse of the State, Resistance of the Villa, Second "End" of Slavery

Was there a social collapse in the fourth and fifth centuries? Undoubtedly there was, but the *villa*, the key site of exploitation, withstood the collapse by changing or by disintegrating in order to be born again in a new form.

A moderate form of the *colonate* became current as a relation of production over a wide area. Changes occurred in the state and in the nature of gang slavery. The ruling-class coalition that had dominated the state now began to give way to make room for a new type of coalition, which before long would eventuate in the feudal system. One form of exploitation was beginning to give way to another form as well; more precisely, the domiciling of slaves, a process that began in the third century, had begun to accelerate, reaching significant proportions by Merovingian times.

The Augustan state, which owed its broad social base to the ethnic and social differentials, the hierarchical system, and the relatively wide distribution of the profits of slavery and imperialism, could not endure once the division of society into two classes (the powerful and the poor) was nearly complete, culminating the logical process of concentration of property, which went hand in hand with the emergence of patronage and the subjection of the peasantry. Ultimately, the Augustan state necessarily turned into its opposite and asserted itself as a despotic power, which attempted to fix the entire social structure and division of labor. Moreover, this growing despotism only hastened the demise of the state by succeeding in what it set out to do, perfecting the *villa* and establishing the manorial system. Even though a powerful state continued to be in the collective interest of the lords, their power made it impossible for them not to deny that state individually. One consequence of this state of affairs was that new alliances were sought, and ultimately a new type of ruling coalition was forged. Another consequence was a phenomenon that first appeared in the fourth century, which seems incomprehensible at first glance: the latifundists, the patrons fought against the state—and the state struck back at patronage; as a result, latifundists frequently entered into alliances with the Germanic tribes.[73]

In the fifth century we find clear indications of a quarrelsome collusion among barbarian chieftains, latifundists, and "Roman" military leaders (with shifting dominance), collusion, in other words, among all manner of the powerful: wealthy landowners, the army, the "conquering" barbarians—the point was to make room for these conquerors in the "club" of exploiters of the peasantry. Was this initially collusion against the state?[74] No, things were not so simple! From the beginning it involved the slow formation of a new ruling coalition: landed power, military power, and barbarian power tended to mingle with one another. The older form of power, the Roman state, reduced to impotence by the transformation of the social and ethnic structures of the empire, was destined to disappear. Inevitably its demise was accompanied by tremors and crises, but these were no more than death rattles. It is generally held that the landed nobility had at first wanted to enhance its independence from the state by forging alliances with the military and the barbarians. Obviously this was true, but the explanation is superficial: the crucial point was to carry on the exploitation of the peasant masses, that is, to maintain a certain social order and, ultimately, to insure the survival of the *villa*. For the latifundist, independence of the state was not an end in itself; rather, the weakness of the state, due to the collapse of its social base, obliged the ruling class to look for another way to organize its power over the exploited class. This new form of organization, moreover, stood in contradiction to the old form, the coalition embodied in the imperial state.[75]

This alliance between the landed and military nobility was necessitated by the new forces that surged forth from Germany—and yet something seems to be missing! The Roman Church and the Roman state had long been in league. Initially the Church had to attempt to halt the advance of the pagan barbarians. But who in Gaul was Christian? Certainly not the peasant masses—does not the very word "pagan" mean "peasant"[76]— who were to be converted only at a much later date. Often Christianity is held to have been a liberating ideology, even a slave ideology. And no doubt it was originally, at the time it first made its way into Italy, but by the fifth century Christianity was the ideology of the ruling class, of the landowners, having replaced the Augustan ideology, and though for some centuries hence it would continue to harbor a dream of empire, it was to become the ideology of the feudal system (one has only to think of the word "lord").[77] The alliance between great landowners and barbarians (but now with the latter in a position of dominance) emerges clearly in the conversion of Clovis after Tolbiac. The old ruling class perceived that it need not fear overthrow of the social order, that it need not give up its position but only move over to make room for the newly arrived barbarians: the "God of Clotilda" was the God of the latifundists, and the *villa* had nothing to fear from these barbarians turned Catholic.[78] This does not mean that the *romani* masters did not suffer violent treatment at the hands of victorious tribes: many a great family was expropriated, massacred, or enslaved, but these martyrs are to be seen in the context of the antagonistic process whereby a new ruling class was formed.

This being the case, what can we say about the argument that the German conquerors revived the old collective freedoms? Conquerors? The tribes that "conquered" the western empire were not hordes of fearsome warriors who swooped down from the forests of Germany, legends to the contrary notwithstanding. They were tribes weakened, vanquished, and decimated by the razzias of the slave system. There were no wars of conquest, but at first only a slow and almost peaceful penetration of an empire whose central structure had crumbled, by Germans astonished to see the walls fall before them, where once they had approached in respectful awe.

In 406, when large-scale invasions were launched along the Rhine, what lay before the barbarian invaders? Enfeebled cities and certain *villae* must have tried to defend themselves from behind their stockades, sometimes successfully warding off the attackers with the aid of barbarian troops. After the Bacaudae insurrection in the early fourth century and continually thereafter, the countryside must often have been effectively in the hands of bands of fugitives of one sort or another, in some cases well organized, the barbarian tribes being just one such group among many. When there was fighting, it was against the cities and of course against the *villae*.

Did the invaders bring with them the freedom and the surviving traditions of the ancient agricultural commune? Marx and Engels thought so.[80] The legend of the barbarians as fearsome warriors is often played off against this other legend, of free men introducing their "new commune" into the conquered territories.[81] How important were the Germanic social relations, as modified by the peculiar organization of the field armies, in the genesis of the social relations of the early Middle Ages? One must not, in my view, underestimate the importance of the organization of the barbarian tribes, with their tendency to establish chieftainships that, though hereditary, were still more or less under the control of the assembly of free men, the "people," that is, all those who had the right to bear arms, hence to share in the distribution of booty in accordance with the traditional rules (one has only to think of the actions of the Frankish warrior in the presence of Clovis in connection with the Soissons vase episode).

Charles Parain has written that "the German barbarians, in the course of their gradual occupation of the Roman empire, settled, or, more precisely, reestablished on Roman soil a free peasantry organized in village communities."[82] There is no doubt that beneath the patina of Romanness, particularly in Gaul, the old collective tribal structures remained vital and surely were reactivated by the barbarian invasions. But there is no cogent reason to attribute the revival of collective freedom, the growing importance of the *vici* (villages in which private ownership of the *ager* went hand in hand with powerful collective rules and even collective appropriation of the *saltus*—as in the "new commune," daughter of the "agricultural commune" of which Marx speaks), and the role of the village chieftainship[83] to the outside aggression. To see the fall of the empire as a consequence of the Germanic conquest is an error that mirrors the error of seeing the revival of the collective freedoms of the peasantry, the decline of patronage, the diminished size of the *latifundia*, and the reduction of the various levies on tenants as stemming from the same cause. These brief interludes of social progress were a phase of the class struggle, even if it is true that the invasions played an essential role in the evolution of the balance of class power.[84]

During the reign of Commodus there occurred in Gaul a peasant insurrection of considerable importance. It was to last until the end of the fifth century, and subsequently to start up again. In approximately the year 300 Gaul seems to have been in the hands of these rebels, known as the Bacaudae.[85] Diocletian was obliged to send his colleague Maximianus into battle against them, conferring upon him the imperial dignity for the occasion. Defeated in battle in the open field, the Bacaudae did not, it seems, disappear, but they did abandon the tactics of the "battalion" and revert to those of the "guerrilla." In the fifth century Gaul was not an orderly country that suffered an invasion by barbarian forces, but a country in which, as soon as one left the safe harbor of the cities, the *villae*, and perhaps the *vici*, Roman order gave way to "the anarchy of the Bacaudae."[86] Does not Salvianus speak of fugitives who took refuge among the barbarians or Bacaudae in 440?[87] "There, one lives according to the law of nature. There, no prestige is lasting. There, capital sentences are delivered under an oak tree and written on the bones of the guilty. There, peasants plead and private persons render judgment. There, anything goes."[88] Indeed, in Armorica, for example, it seems that rebellious slaves and peasants created an autonomous "state" organization, expelling the Roman officials, expropriating the landowners, reducing the slaveholders to slavery; they organized a judicial system and an army.[89]

For some writers, "brigandage" is a word to cover all, or virtually all, of this.[90] This is the interpretation that today's historians have placed on the words of yesterday's ruling class, as though tomorrow one were to view the "terrorists" of the wartime resistance in France through the eyes of the Vichy government, or the Algerian "bandits" through the eyes of a French general, or the Polish "hooligans" through the eyes of the Gomulka regime! The rebellion of the Bacaudae did not end with their failure in battle, nor in the fifth century, nor was it ever entirely wiped out, as Georges Duby rightly observes in his remarkable but all too brief comments at the end of the foreword to the *Histoire de la France rurale*, in which social conflict is given too small a place; even agreeing with him that this history is of necessity "poorly known, distorted"— since it is not the villager who speaks, but his masters[91]—we must stress that it is nonetheless history.

It is obviously important to identify exactly which strata of society were involved in the rebellion. Unfortunately, few historians of the late empire discuss the Bacaudae, no doubt by design, or, when they do discuss them, they disparage them as mere brigands. However, we do find, particularly in the work of M. I. Finley and E. A. Thompson, that slaves and free tenants cooperated, not surprisingly given the tendency for the lower strata of the peasantry to be lumped together in a subjugated class (in the new sense of the term, referring not to a legal status but to a de facto situation), a growing proportion of which (relative to the gang slaves) worked primarily[93] on their own familial plots and lived in independent dwellings. Still, slaves perhaps (probably?) continued to play the leading role in the Bacaudae rebellions.[94]

The Bacaudae of the late third to the fifth century may be compared with the Circumcellions in Africa.[95] There have been attempts to paint these latter rebels as mere brigands driven by religious fanaticism (Donatism) or to emphasize the anti-Roman, anti-imperialist character of this native movement. It is true that these rebels were violently anti-Catholic, but was this not because the Church was the church of the slave masters, the church of the great landowners?[96] It is true that they were anti-Roman, but the social order was inseparable from the imperialist order. There seems no reason to doubt that we are looking at a social insurrection that took the "usual" forms of war against the masters, the Romans and their religion.

Who were these rebels, and where did they get their name, *Circumcelliones*? The term, as J. Gagé has pointed out, probably comes from the fact that they were prowlers who crept round the cellars (*circum* + *cella*),[97] but it is not clear that Gagé is right in his estimation that they were recruited from among agricultural laborers for hire, those who moved about from farm to farm according to the season. His evidence is an imperial edict of 412, which treats them neither as slaves nor as *coloni*. But is there any reason why they could not have been fugitive slaves on the loose for rather long periods, slaves or *coloni* who had broken the ban, "maroons" (runaways) as fugitive Negroes would one day be called?[98]

If one looks over the evidence, this conclusion seems likely. Owners of land and slaves seem to have been afraid that slaves everywhere would free themselves with the aid of these rebels, thus swelling the ranks of the insurgent armies. Saint Optatus[99] gives us a good idea of the fear felt by those who held title to slave estates or slaves, or promissory notes secured by such property: "Everyone made haste to waive even the largest of these debts, and it was held a boon to have escaped [the rebels'] blows. Even the roads were no longer safe: masters were hurled from their carriages and ran like slaves before their own valets, who sat in the place of their masters. At their behest and command, the situations of master and slave were reversed." After the experience of such an "inverted world," it would be surprising to find that the slaves returned on their own to the "tender mercy" of their lords!

Similarly, we find Saint Augustine asking: "What master then did not have to fear his slave? . . . Who, therefore, dared so much as to threaten one of these destroyers or their protectors? . . . For fear of the club, the fire, and imminent death, men tore up the deeds of purchase of the vilest slaves and granted them their freedom. . . . Heads of family of honorable birth and refined education were beaten to within an inch of their lives or chained to millstones and by the scourge of whips forced to turn them, like animals."[100] The role of the slaves in the revolt is clear, and the millstone that the master (the "head of the family" in the classical sense) is forced to turn symbolizes the "inverted world." The vengeance wrought was typical of the vengeance of slaves (not to be confused with their aim, as is too often done!), and Saint Augustine cannot help but highlight the terror of the "wealthy."

The imperial state was born amid the great slave revolts of the late republic. Social order had to be maintained after the advent of imperialism and the slave system. The possibility of doing so depended on an alliance of the ruling class (landowners and financiers) and on the existence of a broad social base for the state, undergirded by a system of stratification and differentiation that allowed all citizens a share in the profits taken from the slaves and the provinces. Owing, however, to monopolization of the land, subjugation of the peasantry, and the concomitant coalescence of all of society in just two classes, the social base of the state shrank, and before long the *villa* came to epitomize the economy and society as a whole: hence the imperial state withered away, and insurrections and barbarian invasions ensued.

In the fifth century, as previously in the third, the rebellions of the fugitive slaves and *coloni* and the barbarian invasions often resulted in *villae* being set afire and destroyed; for a time, the *villa* ceased to be the unit of exploitation (of men and land). Thus formerly dependent slaves and *coloni* must (often? sometimes?) have found themselves (de facto) free peasants settled on plots of their own: the *coloni* simply went on working the land they had been working, while the slaves carved out plots from the lands of the estate. Eventually, of course, the masters would return, but by then the form of exploitation would have changed, as compared with the old *villa* system, and for a time would be more moderate. Often the *villa* was hard pressed to "hang on."

In the face of rebellion and invasion the landowners put up a brave front, loosening the fetters somewhat, reducing the exploitation of the *coloni*, changing the size and shifting the boundaries of the estate. New *villae* appeared, but the *villa* as such did not disappear, even if its owner changed. A new latifundian aristocracy was born of the "alliance" among the barbarian chieftains, the Gallo-Roman landowners,[101] the "Roman" generals, and the clergy. The new aristocracy tried hard to restore order by repressive means, by slow and drastic measures of which we hear but faint echoes. Whenever the peasants mounted collective resistance to the system, the landowners resorted to such measures. Order was restored, but it was not the old order based on gang slavery as the dominant form of exploitation. Though this endured a good while and now and again even made a strong comeback, by the end of the early Middle Ages it was clearly becoming peripheral. Why? Before we attempt to answer this question, basic for an understanding not only of this period but also of later ones, we must pause to describe the fundamental cell of the new society, the Merovingian *villa*, as it emerged in the century following the troubled fifth, and as it developed throughout the early Middle Ages up to the time of Charlemagne's attempt to found a new empire.

III. Forms of Exploitation in the Early Middle Ages and Challenges to Them

It has become virtually impossible to describe the early medieval *villa* since the demise of belief in the traditional *villa* and the "classic" manorial system, with its demesne cultivated by serfs under *corvée*, and its manses devoted to reproduction of the labor force. Let us not grieve overmuch for its demise. Since it enabled Marx to work out the theory of the feudal mode of production, it did not live in vain! It is often said that no historian today accepts the idea of the feudal mode, an abstraction utterly devoid of interest.[102] It is true that attempts to make of this theory a model of nearly universal applicability, or even a description of a typical case, often led to the mouthing of textbook banalities. But as Marx saw it, the feudal mode of production was not a description of a social formation! It was merely a way to identify a fundamental social relation. This was useful for thinking about medieval social formations. It was also useful for casting doubt upon (and even demolishing) the very concept of the F. M. P. itself. Now, this is a concept that lurks in the mind of all historians, whether consciously or not, even those historians who have revealed what prodigious variety the real history holds, thereby helping to overthrow the dogma that the classic notion of the feudal mode had become.

To put all this in plain language:

1. an abstract model need not be useless;

2. nothing could be more absurd than to confound the (or a) feudal mode of production with a description of the social formations of the Middle Ages;

3. *at the very least*, we need to take another look at the traditional concept of the feudal mode of production itself.[103]

How can we explain the prodigious diversity of reality without succumbing to the flaccid "anything goes" school of history, and yet without pretending to give an exhaustive account—which is quite plainly out of reach (still more out of *our* reach!)?

To begin with, we shall try to construct a new abstract model, allowing for some of the diversity revealed by historical research: in other words, we shall attempt to characterize one sort of Merovingian or Carolingian *villa*, presumably typical (in certain regions anyway) of the times. Having done this, we shall underscore the fact that in reality there was a very wide range of estate types by mentioning at least one attempt to establish a typology. Finally, we shall say a few words about the free peasantry outside the domain: the allodialists.

Before getting on with this program, however, it is worth mentioning that the old scheme erred in two respects (at least): it failed to take note of the continued existence of large numbers of chained slaves (of what we earlier called a "post-slave system," in other words), and it made too much of the *corvée*. These are really two aspects of the same error, because the blunder in regard to the slave system explains how the theory of the generalized *corvée* came into being, since obviously some portions of the estate were still directly exploited by the lord. Having said this, let us try to see what new scheme may be established, bearing in mind the wide variety of types of estate that seem to have coexisted, between the Rhine and the Loire surely, but also in Latium, about which we possess extensive knowledge thanks to the work of Pierre Toubert: "the" Merovingian, and, later, Carolingian, *villa*.

A) Complexity of Social Relations in the Early Medieval Villa

In the Merovingian or Carolingian *villa* we find, to begin with, a relatively large group of slaves.[104] These prebendal slaves lived "on the bread of their master," in outbuildings off the courtyard, and worked in teams. The lord "held them in hand" (*servi manuales*), i.e., in his power, or had them "at hand." In this we see the continuation of the old form of gang slavery: these slaves worked the reserved portion of the estate or demesne. Even if their relative importance probably cannot be compared with the importance of slavery in the second-century *villae*, the number of prebendal slaves seems nevertheless to have been noticeably greater than during the period of social and ethnic unrest (Bacaudae, invasions) during the late third, second half of the fourth, and fifth centuries.[106]

All historians today agree on the importance of these ancient forms of rural slavery during the early Middle Ages, i.e., from the fifth century to the end of the ninth century. In the case of Spain, Pierre Bonnassié has studied the Visigothic codes[107] and notes that of the 498 legal texts known to us, 229 concern problems of slavery. He adds that similar proportions hold for Salic law, the Burgundian laws, and Frisian law (not drafted until the time of Charlemagne). This is to say nothing of the frequent references to slaves in literary texts and tales, as well as in conciliar decrees and penitentials.

Where did these slaves come from? It is clear that the usual attrition of the servile work-force due to death, emancipation, or escape was compensated by subjugations on a fairly large scale. Since the number of people entering servitude and the number of slaves lost in one way or another varied over time and did not exactly balance each other, there must have been wide variations in the size of the slave population from one period to the next.

Subjugation was effected in the time-honored ways: judicial condemnations—Bonnassié has described the early medieval judicial system as a machine for enslaving poor free men; sale of children, of considerable importance during periods when poverty was on the rise;[109] and, above all, war. War in the Merovingian and Carolingian eras was primarily a "manhunt":[110] after an invasion a whole people might be reduced to slavery (as in the case of the subjugation of the Celts after the Anglo-Saxon invasion of the British Isles in the fifth century, except for those who were able to flee to Cornwall and Wales); or kings might organize slave-hunting expeditions, such as those carried out by the sons of Clovis in Germany or by Dagobert in Gascony (the Frankish army brought back large numbers of slaves, chained two by two, "like dogs"); or a people reduced to slavery might be deported, as happened to the Saxons following the wars of Charlemagne; or there might be tribal wars between provinces (the inhabitants of Berry against those of Orléans, of Orléans against Poitou, and so on), useful only for rounding up slaves and livestock.

Is it possible to arrive at any idea of the number of slaves (both prebendal and domiciled) relative to the number of free men, as it varied over time? As a working hypothesis, Bonnassié suggests that the total number of slaves amounted to somewhere between 10 and 15% of the number of free men. Why not! The figure seems quite reasonable, but the fact is that no one has the slightest idea. And this is to say nothing of variations from region to region, which must have been considerable. As far as changes over time are concerned, I think the following hypothesis is warranted: slaves fled in large numbers during periods of social unrest and invasions, or whenever the state entered upon a period of crisis or collapsed, and the same holds true for large-scale emancipations and for domicilings.[111] The number of enslavements depended not only on the success of razzias, but also on rapid restoration of order after an invasion (as in the case of the Anglo-Saxon invasions in the fifth century), on the possibility of subjugating free peasants, and on the repressive power of the state. From this it follows that there were relatively few rural slaves, and especially prebendal slaves, during the ethnic and social unrest of the third century (Bacaudae, invasions), and later during the "final" crisis of the second half of the fourth and the fifth century. By contrast, the number of slaves increased with the establishment of barbarian kingdoms, which combined repression internally with military forays externally. There may have been a considerable number of both escapes and domicilings in the seventh century (at least in its second half), followed by a resurgence of the slave system with the Pepins beginning in the early eighth century and of course with the empire of Charlemagne. After the collapse of the imperial venture and its associated state organs, and the ensuing social and tribal unrest coupled with the Viking, Saracen, and Hungarian invasions in the second part of the ninth and early tenth century, slavery declined once again.[112]

In addition to slaves, the Merovingian and Carolingian *villa* also harbored *coloni*. Had their situation changed greatly since the later empire? And if so, how? They were still free men and seem in general to have held land and (though perhaps less often) to have been held by the land.

Did being bound to the soil mean being subjugated by their master? Marc Bloch observed that where an imperial constitution said, "Let him be returned to his native land," the code of Roman law drawn up for the Visigothic state in the early sixth century said, "Let him be returned to his master."[113]

It is likely that first the crisis and later the collapse of the Roman state ultimately vitiated the fourth- and fifth-century landowners' claim that the peasant was tied to the soil. With the advent of the barbarian kingdoms, however, was there perhaps a reinforcement of the manorial system, a trend that (after a reversal in the second part of the seventh century) was renewed in Gaul as the Carolingian empire rose to its zenith? Still, despite the probable restoration of the colonate, the chance of escaping and joining a band of fellow fugitives probably remained high enough to explain why the law changed so as to accommodate the reality: in Sabine, for example, "the right to decamp was expressly accorded to the free *colonus* and even to the slave domiciled and emancipated by his master upon grant of tenure. . . . Around the year 750, then, while the *colonus* still held land, the land no longer held the *colonus*"[114] (whereas, by contrast, in the later empire the law tried desperately to shape an increasingly anarchical social reality). Nevertheless, the hypothesis that I shall put forward is that with the Carolingian order came a relative increase of the dependence of the *coloni* on the land, and hence on the master, as well as an increase in the burden of required services; moreover, liberation, real though certainly in a relative sense, did not come until the social crisis of the ninth and early tenth century.

We also find new forms of protection on the estate, transformations of the earlier forms of patronage. These represent a first stage of evolution of the system, a resumption of the late imperial trend toward subjugation. Through violence, whether overt or covert, smallholding peasants were obliged to sell or hand over their land to great lords, both secular and religious, and then take it back in *precarium* (whence the French *précaristes*), often with a premium to pay in the form of various *corvées* (when they were not simply reduced to slavery, primarily by judicial means!). To be sure, some peasants, and in certain cases entire *vici*, did come forward to ask "freely" for protection, that is, for de facto subjugation, but often the protection was sought from the very same persons against whom it was needed, or "from their brothers"! Thus there was a recommencement of the same trend toward protection that had led to the subjugation of a portion of the old Gallo-Roman peasantry: the revival of collective liberties in the *vici* and the de facto liberation of many peasants during the period of unrest in the late fourth and fifth centuries had replenished the "stock" of those in need of protection!

The "classical" *villa*, with its demesne and its tenements, was not constituted merely (or even primarily) by dismemberment of the directly exploited areas of the old estate, but by expansion, thanks first to the patronate during the late empire, and, later on, during the early Middle Ages, to protection and the *precarium*, which became perpetual. This preliminary development was coupled with the domiciling of slaves.

The *colonus* of old and the new beneficiary of the lord's protection had the status of free men; alongside their free (ingenuous) tenures, however, we witness an increase in the number of tenures often referred to as servile. Domiciling of slaves dates, as we have seen, from the late empire. Although our knowledge of its importance at that time is limited, there is no doubt that it was on the rise, though irregularly, interrupted at intervals by significant revivals of gang slavery.

One problem here, it would seem, has to do with the continuous spectrum of situations from the chained slave to the slave granted both emancipation and a "large" tenement. The image of the eighteenth-century plantation in the Antilles comes to mind: the Negro "yard slave" was given a hut and a bit of land, no doubt quite limited in size but large enough to permit the raising of food crops; but he was still sent to work, chiefly in gangs, on the estate (some of the men still being housed together in large barracks in some cases). Such situations may well have been common in the early Middle Ages. It is difficult to distinguish between the situation of a man with a small servile tenement but still subject to *corvées* that differed but little from the old forms of gang labor and the situation of the *servi manuales* with their *portiuncula*.[115] A whole gamut of cases must have existed, with a wide range in the size of tenements granted to former slaves and a wide variety of *corvées* and services to be rendered to the master. What is more, the master frequently had the right to take the sons of "domiciled" slaves to fill out his complement of slaves "at hand," which shows that to domicile a slave was not to break irrevocably with the past as far as heredity was concerned.[116] Finally, the example cited by Georges Duby from the law of the Alemanni (compiled in 717–19), to the effect that slaves of the Church must pay a fixed tribute, slave women being obliged to carry out all the required tasks, and males being obliged to work "three days on their own account, three days on the demesne,"[117] is not to be regarded as anything more than a typical case at best. In general, domiciled slaves owed (at least initially) a payment in money, in kind, or in labor larger and above all less certain than that owed by free men. The case of the *villa* of Staffelsee in Bavaria is often cited as one in which the difference between free and servile *manses* was considerable: the free tenants (or those in free *manses*) owed up to 36 days of *corvée* per year, a trifle, while servile manses owed three days of *corvée* per week. From this it is supposed to follow that during the eighth and ninth centuries an abyss separated free tenants from domiciled slaves. This cleavage was increasingly obscured, however, by the settlement of free men in servile *manses*, marriage, and so forth.

In some cases, moreover, the domiciled slave was emancipated without bringing about any real change. Frequently along with his emancipation he had to renounce his freedom by undertaking certain obligations, particularly in the form of rather nebulous *corvées* and payment of a head tax known as the *chevage*, which was a reminder of his subject status (as distinct from that of the free tenants): this went by the name of manumission with obedience (*cum obsequio*).[118] Furthermore, the burden on the free tenants no doubt increased greatly between the Merovingian and Carolingian periods, as did the burden on the peasantry as a whole:[119] the late imperial trend toward homogenization of the peasantry through domiciling of slaves and subjugation of free men resumed, now even more far-reaching in its effects, though there were phases of acceleration, stabilization, and reversal.

With the help of Pierre Toubert,[120] we can avoid oversimplification. As early as 750 or so in Sabine, he notes, "the *colonus*, quite generally, was one who had the hereditary and pacific enjoyment of a *casa colonica*, a complete peasant farm centered on the nuclear family: *qui in casa residet, qui casam regit cum uxore, filiis ac filiabus*, etc.," i.e., domiciled slaves as well as all free tenants; as Toubert observes, moreover, sometimes the word *colonus* was applied to a freedman provided with a modest *portiuncula*. The only criterion was the domicile (*casement*), since prebendal slaves (*servi manuales, servi familiares, servi qui intra casam serviunt*) were never characterized as *coloni*. This is reassuring, for it tends to confirm our idea that on the whole the major question was that of domiciling: once the genuine independence of the hut had been acquired, fusion with the various sorts of free *coloni* or tenants ultimately followed. A prebendal slave with a *portiuncula* was still far from a tenant because the gang slave generally still lived in the barns or dormitories of the *villa*, ate the master's bread at the master's table, and, though free to procreate, was not permitted to live as part of a nuclear family (though women may have been allowed to live with their children in more independent huts, with male slaves living with them in more or less stable circumstances).

The tenant or *colonus*, on the other hand, frequently lived on his own land in his own separate hut: moreover, it seems to me that in some cases the scattered dwellings of these peasants reflect concessions won during the periods of social and ethnic unrest around the turn of the

fifth and tenth centuries. These concessions, in turn, led to further liberation (the Merovingian reaction, followed by the even more important
Carolingian reaction, probably did not succeed in regrouping these scattered tenants, a failure that would explain the need for prebendal slaves
and hence for razzias and reductions to slavery by legal means; on the
other hand, *incastellamento* and banal seigniory, beginning in the second
half of the tenth century, were more successful in regrouping the scattered peasants).[121]

Moreover, these tenures seem to have been *censives* (with a fixed *cens*
or dues proportional to the harvest) more often than classical manses
with *corvées*, as in the *villae* of the "Parisian" type, at least during the
seventh and early part of the eighth centuries, not only in Latium or
Italy, but in Provence, Catalonia, and the Loire region as well.[122] Did the
"classic" manorial system spread more widely during the Carolingian
reaction?

A priori, the era of Charlemagne and Louis the Pious seems the better
known, thanks obviously to the capitulary *De Villis*, the polyptychs of
a number of monasteries, particularly that of Irminion, and a good many
charters; in consequence, the danger of hasty generalization from these
few texts is the greater: indeed, it was from such information that the
"classical" *villa* of this period of restoration of the state was deduced,
and it was long accepted that the *villae* were the principal, and virtually
the only, mode of exploitation of men and land during this time! To be
sure, the classical *villa*, with its demesne worked by prebendal slaves
and tenants under *corvée*, its variety of workshops providing for quasi-
autarchy, and its free and servile tenures, had the advantage of clarity.
Historians of old, as we mentioned earlier, failed to see the prebendal
slaves (neglected in the inventories) and hence arrived at their classical
system, in which the demesne and the *manses* were closely associated:
the classic feudal mode of production. Once the large number of *servi*
had been recognized, thus forcing acknowledgment that the economy
of the demesne was more independent than had been thought, it became
necessary to acknowledge the presence of other workers as well, because
prebendal workers of free status who nevertheless belonged to the demesne were also found; they were recruited from among the surplus
population of the *manses* and lived on food provided by the master and
in his house or its dependencies. There were also quasi-wage-laborers,
constituting what was merely a reserve labor force, highly unstable, but,
in view of its mobility, quite practical. These workers were paid with a
meal and a room, did not belong to the demesne, and frequently roamed
the countryside in bands. In some cases these roving bands actually
amounted to seasonal migrations of whole village communities, while

in other cases they more nearly resembled a more or less permanent horde of vagabonds, hence already a free labor force: free, that is, to hire itself out or starve.

The typical system, moveover, was certainly not as widespread as had been thought: on the one hand we find surviving small- holders, peasant communities, allodial holdings of medium to large size, and on the other hand domains of widely varying types, with a system based on censive tenures having been common, as we have seen, in the seventh century. However, there is reason to think that during the Carolingian era the *villae* of the imperial aristocracy were economically and socially dominant relative to all the rest, that is, to the various other forms that grew up around them, and that this system spread in two ways: by "contagion" from more Romanized to more "savage" zones, and above all by the tendency of the *villae* to grow larger, with the master of the great estate extending his protection[123] to the peasants of the surrounding country-side (through the *commendise*). Little by little these peasants were thus integrated into the manorial system of exploitation, first by payment of an annual levy (*chevage*), later moving from this protected status to a dependent status not very different from that of the domiciled slave.

B) The Diversity of Types of Estates

It is now clear that the tendency toward larger estates and wide diffusion of the manorial system did not give rise to a *single* typical estate form, the form commonly depicted by historians on the basis of what was apparently a type of estate frequently found in the area between the Rhine and the Loire. If we turn our attention to Italy, we find that many different types of estates existed there. These are relatively well known thanks to the work of Pierre Toubert in particular.[124]

Toubert distinguishes three estate types in eighth- and ninth-century Italy:

First, there was the "pioneer" type, characteristic of central Italy and the lower Po Valley. Here we find no well-defined "master's house," few large manorial buildings, and no large reserve of arable land. Two different sectors were juxtaposed without integration: one was chiefly pastoral, along with a few vineyards or olive groves—this was the sector from which the profits of the estate were derived; the other was the peasant-worked sector, i.e., the portion of the estate tended by free tenants under no obligation whatsoever to provide *corvée* labor. These free tenements are said to have expanded at the expense of the manorial *manse*, which depended chiefly on pastureland and orchards.

A second type of estate, perhaps older than the first, contained a reserve in which the emphasis on vineyards and olive groves was markedly greater, with forest and pasturing still important and grain growing virtually nonexistent. The organization of direct exploitation centered on a master's house and other buildings, together with a variety of high-level technological equipment, representing a considerable investment in fixed capital, which required regular maintenance. *Corvées* were required of the tenants only a few weeks per year, but they were of course well-chosen weeks, falling, for example, during the seasons of olive picking or grape gathering.

Finally, the "classical" type of estate typically involved grain growing, where the soil was suitable. Individual tenements were flanked by vast grainfields, directly exploited by the master. Only in this case do we find the "classic" relation between tenements and demesne.

Gang slavery, therefore, was of no importance in the "pioneer" domain, where there was no "master's house" and no *villa* (in the architectural sense); it seems to have been dying out in the "classical" case, probably via domiciling; and doubtless it persisted in the "old" system as a way of providing labor for the upkeep of the vineyards and olive orchards. But there is no point in generalizing on the basis of eighth- and ninth-century Italian types. What we must stress is merely this: in the "frontier" zones, where there was a transition from the estate based on forest and pasture to tenant cultivation, the changeover may not have been exclusively, or even primarily, the result of a decision made by the lord, but rather a consequence of manifest encroachments. Demographic pressures had made it "necessary" for the peasants to resort to such measures, and, what is even more important, existing circumstances had made it possible: namely, the absence of the *casa dominicata*, the center of surveillance, control, and repression, together with the presence of vast areas of "free" uncultivated land. Under these circumstances it is easy to see how the estate could have disintegrated, even under the Carolingian system, favorable to it in so many respects.

C) A Free Peasantry

Thus we find no one type of great estate; not only that, but in the pores of the manorial economy, we do find many free peasants, property-owners joined together by solid communal ties, much as today we find small businessmen in the pores of monopoly capitalism. How many free peasants were there? No doubt their number was considerable. If, contrary to the ideas of Engels and Marx, the barbarians were not themselves the bearers of freedom, it remains true that the social crises of the third and above all the fourth and fifth centuries, as well as the collapse of the imperial state, were liberating influences. Fugitive slaves, domiciled slaves, and *coloni* found ways to enjoy some measure of real freedom and made themselves masters in their own homes, often collectively. Lately become allodialists, the Frankish peasants were free men on their own land, largely because as members of the Frankish nation they had remained warriors. The trend toward subjugation of the peasantry did surely resume with the Carolingians, but despite this social reaction, coupled with the tendency toward military specialization, new forms of patronage, and legal or de facto expropriations, free allodialists probably remained in the majority during the Carolingian era, counting both Franks and native peasants.

We know from the military capitularies of 807–8 how Charlemagne sought to preserve a recruiting system in which poor freemen could enlist in his armies, and we also know of the oath-swearing ceremonies organized by the emperor, whereby he attempted to reestablish a direct tie between himself and the whole of the Frankish nation, including the poor. The clear impression we get from all this is that, far from being a system based solely on great estates, the Carolingian world was one in which a large role was played by smallholders (in some cases tenants of a great landowner), tightly bound together in village communities in which power was exercised in assemblies of the populace (like the Spanish *concejos*), providing in some cases for periodic redistributions of land (as with the *ceorls* of the Anglo-Saxon communities).[125]

The free peasantry, often grouped in sturdy peasant communities, was held together by collective labor practices (particularly in regions with long, narrow fields[126]), as well as by cultural ritual. Peasant culture of the early Middle Ages is characterized negatively by its resistance to Christianity—the Roman religion, the religion of the great (Christianization of the countryside, which got under way in the fourth century, was far from thorough at the dawn of the tenth)—and positively by the legacy of autochthonous paganism, and even perhaps by slave-transmitted rituals. This pagan heritage made itself felt in festivals (the festival of the winter solstice, which coincided with Christmas, the festival of the summer solstice, which coincided with Midsummer's Day, ritual baths, nocturnal games, dances, songs—all rituals judged obscene and pitilessly persecuted by the Church).

The free peasants of the village communities, some say, were also responsible for technological progress in the early Middle Ages: peasant collectives are said to have carried out landclearing, popularized the wheeled plow, and built mills *prior* to the rise of banal seigniory.[127]

D) From the Carolingian "Reaction" to the Social
Struggles of the Ninth Century: The Crisis of the
Manorial System and the "End" of Slavery

Must we then give in to the "revisionist" estimate of the place of the allodialists in Merovingian and Carolingian times and go so far as to relegate the estate to a position of secondary economic importance, or perhaps to view it as anomaly? I do not think so. On the contrary, I believe, first, that between the fifth and seventh centuries the social structure was based chiefly on free peasants and tenants, relatively little exploited (as compared with previous periods). The social and political breakdown in the west at the end of the Roman Empire explains the rise of this social structure, on the basis of which the Carolingian state established itself. But, second, I believe that the tendency, particularly during the eighth and the first part of the ninth century, was toward a revival of the great estate, gang slavery, subjugation of the poor free peasants, and increase in the burden on the poor tenants. That Charlemagne made such prodigious efforts[128] to maintain military ties with these peasants becomes comprehensible if we suppose that their condition had deteriorated so seriously that they found it difficult to play their traditional warrior role, not a few of them having fallen prey to de facto subjugation (again!) or been caught in the toils of a system in which they were required to provide services or pay rent.

Even in the Carolingian era the tendency toward extension of the great estate had been vigorously contested, often by organized free peasants, whose struggles have been discussed by Georges Duby in his foreword to *L'Histoire de la France rurale*, peasants who emerge from "the prescriptions of the Carolingian capitularies, repeated time and again because they failed time and again to have any effect, expressive at once of the anxiety of the well-off at the thought of so many outlaws lurking in the bushes at the edge of the clearing and of their own inability to control them." We find other indications of this peasant resistance in clandestine village oaths, ritual bacchanalia, peasant guilds capable of organizing resistance first against the Normans and later against the lords, outbreaks of "brigandage"—that brigandage of the Bacaudae which "lived on, despite repression to one degree or another, all over the medieval landscape, as one of the avatars of an obstinate resistance to oppression: oppression by the State, oppression by the lord, oppression by the rich."[129]

However, while the Carolingian order was on the rise (during the eighth century), and later under Charlemagne and Louis the Pious, during the apogee and early stages of the decline of that order, the balance of power was favorable to the masters of the *villae* and unfavorable to their tenants, whether freemen or domiciled slaves, and this led to a further withering away of the differences between free and servile tenures. There had previously been a tendency for the connection between the status of the man and that of the tenure to be destroyed because of mixed marriages and inheritance, and little by little the peasantry of the estates (then growing in proportion to the other inhabitants) became increasingly homogeneous; former *coloni* and free tenants were no longer distinguished from domiciled slaves on the one hand, and *protégés* in the strict sense on the other hand (except, of course, if the latter had been and were still warriors[130]), so that only the *servi manuales* stood apart. Manorialization continued, *in spite of and because of* the restoration of the imperial state. "In spite of," because the reconstruction of a coalition of the powerful around a centralized state having some degree of autonomy from the ruling class could only be accomplished by concentrating the royal powers in the hands of the state, hence by submission of the powerful to that state, to their state. "Because of," because the restored imperial state made internal repression possible and accelerated the concentration of lands in the hands of the imperial aristocracy, while at the same time aggravating exploitation, facilitating fruitful sorties for pillage of treasure and men (revival of slave razzias), and reestablishing imperialist superexploitation.

But the social basis of this state continued to be quite narrow: the Frankish nation, a people of free warriors; descendants of Gallo-Roman peasants who had been able to press their claim to certain collective freedoms at the time of the Bacaudae insurrection and the invasions; the people of the *vici;* and peasant owners of small- to medium-sized plots— all these groups had, despite their resistance, gradually succumbed to logic of the large estate. War, hence pillage and razzias, once again became increasingly the specialized province of a few. When matters had evolved to the point where only a small number of men of war remained, and the masses of peasants were unarmed, hence increasingly dependent, the state could not but wither away (in a resumption of the same process that had been at work during the late empire). This explains Charlemagne's great fear at a somewhat earlier date, when he saw the direct tie between the state and peasant warriors, allodialists and even freeholders (often the same man was both) breaking down, for this tie formed the "warp" of the social fabric, the social basis of the state. It also explains why the collapse of the Carolingian state three-quarters of a century later was attended by uprisings and invasions, which further reinforced the process of decomposition, thereby sealing the fate of the last attempt to create an empire in the West. Moreover, this structural change was bound up with the final transformation of slave relations of production (post–slave system). The gang slaves fled the estates or were domiciled, domiciled slaves were emancipated, tenant ties were relaxed, and *corvées* became more difficult to impose! I am quite ready to believe that this ultimate end of the slave system coincided with a crisis in the manorial regime, i.e., in the survival of the ancient *villa* system: in short, there was a crisis of serfdom and the *corvée*, a crisis of what might be called the first feudal mode of production, the mode that Marx and the historians of his day were describing. One has no choice but to correlate all these crises with the crisis of the state.

Among the various "proofs" that there was indeed a wave of individual and collective emancipations of the *servi manuales* in the late ninth and early tenth centuries, we may cite written sources from central and western France, which make mention of a peculiar social category, the so-called *colliberti*. The term persists in the texts through the twelfth century. Much discussion has been devoted to the origin of the *colliberti* and their place in society.[131] It seems likely that originally they were emancipated as a group in the late ninth and early tenth centuries, whence their very name, *con-liberti*; at the same time, ties with the master were maintained. The *colliberti* were probably descendants of gang slaves who had not been domiciled, large numbers of whom still remained on the Carolingian demesnes. The *servi*, or serfs, on the other hand are said to be descendants of former domiciled slaves. In the eleventh century the *servi* on their tenements probably had the advantage over the emancipated slaves without tenure. Later, with the fusion of all the dependents into a single, relatively homogeneous mass, the differences between the two groups tended to disappear (with the *colliberti* coming to hold tenures, for example), and soon the word *colliberti* vanished (end of the twelfth century). What interests us here, however, is the wave of collective emancipations associated with the unrest of the late Carolingian era.

The intestine wars among the great, chiefly the sons of Louis the Pious, and the invasions do not explain the demise of the empire and of the revived central administration, even if they do ultimately count as contributing factors. Concentration of the *villae* and subjugation of the peasant masses, however, reinforced by the revival of the state, do explain why the revived state was doomed to failure. To begin with, the unrest of the ninth and tenth centuries marks a key phase of the class struggle. The old ruling-class coalition, a social impossibility nonetheless reinstituted for a brief period, once again modified, temporarily, the balance of power between the ruling class and the peasant masses, the more so in that the masses were not yet "serialized," with consequences we shall now detail.

From the standpoint of the exploited masses, there was strong resistance to submission to lord and master, strong opposition to shouldering a crushing burden of dues and obligations. Against the master who violated the *lex*, i.e., abused his power to exploit his tenants, the latter revolted, aided by the serfs and by slaves still working in gangs. We are familiar with such *conjurations* (sworn conspiracies) of serfs and freemen by virtue of the laws concerning them, which forbade conspiracy and attempted to disrupt alliances. The law made it incumbent upon the masters to crush rebellion, and it seems that they did so brutally.[132] Here was a switch to open rebellion on the part of peasants who had hitherto carried on their fight chiefly by surreptitious means: "inertia, dissimulation, indulgence bought from the steward, and the threat of flight into nearby wastelands, where pursuit was impossible, there to join the bands of outlaws."[133] Moreover, in the ancient *vici*, the peasant communes, which either stood outside the estate or survived within it once they had been wholly or partially engulfed, the possession of collective rights and the existence of solidarity in the parish gave rise to guilds, associations held together by oaths against the despoilers. This explains the fear of these conspiracies and rebellions, out of which grew the stereotype of the peasant as a creature predestined to evil, ugly and besmirched, a dangerous enemy.[134]

From the standpoint of the masters, the situation called for brutal repression whenever possible. But there was also a reduction in the size of the demesne, the portion of the estate directly by the master, not merely relative to the portion held in tenure—this could only have been accomplished by increasing the share of the latter—but absolutely. Domiciling of the last remaining men who "lived on their master's bread," the *servi manuales*, along with collective emancipation of the whole slave gang, the reduction of the *corvée* (the last surviving form of the old slave system), and the reassertion by the peasant communities of their ancient rights, doubtless accompanied by a resurgence of a free peasantry, of allodialists—all these things led to the collapse, and dismemberment of landed seigniory, which in its old form had been a system of exploitation complex in its workings yet capable of laying hold of a considerable portion of what the peasants produced.

Thus it is possible that between the final demise of slavery in the West (accompanied by crises of the manorial economy and governmental authority) and the forging of a new coalition by the masters based on a new type of seigniory, there intervened a period of unrest—not only a time of insecurity, when vagabond bands of robbers, both native and foreign, roamed the countryside, but also a time of collective freedom, of revenge by the free peasantry, and of reduced exploitation. Around the year 900 there doubtless came "a unique moment when the ancient system of exploitation, based on slavery, had totally disappeared, and the new feudal system of exploitation had not yet been born,"[135] a moment that may be seen with particular clarity in southern Europe, where the slave system did not fade away with the rise of serfdom, there being instead continuity between the old and the new mode of exploitation. Is this moment any more difficult to discern in northern Europe, where the slave system was transformed into the system of serfdom by way of domiciling? Perhaps not, because there the social crisis was a crisis of the manorial system, i.e., just as much a crisis of gang slavery as of *corvées* or rents in kind.

The point is not to erect a myth of a golden age of freedom for the peasant at the beginning of the tenth century. But were not the egalitarian heresies of the eleventh nourished by mythical memories of such a golden age? The tenth century witnessed the rise of a new feudal order. The crushing of the peasant revolt in Normandy at the end of the tenth century is indicative both of the fragility of the new order (there was a mass uprising against it) and of its substantial solidity (the revolt was crushed). Doubtless there was an aggravation of the class struggle as the tenth century gave way to the eleventh,[136] with the masters in control: the revolt was caused by exasperation with the new order. A century earlier there had been a liberation movement of the *servi* and the subjugated peasantry: the balance of power had changed.

IV. The Elaboration of a "New" Feudal Mode of Production

In the end the independent peasantry, after losing ground under the Carolingians, probably regained its predominance at the beginning of the tenth century: the interlude of imperial restoration had ended in failure. With the collapse of the central state, the manorial system and serfdom in its "classical" form had also collapsed: hence the demise of F.M.P.$_1$!

However, following the "break in the tenth century"[137] and/or early eleventh century (depending on the region), a new type of coalition was forged by the masters, feudalism, and a new type of seigniory was established, based on the possibility of employing new forms of exploitation, not merely of a portion of the peasantry, but of practically all the peasants of Europe. Already during the Carolingian reaction there had been a tendency to homogenize the peasantry by "downgrading" the poor freemen, both allodialists and tenants. This trend continued in the social crises of the ninth and tenth centuries, with the liberation and emancipation of the gang slaves, the reduction of *corvées*, and perhaps the mingling of allod and tenement. The new mode of exploitation was able to capitalize on this homogenization in order to spread. The individual rate of exploitation may have been lower, but now exploitation extended to all men, save for such specialized groups as priests and warriors, yielding a total product sufficient to "stimulate" a commodity economy, and soon a monetary economy based on the surplus.

We have at present a good knowledge of the two major forms of this *new* feudal mode of production, namely, encastlement (*incastellamento*)[138] and banal seigniory; we also know when these forms crystallized, in relatively brief periods that we can pinpoint quite easily in each region (usually no more than the space of a generation). Both forms were associated with military force and local political power, generally more or less continuous with the remnants of the Carolingian administration. What occurred was not a restoration of the central power but a tenacious resistance or restoration of local power, backed by military force. Was this a restoration of order, a reaffirmation of control by "direct political violence" exercised by armed men? Was the triumphant violence of the castellans based on a profound transformation in military technology, which gave the mounted warrior, equipped with stirrups and hence able to wield heavy weapons (the long lance, the cuirass),[139] a clear-cut superiority over peasants "armed" with scythes, pikes, and cudgels?

Such a view has often been upheld, to the point of making the use of the stirrup in the West the cause of feudalism.[140] This is naive. Instead, it was the new feudal structures that gave rise to the heavily armed warrior, chiefly for the purpose of combat between knights. Indeed, how effective would such a knight have been in the guerrilla warfare necessary to quell the free peasantry of the ninth and tenth centuries? In the forest and scrub, peasants armed with guisarmes and bows could hold out indefinitely against the clumsy knight. It was not heavy weaponry that triumphed! Forget the idea of the lord armed as at Crécy riding out to subdue the allodial peasant in order to impose the new feudal charges upon him; in fact the peasants were subdued in police actions of the counter-insurgency type, carried out by small groups of men on foot flanking a mounted sergeant!

The ability to construct fortresses and to breed horses for combat, on the other hand, did give an undeniable edge to the lord. However, this ability presupposed the existence of relations of exploitation.[141] There is reason to believe that the material power of the knights and castellans was based on existing social relations, on relations of production associated with the "old" form of landed seigniory, which survived to a sufficient extent to provide a surplus for the aristocracy; these were also political relations, since the men in question were frequently descendants of the representatives of the count, Carolingian *voyers*, *viguiers*, or *vidames*.[142]

Still, there must have been more involved than mere coercion, more than organized military power and violence exercised by those who held the fortresses and by men on horseback against the feeble peasant with his guisarmes. Banal seigniory was brutally imposed in certain regions, but, as we shall see, there were also families who came "voluntarily" into the *castra*, or fortified villages, at the time of the *incastellamento* of southern Europe. This was voluntary servitude, in the sense of La Boétie, of masses frightened by robbers and by social upheaval itself, by "Saracens," whether genuine or counterfeit, by Normans and Hungarians, and attracted by "valid" domiciling contracts (which must have given an impression of security in these troubled times): people were reassured as well as confined by the walls of the fortress. Bear in mind that the old system of tenure and domiciling, the large numbers of fugitive slaves and serfs, and the power and numbers of the allodialists all contributed to a rather wide dispersion of the population. Hence the family living in geographic isolation was in a position of weakness, even if collective bonds remained intact, in the face of groups of vagrants or, even more, the men of the castellan. Thus, while the submission of some peasants to their new masters was merely formal, whether subjugated where they lived or forcibly carried off and brought to heel by violent means, others submitted genuinely for the sake of security or food for their families.

Banal seigniory has recently been given a clear definition. It took shape in the late tenth and early eleventh centuries within the limits of what had been the Carolingian Empire, where it came to constitute the basic element of the political order (save for certain regions, in which royal power was more successful in holding the magnates in check, as in England in the eleventh and twelfth centuries). Banal seigniory (the term is due to Georges Duby[143]) involved the establishment of political power based on the possession of fortresses, and, more generally, on the force of arms. The restoration of public order thus had two compenents: first, the installation of a coercive political power and the seizure of public domains, and subsequently the establishment of the powers of the ban, i.e., of seigniorial rights associated with the administration of justice and with certain economic monopolies (mills, ovens, etc.) by military chiefs, in virtue of their possession of a castle.

As J.-P. Poly has pointed out, the castle did not serve as protection against invasions, which had on the whole ceased by the time the fortresses were built, and, though it did of course serve to protect the castellan against his peers, chiefly "it loomed over the *villa*, dominating the land and all the peasants, whatever their condition. And since now the magnate came to take up residence in his castle, he made it the collection center for all those new dues which he claimed were owed him and which he was then extending, or trying to extend, to all who lived in the shadow of his Roque."[144] The "private" castle was essential to the power of the ban, as the means of exercising the power to command all the freemen of the surrounding region; with the transformation of this political power into the means of exploitation, the castle made possible the extraction of surplus labor from all, or almost all, the peasants.

Clearly, this new fiscal system, or the extension of the old one, was one of the most important ways of confiscating the surplus. The various exactions—the *taille* or the *tolte*—were almost always arbitrary. As Duby explains, the power of the ban was so extensive as to permit seizure of whatever could be carried off from the peasant's dwelling: money, harvest, livestock, and labor. Even a new type of *corvée* was established, connected with the old military obligations of freemen and having nothing whatever to do, so far as its origins are concerned, with the servile *corvée*, a survival of the slave system. Equally arbitrary were the rights of justice and the economic monopolies which fell on top of the other "exactions." As Pierre Bonnassié has put it, "the former freemen were thus subjected to a regime of strict dependence, which was to form the basis of the new servitude, of a wholly novel kind utterly different from the old."[145]

What about *incastellamento*? Toubert's work has disclosed its importance in Italy (Latium and Sabine), but it is increasingly clear that the phenomenon was also important in the south of France, and even in the more mountainous regions. Encastlement involved the establishment of fortified hilltop villages, perched on previously uninhabited peaks. Its inception marks a break between the old system of scattered, open settlement, and a new system of concentrated and fortified dwellings, enclosed by the walls of the new *castra*, or *castelnaux* (as they were called in the south of France).

Encastlement is inconceivable in the absence of a desire on the part of the lord to bring men together in groups, by enticing them, not so much one at a time as in families (often in the broad sense) or even whole communities headed by a "chief," frequently a priest: "Quite the opposite of a bunch of vagrants or miserable wretches."[146] This confinement was not accomplished by forcibly locking up vagabonds, bands of thieves, or other "asocial" types, but rather by appealing to "good folk," in some cases to the small allodial peasantry, rural craftsmen, or substantial free tenants. They came, sometimes from afar but usually from the region itself, to be assigned a space where they might build a dwelling in stone, in the shape of a regular rectangle whose dimensions were fixed by the settlement charter, as well as a small garden plot, of similarly regular shape, against the outside wall of the enclosure, a small vineyard, and a number of parcels of arable land on a variety of soils (the size of which depended, in some cases, on the size of the family). The village was always surrounded by a wall, and the dwellings were always located in accordance with a regular, predetermined plan, centering on the church and the fortress.

Though the hilltop site was often new, the land, of course, consisted largely of previously cultivated plots. The lord had first to regroup the peasants who had worked these parcels (who must have been free, moreover, either to accede to the new grouping and charter or else decamp). Was some land deserted and other land cleared to make way for new arrivals? Beyond any doubt, colonization was an important aspect of the new developments, but it almost never went without a restructuring of the existing pattern of cultivation. One portion of the land was always reserved for intensive cultivation, devoted either to the production of a variety of food crops or to the production of marketable commodities (oil-yielding crops, grains), and another portion was left uncultivated, reserved for foresting, gleaning, and raising livestock—a rather rigid specialized structure. Most important, proof that power was primarily of a political nature is furnished by the fact that space was now closed: no longer were there interstices between one cluster of plots and the next, and each cluster was dependent on a *castrum*.

What caused these changes? The Saracen and Hungarian invasions must be ruled out: these were practically finished when encastlement got under way in the middle of the tenth century. Furthermore, it is clear that spontaneous regrouping of a peasant community never occurred. Obviously, what we are looking at is a decisive moment in the social struggle, an initiative by the lords to assume, or to restore, control over the whole of the peasantry, an extraordinary moment in which a new form of social control was crystallized, a control based on a regimenting of cultivation, a radical and lasting restructuring of the tilled land, and on a new mode of organization in the sphere of production, all of which was epitomized in the material structure of the whole complex, with its strict enclosure and its planned pattern, centered on the military and religious institutions.

Naturally the lord profited from this operation. Did he assume control over men in order to extract surplus labor? How was this extraction accomplished? The second question is not difficult to answer: the forms of exploitation were similar to those of banal seigniory, perhaps without the arbitrariness, but with greater integration of dues connected with lordship over the land and dues associated with the exercise of political and judicial power. As to the first question, apart from the obvious aspect of the answer (yes, control was exerted in order to extract surplus labor), we also come across the notion that control was an end in itself (the extraction of surplus labor being merely the means of reproducing that control); but this is a question which goes beyond the phenomenon of encastlement!

How was it possible for encastlement to spread over large areas? How could the lords have won, when the Carolingian reaction had failed to subdue the free peasantry, and when, as we have seen, there seemed to be movement at the turn of the tenth century toward liberation through violence? "It is the very peoples themselves who allow themselves to be gobbled up, or, rather, who offer themselves up for the gobbling, for if they ceased to serve, they would be rid of servitude; it is the people who subjugate themselves, who cut their own throats, who, faced with the choice between serfdom and freedom, abandon liberty and take up the yoke."[147] Indeed, it is not wrong to say that in part the peasants came voluntarily to seek the refuge of the fortress, the protection not only of other lords, but also of their own lords: *servi fugitivi*, brigands, vagabonds, and other rebels against the social order. Anarchy produced power, and social conflict associated with the crisis of the state created anarchy! Otherwise things would have been too simple! Rather than contrast voluntary servitude with forcible constraint, however, one must understand that the violence of the lords found support in social groups bereft of stability and security and afraid of famine, in *families* which in the long run preferred order, security, and servitude to freedom, and the lords found their thugs among the vagabonds and the former *servi manuales!* The class struggle has its own internal dialectic.

But this question takes us beyond the temporal horizon of our study (we shall have more to say on this point). We must first try to understand the whys and the wherefores of one of mankind's most glorious victories: the end of the slavery of the ancient and early medieval world. Was it not this victory, moreover, that led to the defeats represented by banal seigniory and encastlement? Undoubtedly, but was not the encastlement of all, wherever it took hold, on the whole an improvement over the slavery of some?

Outline of the Following Chapters

It is easy to see how the domiciled slave whose tenement was large enough and whose time was not completely monopolized by *corvées* (clearly two sides of the same coin) gradually lost the characteristics that distinguished him from the free tenants. This gradual merging was only accentuated by the loss of autonomy that the free tenants seem to have suffered during the late empire and early Middle Ages. At the same time, it is not hard to understand how the strict prohibition against sexual relations between freemen and slaves (save for relations between the master and female slaves) gave way, because of domiciling, first to tolerance of such relations and later to acceptance of the validity of religious marriage. It also becomes clear why the master was soon forbidden to punish his domiciled slave by beating, mutilation, or death. The transformation of the domiciled slave into the "serf" is not the problem. Marc Bloch, for example, showed some time ago[148] how a similar de facto situation led to convergence in the legal status of the two groups: marriages between members of both, as well as occupation of servile tenures by freemen, brought the domiciled slave and the free tenant close together.

The fundamental question is this: Why did the masters domicile their slaves? Or, how did the slaves manage to get themselves domiciled? Of course the progression gang slave to domiciled slave to serf, i.e., via domiciling, was not a necessary one. The master could allow his slave gangs to break up or wither away by attrition, by not replenishing the stock through breeding, purchase, or capture. The two questions are almost identical. In both cases slave gangs and direct exploitation were replaced by tenants as much as possible in a position of dependence. The only difference between domiciling and failure to reproduce the slave stock was this: with domiciling the same man who had been the slave became the dependent, while in the latter case it was a different man. Hence the second solution to the problem is predicated on the existence of a supply of subject peasants at the master's disposal. This explains the connection between the end of slavery and the subjugation of the peasantry. But the question of the subjugation of free peasants (de facto and de jure) is not primary for us in the present context.

During the late empire, as we have seen, domiciled slaves did exist, and a wave of domiciling took place.[149] Doubtless it was not so important a factor in the decline of slavery as the destruction or withering away of the slave stock, which was supplanted, often over a long period of time, by *coloni*. During the early Middle Ages, on the other hand, domiciling seems to have intervened quite frequently between gang slavery and serfdom. The difference can probably be explained by the size of the dependent labor force at the disposal of the master; accordingly, mere demographic differences were trivial or unimportant, and what mattered most were differences in the balance of power that permitted the subjugation of the free peasantry: at certain point in the early Middle Ages, there were strong peasant liberation movements.

Hence one frequently noted difference between the two periods has to do with the relative importance in each of the two modes by which slavery declined (domiciling on the one hand, attrition of the slave stock accompanied by substitution of dependent labor for slave labor on the other hand). In general, however, analysts of the decline of slavery between the second and the tenth centuries place the accent on the same set of causes (some stressing general causes valid for any slave system[150]). Thus there is no need to distinguish two types of analysis, one for the end of the empire, the other for the beginning of the Middle Ages, except where a particular theory explains only one of the modes of decline (we shall see that this is the case with M. I. Finley,[151] who does not account for domiciling). In a similar way, we shall put forth a general cause in no way specific to any particular period, though it may operate according to quite different modalities in different historical eras.

What approach are we going to take?

To begin with, we shall interrogate other historians who have written on the subject (chapter 2). In particular, we are going to be looking at the work of historians whose profoundly new approach to the interpretation of history has excited our interest, the historians of the *école des Annales:* in our case, since we are concerned with rural history, and particularly with French rural history, and with slavery and the early Middle Ages, we shall of course be turning to the work of Marc Bloch and of his successor Georges Duby. Some readers may find these choices surprising, for neither man is a "specialist" in slavery (though Marc Bloch did lay great stress on the question). But this is precisely why we have chosen them. For the interpretation they give is a global one, and the question that interests us is that of the transition from one mode of production to another. Nevertheless, we shall not on that account neglect the work of so important a specialist as Charles Verlinden, whose views we shall have occasion to criticize; what is most interesting in his work, however, is its factual content, "theory" playing a quite limited role. (As for the late empire, the very important argument of M. I. Finley will be analyzed later on, in chapter 4.)

In the background, of course, we will have occasion to run across the somewhat outdated views of H. Wallon and E. Meyer,[152] and, above all, the work of Max Weber,[153] as well as that of Fustel de Coulanges,[154] M. Rostovtzeff,[155] and Ferdinand Lot.[156] Of more recent date is the debate surrounding the "new economic history" and its approach to slavery, focusing on slavery in the Antilles and in America between the seventeenth and nineteenth centuries, and particularly on the profitability of the slave system in that era—this is a debate we cannot avoid.[157]

Special consideration will be devoted to certain Marxist historians (chiefly to one of the most important of them, Charles Parain) in chapter 3, where we will criticize a mechanistic interpretation of historical materialism. This critique is to be read as an application of the remarks made in the introduction. Such criticism is, in our view, indispensable, for the transition to feudalism cannot be understood unless class struggles are brought to the fore.

Finally, following these two critical chapters, we shall take a more "positive" approach in chapter 4—"positive" in the sense that we shall attempt to verify a hypothesis by investigating whether it and it alone provides a perspicuous account of the transition process. No decisive facts will be adduced (seldom do we find any facts accepted by all authorities, particularly in this area, where empirical research has had other focal points); rather, we shall reflect on the notion of causality and reconsider Marc Bloch's question, "How and why did the slavery of the ancient world come to an end?"

Doubtless it is true that "everything affects everything," that everything acts, reacts, and retroacts on everything else in any complex system. The danger in this view, however, is that it is likely at best to yield a structuralist, not to say structuralo-Marxist, "mishmash," in which everything is said and nothing explained. Certain determinations are principal, primary, driving forces. The other elements of the causal system (secondary determinations) exist only through the principal elements, in their essence, their form, or their effectivity (*effectivité*). Only in this sense can Engels's assertion that the economic base is "determining in the last instance" be understood. Of course this assertion gave rise to an *economic mechanism* that dominated the field for a time); *social mechanism* is a danger equally to be avoided.

By showing that social struggles explain the end of the slave system (*Gutsklavenwirtschaft*), we do not wish to give an analysis based on "linear causality." Once the class struggle (not only of the exploited against their masters, but also of the masters against the exploited) has been brought to the fore (as the locomotive, and not merely the midwife, of history), we shall see how the various explanations in terms of productivity, profitability, demographics, or statistical variations in the slave trade are reborn (genuinely reborn and not merely adapted to fit the interpretation): we shall understand why, superficially, today's orthodox interpretation of history can provide an explanation.

Why has the class struggle traditionally been presented as a sort of "hors d'oeuvre" served up alongside the main dish, the real meat of the matter? Because, in the first place, source material—the raw stuff of history—is sorely lacking in this regard. The sources with which the historian ordinarily works are produced by the masters or by their clerks and executioners, their retainers of one sort or another. The pen was not wielded by Spartacus, still less by some unknown slave or dependent peasant risen in open—or more frequently silent—struggle against his master. Historians are never sufficiently attentive to this bias. Then, too, what historical research has been done has reflected the needs of the ruling class of the historian's own time, providing ideological reassurance. The historian, like the chronicler or journalist, frequently writes for a master or for the masters.[158]

Research is guided by reigning theories of history. For a long while history focused only on battles among the great, on their wars and tournaments, on the meretricious or, at any rate, the visible (which could not be ignored). The work that has gone into building up a history of the hidden depths has made it possible to bring to light slow changes in material life (an indispensable achievement, to be sure), but not as yet the struggles of men that ultimately determined that material life. Conflict—often muffled, hidden, clandestine, surging into the limelight, into view, into "history" only on the necessarily infrequent occasions when armed insurrection breaks out—is what historians ought to be trying to tell us about: the history of the class struggle, yet another history of society's hidden depths.

2

The intersection of ss *supply and* dd *demand curves showed no signs of moving toward the vertical axis of zero slavery!*
Paul A. Samuelson, *Economics*

Questions to Historians about Economism

The "economistic" line of argument may be summed up by citing Engels's "definitive" formulation: "Slavery no longer paid; it was for that reason it died out."[1] In this chapter we shall be criticizing this line of argument in its various guises, except for those associated with mechanistic Marxism, consideration of which is postponed until chapter 3.

It bears emphasizing that in the present chapter we shall be attempting an internal critique of the "economistic" arguments. We shall argue first that the very idea of large landowners making economic choices on the basis of rational calculation is mistaken (section I). After that we intend to engage the authors whose work we are criticizing on their own terrain, in order to show that comparisons between the slave system and the system involving domiciled slaves, *coloni*, or serfs on the basis of productivity (section II) or profitability (section III) do not work out in favor of the latter. Then we shall give a similar critique of arguments in terms of reproduction of the labor force (section IV) or reproduction of "economic conditions" (section V), such as those advanced by Marc Bloch. Finally, we should probably have included a separate chapter devoted to refutation of the arguments of those who see Christianity as the cause of (or as a crucial or important factor in) the end of slavery (section VI), but economism, or vulgar materialism, and moralism, or ideologism, are inextricably associated, two sides of the same coin.

Let us begin by rehearsing the argument of Georges Duby,[2] which adduces several interdependent causes to explain the domiciling of slaves. Basically, Duby is drawing heavily on the earlier arguments of Marc Bloch.[3] Duby writes:

> Both the appearance and proliferation of peasant tenements in the seventh century were the result of a far-reaching *innovation*, a new method of utilizing dependent labour. In this period great landowners seem to have been *discovering* that it was *profitable* to marry off some of their slaves, settle them on a manse, and make them responsible for cultivating its appurtenant lands and feeding their own families. The process would relieve the master by *reducing costs of staff maintenance, generate* enthusiasm for work on the part of the servile task-force, increase its productivity and ensure its replacement, since these slave couples would be entrusted with seeing to their children's upbringing themselves until they became of working age. By degrees this last advantage probably turned out to be the most important. Slaves became increasingly *rare* on the majority of western European markets all through Merovingian and Carolingian times. Possibly this decrease stemmed from a growing strictness in religious morality in relation to the enslavement of Christians; more certainly it was the outcome of an expansion of trade with the southern and eastern Mediterranean. Most of the slaves procured through war could be sold outside Latin Christendom and *their market price was rising,* with the result that landowners *had an interest* in having them brought up locally. The best way to manage this was to leave the matter in the hands of the parents, so as to obtain slaves from domestic procreation and let them live in their own homes.

Duby's analysis of the seventh-century situation does not differ fundamentally from the analyses given by a number of historians of the first "end" of slavery in the late empire. The "economistic" arguments are identical, though of course adapted to the circumstances. We have chosen to cite Duby's because it is a clear statement and an excellent synthesis.

Marc Bloch had earlier explained that in *all gang-slavery systems* we find that (*a*) the slave is a poor worker, returning a low yield; (*b*) he is perishable capital, for the death or illness of the slave entails loss of the sum it cost to buy him and forces the master to purchase another slave; (c) breeding could hardly be counted upon to replenish the slave force, for under the prevailing conditions it was too precarious an affair; (d) this was not serious as long as slaves were available in abundant supply, hence at low prices. Many slaves could be wasted on small jobs and if one died he could be readily replaced; (e) when the difficulty of replacement increased and the slave's value rose, landowners turned to the tenement system.

With the tenement system, on the other hand, we find that (a) the worker produced a greater yield on "his own" field and even on the demesne (if the *corvées* did not produce an excellent yield, still it must have been superior to the yield of the old system, for the domiciled slave would have been afraid of having his tenement revoked); (b) "since the slave lived in a better-organized family, he was more certain of perpetuating his family lineage."

Several arguments are intertwined in the Bloch-Duby thesis summarized above, and several questions arise: questions of the strictness of religious morality, of economic rationality, of the gang slave's productivity, of the profitability of slavery, of the feasibility and cost of breeding slaves and of fluctuations in the slave trade. We encounter the same arguments in discussions of slavery in the late empire and the early Middle Ages, as well as in analyses of the end of slavery in nineteenth-century America. Let us now attempt to show that, presented in this form, they are not convincing.

I. The Question of the Rationality of the Great Slaveholding Landowner

Duby refers to an innovation, a discovery made by the great landowners. Accordingly, they must first have carried out calculations to show the profitability of gang slavery as compared with that of the domiciled slave.

Now, such a calculation is difficult to perform. Surely the great landowners were able to see that gang slavery yielded profits, but from there to a comparison of the profits of the two systems is a major step. To carry out such a calculation in the case of slavery in the southern United States, Conrad and Meyer were forced to make assumptions concerning the average life span of a slave, his cost, the cost of necessary additional investments, the interest rate, the annual yield on the slave's productive activities, and the number of offspring produced.[4] So it is reasonable to ask what sort of economic reasoning the great Roman or Merovingian landowner was capable of undertaking.

The question is a difficult one to answer, for the problem is not merely to determine whether the masters were capable of carrying out roughly accurate economic calculations. Merely to venture onto this terrain is enough to raise serious doubts in our minds (though obviously not on account of any supposed intellectual deficiencies of the ancients): M. I. Finley has pointed out that one of the most thorough estimates of farm income, in the judgment of modern historians, that which Columella made of the income of a two-hectare vineyard,[5] allows for the purchase price of the land and of the slave vine-dresser, the cost of vines and props, and even the two years' revenue lost while waiting for the vines to mature, but neglects the farm buildings, equipment, ancillary land, slave-maintenance cost, depreciation, and amortization.[6] Far more serious oversights are to be found in other examples. However, masters may well have decided whether or not to domicile slaves, for example, on the basis of mistaken calculations.

Beyond this, the question is whether the notion of economic calculation then had anything like the significance attaching to it today. To be sure, in the calculation alluded to above, Columella does arrive at a precise rate of profit (33.3%) and, commenting on a common theme of the day, explains clearly that to use a steward and slaves is superior (under certain conditions[7]) to renting, because the former method yields greater profits. However, was not such a purely rational or modern argument rather unusual for the time? A near contemporary of Columella's, Pliny the Younger, mentions in one of his letters[8] that he is planning to buy an estate alongside one he already owns, which happens to be available at a low price on account of poor management by the owner and his tenants. According to Pliny, the primary reason for making the purchase is the beauty (*pulchritudo*) of the estate; although he does observe that he will be able to visit both estates in the same day, make do with a single agent (*procurator*) and even a single steward (*actor*), and keep up a *villa* suitable for receiving a visiting senator, he has not a word to say about the size of the property, the income it brings in, or the crops grown. It will be objected that he was a dreamer! Perhaps— and further evidence of this sort could be adduced without constituting a proof. Still, it may be said that at this time rational economic considerations did not stand out clearly from other motivations. Why were land and slaves coveted? Among other reasons we may cite a taste for land and for the honor that it brought in greater abundance than did other kinds of "investments," family and civic tradition (which encouraged the maintenance of family holdings and agriculture, the time-honored activity), the desire to provide for a daughter's dowry, the power and pride derived from holding large numbers of slaves, aestheticism, ostentation, the obligation to own a sumptuous *villa* for receiving important guests, the pronounced taste for sojourns in the country, the importance of property in land and slaves for administrative and political careers. In short, use value and exchange value were inextricably intertwined, and the situation was one in which income was attractive only as it related to "unproductive" expenditure, the sign and instrument of grandeur.

A caution is in order at this point, however: the foregoing is not to be interpreted as suggesting in any way that the masters were uninterested in the profits they drew from the exploitation of men and land! This may have been truer for the Merovingian and Carolingian aristocracy (in regard to the latter period, Duby makes mention of indifference to economic realities), but the Roman master needed to know only that his estates were bringing in substantial sums (and this was clearly the case for the slave *villae*), in other words, sums that would enable him to live "nobly" (a socially necessary income!).[9] Beyond that he did not concern himself with profit rates, amortization, and the like; he performed no economic calculations.

For gang slavery to be abandoned, probably more was required than a calculation (which would have had to be incorrect, moreover) showing that a system of exploitation based on domiciled slaves or *coloni* would have increased the rate of profit by 5 or 10 percent. Was not what was needed most likely the realization on the part of the landowners that they had no option but to shift to such a system if they did not wish to see their social position—and, in particular, their level of expenditure—abruptly lowered and their continued existence as a class threatened?

II. The Question of Productivity

A typical example of ultra-economism in explaining the transition to serfdom is provided by the argument of S. Mazzarino. As he naïvely expresses it, "under these conditions, slave labor in an economy based on large estates cannot be as productive as is sometimes thought. The masters become aware of the important fact that the domiciled slave, with his wife and children, develops an affection for the soil and produces more. Obviously the master does not immediately draw all the consequences of this observation; but there is no doubt that the most intelligent masters do notice the fact."[10] In other words, as Mazzarino himself puts it, "for a variety of reasons it becomes a matter of importance to *interest* the slave in production, to give him a family and a *peculium,* and so the slave barracks are consigned to oblivion."[11] This analysis is a caricature of what Duby refers to as "technological innovation" or discovery: "the masters become aware. . . ," "the most intelligent masters notice." It also involves a confusion of productivity with profitability: even if the gang slave is less productive than the domiciled slave, does it follow that the master derives a greater profit (a greater total profit or a higher rate of profit?) from the second arrangement, so that he will inevitably choose it over the first? Duby avoids this elementary error, as does Ferdinand Lot, who also maintained that the productivity of slave labor was low.[12] Let us look at this argument more closely.

To answer the question of how productive servile labor was in comparison with other forms of labor would require, as a preliminary, having a clear, operational concept of what productivity is, as well as the data needed to measure it. Leaving the problem of measurement aside,[13] there remains the concept itself. Suppose we have a slave *villa* of one hundred hectares, with two hundred slaves working in teams and centralized organization of the labor force, with one thousand "tools," and with an output of four hundred tons of corn in a year's time. Assuming that all other inputs remained unchanged, we would have to imagine an increase or decrease in output due solely to a changeover from gang slavery to a tenement system in which serfs organized their own labor and cultivated their own land (along with supplying *corvée* labor on the demesne). The resulting change in output would be an index of the productivity of the particular factor we have been calling "domiciling." Here we are not interested in the possible effects of other changes, such as the change in legal status (from slavery to serfdom or freedom, coupled with ownership of a small plot or possession of a hereditary tenement, whether servile or ingenuous), but only in two aspects of the transition: first, the change in social relations (from gang slave to domiciled slave or virtual serfdom, as we have discussed above), and, second, the change in the manner of working the land (from direct exploitation by slave gangs to individual exploitation of small plots, the changeover being complete in the extreme case where the demesne is eliminated altogether).

The economistic argument assumes that masters were able to carry out a comparison of this sort. More than that, they would have had to do so within the framework of the existing type of estate (unless we are willing to go so far as to imagine the possibility of reversible experiments in socioeconomics, allowing for a changeover to domiciling, comparison of the results, and depending on the outcome, a possible return to gang slavery). Hence the comparison would have been a very rough one (all the "inputs" would have changed), to say nothing of the fact that the period during which all this is supposed to have taken place was to say the least somewhat troubled.

What is more, supposing that different outputs were obtained, how do we account for the difference? Did men work more days per year, or more hours per day? If so, why did the domiciled slave, the serf, or the free tenant work those extra hours or days? Possibly rather than work longer hours they worked more efficiently: in other words, the gang slave may have produced either more or less per hour than did the domiciled slave on his own tenement. Once again, it is impossible to be certain a priori what the meaning of a given change was; if it is assumed that under gang slavery labor was less intense, i.e., produced less in a given period of time with the same material and so forth, it is imperative that clear reasons for that assumption be stated.

Note, in this regard, that we are concerned not with the labor of an individual slave, but rather with that of the collective laborer (that is, with the productivity of the entire slave gang, including the foremen). Working in gangs on a large estate would have made it possible to take advantage of the efficiencies of large-scale operation, division of labor, and centralized organization. These often noted characteristics of gang labor certainly increased its intensity. Not that these advantages were obtained free of charge. That is, for example, specialization may well have increased the slave's output per hour, but only with increased demands on mind and body resulting in greater wear and tear on the labor force, hence at a cost in human terms that is difficult to pin down (a shortened life span is only one aspect of the problem, along with illness and the like).

This leads us from the question of productivity to the larger question of profitability. The work force produced more but at the price of increased wear and tear (bear in mind that the labor in question here is not the same labor that enters into the production function).

All those who have employed productivity arguments in their reasoning about the end of slavery are committed, implicitly or explicitly, to a theory of the causes of the increased productivity of the free tenant or serf. Why would he have submitted to working a longer portion of the day or year or to a greater intensity of labor? The answer to this question is said to be obvious: the serf on his tenement, the domiciled slave, the *colonus*, the free tenant, the landowning peasant are all supposed to have had a direct "interest" in production, in both quantitative and qualitative senses.[15]

Marx, too, explains that "compared with the labor of the slave, the labor of [the independent worker] tends to be more intensive, hence more productive. The slave works under the spur of fear, not for his existence, which, though not his own, is nevertheless guaranteed. The free worker, on the other hand, is driven by his needs."[16]

To consider first the question of fear, it is wrong to imagine the slave in the imperial *villae*, or for that matter on plantations in the United States or the Antilles in the eighteenth and nineteenth centuries, as motivated solely by its omnipresence. As we have seen in our account of Columella's model, there were also various material and psychological stimuli, a whole spectrum of "rewards" and genuine promotions within the hierarchy of slave society. Conversely, the "free" worker was no stranger to fear, since he had to face a whole range of sanctions in many guises. Having said this, we must add that despite Columella's idyllic picture, the slave in ancient or early medieval times was subject to physical punishment and even death at the hands of his master.

Here, with wage labor out of the picture, we are interested in studying fear in connection with the gang slave as compared with the domiciled slave, and the domiciled slave as compared with the serf. As a social type, the domiciled slave was evolving relatively rapidly toward serf-dom.[17] Probably the master retained power over his body, but his relatively greater economic autonomy must have considerably reduced the master's power as compared with its absolute forms, until ultimately its exercise became exceptional and unsanctioned. Once it is recognized that in this respect the evolution from slave to serf entailed considerable change, it becomes clear that the goad of fear, direct compulsion, was not insignficant. This was particularly true in that the slave had to fear for his life, not only in cases where, as Marc Bloch pointed out, slave labor could be used wastefully (just as the inmates of concentration camps could be worked to death), but also where slaves were bred (a few of them might be punished, mutilated, or killed as examples to the rest).

Turning now to the question of needs, how effective a goad to productivity were the needs of the worker? The needs that "drove" the independent worker did not always lead him to favor goods over rest and leisure. We must be on our guard not to think of the independent peasant in the early Middle Ages as a dynamic and energetic capitalist entrepreneur. What reason would he have had to work over and above what was necessary to satisfy the "natural" needs of his family, whose desires were "simple"?[18] More than that, his tiny plot would have been subject to rapidly diminishing returns.

Marc Bloch gives an interesting, though contradictory, argument to explain why *corvée* labor on the demesne could be made to yield more than slave gangs working the same land: the peasant could be threatened with repossession of his manse. Who can doubt that such threats were effective? But the gang slave was subject to other threats, no less "stimulating" to productivity.

Let us take a step beyond considering the individual worker in isolation. Use of the slave gang on the *latifundia* allowed for certain economies as a result of division of labor and, more generally, cooperation. I do not wish to exaggerate the importance of these economies—quite the contrary.[19] I merely want to point out to the advocates of the economistic line that there is surely a contradiction in their emphasizing the technical advantages of mass production to explain or justify large industrial operations with centralized management and division of labor— the modern equivalent of the slave gang—while stressing the equally technical advantages of the small individual parcel of land, worked autonomously, over the centralized management of slave gangs on the *latifundia*. To take this line is to pin the whole argument on the peculiar characteristics of agriculture in general or of certain crops in particular.

The gravamen of the charge is not to reject Smith's old argument that the division of labor is relatively insignificant in agriculture because of the seasonal nature of the work, but merely to point out that an increase in the size of the directly exploited demesne and the use of slave gangs could raise yields enough to compensate for a possibly lower intensity of labor. As Marx and Engels were aware, moreover, with the tenement system division of labor is limited by the fragmentation of the work effort.[20] Did not Marx write that "propietorship of land parcels by its very nature excludes the development of social productive forces of labour, social forms of labour, social concentration of capital, large-scale cattle-raising, and the progressive application of science."[21] Gang slavery on the *latifundia*, on the other hand, allowed not only social and technical division of labor but also centralized organization, economies of scale, and other advantages associated with the possibility of using "indivisible equipment," i.e., equipment that could not be adapted to use on the *microfundia*.

Having mentioned equipment, let us take note of the argument (not put forward by Duby or Bloch) that the low productivity of slave labor was due to the difficulty of introducing machinery into a slave labor system. Was slavery a fetter on technological progress, an impediment to the development of the productive forces? We shall have occasion to come back to this question. For now the important thing is to note that even if it is conceded that slave relations of production were an impediment to technological progress, this has nothing to do with why the masters turned away from slavery. Indeed, slavery precluded the introduction of a new machine (a water mill, for example) only because the machine would have produced less profit for the master than the slaves it would have replaced. Under these circumstances the masters as a class would have had no interest in giving up slavery. Technological progress was not an end in itself; for the exploiting class the only end was the size of the surplus extracted, and if this was greater without the water mill, why would the masters have abandoned slavery?

To hold that the end of slavery was the cause of technological progress is not at all the same thing as to hold that the cause of the end of slavery was that it impeded such progress!

Obviously it is quite difficult to give convincing evidence regarding the productivity of the gang slave as compared with the domiciled slave. As Finley has noted, it was not until the fourteenth century that yields equivalent to those of the Roman *latifundia* were obtained in France.[22] This proves little, however, since we have no idea how many slaves were at work on each acre of land. Possibly more men were used per acre on the great estates of the second century than on the Merovingian *villae*. From the eleventh century onwards, however, the number of workers per acre in France must have been at least as great as in imperial Italy during the second century, and the relatively low yield in the Middle Ages is thus an index of low labor productivity.

To conclude our remarks on this topic, let us turn to the current debate concerning the productivity of the gang slave in another time and place, the black slave in the southern United States. The celebrated work *Time on the Cross* by Fogel and Engerman, which gave wide currency to the notion that slavery was an efficient institution and slaves good workers, quantitavely and even qualitatively, and which provoked a great hue and cry when it appeared, undoubtedly rests on quite a few dubious assumptions; still, their results are enough to cast doubt on any naïve claim that gang slavery is always inefficient. Such a claim cannot be taken seriously when it is stretched to the point of making this supposed low productivity or impediment to technological progress the *cause* of the end of slavery and the reason for the domiciling of slaves.

On the question of the relative efficiency of slave agriculture, Fogel and Engerman were led to the conclusion that in the pre–Civil War period, slave labor was "superior,"[24] which they explain not by a greater number of working days in the year (on the contrary, slaves at that time seem to have worked fewer days) or a greater number of hours in the working day, but rather by "the organization of the work force in teams that worked intensely, were highly coordinated, and operated with precision."[25]

Much of their article would be worth citing here, particularly the part in which they emphasize the importance of the division of labor among the teams and within each team, the fullest utilization of each individual (for example, of pregnant women and women who had just given birth), and the advantages of centralized, disciplined, and strict organization, not in order to apply their argument "as it stands" to the medieval case, but to bring out the fact that centralization, specialization, and discipline made for increased returns on the human machine, the collective worker. Once again it should be noted that such intensive use of the labor force added to its wear and tear, so that the argument must be couched in terms of comparative profitability (rather than say the work force yielded a greater product for the same amount of labor, one should say instead that a greater product was obtained with labor of a different kind) and exploitation (since in both cases there was a master).

Of course the relevant comparison for our purposes is between the slave system and systems based on serfdom or small freeholds, not between slavery and wage labor (with centralized management, division of labor, and so forth). The latter is the comparison undertaken by Fogel and Engerman, which would explain, as they show, why slavery apparently failed to prove its "superiority" in the United States under nineteenth-century industrial conditions. This failure had nothing to do with the specific technical characteristics of the slave system. Rather, it merely reflected the fact that the two systems now being compared were both of the same type (i.e., centralized, strictly organized, specialized, and disciplined).

It is not our intention to turn the productivist argument on its head and play the Fogel and Engerman of antiquity. Our point, to put it mildly, is merely that it remains to be proven that the productivity of the ancient slave system was low. Moreover, when it finally did become clear that the slave was relatively inefficient, the reason, as we shall see, was not the one the economists propose.

III. The Question of the Profitability of Slavery

On the subject of American slavery, Paul A. Samuelson has written that "among historians, most of whom know little economics, a myth later grew up that slavery in the decades before the Civil War was *becoming economically unprofitable*. According to the myth, if Lincoln could have been a little more patient, the South's peculiar institution would have collapsed of its own weight "[26] The same myth is prevalent with regard to ancient slavery.

Was it *profitable* for the masters to domicile their slaves? What mattered to the master (assuming he behaved in an economically rational manner) was the surplus product he extracted from exploitation, and not the

productivity of the worker in any direct sense. Is there warrant to suppose that domiciling or, more generally, tenancy with payment of rent
in kind or money as well as labor services (*corvées*) on the demesne
(serfdom) was more profitable than direct exploitation of the entire estate
by gang slaves fed on "the bread of their master" in a common refectory
and housed in the master's barns (if not in huts of their own)?

A) Comparing the Profitability of the Two Systems

The productivity of the peasant on his own tenement is supposed to
have been higher than under the system of direct exploitation by slave
labor. Although we have criticized this assumption above, let us assume
for the moment that it is correct. There was plenty of opportunity for
chicanery of one sort or another to affect the portion of this increased
product that was actually remitted to the master. Fraud is a constant
theme in the history of peasant tenancy, as is the surveillance that was
established in an attempt to control it. But surveillance was of course
far more difficult with tenants than with gang slaves or, more generally,
with a centrally managed work force.

What about *corvées* on the demesne? Doubtless this was the worst of
all possible systems from the master's point of view. All in all, the threat
alluded to by Marc Bloch (of revoking the tenure of the peasant who
was remiss in performing his *corvée*) was "slight" compared with the
threat hanging over the slave (death). It would seem, moreover, that the
threat of revocation was hardly ever carried out, and so it must soon
have come to be regarded as empty. The truth of the matter is that the
domiciled slave, who before long became a serf like any other, enjoyed
considerably greater autonomy than the gang slave. Duby himself points
out that the *corvée* laborer was particularly "lazy" and prone to "pilferage," but that he was far better fed than the slave working on the
demesne: "greedy manual laborers, quick to filch and slow to bend their
backs," is Duby's description, not to be improved upon.[27] The reader
may be imagining that the profitability of *corvée* labor was comparable
with that of gang slavery, but reduced to a few days per week. This is
wrong: the tenant's power vis-à-vis the master was far greater than the
slave's, even if the tenant remained formally a slave or, after emancipation, continued to labor under the regime of the *manumissio*. To eat
his own bread in his own hut was no small thing, particularly since the
masters were very soon reluctant to intrude their power beyond the
boundaries of the serf's garden.

In Duby's eyes, moreover, laziness, fat living, and pilferage account
for the decline of the *corvée* and for commutations from the twelfth
century onwards. The demesne, cultivated either by the domestics of

the *familia*, successors of the nondomiciled slaves, or by hirelings watched over by a steward or farmer, was quite productive, moreover.[28] I am aware that Duby's point is to show that the productivity of the gang slave was less than the productivity of the serf, which in turn was less than the productivity of the wage laborer. The truth, however, is that the hireling who was fed by the master—and very badly, I might add, compared with the *corvée* laborer[29]—was in fact the brother of the domestic who supplanted the nondomiciled slave. The earliest wage earners were even lower in status than the slaves of the *familia*. The fact that the hireling would before long be earning a few coins in addition to his food does not alter the fact that on the whole he received no more food than the *servus* of the *familia* (hence much less than the tenant serf who grew his own food on his tenement—and probably lived relatively well, surely eating far better than the domestic while on *corvée*). Moreover, both hireling and slave did far more work than the peasant on *corvée* (two to three times as much![30]).

B) Costs of Upkeep

Domiciling, in Duby's words, "relieved the master by reducing costs of staff maintenance."[31] What costs? Well, obviously the gang slave was fed the master's food from the master's kitchen, while the domiciled slave ate his own food from his own kitchen.

But the food that went to the gang slave was not bought outside the *villa*. As we know,[32] even under the empire in its mercantile period, the *villa* aimed to achieve the maximum possible autarchy, at least with regard to consumption (although it may have sold a part of what it produced outside). The degree of autarchy increased, moreover, during the late empire and early Middle Ages. Landowners did not have food for the slaves brought in by nearby merchants at great expense—far from it! Working in gangs, the slaves themselves produced what they ate on the master's land. Domiciling also required land and labor for the production of subsistence items. If it is true that the domiciled slave was better clothed and fed than his brother the gang slave, and if his overall productivity (counting work both on the tenement and in *corvées*) did not increase, then more labor was required to produce what the workers needed to survive.

Even if necessities were imported from outside the *villa* in exchange for money, something must have been produced in return. Exactly the same analysis in terms of quantity of land and labor must still hold good. Or, rather, not exactly the same analysis—for there might have been problems with cash flow (that is, problems with the *villa*'s balance of payments), but in fact there were none since no actual disbursement of cash was made. Granting this, the argument as it stands is empty, or, rather, it merely asserts that the ratio of rate of consumption[33] to productivity for the gang slave was greater than the same ratio for the serf (or domiciled slave)—and this is not obvious, to say the least.

C) Costs of Supervision

Both Duby and Bloch (apparently) neglect the costs of supervising the work force. This is curious, since these costs are among the most substantial points in favor of their argument, as Marx observed in the third volume of *Capital*. As is well known, Marx distinguishes between two aspects of management and supervision. On the one hand there is the general problem of cooperation, "determined by the nature of all combined social labour,"[34] such as the work of the orchestra conductor, for example. On the other hand, there is the "labour of supervision and management, arising . . . out of an antithesis, out of the supremacy of capital over labour, and being therefore common to all modes of production based on class contradictions like the capitalist mode."[35] Hence this type of labor has a "twofold nature," only one aspect of which is productive: "Now the wage-labourer, like the slave, must have a master who puts him to work and rules over him. And assuming the existence of this relationship of lordship and servitude, it is quite proper to compel the wage labourer to produce his own wages and also the wages of supervision . . . 'just compensation for the labour and talent employed in governing him and rendering him useful to himself and to the society.' "[36]

Accordingly, Marx could write that "this supervision work necessarily arises in all modes of production based on the antithesis between the labourer, as the direct producer, and the owner of the means of production. The greater this antagonism, the greater the role played by supervision. Hence it reaches its peak in the slave system."[37] It follows that the slave system (*Gutsklavenwirtschaft*) entails more "hidden costs" than systems with less severe class conflict.

The argument that the man holding the whip must also be fed merits further attention. Undeniably the overseer's pay must be counted as a cost of the slave system (to the master), so that the question becomes one of determining whether or not centralized management of slave manpower, with supervision, allowed for a sufficient increase in the master's share to cover this additional cost.

The problem pertains not only to gang slavery but also to wage labor in large factories with division of labor and centralized management and control, as in British industry in the eighteenth century, for example. Even earlier the same question may be asked in connection with rural wage labor and the gangs of hirelings who came to work the demesne in the twelfth century, supplanting the *corvée* labor of serfs who, thanks to the independence they enjoyed on their tenements, were shiftless, intractable, and thieving.

In *What Do Bosses Do?*[38] Stephen Marglin has given a good explanation of why the factory system was superior to the putting-out system from the standpoint of the bosses: the factory reduced waste, pilferage, and major theft and enabled the boss to counteract the "rational" behavior of the worker who "withdrew" his labor once he had achieved a certain income level, behavior that had disastrous effects on the business, while at the same time providing the boss with a way of coping with worker "idleness." Both the modern system of concentrating workers in factories and the medieval system of concentrating hirelings or gang slaves on demesnes served to increase the surplus accruing to the masters. Thus gang labor is profitable, and that is why it was reintroduced in the new form of wage labor on medieval estates, in the factories of England in the early days of capitalism, and later on in all parts of the world.

It would seem that Marx, too, believed that large factories outperformed small industry for the same reasons that the slave system was more profitable than serfdom in spite of the hidden costs of supervision. He has good words for the "remarkable quick eye" of Steuart, who asked: "Why do large undertakings in the manufacturing way ruin private industry, but by coming nearer to the simplicity of slaves?"[39]

In the course of our earlier criticisms of "economistic" historians, we maintained that the gang slave could produce more than the domiciled slave (counting both tenement and demesne) in a comparable period (per diem, say) and on land of comparable size and fertility. Thus we have been arguing in terms of men, days, and acres. Bear in mind, however, that the extra daily output was obtained because the slave worked longer and harder than the serf. Marglin may be right in saying that productivity must be calculated for the same "output" (corn) and for the same "inputs" (land and labor), but the point is that the gang slave did not supply the *same kind* of labor or the same quantity of labor. If we take as our labor unit one hour of labor of a given intensity on one hectare of land, we would find that the gang slave produced more, but also that he expended more of himself: that is, that he worked more hours at a given intensity or worked more intensively for the same number of hours. In this sense, and this sense only, the productivity of the gang slave was not higher than that of the domiciled slave (nor, for that matter, was the factory worker's productivity greater than that of the worker at home under the putting-out system).

What mattered to the master, however, was the difference between the quantity of corn produced and the quantity consumed by the worker. If the labor of the overseer was not productive, it was profitable.

D) Consciousness and Violence

The slaves, of course, were well aware that their share of production would increase as a result of domiciling and (or) that domiciling would enable them to reduce the duration and intensity of labor needed to provide for their own subsistence and to produce a surplus for the master. And *these were also goals for which they fought*. As the bourgeois economist sees it, the domiciled slave eventually produced more (deliberately!) and hence increased the absolute amount of his own share, even if that meant increasing his master's share as well (possibly even more rapidly than his own). The truth is otherwise: the domiciled slave sought, and what is more, obtained, a redistribution of the product of his labors, as well as of the work load—even if his goals were broader still.

The masters, moreover, were well aware that gang slavery yielded large profits. Doubtless the great landowners of antiquity were incapable of calculating the profitability of slavery as compared with that of other systems, but they knew that they were making huge profits and spent them lavishly. As M. I. Finley has observed, the literary tradition according to which ancient slavery on the whole yielded little or no profit, whether absolutely or in relation to serfdom (an opinion accepted by historians influenced by "economism" along with Schtajerman or Duby, and, in the wake of Max Weber, by Salvioli and Lot[40]), "would have astonished Greek and Roman slaveowners, who not only went on for many centuries fondly believing that they were making substantial profits out of their slaves but also spending those profits lavishly."[41]

The controversy is an old one: E. Meyer[42] and W. Sombart[43] long ago stressed the profitability of the slave system. Can anything be added to the debate by drawing upon the more recent controversy concerning slavery in the southern United States? Caution, to say the least, is in order in comparing two societies so radically different, and we do not intend here to rehearse the impassioned discussion that followed publication of Fogel and Engerman's *Time on the Cross*. Even if it has not been proven that the productivity of the black slave in America was greater than that of the wage-earner, it does seem certain that "profit relative to capital invested was higher on plantations in the South than on farms in the North."[44] The great landowners in the South, moreover, agreed to give up the allegedly exiguous profits of slavery only after waging a war to defend them: scanning the ledgers of northern farmers seems not to have convinced them!

IV. Reproduction of the Work Force:
Razzia and Breeding

Profitability cannot be discussed without distinguishing between the different methods of obtaining workers and the different costs associated with each. If we believe Bloch and Duby, *one* slave system was profitable, namely, the system that combined gang labor (with common feeding and lodging and centralized management of the work force) with the razzia. This system is comparable with the concentration camp. A reserve army of laborers was always at hand, either inside or outside the territorial limits; slaveowners had only to draw on this reservoir of manpower (via the razzia) to capture new slaves at minimal cost (including the cost of shipment). Since the reserve was viewed as virtually unlimited, the "production" price of the slave was equal to the cost of capturing him plus the "normal" profit of the raider (which was held down by competition among raiders when there was no collusion or monopoly). Slaves were *wasted* in consequence, as Marc Bloch has rightly pointed out. In the extreme case (infinite supply, zero cost of capture) it would make sense not to feed the slave at all, but rather to replace him every day (the same holds true if one is deliberately trying to exhaust a limited supply, as in Hitler's death camps). Hence little or no expense was wasted on the upkeep of the work force, which was systematically destroyed by work beyond human endurance and fed poorly if at all. (Nazi leaders are often said to have been irrational because they systematically destroyed the work force in the concentration camps. Not at all, for their objective was to exhaust the available supply, perhaps because they regarded it as renewable; Jews and Gypsies were to be replaced first by Slavs, and then by other nationalities.)

Breeding of slaves was, of course, incompatible with such a system. Since the master did not even maintain the existing work force, how could he have been expected to accept the cost of reproduction by breeding! Obviously families were forbidden, but as reproduction could take place outside the family, abortion and infanticide were encouraged or made mandatory, either by pressure on the mother or by more direct means (systematic liquidation of children). More "moderate" systems of this kind still discouraged childbirth and rearing, but not so systematically.

Another type of slave system existed, however, a system that reproduced itself. This grew up under circumstances of two kinds: either razzias abroad continued but the price of slaves rose (owing to increasing costs of capture or a monopoly of the supply), making breeding of slaves a profitable undertaking, or else the supply from abroad dried up and all slaves were raised on the estate. Waste was eliminated in systems of this kind, and the work force was maintained and reproduced; enough food was provided to sustain life, the amount of work required was adjusted in light of the danger of exhaustion, and childbirth was encouraged. In reality, of course, we do not find a sharp discontinuity between the two kinds of system, but rather situations intermediate between these two extremes, systems either more or less prodigal of slave manpower. Here we are interested in the question of the profitability of the breeding system and its compatibility with gang slavery.

There is no need to repeat what we have already said about profitability. We shall content ourselves with pointing out that the "concentration camp" system obviously allows for superprofits. Though the productivity of the slave may be reduced by exhaustion, it can be increased by terror, and, most importantly, the surplus is very large relative to the portion going to the worker. The breeding system also turns out to have been profitable wherever it was used, not only in the later empire (during which, as we shall see later on, there was breeding, widespread opinion to the contrary notwithstanding) but also in America and the Antilles.

The slave system with breeding was more profitable than serfdom (cf. above), and at least as profitable as wage labor. When Ferdinand Lot writes that "breeding of slaves was costly: up to the age of thirteen, at least, the slave represents expenditure without return; his forces are quickly spent and he dies young," he is confusing the two systems, for under the system of breeding waste is avoided and the slave is taken care of. As work by American historians on slavery in the southern United States has shown, the slave was not more quickly worn out than the wage laborer of the period and did not die younger. Masters took care of their slaves just as they took care of their horses. Like any other valued possession, the slave was protected as a part of the master's patrimony, perhaps even the most substantial part (whether from the standpoint of profitability or from that of prestige).

The reader should take care lest Bloch's phrase "perishable capital" mislead him into supposing that the slave master was at a disadvantage with respect to the capitalist employer, in that he had either to buy his human "capital" or to finance its breeding himself, paying for food, clothing, etc. In a system with breeding, the cost of buying a slave had to adjust to the cost of producing one (when the market price was high, everyone bred his own slaves; when it was low, when a good cheap source of supply existed, it was possible to resort to the other system, the one that made no provision for reproduction of the work force). The cost of reproduction is one borne by both slave masters (who paid to feed the children of their slaves) and capitalists (who pay workers enough to raise families). In concrete terms, the master who bought a fourteen-year-old slave paid approximately what it cost to feed him for those fourteen years (for if the price were higher, the master would switch to breeding, and if the price were lower, he would forgo breeding altogether); whether he chose to buy or to breed, the master did not have to "pay twice over."

True, slavery did require the master to make an initial investment. Even if we confine our attention to the case of a *villa* able to reproduce its own work force (with either simple or expanded reproduction), with daily distribution of the socially necessary minimum quantity of subsistence goods to each family (scarcely to be distinguished in this respect from the pay of a wage-earner), still the master had somehow to acquire his slaves in the first place. In the system without breeding, the *instrumentum vocale* does not reproduce itself any more than the *instrumentum mutum* does, and the investment must be renewed. To put it another way, "in the slave system, the money-capital invested in the purchase of labour-power plays the role of the money-form of the fixed capital, which is but gradually replaced as the active period of the slave's life expires."[46] The velocity of capital circulation is lower than in the case of wage labor, but this is of little interest in comparing slavery with serfdom. In this regard it might be possible to analyze serfdom as a slave system in which the work force reproduces itself, the initial investment having been relegated to the distant past. Such an analysis assumes, however, that gang slavery was compatible with breeding, a point that has often been questioned.

Thus the observations we find interesting are those that stress the connection between the low profitability of the slave system and the high cost (not to say impossibility) of breeding slaves in a gang-labor system. In consequence, it is argued, there was a transition to serfdom by way of domiciling, which became indispensable as a way of reducing the cost of reproducing the work force on the estate. From this it is supposed to follow that there was a connection between the slave traffic and gang labor (and ultimately the slave system as such, since domiciled slaves gradually became serfs), constituting one kind of system, and on the other hand a connection between breeding and domiciling, consituting another kind of system (which eventually grew into serfdom).

This analysis is based on the assumption that it can be shown that breeding was not practiced in the labor gangs of the late empire, and, more generally, that it is difficult if not impossible to have both gang slavery *and* breeding. When the slave trade dries up, or at least when the price of a captured slave exceeds the cost of producing a slave (whether because the supply dwindles, capture becomes more difficult, transport must cover greater distances, the raider's profit margin rises, or demand increases), domiciling presumably flourishes.

A) Breeding and the Slave Gang

Contrary to what Max Weber believed, child-rearing was widely prac- ticed in the slave gangs of antiquity during certain periods, notably when trade in slaves was diverted from one region to another (as was the case in central Greece, when the slave traffic gravitated chiefly toward Italy[48]) or decreased in volume.

An interesting case in point is that of Trimalchio, the slave in the *Satyricon* who became a potent financier and landed magnate. The ban- quet in Petronius' tale is brusquely interrupted by the arrival of a sec- retary from Trimalchio's estate in Cumae, who details for the owner what his property is bringing in. We are told that seventy children have been born to the slaves of the estate, five hundred oxen have been put in harness for the first time, one slave has been crucified for blasphemy, and so on.[49] Like others of his class, Trimalchio took a great interest in childbirth as a means of producing wealth and no doubt encouraged it.

How? Stimuli were not lacking. As we have already seen, Columella in the first century allowed a mother of three children exemption from work on his estates and set her free if she produced still more children.[50] Births could thus be encouraged by going easy on mothers and dazzling them with visions of ultimate emancipation and the like—for this, the "standard" family was not indispensable and probably not even as ef- ficient as we like to think when compared with systematic child-breeding on veritable stud farms.

To be sure, no such branch in the social division of labor really de- veloped in antiquity. Despite these few examples and the many theo- retical possibilites, the landowners of the time do not seem to have systematized slave-breeding, either in their *villae* or on specialized stud farms. Why not? The answer is simple: we agree in part with Georges Duby when he writes that breeding was useless,[51] in view of the price of slaves captured by soldiers and pirates. More precisely, let us say that breeding was *generally* useless because the price of the captured slave only occasionally rose as high as the cost of producing a slave, and still more rarely exceeded it.

Generally useless, then. But not impossible or virtually impossible in the conditions of the slave gang—as Max Weber would have it[52]—nor even very difficult, as Marc Bloch believed (breeding being too tenuous under such conditions[53]) and as Perry Anderson has argued (used temporarily after the demise of the large-scale slave trade, the "expedient" of breeding could not serve as a long-term solution.)[54]

Furthermore, it is well known that in the early part of the nineteenth century, when slave trade with the Antilles and the southern United States was interrupted (or when the difficulties of carrying on the trade increased the price of importing slaves, if for no other reason than because of the increased risk), systematic breeding was used with excellent results, either on the plantations themselves or on stud farms more or less specialized for the purpose.[55] The switch to breeding, moreover, in no way entailed the end of gang labor as the chief method of working the plantation.

But the example might seem to undercut our argument—for is not the point that in the Antilles, for example, the system used was one in which families were housed in their own huts? We have already pointed out that this was the case.[56] But the slave huts were generally quite close together and provided with nothing more than small gardens. Nor were they always family dwellings in the true sense, because the still extant system known as the "visiting union," in which the woman and her children are settled in a fixed location and the "husband" is allowed to visit sporadically, was probably then in force (though not officially recognized). This system may have been as effective for reproduction as the "standard" family, even if the appurtenant garden provided no more than a dietary supplement.[57] It bears repeating that a similar system was probably in use in the early Middle Ages; between the system of gang slavery with barracks and common dining hall and the system of the domiciled serf, often emancipated, provided with an "adequate" tenement, and relieved of all but minimal labor obligations, a whole range of intermediary situations existed. The two periods are contrasted in the following respect, however: in the early Middle Ages domiciling was synonomous with increased autonomy and marks a stage on the road to serfdom, indeed to an independent peasantry; the huts in the Antilles coexisted with a gang-labor system and were in no sense a sign of evolution toward serfdom. It was not directly because it had become a useful, not to say a necessary, means of assuring the physical reproduction of the work force that the great landowner in Merovingian or Carolingian times was obliged to grant a tenure to his domiciled slave and finally to make him a serf. In other words, the cause of domiciling, a *social* change, was not *natural*, not demographic or technological (e.g., in the sense of a presumed incompatibility between "barracks living" or gang labor systems and breeding).

More than that, population and slavery are connected in an opposite sense. Not only did the *scarcity of men* not give rise to a trend toward slavery, it may, on the contrary, have led to a revival of slavery in the early Middle Ages, for every isolated individual was then in danger of being reduced to slavery, and at a time when labor was scarce, wealth was equivalent to power over men (as Georges Duby would agree). And whose power over men was greater than the master's power over his slave gang?

As we shall see, however, *scarcity of manpower* is, to say the least, insufficient to have caused the end of slavery, the real cause having been the *social scarcity* of *servile* labor power,[58] which was related to the struggles of slaves against their masters, their legal status, and, above all, against the real, objective conditions of their existence.

B) The End of Gang Slavery and the Slave Trade

If breeding was incompatible with gang slavery and maintenance of the slave system required an abundant supply of cheap slaves, then declining slave traffic should be indicative of a transition to serfdom.

Max Weber's version of this argument runs as follows: when Rome's slave-producing wars came to an end, the Romans had to turn to slaves domiciled with their families, who provided for their own upkeep and reproduced themselves, or to *coloni*, because the masters could not rely on breeding as a solution to their problem. Hence ancient slavery is supposed to have come to an end after the wars of conquest ceased. In this stark form, and even in Perry Anderson's toned-down version,[59] this position is difficult to maintain, because systematic Roman conquests followed by sales of huge hordes of slaves ended in A.D. 14. The supposed effects of the dwindling supplies of slaves did not make themselves felt, however, until two centuries later. Even allowing for the conquests of the late first century (Trajan), after which the borders of the empire were stabilized, still we must wait a century before the slave system begins to lose ground! Finley[60] has observed that in southwestern Gaul, for example, the date when the work force on the largest estates ceased to be predominantly servile can be fixed as the early third century, not before. When slavery began to lose ground, furthermore, it was still possible to recruit German slaves, and such slaves were in fact recruited on a broad scale.[61] Piracy and trade were still flourishing, certain provinces are known to have derived their wealth from the export of slaves,[62] and some servile manpower was even provided by military action along the borders of the empire. To these sources of slaves we may add certain others: subjugation of the local peasantry, capture of fugitive *coloni*, reestablishment of slavery for debt and even for adultery.[63] If it is certain that the importance of gang slavery decreased as compared with that of the *coloni* and that the volume of the slave trade diminished, was this because the number of slaves offered for sale on third-century markets had decreased? Even if nothing like the enormous hordes of slaves rounded up by the Roman armies in the pre-Christian era now flooded the markets, so that there was no question of a return to the system where the slave had scarcely any value and so could be wasted, still it was possible in the third and fourth centuries to bring new slaves to a market already stocked through breeding, hence at costs near the cost of production. If such practices were not encouraged, was this not because the demand for gang slaves had decreased?

As Perry Anderson has observed, following Weber,[64] the price of slaves seems to have fallen in the third century. Assuming a reduced supply, it must be that demand also plummeted. Why? Anderson's view is that, in the second century, when the cost of slaves was high, the landowners must have become accustomed to a different system. Unfortunately for this theory, the slave system declined not in the second century (when the cost of slaves was high), but chiefly in the third. The sequence of events was not constriction of supply (early second century), "end" of prevailing slave system (second century), cessation of demand for slaves and fall in price (third century). When the slave trade slackened (second century), the slave system (with gang slavery) in fact continued to do well, with some changes in the mode of production of slaves: razzias were supplemented by breeding, which explains why the price of a slave rose to the level of the production cost. Then the price plummeted in the third century because of the crisis in the slave system.

Further indications that fluctuations in the slave trade cannot be regarded as causes of the end of slavery come from study of the Merovingian and Carolingian periods and the subsequent disappearance of rural slaves in the tenth century, particularly in France. In these periods, too, the causal analysis outlined above runs up against the "classic" difficulty: how can we tell whether reduction of the slave trade caused the end of slavery, or whether the crisis in the slave system caused the end of the slave trade, when both trends emerge simultaneously, precluding deductions of the sort that would be permissible if there were a time lag. Fortunately, there are periods when trade did not slacken but slavery disappeared in certain areas.

Duby, as we have seen, affirms that "slaves became increasingly rare on the majority of western European markets all through Merovingian and Carolingian times."[65] Doubtless this assertion is too broad, since there were most likely periods of decline in western Europe (seventh century?), as well as periods of revival of gang slavery (mid-seventh century, mid-ninth century) and a period during which the system broke down (second half of the ninth and first half of the tenth century). The interesting point for us, however, is that Duby rules out a fall in the slave trade as a cause of the decline of gang slavery in the countryside.

Duby is, of course, perfectly well aware that during the period of the invasions, "the captives of the barbarians replaced the captive barbarians," to borrow the words of R. Fossier,[66] and that historians are agreed that the fifth and sixth centuries saw a considerable increase in the slave trade, as well as an expansion in the area of recruitment.[67] He is also aware that during the following period, from the time the sons of Clovis made their forays into Germany and Dagobert into Gascony until the time of Pepin's campaigns against the Saxons, significant numbers of slaves were brought back.[68] Under Charlemagne, finally, enslavement of individuals (many of them Saxons) and later deportation of entire groups reached considerable proportions. Enormous numbers of men were captured in ninth-century raids into Bohemia and beyond the Elbe (among the Slavs, whose name eventually came to be applied to slaves in general), and later Viking raids delivered up Irish, Flemish, and Polish captives.[69]

If, during the Carolingian era, hordes of men were subjugated to provide manpower for the *villae* of the imperial aristocracy,[70] it is also true that razzias and the slave trade continued to flourish during the ninth and tenth centuries, when slaves in general merely passed through western Europe en route elsewhere. Captured in privately or publicly financed forays, slaves were taken to interior markets at Verdun, Metz, and Valenciennes in the ninth century, Rouen, Göteborg, and Augsburg in the tenth, as well as to Barcelona and Venice, where they were bought by middlemen and shipped to users all along the shores of the Mediterranean. Verlinden points out that during the tenth century the flow of Slavic slaves into the caliphate of Cordova reached a peak and that western Europe balanced its trade with Byzantium thanks to Muslim money obtained through the export of slaves.[71]

For Duby, then, it is no longer curtailment of the slave trade that explains the decline of slavery, but rather the fact that the *price of slaves was increasing* because of sales to the Muslim world, pushing the cost of slaves out of the reach of Frankish landowners, who were thus forced to resort to breeding, hence to domiciling. Prices, however, must also have been high for Muslim buyers, even higher than in Europe owing to lengthy voyages and the profits of middlemen.[72] Let us suppose, for the sake of argument, that the buyers were wealthy enough to lay out larger sums for slaves than the relatively poor Franks could afford (an assumption that is arguable, since Frankish landowners did have caches of money, and if they did not make use of them, the reason is that there was little opportunity to buy outside the estate; had they wanted slaves, they could have dipped into their cash reserves); beyond a certain price, however, the Muslims, too, should have switched to breeding! That they had the wherewithal to buy slaves on the market does not rule out their changing over to breeding if the price of slaves exceeded the cost of production, and therefore, on Duby's view of the matter, they should virtually have been forced, once the price of captured slaves had reached a certain threshold, to resort to domiciling in order to practice breeding. But nothing of the sort occurred.

The situation in France in the tenth century is particularly revealing, because we know that by then slavery there had disappeared. Can this have been related to some reduction in the slave trade during the late ninth or early tenth century? Certainly not, since, as we have seen, the slave trade was at peak during this period, and the trade routes crossed or skirted France! Never were more Slavs being shipped to Cordova to be sold into slavery than during this period.

Later on, when there was an influx of Moorish slaves into Christian Spain during the early years of the *Reconquista* (late eleventh century), there was no reversal of the flow of slaves (which now should have been into France) and not the slightest revival of rural slavery in France (though there were urban domestic slaves in the south). In theory there was nothing to prevent the export of slave "merchandise" outside Spain (trade was easier now than it had been in the tenth century!). Verlinden observes that Spain saw a revival of slavery in the eleventh and partic-ularly the twelfth and thirteenth centuries, which he connects with the abundant supply of Moors. But how, then, do we account for the fact that this slavery spread only very slightly into southern France and virtually not at all elsewhere? Even in Spain, the flourishing of slavery probably did not involve a revival of gang slavery in the countryside, but rather the use of domestic servants, frequently in the towns.

To sum up, then, our view is that revival of the slave trade within or near the borders of a country in which the slave system has disappeared does not bring that system back to life, and furthermore, a slackening of the slave trade in a society in which the slave system is flourishing does not destroy that system.

V. Marc Bloch's "Economic Conditions"

Marc Bloch, in his book *Feudal Society* and his article "Comment et pour-quoi finit l'esclavage?"[73] makes two comments that cannot be classed together with his reflections on the inefficiency of servile manpower or fluctuations in the slave trade (and in the price of slaves) or the effects of the Christian religion. We shall discuss these remarks in the next two subsections.

A) Nonmonetary Economy and Serfdom

Bloch writes that "economic conditions precluded the exploitation of excessively large demesnes with the help of hired labour or workers maintained in the lord's household, [and so] it was better for the lord instead of keeping all the plots of land in his own hands to have permanently at his disposal the labour and resources of dependents who were in a position to maintain themselves."[74] This assertion is at once clear and obscure. Clear, in that obviously the dependents referred to are serfs (or domiciled slaves), who rendered services in labor and provided for their own upkeep; economic conditions, accordingly, produced serfdom by precluding the use of hired labor or workers maintained in the lord's household (prebendals and slaves who "lived on their master's bread"). But this raises another question: what "transformations of the economy favored the dissolution of the great teams which but a little while before had served to cultivate the now sub-divided *latifundia*"?[75]

The economic conditions Bloch had in mind were clearly the decline of the monetary economy, the serious curtailment of trade, and the sluggishness of commerce in the West (neglecting here the question of whether the decrease in the monetary mass—due to a trade deficit with the Orient?—contributed to the curtailment of trade, or whether the "sluggishness" of commerce led to a decline in the use of money).

Bloch's argument is not valid. Indeed, he himself explains[76] that "economic conditions," the absence of monetary circulation, precluded the use of hired labor but reinforced the other two possible systems, "prebend" and "tenancy": "The weakness of trade and of monetary circulation had a further consequence of the gravest kind. It reduced to insignificance the social function of wages. . . .Two alternatives offered: one was to take the man into one's household, to feed and clothe him, to provide him with 'prebend,' as the phrase went; the other was to grant him in return for his services an estate which, if exploited directly or in the form of dues levied on the cultivators of the soil would enable him to provide for himself."

Now, the position of the gang slave was quite similar to that of the prebendal, both being fed at the master's table with the master's bread. The sluggishness of trade and the money economy either reinforced this system or was compatible with it.

B) From the End of the Market Economy to the
Subdivision of the Estate and from
Subdivision to Serfdom

Domiciling, it is said, was a consequence of the need to subdivide the estate, which could not be exploited directly with the gang of slaves: subdivision, Bloch argues, dates "from the very period when the slowdown in trade was most pronounced," and was "motivated by the absence of any kind of market for the harvest."[77]

Large Roman estates raised crops for sale on markets: they produced commodities. By the early Middle Ages the markets had been curtailed considerably, the towns, reduced to mere burgs, no longer served as outlets, and roads and transportation were lacking. In other words, surplus labor could no longer be "realized" on the marketplace, commodities could no longer be produced, hence direct exploitation of the estate by gang slaves became impossible (or at least inconvenient). The surplus had to be extracted in other ways, directly in the form of *corvées*, services, or goods delivered to the castle.[78]

This may well be the best possible line of argument. But it is a mistake to regard the end of the merchant economy as the cause of the abandonment of direct exploitation, which in turn is presumed to have been the cause of the end of gang slavery. On the contrary, historically, what "made" the directly exploited great estate was slavery, which was thus an important cause of the growth of the urban merchant economy.[79] The manner of exploiting the land does not determine the manner of exploiting men, but rather the reverse.

Gang slavery can coexist with a "less" mercantile economy: thanks to the division of labor, the slave gang can produce, in workshops on the estate and in the fields, subsistence goods for the workers and luxury goods for the lord, just as *corvée* labor did on the demesne (together with a salable portion of the product, which never vanished altogether[80]). For the master the only question was that of the surplus. With gang slavery, three systems are possible a priori: a perfect mercantile economy, in which the master sells all that is produced and buys subsistence goods for the workers and various other commodities for himself and his retinue; an imperfect mercantile economy, in which the gang slaves produce their own subsistence and the surplus is sold; and, finally, a nonmercantile economy (or an economy in which the role of trade is small), in which the slaves produce their own subsistence along with a surplus product which is not sold and therefore must take the form of goods immediately usable by the master and his retinue. The first of these systems never existed, and the second was that of the classical *villa;* there is nothing absurd about the third system, however.

Indeed, in the system that was to take concrete shape, the surplus product would be extracted from the demesne or the workshops via *corvée* labor, i.e., via the remnants of the old system of gang slavery, while the workers' subsistence would be produced on the tenements. Technically, it would have been possible to produce subsistence goods for the villeins by means of gang slavery, for the simple reason that subsistence goods were produced in just this way throughout the early empire! Conversely, the *corvées,* remnants of the slave gangs, produced goods a portion of which were consumed by the master and his family, while the rest of this surplus product would have been available for sale so as to enable the lord to acquire such scarce items as weapons and spices. Here again the problem of the sale of the surplus produced by *corvée* labor crops up—where could it be sold? To put it another way, the workers' subsistence, which technically could have been produced by gang labor, was obtained from the tenements; as for the surplus, the problem was simply shifted to a new sphere, since the *corvées* on the demesne produced goods for which no market outlets could be found!

Furthermore, there was evidently some uncertainty on this score in Marc Bloch's mind, since in 1931 (in *Les Caractères originaux*) he explained the subdivision of the demesne during the tenth and eleventh centuries as the result of a curtailment of markets,[81] which led to the end of the *corvée.* But to assume that this was the case amounts to a concession that domiciling together with *corvée* labor in the early Middle Ages did not solve the problem of realization of the surplus: both the gang slaves of the *villa* and the *corvée* laborers on the demesne produced a surplus that was virtually impossible to sell.

The extent of Bloch's uncertainty is attested by the fact that in *Les caractères originaux* he explains that conditions were the same throughout Europe during the tenth and eleventh centuries, and yet neither in Great Britain nor in Germany was there a diminution in the importance of the demesne in this period; unable to explain this contrast, he frankly confessed his inability to find the underlying cause. Two years later, however, he held that it was the economic renaissance, the revival of trade and the monetary economy in the tenth and eleventh centuries, that transformed the lord into a rentier of the soil and impelled him to subdivide the demesne. Of course Bloch was aware of how effectively he had demolished his own argument, since subdivision was also supposed to have been a product of the economic slowdown of the ninth and tenth centuries! Accordingly, he concludes that economic explanations always cut two ways![82]

VI. The Moral and Religious Factor

One frequently adduced argument was touched upon, as we saw at the beginning of this chapter, by Duby, who treats it with a certain skepticism: namely, that Christianity—and even earlier, according to some authors, Stoicism—was the cause, or one chief cause, of the end of slavery. With this argument we leave the realm of material causation behind and move on to an attempt to give a superstructural explanation of a social change. Does this mean standing history on its head? Not necessarily; indeed, it would be possible to attribute to Christian or Stoic morality a role, even an important role, in causing the social change in question without thereby ruling out a materialist analysis of the inception and spread of Christianity (or Stoicism). An antislavery ideology born in struggles by slaves against the slave system may well have produced a "feedback effect" on social relations in that system. However, such a materialist interpretation is not often given, except, of course, by Marxist historians,[83] and most proponents of the religious hypothesis are either idealists or believers in history as revelation.

We would not bother to discuss the question had Marc Bloch not chosen to rely heavily on it. In "Comment et pourquoi finit l'esclavage antique," in fact, he argues that "it was no small thing to have said to the 'talking tool' (*instrumentum vocale*) of the old Roman agronomists, 'You are a man, you are a Christian.' "[84] Ultimately moreover, slave marriages were accorded religious validity, as were marriages between slaves and free tenants. Above all, emancipation became a work of piety (and what is more, a work which could be accomplished without serious loss of power over the man—thanks to the practice known as "manumission with obedience"— and which brought with it certain financial advantages).

As Marc Bloch himself notes, however, "religious opinion" had no wish to overturn the "established social order," the legitimacy of slavery was recognized by the Church, and "clergymen as individuals and the Church itself as an institution became very great landowners, possessing huge numbers of slaves."[85] Much of the thrust of the religious argument is vitiated by these two remarks. But there is more:

As M. I. Finley has pointed out, after the conversion of Constantine and the rapid integration of the Church into the structure of imperial power, we find no trace of a demand for the abolition of slavery, of a law in which the influence of the Church might have made itself felt, or of any desire to get rid of slavery, even gradually. Indeed, it is to the most Christian of all the emperors, Justinian, that we owe the most thorough body of laws concerning slavery.[86]

Whenever we find, in the writings of Church dignitaries or future saints during the late empire and early Middle Ages,[87] appeals to masters to emancipate their slaves, we discover that they amount to nothing more than the usual appeals to men of wealth and power to abandon their earthly goods, slaves included, in favor of wealth of another kind, mainly when facing death. Slavery in itself was not condemned, any more than private property—quite the opposite.

Church doctrine regarding slavery derives from Saint Paul (I Corinthians, Ephesians, Philemon). It was Paul's judgment that if the masters owed it to their slaves to treat them humanly, slaves owed it to their masters to obey. In subsequent centuries, moreover, this "proslavery" doctrine of Paul's was interpreted in a manner most favorable to the masters! Thus, in his letter to Philemon, Paul sends a *servus fugitivus* back to his master, whom he counsels to treat the slave mildly. Sixth- and seventh-century councils, basing themselves on this letter, refused slaves all rights of asylum. The Church accepted and propagated the idea that slaves were collectively responsible for their fate: had they been free of all guilt, would God have kept them in so frightful a situation? Guilty of what? At the root of the condition of the slave or his forefathers lay a sin. Or else, as Isidore of Seville believed, slavery was expiation for an original sin in some way more serious for the slave than for other men(?), and masters had by "divine" will been set over the slaves, who by their very nature were liable to act in evil ways, in order to chastise them, thereby allowing the good to reign supreme.[88] We find this doctrine expressed as early as the late sixth century in the writings of Pope Gregory the Great (*Moralia in Job* and *Regula pastoralis*).[89] Slaves are predestined to evil, and it is because of their propensity to sin that they are slaves.

As Marc Bloch reminds us, the Church (and clerks as individuals) owned many slaves in the late empire and early Middle Ages. Were the slaves of the Church at least better treated than other slaves? It would seem that the Church treated its slaves no differently from other masters. In 675 a council issued an order to members of the clergy to stop mutilating their slaves, proof that prior to this date, in any case, such punishments were practiced!

It cannot be denied that there were emancipation movements. If we take the emancipators at their word, emancipation was a work of piety. But if the movement itself is beyond doubt, particularly in certain periods (the ninth century, for example), there is no reason always to believe what the masters have to say about it. Thus, Pierre Toubert[90] has described a widespread movement in Sabine which ultimately led to the elimination of slavery on the eve of encastlement (late ninth to early tenth century). In his view, the most important aspect of this movement, today least in evidence, was the purchase of manumission by domiciled slaves, generally as individuals. Prebendal slaves, on the other hand, could obtain their freedom only thanks to "the pious generosity of their masters,"[91] and, so Toubert tells us, "there is no need to deny the psychological motive (of these emancipations *pro remedio animae*)."[92] Perhaps, but the same moral considerations ought to have impelled the masters to emancipate their *servi casati* free of charge, and this they did not do: manumission was always bought and paid for by domiciled slaves. More than that, Toubert describes the situation in these regions during this same period, the second half of the ninth century, as one of "social crisis,"[93] marked by brigandage and bands of "guerrilleros." Can we make so bold as to presume that there was a connection between these "pious" emancipations and the social conflicts of the time?

Still, it is true that the Church encouraged and even consecrated manumission (*manumissio in ecclesia*). More than that, the lives of the saints are filled with instances of mass emancipations and redemptions of slaves, which must have moved the faithful to imitate these actions.

Having said this, we may ask how the Church itself behaved in regard to the emancipation of its own slaves. Manumissions of slaves of the Church were rare, even strictly forbidden by the councils. Why such harshness? Because the slaves of the Church were the property of the poor, and to set them free would have impoverished the paupers.[94]

Verlinden has observed, sternly, that during the late empire and early Middle Ages, the Church always favored the rights of the master over those of the slave,[95] save, of course, when the master was a Jew or a heretic. By forbidding heretics and Jews to own slaves, the Church attempted to secure a monopoly of property in slaves for members of the Christian faith! In spite of these interdictions, proclaimed time and time again by the Church,[96] Jewish merchants, often encouraged by the "magnates," established a virtual monopoly over the slave traffic, and the criticisms of the Church were directed solely at this monopoly: the Church feared (rightly, moreover) that the merchants would take advantage of their position to convert their slaves to Judaism.

Then there is the argument cited by Duby (in particular) which runs as follows:[97] while it was still possible to keep slaves who had become Christians, little by little the Church won agreement that Christians were no longer to be enslaved, so that as the world became more and more Christian, it became increasingly difficult to obtain new slaves. In fact, this new strictness was slow to take hold and did so only when it did not run counter to the interests of the slave raiders. It became effective as the theater of war moved farther and farther away from the Chris-

tianized West with the Carolingian "peace" and when the slave system
had drained pagan Saxony and contingents of pagan "Slavs" came to
pass through Gaul en route to enslavement elsewhere. At most we might
assume that this new "strictness" increased the price of slaves. This
brings us back to our general criticism of this argument as an explanation
for the end of slavery.[98]

Need we add that Christian morality was quite ready to tolerate the
slave system in Christian Spain during the greater part of the Middle
Ages: are we to assume that the new strictness was less strict on the
other side of the Pyrenees? Even in Rome a *motu proprio* of 1548 justified
the slave trade—were slaves not part of the patrimony and useful by
dint of their labor?—and prohibited manumission of Christian slaves;
the cardinals of the holy city were themselves slaveholders.[99] What is
more, Christian morality was quite ready to tolerate, to say no more
than that, the slave system in the Antilles and the United States; even
in the nineteenth century, it would seem, southern slaveowners were
not excommunicated.[100] What resounding silence marks this long history! When the Church was not busy encouraging slavery, it pointed to
the structures of heaven as justification for the slave system!

The same was true for other religions: holding a virtual monopoly of
the slave trade, Jews in the early Middle Ages were much appreciated
by princes in consequence and seem not to have been criticized by their
rabbis for what they were doing. And Islam! All the gods were thus on
the side of the masters.

Let us conclude where we ought to have begun, with the role of
Stoicism. Writings of the Roman Stoics from the imperial period (few
of which have survived) emphasize the need for masters to behave with
moderation in their own interest (at a time when slaves were becoming
relatively costly, it was a good idea to stop using them wastefully and
to have them reproduce themselves). Furthermore, the same texts encourage the slave to accept his status and to recognize the consequences
of rebellion, violence, and dishonesty.

These ideas of the Stoics had scarcely any practical effect on slavery
as an institution;[10] on the whole, Christian ideas were no more conse-
quential. Far from being instigators of social transformation, these ideas
adapted themselves to the new order. A posteriori interpretations of the
texts, however, have attempted to accredit the idea of a liberating this-
worldly religion; did not Christianity spread initially among slaves in
Italy, and was it not to be expected that Christian ideology would lend
itself to the liberation of slaves? These interpretations are mistaken: the
liberation held out to the slaves was not of this world. On the contrary,
Christian ideas—like those of the Stoics—drove the slaves toward res-

ignation. Later, these same ideas would play an identical role among Negro slaves, as well as with industrial workers. If we think of the class struggle as the locomotive of social change, we might look upon Christian ideas from this standpoint as a brake. There is nothing surprising in this, bearing in mind the alliance between Christianity and the slave state in the past, from the time of Constantine onwards, and subsequently between Christianity and the new masters, as we learn from Gregory of Tours' account of Clovis's miraculous conversion after the battle of Tolbiac.[102]

3

This explains why we find that the more highly evolved the economy and the society are, the more the collectivist principle comes into contradiction with the productive forces.

Valéry Giscard d'Estaing, *La Démocratie française*

Productive Forces and Feudal Relations

Looked at in terms of the modification of social relations (the key level of analysis), the transition from economic formations of society based on the ancient slave system to medieval feudal formations is a long and complex process. The main elements in this process are the rise of the *coloni* in the late empire, the domiciling of slaves, particularly during the early Middle Ages, and the transformation of slaves into serfs, which went hand in hand with the evolution of the *coloni* and the subjugation of free peasants. To put it somewhat differently, the status of slaves rose (domiciling was undeniably a major social change). This was one aspect of a multisecular trend that began at the end of the republic; another aspect was a fall in the status of the independent peasantry (*coloni*, tenants, etc.), hence a homogenization of the masses of peasants in serfdom. This was followed by a slow conquest of property rights in the tenement, abolition of *corvées*, commutation of rents, and the gradual disappearance of serfdom.

When do we first find a social formation that can be characterized as a feudal mode of production? That depends on how we define the feudal mode. If the presence of the social relation generally known, for the sake of simplicity, as serfdom—or, in other words, the presence of a particular type of exploitation of men and land—is taken as the defining characteristic, then it would seem that all the essentials were in place at the beginning of the Middle Ages, indeed, even earlier, in the late empire with the colonate. If, on the other hand, the accent is placed on the feudal system as a whole, with its hierarchy of persons and its abandonment of the Roman notion of property and Roman forms of government and religious ideology, then we must wait at least until the end of the eleventh century, if not until the end of the thirteenth and the crises of the fourteenth century.

The problem is that serfdom was no longer the dominant relation of production when feudalism took hold at the superstructural level! The manorial system, heir to the *villa* system, was in large part replaced (as far as its surplus-extraction function was concerned) by political, judicial, and economic forms of seigniory. *Corvées* and dues in kind, tenacious remnants of the old system of gang slavery, had either disappeared or been reduced in importance as a means of exploiting the peasantry, becoming secondary to banalities, fees of justice, tithes, and so forth— the various concomitants of political power.

If we must continue to speak of a feudal mode of production, therefore, it would seem that at the very least we need to recognize two such modes, the first (F.M.P.$_1$) being characterized by the prevalence of serfdom and the manorial system, whereas the second (F.M.P.$_2$) saw the emergence of a free peasantry (claiming rights over property, household, and person), from which labor was extracted chiefly by way of banal seigniory, or monopolies and feudal dues associated with political and judicial power, which often emerged in the wake of commutation of such old servitudes as *corvées* and natural rents.[1] The economic formation of medieval society is characterized by the predominance first of one, then of the other, of these two types of social relations.

Can we superimpose upon this evolution from slave relations to early medieval serfdom and thence to the peasantry of the thirteenth century, exploited and ruled but not enslaved,[2] the "philosophy of history" found in the Preface to the *Critique of Political Economy?*

It will be worth our while to pause for a moment in order to consider the controversy over "how to characterize a mode of production." Let us first consider the vigorous criticisms leveled by Charles Parain[3] at an article by G. A. Melekechvili entitled "Esclavage, féodalisation et mode de production asiatique dans l'Orient ancien."[4] Melekechvili explains the transition from a classless society to a class society in terms of progress of the productive forces, which gives rise to a surplus product.[5] He goes on to argue, however, that

> the ancient world and the Middle Ages passed through all the stages of social development. . . . : primitive class society, a developed slave system or a developed feudal system. However, there is reason to doubt whether any of these stages of social development is necessarily associated with a *determinate* level of development of the instruments of labor. Surely there is no justification for seeking a *direct* connection between the predominance of a certain type of social relation, whether slave or feudal, and the development of material production, or for thinking that feudal socioeconomic relations *necessarily* correspond to a higher level of development. As we know, the transition from slavery to feudalism in western Europe took place in conditions *more* of decadence than of growth. The prevalence of a certain type of socioeconomic relations obviously does *not always* depend *mechanically* on the level of development of the instruments of labor and techniques of production. The same implements, for example, can serve equally well as the basis of either the slave structure or the feudal structure. . . . It is doubtful whether there was ever in the history of Antiquity and the Middle Ages a jump in the development of the productive forces of such a kind as to insure the decisive predominance of a particular form of exploitation.[6]

Despite the prudence evident in this passage (in which we have underscored the author's cautious phraseology), in our estimation it goes to the heart of the debate: this is because it casts doubt on the necessity of a correspondence between a level of development of the productive forces and a certain relation of production, as well as on the mechanistic version of historical materialism, in the context of a specific transition.

Charles Parain was unable (in 1969—the date is important when evolving views are concerned) to accept this position. The weakness of Melekechvili's argument, he contends, is that it neglects the role of the development of the productive forces in the unfolding of history and holds instead that the class struggle is enough to explain the major historical transformations. Now, to begin with, Parain counters, if during antiquity and the Middle Ages there was never a leap forward as forceful as that which gave birth to class society during the Paleolithic Age, there were nonetheless "smaller jumps that were yet sufficient to require transition from the large-scale slave cultivation of antiquity to the small-scale production characteristic of feudalism in Europe."[7] If this passage makes any sense at all, Parain must mean that technological progress,

or, more generally, the development of the productive forces, was sufficient to make the feudal mode of production a necessary development.
Thus, even if he tips his hat to the class struggle, as usual by citing the
opening sentences of the *Communist Manifesto*, he ends up by reducing
its role to nil, or, more precisely, by arguing that it is completely determined by the development of the material base.

Parain then turns to a second line of attack, criticizing the "panfeu-
dalism" of the Soviet historian, that is, the argument that the vast majority of class societies tend in their initial phases to develop toward
feudalism, slavery being no more than a parenthetical interlude. According to Parain, such a position is tenable only because feudalism is
defined solely in terms of its social relations, hence deprived of its base,
"which is a determinate level of development of the productive forces."

Finally, Parain charges that the Soviet author is led "to reject the
Marxist notion of a progressive series of historical epochs, without which
history would seem to have no logic," namely, the sequence of four
modes of production—Asiatic, ancient, feudal, modern bourgeois—representing social and material progress from one to the next, each mode
containing the following stage in embryo.

To recapitulate, the point of Parain's critique is to berate Melekechvili
for failing to live up to the requirements of strict "orthodoxy." Parain is
attempting to force "real history" into the Procrustean bed of a "philosophy of history," even though Marx and Engels, as early as *The German
Ideology*, emphasized that "viewed apart from real history, these abstractions have in themselves no value whatsoever. They can only serve to
facilitate the arrangement of historical material, to indicate the sequence
of its separate strata. But they by no means afford a recipe or schema,
as does philosophy, for neatly trimming the epochs of history."[8] But
what about real history? How does Parain himself view the transition
to "feudalism"?

On the basis of the passage cited previously, it would seem that Parain
defines the F.M.P. as the articulation of new relations of production with
a higher level of development of the productive forces, associated with
"small-scale cultivation"; his claim that the "jump" in the productive
forces was enough to require new social relations brings Parain close to
the most simplistic of mechanical views, of the sort one might arrive at
after reading the Preface to the *Critique* by itself—we shall call this the
"Menshevik" view, taking the liberty of making an "ironic" leap of
sixteen centuries, as Parain himself has done elsewhere.[9]

According to the mechanistic, adialectical, Menshevik view, the class
struggle is merely a reflection, virtually automatic, of the contradiction
between the old relations of production and the level of development

of the productive forces. The accent is placed on the blockage of further development by the old relations of production; the new social relations are said to be strictly determined by the "material base," and so this base must be constituted prior to the era of social revolution.

Applying such a model, we would be forced to conclude that the development of the productive forces of Roman society, first under the republic and later under the empire, was ultimately blocked by slave relations, marking a point beyond which the ancient mode of production could develop no further. Furthermore, we would have to assume that the material base necessary for the emergence of serfdom already existed during the late empire, social conflict serving only to adapt the new relations to this basis.

A whole historical tradition, both Marxist and non-Marxist, stresses the idea that gang slavery as a mode of production led inevitably to stagnation; though slavery first marked an advance in productive power (through cooperative labor on large estates), it attained a virtually inviolable limit of development once the forms of organization and the technology compatible with slavery as a social relation had been achieved, after which it became impossible to introduce technological advances (such as water mills).

But it can be shown that technological progress was compatible down to the end of the Roman Empire with some of the most brutal forms of slavery in the Spanish mines and on Roman *latifundia*.[10] When we come shortly to compare the level of development of the productive forces during the late empire in the West with that of the early Middle Ages, we shall gain a better idea of the relative dynamism of the ancient slave mode. If the comparison is permissible, moreover, it may be worth noting that when slavery in America had to confront the most technologically advanced system the world had ever known, capitalism, while it is clear that the slave system on the plantations was losing ground, there were nevertheless important innovations, such as the introduction of mechanized cotton picking (though slavery must have impeded its development and widespread use).[11] Genovese, who, unlike the "new economic historians," emphasizes the substandard productivity of slavery as compared with capitalism, acknowledges that, all in all, the planter, benefitting from the advantages of mass production, obtained returns no greater (but no smaller, either!) than those obtained on small farms in the free northern states, which operated in a capitalist economy and made up for their small scale with superior technology.[12] This being the case, there would seem to be no reason why gang slavery, when confronted with a far less dynamic system in feudalism, should have been on the average more of an impediment.[13]

We do not mean to imply, however, that ancient slavery was not in any way a brake on development. On the contrary, slavery was a social relation that hampered progress: it was not the absence of machines in antiquity that forced landowners to resort to slavery, but rather slavery that prevented the use of a good many technological opportunities theoretically within the grasp of the ancients. This was not due to a mental block bound up with an aristocratic ideal and contempt for commerce, gain, and above all the trade of the artisan, but rather to a "social block" bound up with slavery, which indirectly produced a "mental block."[14] On the one hand, it was chiefly slavery of the "concentration camp" type, with very low labor costs (during the eras of conquest, the cost of social reproduction through razzia was less than the cost of "natural" reproduction), that hampered techological progress, and this system tended to disappear once the empire had been stabilized. On the other hand, the feudal mode of production could be just as much an impediment to progress as slavery (though for quite different reasons, and with quite different consequences).

In an article written in 1977,[15] Parain maintained that the relations of production of the slave system began to impede the development of the productive forces as early as the first century, so that it became necessary to replace slave gangs on large estates with *coloni*. We shall have more to say later on about the relation between changes in the material base and the class struggle as described in this article; for now it is enough to note that the explanation in terms of noncorrespondence is said to be "valid for the spread of the colonate," but "still insufficient to account for the dynamism exhibited by the feudal tenant, in contrast to his predecessor (the Roman *colonus*): in the interim the character of the productive forces continued to undergo transformation."[16]

On the basis of this article, it would be excessive to claim that Parain was invoking a "Menshevik mechanism" since he argues only that social relations had begun to hamper further development and uses this "model" only to explain the transition from the slave system to the colonate, rejecting it as an explanation of the transition to the more "dynamic" feudal mode of production.

In point of fact, Parain acknowledges that "the destruction of an obsolete social regime took place before all the productive forces it was capable of creating had developed, and certainly before the material conditions of a new regime had ripened."[17] To explain the collapse of the slave-based Roman empire, he resorts, almost explicitly, to another "model," which we might call "Stalinist."

Also mechanistic, this second model allows for the fact that not all the possibilities for development of the productive forces within the previous mode of production had been exhausted, and that the new relations of production had not yet ripened (had not yet even "blossomed") at the time of the social revolution. The revolution was nonetheless able to succeed on account of crises or convulsions characteristic of the youth or maturity of the previous mode of production (rather than of its end), hence well before it died a natural death, particularly if external events happened to exacerbate internal contradictions (such as military defeat, for example). This being the case, before new relations of production could be envisaged, there must, to the extent that the correspondence and causal relation between productive forces and relations of production holds good, have been a transition period during which the material foundations of the new social relations would have to have been laid ("build the material base of socialism first," as the slogan goes). The sequence of events is as follows: overthrow of the superstructure (the state together with existing legal and political relations), construction of the material base, overthrow of the relations of production.

To be sure, this scheme is no longer strictly mechanistic, since it allows for the possibility of an "anticipatory" social revolution. And surely it is possible to introduce a "dialectical" movement into it, by granting that during the transition period the relations of production begin to change and that the laying of the new material foundations is influenced by the interaction between the base and the relations of production (first a little "base," then a little of the other, then a little more "base"!)—provided, of course, that "in the last instance" the determining factor is economic!

To explain the transition to feudalism according to this "Stalinist" model, one would have to overcome some objections:

1. The collapse of the old system (i.e., the slave system) and the formation of the new relations (colonate, domiciling) occurred at a time when the material basis of new relations of production was nonexistent or barely "embryonic."

2. Furthermore, granting that the relations between master and *colonus* or domiciled slave (and ultimately between master and "serf" in the early Middle Ages) were not yet truly "feudal" or fully developed, relatively significant growth of the productive forces did nevertheless take place (between the sixth and the end of the ninth century); in other words, the material base of feudalism was built "first," and only later were true or fully developed feudal relations constituted. Hence one must show how this development of the material base during the early Middle Ages produced the social transformation of the eleventh and twelfth centuries.

3. Finally, one would have to explain what caused the pronounced technological progress that we find in certain periods. At the beginning of the eleventh century, for example, did lords introduce water mills in order to increase peasant productivity, thereby in part benefitting the peasants themselves (which would explain why the peasants accepted these "innovations," and why the balance of power shifted in their favor, thus making possible an explanation of the "liberation" of the eleventh and twelfth centuries in terms of development of the material base)? Or, to take the opposite tack, did lords introduce water mills solely as an instrument of exploitation, in order to increase their own share of the product at the expense of the peasants, at a time when peasant struggles had considerably reduced the efficiency of the manorial system (in terms of production of surplus for the master) and of the old ways of extracting surplus labor (serfdom, *corvées*, natural rents, slavery or quasi slavery)?

In this chapter we shall attempt to show that the explanatory schema set forth above is not convincing, not because it emphasizes social struggles—although this is the criticism often made by non-Marxist historians—but on the contrary because it subordinates class conflict to economic and/or external factors.

I. The Collapse of the Slave Empire, or the Struggle of the Lower Classes

What caused the collapse of the slave system and the constitution of social relations characteristic of the colonate or of serfdom? What connections are there between the change in the way men were exploited and the end of the Roman Empire?

At times Parain seems to argue that the Roman Empire did not die a "natural death." Borrowing the well-known phrase of Piganiol, for example, he says that "it is possible to maintain that Roman civilization was murdered, and murdered by the barbarian invasions."[18] Violent death at the hands of outsiders would explain why this mode of production was unable to develop its technological potential to the full: the barbarians killed it off before it had run its course.

Of course Parain goes on to point out that the invasions were able to destroy Roman society only because it had been in decay for more than two centuries, the imperial state was working badly, and the social measures that the privileged classes were forced to take in order to safeguard their position aggravated the class struggle.[19] The class struggle does figure in the argument, but its effects are limited and subordinated to an "external" or economistic logic.

This argument does not stand up under scrutiny: the barbarian invasions should not be viewed as a triumphant march of armies but rather as a penetration of the empire, often peacefully and even at the behest of the Romans, by exhausted and downtrodden tribes, astonished to discover that the empire's defenses had crumbled. The Roman Empire died of its internal contradictions, which the invasions served only to magnify.

Was a civilization based on slavery or the colonate "pulled down" by the barbarian invasions? If Parain concedes, as he seems to do,[20] that during the third and fourth centuries the colonate was clearly in the ascendant over slavery, he cannot use the invasions to explain the dismantling of the slave system. The invasions, in this case, could only have finished the destruction of a political-cultural superstructure (Roman civilization) whose underpinnings in slavery had already crumbled. To argue in this way, however, would be tantamount to accepting the strict mechansitic argument that Parain is at pains to reject and would deny his own favorite notion that the slave system was pulled down before it had exhausted its potentialities. Nothing remains to explain the untimely demise of this system of production. In consequence, the "catastrophe" thesis must be ruled out as an explanation of the change in the relations of production, since the only effect of the invasions was either to complete the demolition of a superstructure whose foundations in the slave system had already been destroyed; or to smash a superstructure compatible with the colonate before that relation of production had time to develop fully. Fortunately Parain has other arguments to explain the transition from gang slavery to colonate.

In 1963 in an article entitled "Lutte des classes dans l'Antiquité classique,"[21] he went beyond the relatively limited development of the colonate to stress also the idea "that in this phase of history the class struggle in fact became, in correlation with the progress of the productive forces, the fundamental driving force behind historical development."[22]

In the first place, it is clear to Parain that Roman society was class-based and hence that class conflict played an essential role, though he rightly stresses the danger of exaggerating the divisions within ancient societies. However, the deepest antagonism, that between freemen and slaves, did not always play the leading role. Nevertheless, the other fundamental antagonism, that between rich and poor, must be studied in conjunction with the former; the latter becomes the principal contradiction only when slavery ceases to play the dominant role in the economy.

In Parain's view, even after the slave system had developed (which he believes happened in the third century B.C., much earlier than we have maintained[23]), the class struggle between slaves and freemen[24] was limited by the lack of homogeneity of the slave class, the possibility of individual emancipation which the masters used to "divide and rule," and the absence of "a truly revolutionary ideal" among the slaves (in contrast, Parain explains, to today's proletariat). Rarely did this struggle reach the point of armed uprising. Generally it was limited to "passive or semipassive resistance, perhaps going as far as sabotage, along with escape from servitude, either by individuals or by groups."

Still, this class struggle met with some success, though this, too, was limited.[25] How was this possible? First of all, according to Parain, passive resistance and sabotage hampered production, just as marauding and brigandage by fugitive slaves hampered commerce. Hence profits from these activities were diminished. Profits were further reduced by the financial burden upon the state for repression. Because this constant conflict cut into the profitability of the system, the masters turned from the slave system to the colonate. On this point Parain is clear: "Passive resistance and sabotage . . . were causes of the shift from large-scale slave cultivation to the colonate."[26] Ultimately an anti-slave ideology, most notably in its Stoic version, emerged in the course of continuing class conflict, exposing the "economic absurdity of the slave system."

Finally, when in the course of the general economic decline the condition of the poor approached that of slaves, a "common struggle" entered to a certain extent into the realm of possibility. The ensuing social tensions weakened the state and allowed the barbarian assault to succeed: "While the slave state was undermined from within by a series of social conflicts, the coup de grâce was delivered by the assault of the barbarians."[27]

It is curious that in Parain's 1963 article, in which social conflict, in correlation with the progress of the productive forces, is said to be the motor of historical development, it is not at all clear what connection Parain wants to make between social conflict on the one hand and technical progress on the other. Is the truth not quite different: was it not in a "time of general economic decline" that the alliance between the poor and the slaves was forged, weakening the empire and thus paving the way for the barbarian conquest?

The relationship between social struggles and the development of the productive forces is spelled out in Parain's 1977 article.[28] In agreement with the "brilliant" analysis of M. E. Sergueenko (1953), Parain explains that "from the end of the first century A.D. onwards, the slave system had begun to stand in the way of further development of the productive forces."[29] Specifically, various improvements in farming practice and implements (such as storage of manure in cemented pits, heavy plows, weeding of cereal grains, complex vine-tending techniques) were impeded by the use of slave manpower. These progressive innovations, it is argued, would have required additional effort of the slaves without offering any improvement in their standard of living by way of compensation, so that the slaves fought against any worsening of their working conditions by means of passive resistance and, more insidiously, sabotage.[30]

In other words, "Transition from one mode of production to another became necessary in order to assure correspondence between the character of the productive forces and the relations of production. Hence slave gangs cultivating large estates were replaced by *coloni* settled on small individual farms."[31]

Surely, as we have already said, Parain does not maintain that this was the only reason for the transition to the colonate, the foregoing passage to the contrary notwithstanding. This is fortunate, for it is a mistake to believe that the innovations mentioned above were incompatible with the slave system (all of them were actually used on large slave-worked estates, whether during the first century[32] or, later, on Carolingian *villae* in the early Middle Ages[33]). And this is to say nothing of the regressive aspects of the *colonus* and his tenement as compared with the large estate![34]

In both his 1963 and 1977 articles, Parain contends, more generally, that the effects of social conflict are at most limited and indirect. Conflict, he argues, reduced the efficiency of the Roman economy either by raising the cost of production (or circulation) or by impeding technological progress. It diminished the capacity of Roman society to stand up to the barbarians. Of course Parain is aware that the inefficiency of the slave system was not purely a matter of technology or nature, but bound up with the combat waged by the slaves against it.

However moderate, his position is still an economistic one: the slave *villa*, according to Parain, was abandoned only because it was no longer profitable or because it did not allow for (or hampered) technological progress—owing, of course, to the opposition of the slaves. Here we meet once again with Engels's argument, that "slavery no longer paid, and therefore it ceased to exist."[35] Even if class struggle is acknowledged as one cause of reduced profits, reduced profits are the reason the system came to an end. As we shall see in chapter 4, while this may well have been one reason why the slaves were successful in their fight, mediation through economic factors is not the only way to explain why the slave system came to an end.[36]

Moreover, in explaining that the struggles worked their effects through the intermediary of antislavery ideology, in which slaves were recognized as being different from animals, Parain is assuming that the Stoics did indeed espouse such an ideology and that it exerted a certain influence "from above." But the Stoics were essentially arguing for a modified slave system, one in which it was necessary to reproduce the work force locally, as against the system we have likened to the concentration camp, in which slaves were worked to death; Stoicism, therefore, exhorted slaves to submit to their fate and be patient. Almost the same thing may be said of Christianity, moreover.[37]

Parain's position—that the effects of the class struggles waged by slaves were limited and that external and economic factors were primary—gives us a clear idea of the differences and similarities between a mechanistic materialist analysis and non-Marxist analyses. When Parain speaks of classes and their conflicts in antiquity, and when he characterizes Roman society during the republic and empire as a slave society, viewing the conflict between slaves and masters as the principal contradiction, he seems dogmatic to bourgeois historians. Like them, however, he uses only two kinds of arguments: either economic, in terms of the low profits or technological dynamism of slave society (however these characteristics may be related to class struggle, which is another matter), or geopolitical (barbarian invasions), reconciling the two in his general synthesis.

Parain's analysis is similar, in our judgment, to that of some Soviet historians. Doubtless since Stalin's death the strict mechanism on which he insisted[38] has lost ground,[39] though in some cases not enough, and it would be interesting to examine the many books and articles on the question of ancient slavery that have appeared in the Soviet Union and in the other socialist countries.[40]

Among these one is of particular interest: a book by Elena M. Schtajerman, which has been translated into German.[41] Schtajerman describes the social structure of the empire (in any case, the early empire) as that of a slave system—with the slaves of the *villae* accounting for the bulk of production, and the surplus value extracted from them accounting for the wealth of the cities in which the great landowners resided— and she sees in the decline of slavery the cause of the crisis of the second and third centuries, characterized by the decay of cities, increasing autarchy of the great estates, and so forth. But what caused slavery to decline? Along with the usual external cause (à la Weber[42]), she insists on the low productivity of slavery, which limited the masters' profits.[43]

Class struggles play an important role. Fear of slave uprisings inspired the masters to take humanitarian measures, which further decreased the profitability of the slave system and led to the replacement of slaves by *coloni* (to be contrasted with our own view, that these humanitarian measures became necessary because slave manpower could no longer be wasted as wantonly as before, but that they did away only with "superprofits" and not with profit as such). Fear again led to more drastic repression. The lot of the slave did not improve, indeed worsened as the masters were forced by the dwindling size of the servile work force to resort to more intense exploitation.[44] The crisis gave rise to proliferating social tensions, which further aggravated the crisis itself and dictated the policies of the Severi, and later of Diocletian and Constantine, who attempted to fix the structures of society, particularly in rural areas. Slaves did engage in class struggle, but this, it is argued, was of secondary importance. Class struggle was in no way the cause of the decline of the slave system, a system of production which died because it was less profitable than the colonate, the forerunner of serfdom, and could not survive the dwindling of the slave trade.

Some of the criticisms leveled by non-Marxist historians at their Soviet colleague should, in our judgment, be turned back against themselves. Surely they are right to emphasize the importance of free labor, both by freedmen and *coloni* (who would not be enslaved until the fourth century[45]); and surely they are not wrong when they stress the fact that the *villae* continued to flourish in the East and even in some parts of the West (Africa, Spain, Britain), whether they were still worked by slaves or subdivided among the *coloni*. Surely, too, Schtajerman's attempt[46] to find in the writings of Seneca, Pliny the Younger, Apuleius, Philostratus, and Dio Cassius signs of "bourgeois class consciousness" is all too likely to succeed in imputing to the authors examined the ideology prevalent in the historian's own time.[47]

But all too often non-Marxist historians find themselves unable to accept the characterization of imperial society as a slave society, and unable to concede that social conflict or even slave uprisings were as important as they are said to be.[48] Revealing in this respect is the skepticism exhibited by Paul Petit, for example, in the matter of the rebellion of the Bacaudae in Gaul, as well as other revolts in Africa, Britain, and Egypt. He writes that "certain social movements may have represented the rebellion of the poor and oppressed . . . but choosing among alternative explanations is a delicate matter: were these disturbances nationalist movements, social rebellions, or agitation by antisocial elements, such as may be found in any society, even a Marxist one? This is the problem that crops up in regard to these brigands, or *latrones*, who were surely not always righters of wrongs and defenders of the oppressed, much less spokesmen for the consciousness of a class."[49]

Admittedly the rebellion of the subjugated peasants and slaves in the Bacaudae was neither the Paris Commune nor the October Revolution!

Elements of class war, anti-imperialist uprising, ethnic conflict, and brigandage were inextricably intertwined. Does this mean the amalgam
was not a social conflict? But there was no class consciousness, some
will object, or if there was any, it was decidedly ambiguous. The objection is superficial. Surely what consciousness there was was neither
clear-sighted nor simple. But perhaps never in the history of humanity
was class consciousness more pronounced among both masters and
slaves, and before long among the poor as well, among the *humiliores*
of every description.

We, on the other hand, would direct our criticism of Schtajerman at
her willingness to subordinate the social struggle to economism by arguing that slavery vanished because its profitability was low. On such
a view social conflict is no more than an indicator of "economic difficulties" connected with an inefficient system of production, which had
been able to hold on only because an abundant slave trade made it
possible to use slaves wastefully and which disappeared when the traffic
in slaves dried up. In this perspective, even if social conflict can play
the role of midwife in the birth of a new mode of production, it is never
the driving force behind social evolution; it does not explain the "end"
of the slave system.[50] When Paul Petit writes that "the masters most
likely freed their slaves, in general, because slave labor was less profitable than the labor of freedmen," at bottom there is nothing to distinguish his view from that of Schtajerman, Parain, or Engels! For a critique
of this analysis, we refer the reader to chapter 2 above.

II. "Build the Material Foundations of
Feudalism First"

On the view outlined above, then, social relations typical of the colonate,
the late imperial precursor of serfdom that persisted throughout the
early Middle Ages, as well as the somewhat different relations associated
with the *servus casatus*, were built up in the wake of the collapse of a
type of slave system that had ceased to be profitable and had begun to
hamper the development of the productive forces (owing to class struggle waged by the slaves), whereupon it was attacked from without and
destroyed. However, the slave system collapsed, according to Parain,
before the material foundations of a new system had been fully laid
down. In consequence, the colonate and serfdom are merely transitional
forms of social relations, fruits of the "premature" decomposition of
slave relations.

Before feudal relations could develop, further development of the material basis of society was required. Parain therefore tries to show that

the material foundations were built up during a long transitional phase (which lasted until the eleventh century), and only *after* that could true feudalism develop. Exactly the same pattern is supposed to have been followed in the Soviet Union, only much more rapidly, owing, as Parain explains, to the increased efficiency of manpower.[51]

However, even if we neglect the fact that, for Parain, the social relations characteristic of serfdom (which, for Marx, are *the* relations of production of the feudal mode) are cast out of the sphere of "feudalism" itself, it would still remain to be shown that over the course of three or four centuries (between the sixth and ninth century) the material base did in fact mature, ultimately attaining a higher level of development. We shall attempt to show that on the average there was no "leap forward," not even a "leap less far-reaching" than that of the Paleolithic era![52] At the same time we shall prove that in all likelihood medieval feudalism was not associated with a degree of development of the productive forces (achieved, it is said, "by the ninth century") significantly higher than that of ancient slavery.

We shall see subsequently that, for Marx and Engels, the essential transition was the one that gave rise to serfdom, and that, far from being linked to a development of man's productive powers, it was associated with a regression in those powers.

A) Was There Development of the Productive Forces during the Early Middle Ages?

According to Parain, "between the destruction of the Roman empire and the emergence of feudalism intervenes a period of four centuries, which at first glance seems a long and confused expanse of time marked by a general decline of civilization, much violence, and ruin heaped upon ruin."[53] Beyond this apparent stagnation, however, dynamic social classes were taking shape, and it was these classes of peasants and landowners that would lay the technological foundations upon which, "once the material possibility was at hand, feudalism was built through the usual process of class struggle."

Parain begins by citing numerous advances in the techniques of the crafts, particularly in the manufacture of arms. He then takes note of other innovations that could only have emerged and spread widely in a context of small individual farms, "because they required the users to take care, initiative, and interest in the work: the wheeled plow, specialized types of sickles and scythes, and threshing flails," innovations known in Roman times but slow to spread. Soon, too, there were new hitching collars and new grains (oats and rye), which facilitated use of a larger portion of the arable land. Finally, there was progress associated with the organization of the manor, which made it possible "to retain a substantial part of the advantages of large-scale cultivation": water-powered presses and mills, more highly developed and more wide-spread than before, and later the three-field system of crop rotation, which came just prior to "the emergence of the feudal regime."

Summing up, "by the beginning of the ninth century technological innovations were either in hand or taking hold which made for the economic superiority of feudal agriculture over Roman agriculture." This, in turn, is supposed to explain why a transition to the social re-lations and legal-political superstructure of feudalism was necessary; this transition is said to have been brought about by the struggles of peasants to secure hereditary title to their tenements. What makes the feudal mode progressive is supposedly the combination of the feudal property of the lord, and thus the advantages of large-scale cultivation, with individual property. Parain is quite clear on this point in a 1968 article: "It was felt necessary to combine the advantages of the small farm, in which the producer could show his interest in and enthusiasm for the work and take the initiative (unlike the slave), with the benefits of means of production on a scale exceeding the capacity of the small farm. These means of production were concentrated in the hands of the lord, which made him appear to be 'the organizer and master of the production process and of the whole of social life.' "[54]

As mentioned earlier, the productivity advantages of a system based on serfdom, with family-worked tenements and *corvée* labor on the de-mesne, as compared with gang slavery on the large estate, must be considered. Now we are being told that, in addition to this, the small farm fostered technological progress by impelling the individual small farmer to use new techniques (the prototype being the wheeled plow). Economism always has its amusing aspects: if those who argue along economistic lines maintained their position consistently, they would be forced to contend that the small independent craftsman is more favorable to technological advance than the centralized factory with wage labor. But in fact they tell us just the opposite: economists since Adam Smith, indeed since William Petty, have argued that the system based on large-scale production units with centralized management of a labor force paid money wages but in fact compelled to perform what amounts virtually to forced labor is the crucial factor in the introduction of machinery, technical refinements, etc. As we shall see, Marx does not share Parain's analysis of feudalism: for Marx, the dismemberment of the great estates represents a regression of the productive forces.

Let us take a closer look at the facts.

The wheeled plow with iron plowshare: In the Roman Empire chiefly the swing plow was in use, although in certain regions a heavier implement, mounted on wheels, was found, as we know from Pliny and indirectly from Virgil. The latter may have been a Germanic or Gallic "invention." The invasions may have helped to spread its use in the Roman Empire. It is known that on large Carolingian estates, the plow numbered among the wooden tools. There is reason to believe that less civilized regions were technically more advanced in the use of metal and that the question is chiefly one of the nature of the soil and the size of the fields involved.[55] In my view, small farms favored use of the swing plow rather than the wheeled plow (which was difficult to turn), unless collective practices were well developed.[56] In the Roman Empire, moreover, the swing plow often had an iron share or tip.[57]

Other cultivating implements: No change is evident (except perhaps that iron seems to have been used more rarely in the early Middle Ages) in spades, hoes, pitchforks, sickles, scythes, harvesting rakes, harrows, screens, etc.

Reapers: Pliny reports that "on the large estates of Gaul a large drum equipped with two wheels and teeth is pushed through the cornfield by an ox."[58] Three centuries later Palladius describes a similar machine and adds a few new details. It is shown clearly in a bas-relief in Buzenol-Montauban. This machine vanished completely during the early Middle Ages.

Rotation of crops: Roman agriculture, like that of hot, dry countries in general, relied chiefly on the two-field system.[59] The extension of the empire to the north, apparently, incorporated regions in which it was possible to obtain a second corn harvest after a spring planting. According to Columella, this practice was also known in Italy in the first century. The three-field system grew up during the eighth century on certain large estates in Europe north of the Loire and the Alps. It is not possible, however, to generalize this observation to other regions or types of cultivation. Then, too, the adoption of the new system was probably a limited response to growing misery, in consequence of which men were willing to devote more labor to the same land—either because of demographic pressure or because of social pressure from the lord, who thereby found a use for his surplus *corvée* labor[60]— and more land to grain crops.[61] Moreover, it was probably not until the ninth and tenth centuries that the new system spread to any great degree.

The water mill: According to Parain's well-known article, the water mill first appeared in the first century B.C. and spread during the first century A.D.: this was a first phase in the growing use of this machine, one aspect of a powerful thrust of technological progress in this period.

Thereafter, we must await the fourth century for "an important leap forward, in an era characterized on the whole by a temporary decline of rationalism and science."[62] Parain takes note of mills installed at Athens, Rome, Arles, and on the Moselle in particular, and observes that besides an increase in the number of installations, we also find technological progress and growth in the size of the production unit (at Barbegal near Arles, for example, water supplied by an aqueduct drove eight paddle wheels): this was the second phase in the rise of the water mill—characterized by technological improvements. Parain also clearly identifies a third phase, marked by "accelerated diffusion of the water mill after the tenth century."[63]

When we come shortly to consider the reasons for the introduction and spread of these mills, we shall have more to say about this periodization. For the time being it is enough to point out that not even Parain himself regards the period between the fifth and tenth centuries as one of further development of the material foundations of society, at least insofar as the water mill is concerned. At the time of the siege of Rome by the Goths in 537, someone did have the idea of using floating mills. But this type of mill clearly represented a step backward technologically; Parain himself observes that the power of the floating mill was low, and that it was quite susceptible to variations in the water flow and impeded traffic on the river—a far cry from the mill at Barbegal!

Hence it is quite difficult to form an opinion of the state of the productive forces in agriculture between the fifth century and the end of the ninth century. One thing seems rather clear to me, however: there was no "leap forward" in the laying of the material foundations of feudalism. The most that can be said is that in agriculture there was probably no technological decline, no diminution in the quality, or even the quantity, of implements available for use—at least we must concede that it is very difficult to prove that there was such regression or scant progress; Duby has written that "we know virtually nothing of early medieval tools, which are unquestionably less familiar than those of Neolithic peasants."[64] This being the case, let us accept Duby's own assessment: "We should keep in view the overall picture of a poorly equipped agrarian society forced to tackle the natural environment virtually bare-handed in order to satisfy its basic requirements."[65]

To this we must add the decrease in population, which probably fell to new lows in the seventh and eighth centuries, with plagues, invasions, wars and their attendant devastation, and malnutrition and famine to make the populace even more vulnerable to such shocks. Cultivated lands were deserted and brush and swampland made new inroads, while malaria came to infest the Mediterranean lowlands.[66] Was not "man the most precious capital"? Of course it is not obvious that fewer men working the same quantity of land necessarily produce less per worker, unless we suppose that in agriculture we sometimes have an area of increasing returns. Now, it is in fact quite likely that productivity falls off if workers are spread too thin on the land, just as it falls off if there are too many workers.[67] More than that, the isolated worker would have been in danger from bandits, slave-raiders, soldiers, and the like. Perhaps the dispersion that was linked to depopulation was not so much a direct cause of reduced productivity as it was a factor in increasing the vulnerability of men, tools, and harvest.

Dispersion was not the only reason for isolation. The collapse of the infrastructure of roads and of means of communication generally, as well as the virtual disappearance of towns, left man alone in the face of hostile nature, bands of soldiers, and thieves. Bear in mind that productivity in food production—which, along with the production of a few articles of clothing and tools, had become almost the only occupation there was—depended not only on the means of production used in agriculture, but also on the state of the productive forces in the economy as a whole. Those historians who are at pains to belittle the decline in man's productive powers between the fifth and tenth centuries tell us that when all is said and done, agriculture was the essential thing, and in agriculture there was no decline and perhaps even progress. They then proceed to study pitchforks and swing plows and the like. But agricultural productivity depends on the political and economic environment.

One further point: it might be supposed that malnutrition of the peasants was chiefly or exclusively the result of increases in the amount of the surplus claimed by the magnates, assuming a steady output. But what became of this surplus? The magnificence of the magnates seems modest compared with that of their Roman predecessors. And where are the sumptuous architecture, the fabulous cities, which under the empire had been built out of the surplus extracted from the countryside? Of course the surplus upon which Rome and the Italian cities depended stemmed chiefly from imperialism. But this was not true of all the cities of the empire, as in Gaul, for example.

Accordingly, it seems likely that there was an overall decrease in productivity with the transition from the ancient slave mode of production to the first feudal mode of production, along with massive destruction of the productive forces.

Invoking the authority of Engels,[68] Parain tells us that we must beware of superficial analyses, for "if on the surface the Merovingian era seems to have been one of decline, in the depths of society, by contrast, if we

focus on the masses of workers, we find that the technological foundations were being laid upon which, as soon as the material possibility
was at hand, feudalism was constructed." Not only is it wrong to speak
of such material foundations being laid, but how, we ask, can anyone
fail to see that such surface regression which included such important
items as the virtual disappearance of roads, cities, science, one type of
culture, and civil peace—cannot have been without consequences for
the deepest levels of the social structure?

The collapse of slave civilization surely did not lead to the collapse of
agricultural production. The free peasantry, living collectively, put certain technological improvements into practice, as we shall see. It would
be absurd, however, to overlook the enormous economic cost of this
social revolution, in all sectors of production. Of this Marx and Engels
were well aware.

B) Marx and Engels: Regression?

Let us begin by recalling the view of Melekechvili, of which as we saw
earlier, Parain is critical. The Russian, basing his opinion on the work
of A. R. Korsunsky,[69] maintains that "in western Europe the transition
from slavery to feudalism took place in conditions more of decadence
than of growth in production."[70]

Does not such a position merely echo the views of Marx and Engels
themselves, as set forth, for example, in *The German Ideology?* In ana-
lyzing the transition from the ancient slave system to medieval feudalism, Marx and Engels point out that the change in the relations of
production cannot be explained as the result of the barbarian warriors
"taking possession of the Roman Empire." They register their opposition
to the widespread "notion that up till now in history it has only been
a question of *taking.*"[71]

In fact, everything depends on the level of development of the object
being seized: the fortune of a banker, for example, cannot be seized
unless the taker submits to the conditions of production prevailing in
the conquered country. Moreover, and it is chiefly this that is important
in the present context, "everywhere there is very soon an end to taking,
and when there is nothing more to take, you have to set about producing.
From the necessity of producing, which very soon asserts itself, it follows
that the form of community adopted by the settling conquerors must
correspond to the stage of development of the productive forces they
find in existence; if this is not the case from the start, it must change
according to the productive forces."[72]

Marx and Engels reject the notion that feudalism was imported ready-
made from Germany, that it was only a matter of the conquering tribes

"exporting" social, legal, and political relations that already existed in Germany.

Now we see the problem: if the conquerors have to adapt to the productive forces they find in the hands of the conquered nation, how is the transformation to be explained? "The feudal system . . . had its origin, as far as the conquerors were concerned, in the martial organisation of the army during the actual conquest, and this only evolved after the conquest into the feudal system proper through the action of productive forces found in the conquered countries. To what an extent this form was determined by the productive forces is shown by the abortive attempts to realise other forms derived from reminiscences of ancient Rome (Charlemagne, etc.)."[73]

Hence there are causes of two kinds: the military organization of the Germans on the one hand, and the level of development of the productive forces they found when they arrived on the other. These causes interact with one another, because the conquest had an effect on the productive forces, and the state of the productive forces was one cause of the conquest.[74] The causes in question are either material or strictly dependent on the material base, as is the case for the military organization of the barbarians: Engels says as much in *Anti-Dühring*.[75]

The important point, however, is that the level of development of the productive forces, which is essential for explaining the transition, was falling. As Marx and Engels put it, "the last centuries of the declining Roman Empire and its conquest by the barbarians destroyed a number of productive forces; agriculture had declined, industry had decayed for want of a market, trade had died out or been violently suspended, the rural and urban population had decreased. From these conditions and the mode of organisation of the conquest determined by them, feudal property developed under the influence of the Germanic military constitution."[76] Hence it is the decline of the productive forces that explains the transition to feudalism, or at least plays a part in the explanation. Far from corresponding to a higher degree of development of the productive forces, feudalism, i.e., serfdom as a relation of production and the whole "feudal structure" (which was just a new form of association against the subject class of producers), corresponds to partially destroyed productive forces.

Missing from this account is the idea that, because slave relations were fetters on the development of the productive forces, they were swept away so as to make room for new relations of production corresponding to a higher level of development of the productive forces and to allow for further and freer development of those forces. We have already conceded to Charles Parain that no such idea is to be found in his writings, either.

Also missing from the account of Marx and Engels, however, is the notion that true feudalism required further development of the material base and that this necessary development was accomplished between the fifth and the ninth centuries. For Marx, notwithstanding his jibe to the contrary, feudalism was not the product of the water mill. Unfortunately, although violence does figure in the account given in *The German Ideology*, restored to its proper place, it is the violence of the conquerors; what is left out is the violence of the class struggle, indeed the class struggle itself.

But it is possible to follow a slightly different line of argument: if the violence of the barbarians succeeded only on account of the decline in the Roman economy, and if the decline in the productive forces was largely due to this violence, can it be said that when the productive forces do advance, they do so as a result of the balance of class forces— viewed not as a static balance, but rather as a dynamic equilibrium determined by the actions and reactions of each class on the other?

C) Technological Progress, Free Peasants, and Village Communities

Although we do not find any signs of wide-scale development of the productive forces between the time of the Roman Empire and the end of the ninth century, it must not be concluded that the early Middle Ages were a long period of stagnation! Only in comparison with the ancient slave mode of production was there stagnation and even regression. But after the collapse of Roman society and of whole segments of the Roman economy, the Merovingian and Carolingian eras did witness technological progress (or the spread of known techniques) that it would be a mistake to ignore. Land-clearing took place in many cases much earlier than was long believed (eighth and ninth centuries), particularly in southern Europe. Similarly, irrigation, terraced cultivation, and, as we have already seen, the three-field system in the north appeared before the tenth century, along with the spread of the wheeled plow and, for that matter, of the horse in certain agricultural applications. Water mills came into use prior to the rise of banal seigniory, though perhaps chiefly in the form of collectively owned peasant mills (the same is true of horse- and mule-driven mills).

For insofar as the productive forces developed in this period, they did so in part, perhaps chiefly, thanks to the collective practices of the free peasantry. In other words, the cause of development was not so much the interrelation (by which Parain sets such great store) between manse (hence individual initiative) and demesne (hence economies of scale, centralized organization, and large-scale means of production) in the context of the great estate. Rather, technological progress was made, and new innovations spread, owing chiefly to the efforts of allodialists joined together in village communities.[77] The dynamic of the eighth and ninth centuries was not concentrated in the great estate, with its tenements, *corvées*, and natural rents, but was also to be found outside these estates and no doubt directed against them.

The water mill is a case in point. While there surely were such mills on the Carolingian *villae*, P. Bonassié[78] points out that in Catalonia it was allodialists who banded together to build small, crude water mills. Typically the ownership of the mill was divided into fourteen shares, corresponding to seven days and seven nights of use. These would be replaced by the great banal mills of the lord.

Similarly, in Roussillon in the late ninth century we find water mills, ownership of which was divided into eight parts.[79] Were such arrangements perhaps more common in the south than in the north (where the estates were better able to "hold on")?

Let us beware, however, of unduly exaggerating the role of the "peasant communes." During what was no doubt a long period of time following the collapse of Roman society, the free peasantry occupied a relatively important position, even though the Carolingian reaction worked against it. A high point came incontestably after the collapse of the Carolingian Empire, when all ties of dependence were loosened. Frequently, however, allodialists (or *coloni*, at that time practically independent) lived in isolation. In Sabine the village "did not constitute the everyday context of peasant life," and Toubert cites a text in which the peasant is described as living on his land in biblical peace, in the shadow of his vines and his fig tree.[80] This would scarcely seem to have been favorable—to say no more than that—to collective life, coordinated land-clearing by peasants, construction of terraces and mills, and so on.

In my view, unduly accentuating the then progressive aspect of early medieval "communes" involves a danger of "falling" into the use of a myth analogous to the one in which the small peasant is seen as necessarily efficient or the lord is seen as the effective coordinator of peasant labor.

The development of the productive forces is an extraordinarily complex phenomenon. Care must be taken to avoid fascination with "large-scale" means of production, such as the water mills of the *villae* (and later of the banal seigniories), or with peasant implements or "fixed capital" by themselves. Taking into account, as we must do, the organization of labor, the variety of tools and technologies, and the urban and transportation infrastructure, it must be granted that although the collapse of the ancient economy entailed overall regression, some factors favorable to development were yet present in the *villae* and allodialist communities. In this period, however, social structures were in the main favorable to the spread of earlier advances in peasant implements, as well as to improvement and extension of the area under cultivation (terraces, clearing, and so forth). Our allodialists are not to be confused with the Chinese peasants of modern "people's communes" or with nineteenth-century "tycoons"!

III. "Large" Water Mills: Where Does Technological Progress Come From?

Technological progress over the course of the first ten centuries of the Christian era took a variety of forms, of which the water mill is one of the most visible and best known. What is more, controversy has focussed on the mill to such a degree that a discussion of the question is an exercise in which it is virtually obligatory for medievalists to engage! Marc Bloch's 1935 *Annales* article[81] is regarded as fundamental by all specialists, and Parain's 1965 *La Pensée* piece was clearly written in reaction to it.[82]

Earlier we mentioned the important phases in the history of the profusion of the water mill: it first appeared in the first century B.C. and was further developed between the first century B.C. and the first century A.D., whereupon a long period of stagnation intervened before the fourth century witnessed still further development, followed by slow advances and finally by rapid expansion in the tenth through twelfth centuries; the final phase of this process of diffusion, i.e., the disappearance of the hand mill, would require some centuries more: it was not yet complete in the eighteenth.

A) Antiquity and the Early Middle Ages

Marc Bloch does not explain the innovation of the ancients but seeks rather to understand why the use of the water mill spread so slowly. The reason, he says, is the abundance of cheap slaves that were available to Roman agriculture. Conversely, the same consideration explains the point of the end of the empire and the beginning of the Middle Ages. The population had declined, particularly that portion which made up the slave gangs. Bloch identifies this decline as one sort of constraint upon landowners. The water mill progressed slowly but surely in Europe. Though many large Carolingian estates had water mills,[83] provided there were good streams in the vicinity, still the old human- or animal-powered mills continued to be used.

Parain adds further details to this picture and offers a few criticisms. He explains the initial development of the water mill between the first century B.C. and the first century A.D. as one step in a series of improvements, which he relates to the era's "powerful technological dynamism," of which there were several aspects.

He is not satisfied with the explanation that limited use was made of water mills because slaves were cheap. On the one hand he rehearses Forbes's argument[84] that stimulus to use the mills was lacking because innovations benefitted only the small class of the wealthy and were accordingly predicated upon the imperialist structure of the state. On the other hand, deeming the foregoing analysis insufficient, he stresses the fact that the type of grain grown at this time (clad grain) could be threshed as well as ground, so that the amounts to be milled were small.

As reasons for the fourth-century expansion he gives (apart from the transition from slavery to the colonate) the reduction in the number of slaves in the cities and increased use of unclad grains.

Certain questions remain, however:

1. Between the first century B.C. and the first century A.D., how did it happen that at first the water mill spread even though the slave system was at its height and masses of cheap slaves were being thrown onto the markets? Parain tells us that this expansion was one element in a broad, general process of technological progress, and no doubt he is right, but is this enough? Our view is that the introduction of water mills and the "powerful technological dynamism" of the time can be understood only by relating them to the sudden explosion of large-scale property associated with imperialism and the slave system; in the end the slave system slowed the introduction of further technological advances. Slavery and imperialism made the great estate, and the great estate made possible the introduction of the first large-scale means of production. But the great estate bore within itself the fetters to its own further developments since it depended on slavery of the type we have likened to a "concentration-camp system," where reproduction of the labor force was unnecessary because labor, being superabundant, was expendable; hence further development of the water mill was halted.

2. The expansion of the fourth century must be related above all to the change in the way men were exploited: the decline of gang slavery and the rise of the colonate. This brings us straight back to the explanation of this first "end" of slavery. The change in the way men were exploited "determined" the modification in the way the land was worked. The great estate did not vanish, so that large-scale means of

production could be maintained; the size of the slave gang diminished in relation to the number of *coloni*, and what remained of gang slavery was far removed from the "concentration-camp system" with its systematic waste of slaves: hence the water mill was useful. Here we note the constraint to which Bloch called our attention.

B) The Expansion of the Eleventh and Twelfth Centuries

According to Marc Bloch, the third phase in the history of the water mill got under way in the tenth century and flourished in the eleventh and twelfth centuries. The explanation of this timing turns on the desire of the lords to institute banalities, or monopolies, chiefly of mills, ovens, and presses, for their own profit. Did this desire on the part of the lords meet with the "willing cooperation" of the peasants?[85] Not at all. The gradual victory of the water mill was won, Bloch explains, by force; the lords drove out the hand mills, destroyed them, and enforced use of the banal water mill in their stead. Numerous bitter struggles ensued, for peasant resistance was strong, so strong that at the end of the Middle Ages many old hand mills remained in use (the struggle would flare up again in the wake of the "feudal reaction" of the seventeenth and eighteenth centuries, which was backed by such judicial bodies as the Parlements of Dijon and Rouen, whose opposition to hand mills was openly declared; once again the fight would be tough, particularly in Brittany, where small mills [*moulinets*] were still to be found after the Revolution).[86] Thus technological progress was the child of "a double constraint": on the one hand great landowners were constrained by the dispersal of many slave gangs at the end of the late empire, while on the other hand lords constrained their tenants between the tenth and twelfth centuries to use the new mills, applying "drastic" coercive measures to induce them to do so.

Parain accepts the validity of Bloch's analyses, which highlight the gradual success of the lords' long war in forcibly establishing the banal mill, but only in regions where feudalism was imposed from without, where we find only the formal features and not the essence of feudalism. By this ploy he in effect relegates the conflict over the mills to the status of an insignificant exception. What, then, are the "deep-seated reasons," according to Parain, for the widespread diffusion of the water mill from the tenth century onwards?

To begin with, there is the development of unclad grains. The transition from spelt to wheat, which can only be pulverized with the millstone, was a sign of growing wealth and provided an impetus for using the water mill, because there was more grain to be milled.

Parain is aware, however, that the increased amounts of grain do not necessarily imply the use of a mill owned by the lord. Indeed, as he points out, in places where feudalization remained superficial (in the south), a small community or private estate of some size might make do with a small water mill, generally equipped with a horizontal wheel but always of rough and ready construction. On the other hand, in the north, the cradle of feudalization, we find mills of larger dimensions, providing better yields than the mills of antiquity. The use of such mills presupposes a high population density (which was the case, as land-clearings show), and their construction requires not only advanced technology but also the capacity to carry out such large-scale projects as canalizing rivers and altering their course, as well as building dams.

The undertaking of such projects, Parain tells us, requires landowners who exercise control over broad territories and a large work force, which if need be can be compelled to do what work is required. In this respect the lord had two advantages over the large Roman landowner: his lands lay in one contiguous unit, and his power of command was not limited by the central power.

In Parain's estimation, however, still more needs to be said. So far he has not gone beyond the realm of coercion, albeit coercion corresponding to "legitimate necessities" (the coercion in question is legitimated by the development of the productive forces it makes possible: are we not, once again, being treated to a comparison with another system in which "coercion" is said to be "legitimate"?). But coercion is not the end of the story. As Parain writes: "The long war waged in some cases by lords against the hand mill shows that no policy can accomplish everything by coercive means; to be permanently effective on a broad front in the economic as in the cultural sphere, a policy must meet not merely with passivity, but, to some extent anyway, with *willing cooperation* from those whom it affects."[87]

In places where the feudal regime was functioning smoothly, in regions which were experiencing growth and where the rights of the lord were counterbalanced by rights collectively won by the tenants, "the peasants must have welcomed the introduction of the banal mill with open arms as an indispensable adjunct to their labors, notwithstanding the prior effort demanded."[88] He compares the independent peasant (and even the slave) of the early empire, who (in spite of his slave?) had to devote hours of toil to milling his grain on his small farm, where involuntary underemployment was the rule, with the small farmer and even the serf in the tenth century, who, having plenty of work to keep him busy on his own land, could not but look upon milling his own grain as an absurd waste of time. Finally, Parain argues, the peasant had an interest in being able to use equipment that he could not afford to own by himself, even if the charges made for such use were somewhat heavy. Where peasants stubbornly persisted in using the old mills, they did so because the economy was stagnant, with involuntary underemployment of family members and idle surplus labor.

Thus Parain's view is that the lord organized cooperation in the interest of all, which won for him the willing cooperation of his peasants. The long, hard war described by Bloch is now just a special case, an exception that confirms the rule, typical of a situation of underdevelopment associated with underfeudalization.

Let us begin at once to criticize Parain's rather idyllic view of the spread of the water mill. As early as 1961[89] he explained that the F.M.P. was characterized by the conjunction of small independent farms (and hence of a certain efficiency associated with individual initiative) with wide-scale cooperation organized by the lord and that this made it possible to hold on to many of the advantages of large-scale agriculture, such as water mills and presses.

On this view, then, the water mill was not introduced as a perfected means of exploitation, viewed as such by lord and peasant alike (accounting for the long war over its use), but rather as a means of production which allowed an increase in the productivity of labor for the profit of all, and particularly of the peasant, who saw matters in this light (and therefore willingly cooperated in the use of the mill). Here we encounter what Marx called the "two aspects" of management and supervision, which come into play once again when division of labor is introduced into manufacturing and when machines are introduced into the factory. Parain greatly diminishes, indeed neglects, the third aspect of introduction of the banal mill: systematic exploitation. He does not say that the mill increased the productivity of the peasant and hence, assuming unchanged living standards, the surplus of the master. Instead, he assumes that it was the standard of living of the peasant that improved. Accordingly, the peasant would have had an interest in the change except in regions where he held as a *precarium* a piece of land too small to absorb the full labor potential of his family and therefore had time to spare for the milling of grain.

Which of the two accounts is true?

We believe that, although the medieval water mill[90] obviously increased the productivity of labor at the mill, it was practically never in the interest of the peasant to use it. Looking at the relations between lord and peasant, the banal mill, no matter what energy source was used to drive it,[91] was nothing but a means of exploitation.

We know that this was the case for other banal dues: the banal oven, of course, and still more clearly such obligations as that of using the lord's bull or boar or "hiring" the horses of the castle for threshing wheat (in the south). Then, too, sale of some products was forbidden during certain weeks (in the case of wine this was known as the *banvin*) so as to reserve the monopoly to the lord. Other products, such as beer (in England), had to be bought at the castle. Furthermore, there was a whole series of rights and monopolies that stemmed from the power to issue orders and to coerce (the word *ban* itself meant order[92]). The same holds true of the various dues pertaining to the use of forest and wasteland, the power to judge and the right to strike coinage, and so on. The ban was merely a new form of exploitation, which did not totally supplant the old forms but was added on top of rights of landed lordship that had fallen into desuetude.

Is there any reason to think that the mill, and the mill alone (along, perhaps, with the press[93]), benefitted the peasant? We have tried our hand at the game of quantitative history, notwithstanding the absurdity of the attempt as far the eleventh and twelfth centuries are concerned, in that so much of the economic data is unknown to us, the rationality we impute to the medieval peasant is to an absurd degree our own (at its best!), and the medieval notion of time (and labor time) is so different from ours—one is forced to do a good deal of hypothetical speculation. Assuming milling dues between one-tenth and one-twentieth and yields of between three and seven quintals per hectare per year (allowing for fallow periods), we made calculations in three cases, corresponding to three categories of peasants (case 1: "average" peasant; case 2: "rich" peasant; case 3: poor peasant). From our results it would seem that the banal mill was disadvantageous not only for the poor peasant but also for the average peasant, i.e., for more than 90 percent of the peasantry. It was not even clearly advantageous for the rich peasant! Furthermore, the hand mill was not the only one in use: allowing for the use of mills driven by donkeys or horses, always within the grasp of the rich peasant and in many cases of the "average" peasant—in the case of the donkey— particularly if the mill was collective or communal,[94] it becomes clear that the banal mill could only have been imposed by force, since it was almost never in the interest of the peasants, properly understood.

Finally, while the great water mills that were forced on the peasantry by the power of the ban, by coercive means, did indeed represent one form of technological progress (since they increased the productivity of the miller's labor), they were not the only possible form but rather the type enforced by existing social relations. Smaller horse-driven mills, to say nothing of small-scale water mills of the sort that ninth-century allodialists built collectively (usually, it would seem, with horizontal wheels, but in some cases·even with vertical wheels), could be situated close to where the peasants lived and operated with nearly equivalent technical efficiency. Far less costly to finance, such small mills would have obviated the need for time-consuming travel to the banal mill. But they were feasible only in conjunction with a social organization that allowed for collective practices. Large-scale milling machinery was inextricably bound up with the new feudalism. In sum, such machinery is the first in history to exemplify the fatal fascination exerted on our imaginations by productive apparatus conceived on a grand scale and forced upon men then as now by the existing relations of exploitation:[95] the reason for our fascination is that we mistake the machines actually constructed for the progressive solution to the problems of production, whereas the truth is that they are but one solution among others, one avenue along which the development of man's productive potential might have proceeded, and very likely not the optimum one even from the standpoint of production.

In an appendix to this chapter we have given some indications of the "proof" of our contentions concerning the relative cost of the banal mill for the peasants.

It is nonetheless true that the introduction of banal mills, ovens, and the like was experienced in very different ways by the wealthiest peasants, or *laboureurs*, and the poorest of their fellows. Fossier contends that the mill played a part in splitting the peasantry into two groups, ruining those who could not afford to pay the 10 percent additional dues.[96] More precisely, it must have squeezed the poor still more than before, while setting apart from the rest the 5 to 10 per cent of the peasantry that tended more and more to work for the market, owing to the relatively large size of their farms. Doubtless Parain is right to distinguish regions in which large-scale tenements were found from other areas. It is clear that the poor and average peasants were the ones who fought against the mills, and against whom the lords waged their long war.

Perhaps the most serious threat to the villager from the banal mill was that it imposed new limits on his independence. Indeed, once his *moulinet* was destroyed, the peasant was at the mercy of whoever owned the mill.[97] How then, if we allow for the dues, the time wasted in transport and waiting, the danger of thieves, and the cost of increased dependence, can we fail to see that it was plainly in the peasant's interest to hang on to his hand mill?[98]

The war of the mills itself makes clear where the interest of the peasants as against that of the masters lay: the smashing of the hand mill took eight centuries! No historian denies that this war was waged, and yet in the end only Bloch drew the unavoidable conclusion: technological progress was the fruit of harsh coercion by the lords. Perhaps the image of this war that sticks most firmly in mind is that of the abbot who paved the hall of his monastery with confiscated millstones.[99]

But why did this history unfold as it did? Why was it particularly in the eleventh and twelfth centuries that lords attempted to enforce the use of a new means of exploitation, the banal mill?

The spread of the water mill, we believe, should be seen as a reaction by the lords to the peasants' conquest of rights to their own tenements and reductions of the dues associated with the manorial system. The peasants won these victories in widely scattered and hard-fought contests over a troubled expanse of two centuries, the ninth and the tenth, a crucial phase, as was mentioned earlier,[100] in the class struggle of the peasantry. For the lords to respond as they did a new coalition of the masters (the feudal superstructure that supplanted the Carolingian attempt to rebuild the state) had to be forged. Seigniory in its new form was based on new ways of exploiting the peasantry, such as monopolies, the administration of justice, taxes connected with the exertion of political power, and Church tithes, rather than on the old dues associated with the tenure of land or *corvée* labor. These new means of exploitation, and in particular the mills, were introduced and imposed by force. By force and for the profit of the master, at the expense of the peasant and above all the poor peasant. Did the mill ultimately lead to an increase in the total product by dint of saving labor? Perhaps, but that was not why it was introduced! It was above all a way of redistributing income, increasing the surplus that accrued to the masters.

The peasants, of course, kept on fighting throughout the twelfth century. So far was this true that we may look upon charters of exemption, land-clearing, and new types of tenure (*cens, champart*) obtained in the twelfth century as a "peasant reaction" to seigniorial exactions[101] and to the spread of banal seigniory and economic monopolies. To my mind, however, these new charters, or contracts, are indications of the new (and temporary) balance of power rather than of a crucial phase of the struggle. Essentially they were a codification, a regularization of the various kinds of dues, limiting the lord's arbitrariness but at the same time crystallizing his rights and legitimating his exactions, which henceforth seemed to have been accepted by the masses and made objects of a contract, items of negotiation. The feudal mode of production had given rise to a solid political-legal superstructure. Socially, feudalism was based on systematic differentiation (the feudal hierarchy) and increasingly on the fragmentation of the peasant class. No longer did this superstructure overlay the mode of production described by Marx, with the natural rents and *corvée* labor associated with landed seigniory; rather it capped a complex weave of various modes of exploitation of the peasantry, in which banal seigniory, mills, and other monoplies, the administration of justice, the tallages, and the tithes of the Church played an essential part, albeit still founded on the master's indissociable rights over land and men.

What was the cause of this form of technological progress? The inroads made by the mills cannot be attributed to the role of the lord as coordinator of the common interests and promoter of increased productivity. Each phase in the advance of the water mill can be related to a prior modification of social relations and to the use of violence by the exploiting class in order to hold on to or increase the amount of its surplus. These were the reactions of the masters to the problems associated with each particular way of exploiting other men: in the third and fourth centuries, for example, when gang slavery suffered a first marked decline, again in the eleventh and twelfth centuries, when a flagging manorial system had to be replaced by a new means of extracting a surplus, and yet again when pressure to increase that surplus was felt at the time of the "feudal reaction," to say nothing of the fashioning of a new technique of exploitation with the gang slave system on the emergent great estates at the end of the Roman republic and in the early days of the empire.[102] Thus technological progress was a byproduct of social struggles, and the form that progress took was determined by social relations. The large-scale mills were not the only possible type of machinery, nor were they the most efficient socially or even technically. Their use, as against implements adapted to the family or collectivity, was enforced by the dominant social relations and by war.[103]

Appendix: The Banal Mill—Advantageous to
the Peasant or Not?

Calculations of the sort we are about to engage in are not to be taken literally. Our only purpose in carrying them out has been to show that historians have no reason for contending that the large-scale water mill, imposed by the power of the ban, was advantageous for the majority of the peasantry because it eliminated the "waste" of time involved in operating the family mill. The point, moreover, is not to criticize technological progress in itself! Rather, we wish merely to make explicit one step in a lengthy argument, several aspects of which were touched on in the Introduction:[104] technological progress is a by-product of social struggles; it was enforced by the masters in forms consistent with the then dominant social relations, either as a means of increasing the rate of exploitation (which had been reduced in consequence of class struggle by the exploited classes) or as a way of implementing a new form of exploitation (the old form having been destroyed by social conflict: this is the case with banal seigniory).

I. Dues of the Banal Mill

It is known that lords profited handsomely from their mills, and more generally from the power of the ban (mills, ovens, presses, cattle, to say nothing of the administration of justice and the power to strike coinage). Taken together, these profits came (during the eleventh and twelfth centuries) to account for a far larger share of the lord's income than the dues he received from his land. Duby cites the example of an estate on which the mill, oven, and gleaning dues yielded five times more corn than the peasant tenures.[105]

The profits derived from the power of the ban represented a heavy burden on the peasantry. Of course these profits varied widely from place to place. It would be interesting to know whether the variation in the total surplus product extracted (in seigniorial dues from land and from banal rights, as a percentage of the total product) was smaller, in other words, whether the rate of exploitation was to some degree "stable." It would also be interesting to know whether banal dues varied in compensatory fashion (when oven dues were high, for example, were milling dues low?).

For the south of France, we must allow a share of $1/16$ for the milling dues alone, and $1/20$ for oven dues. It is not out of the question that dues were (much) lower in the south, where banal seigniory was less deeply rooted, than in the north, where that form of social organization had supplanted a doubtless more stringent estate economy.[106] However, Guy Fourquin reports low milling dues for the region between Champagne and Burgundy, amounting to between $1/16$ and $1/24$ (but $1/8$ or $1/9$ for the press).[107] Fossier speaks of dues of 10 percent of the grain brought in for milling or baking.[108] For milling dues alone, J. Ellul gives a figure of $1/16$ of the grain, but he adds that sometimes the figure was much larger.[109] We hear talk of a mill tithe, and it would seem that dues as high as $1/6$(!) or $1/8$ were not unknown.[110] Let us assume dues between $1/20$ and $1/10$ for the banal mill.

To get some idea of the cost of milling to the peasant, however, we must add transportation costs (in terms of time lost en route to the mill). Distances to the banal mill were often great, and this was—and would long remain—a source of great discontent for the peasantry. The zone on which each mill drew (each large banal seigniory having several mills) was fixed at roughly the area within a radius equal to the distance that a donkey laden with grain could cover in half a day. To judge from the *cahiers de doléance* of 1789, however, it would seem that in some cases the distance to be covered was even greater. To this wasted time must be added time lost waiting at the mill, often considerable, to say nothing of the danger of being attacked along the way by thieves (the peasants often traveled in caravans). Sheaf after sheaf, this journey had to be repeated countless times (and the poor peasant might even be forced to carry his grain and flour on his back, unless he could borrow or hire his neighbor's donkey).

We shall give shortly an approximate estimate of the cost of transport and waiting. Also to be taken into account—perhaps the most important factor of all—is fraud by the millers. This seems to have been of great importance at all times. Against the multifarious variety of deceit and extortion the peasant had to face, he was virtually defenseless, since he could not monitor the milling and the miller helped himself to his share before returning the flour. Nor could he take his grain elsewhere or complain to the lord, who profited from the fraud, whether directly or indirectly (by increasing the dues paid by the miller). Fraud was one of the peasants' constant complaints, along with the time they wasted traveling back and forth to the mill.[111] How are we to evaluate its magnitude, since neither the tales of the peasants nor the protestations of honesty by the millers prove anything? Still, since conditions were extraordinarily favorable to fraud, how can we help believing that if the legal rate was $\frac{1}{16}$, the actual rate must have been something much nearer $\frac{1}{10}$!

II. The Time "Wasted" in Milling by Hand

To arrive at an estimate of what advantages use of the banal mill might have held for the peasant, we must of course begin by estimating the efficiency of hand mills, and then try to determine how much grain the peasant family consumed each day, hence how much needed to be milled. We shall see that to have a rough idea of how much bread per day might have been consumed by a monk, a prebendal, or a hireling is not enough. What we have to try to find out is how much a peasant family produced on a tenement of average size, large enough to be regarded as self-sufficient; more precisely, we want to know what the family had left after paying the lord of the land his due.

A) Efficiency of the Small Mill

What was the significance of "those long days once wasted" in milling grain by hand? "To see the extraordinary economy in manpower achieved by such a mill, it is only necessary to compare these figures [for water mills] with the quantity of corn ground by two slaves with a rotary hand-mill in one hour: 7 kilograms, or 70 kilograms in ten hours."[112] That is indeed a good deal of time! What are we to think about this yield?

Gimpel, it seems, took his data from a work by R. J. Forbes.[113] Caution is in order, of course, in making use of any such figures, because there were several types of hand mills.[114] Nothing will be said here about the old-fashioned back-and-forth mill. Rotary hand mills changed from one era to the next, and even in the same period we find many different kinds. To name a few, there was first of all the hourglass-shaped "classical" mill (found at Pompeii), which was very heavy, relatively inefficient, and almost always driven by a donkey or a horse, though sometimes by fugitive or rebellious slaves; there were mills with flat grindstones, which were lighter and more efficient; and similar mills with vertical cranks. Technically, these flat-stone mills are quite remarkable, surpassed only be gear-driven mills.

The gear-driven mill was perfected in the time of Vitruvius (first century B.C.). This,and not the use of water power, was the great innovation, since very ancient water mills are known. These, however, were equipped with horizontal wheels driving horizontal millstones with no speed reduction (direct transmission). Then, too, the Vitruvian system could be used in mills operated by slaves or soldiers. It has been possible to piece together a crank-driven geared mill of large scale: such a system may have been used where a mill was indispensable even though water was lacking (fortifications, for example). This type of hand mill could grind up to 100 kilograms of grain per hour with four to six men![115]

Did small mills of this type exist during the late empire? Technically they were feasible, and examples have been reconstructed (the so-called Saalburg mills). We find such mills in the Middle Ages. A well-known column capital in the Vézelay cathedral represents, as it seems to me, a small hand mill with vertical wheel of quite "modern" construction. We have a rather good idea of the yield of such mills, which were still in common use (without major changes) in the eighteenth century: 7.3 kilograms of flour per man-hour.[116] This is a very high figure, far too high for the typical twelfth-century case.

In fact, the mills used by peasant families during the eleventh and twelfth centuries were no doubt small and simple in design, and easy for one person to operate (frequently a woman, even an old woman). Roughly similar mills are still in use today in underdeveloped countries in the regions of "corn civilization." Then as now, a yield of between 3.5 and 4.5 kilograms of grain milled per man-hour seems a reasonable figure.

Alongside the hand mill, of course, the peasant could also make use of mills driven by donkeys or still larger mills driven by horses (in the latter case, this would have required collective ties or a fairly comfortable level of wealth). Such mills were predominant in the Roman Empire. A properly harnessed horse (for example, during the Middle Ages) can produce 35 kilograms of flour per hour,[117] and a donkey or mule approximately 80 percent as much.[118] Frequently peasants had at least the temporary use of a donkey. Granting this, the "long days spent in milling" largely evaporate! For the time being, however, let us set aside the possibility of using animal power, since we know that western peasants used the hand mill (when they could) until the eighteenth century.

To estimate the cost of hand milling, we must make allowance for the depreciation of the mill. The fact is that these mills, which were relatively simple to build, were not very costly[119] and, what is more, had an extremely long lifetime.

*B) Amount of Grain Set Aside
for Family Consumption*

How much grain had to be milled each day in order to produce enough bread to satisfy the requirements of daily consumption?[120] In 305 Diocletian set the daily wage of a worker not provided with board at 3.75 kilograms of grain, which corresponds to approximately the same weight of bread.[121] For seventeenth-century France, Fernand Braudel tells us, we must allow 12 quintals per family of 4 per year, or 3.3 kilograms per day, or perhaps less, since he also mentions a figure of one pound per person per day [122] We thus have an impression of a certain constancy of consumption over a very long period of time, with variations within a given period being primarily social. What was the situation in the early Middle Ages? Michel Rouche depicts a ravenous people, terrified at the thought of eating less than 1.5 to 1.7 kilograms of bread per day (in the Carolingian era).[123] For a family of two adults and four children,[124] this would come to 5.25 kilograms. Even higher figures are possible, up to seven kilograms of wheat bread for a family of hirelings in the year 800 or thereabouts.[125]

It is clearly impossible, however, to deduce the bread consumption of a peasant family from that of prebendals, monks, or hirelings. The family ate no more than it produced, often far less! It is difficult to say, moreover, just what a tenant farmer did produce.

The size of the tenement varied widely in all periods, as did the number of people a given plot of land had to support. Our calculations must accordingly allow for three cases. Given a family of two adults and four children, the amount of cultivable land available may have varied in many cases from as little as 1.5 hectares for the "medium poor" family to 3 hectares for the average family (sometimes said to be "well-off") to 10 hectares for the "rich" family.[126]

This leaves the problem of yields, to begin with in terms of the harvest/seed ratio: except for Carolingian times,[127] these values are relatively well known.[128] Though they varied considerably from one year to the next, it is possible to eliminate variations due to weather conditions, whereupon one arrives at a range of between 4 to 1 and 5 to 1 (or 3 to 1 and 6 to 1).[129] What this means in terms of yield per hectare is hard to say. We may assume, however, that it was customary to plant 2 quintals of seed per hectare. It would seem, then, that at best one hectare of land planted in wheat could have yielded 12 quintals; we will allow up to 14 quintals as a possible figure, and 5–6 quintals as a "worst case" (though in a "normal" year). Only half of the arable (or in some cases two-thirds) was under cultivation, however, while the rest lay fallow. This would give yields of only 3 to 7 quintals per hectare of arable per year.[130] (Seven quintals per hectare per year was no doubt possible in a "normal year" only if fields lay fallow just one year in three and were planted the other two years in crops that could be baked into bread, such as autumn wheat and a spring cereal.)

On these assumptions, we have the following table of corn production:

Corn Production		
Size of tenement	Annual yield per hectare(quintals/hectare)	
	3	5	7
1.5 ha	4.5	7.5	10.5
3 ha	9	15	21
10 ha	30	50	70

If we assume that the weight of bread obtained was equal to 80 percent of the weight of the grain and that the amount due the landlord (not counting banalities, multures in particular) was 15 percent,[131] we arrive at the potential daily consumption of bread per adult male and per family:

	Potential daily consumption (in kg.) for annual yield (quintals/hectare) (family consumption in parentheses)		
Size of tenement	3	5	7
1.5 ha	0.24(0.84)	0.4(1.4)	0.56(2)
3 ha	0.48(1.64)	0.8(2.8)	1.12(4)
10 ha	1.6(5.6)	2.72(9.5)	3.725(13)

Consumption of large quantities of bread (between 1.5 and 1.7 kilograms per adult male per day) was thus impossible where 3 hectares or less of land were available! Now, a plot of 3 hectares is sometimes said to be almost adequate, and some say such a plot was typical of the well-off peasant, in any case in all the northern provinces (in the south, peasant plots seem to have been larger). This allows nothing extra to feed an ox, however! We can drop the 1.5 hectare case: the ratios are too small to permit subsistence on the bread produced (in some cases the peasant could hire out his labor or live on what he could glean, eating honey or "roots" or what meat could be had without land—fowl, goats, acorn-fed pigs). On the other hand, with 10 hectares it is clear that more than enough grain could be grown to provide for home consumption (allowing some extra for oats for the horse, a variety of other foods for the family, and products for the market). If, however, we assume that a family of this size could live on 3 hectares between the tenth and twelfth centuries, we must accept consumption patterns of all three kinds. The poor peasant could not have eaten more than 750 grams of bread per adult male (if he managed to hire out his labor); he ate other things. The "average" peasant could hardly have eaten more than a kilogram of bread (which rules out the 3 quintal/hectare yield case as inadequate for survival, landing us back in the situation of the poor peasant). The rich peasant may have consumed up to 1.5 kilograms, but by virtue of his very wealth could have eaten other foods as well, thus consuming less than 1.2 kilograms per adult male.

Accordingly, we may assume that, allowing only for personal consumption the amount of grain to be milled was between 3 and 5 kilograms.

Thus the milling time per day was as follows:

Milling time per day		
	Amount milled per hour	
Amount to be milled	3.5 kg/hr	4.5kg/hr.
3 kg	51 min.	40 min.
5 kg	1 hr. 25 min.	1 hr. 6 min.

III. Estimation of Average Costs

If we accept the foregoing, we still have to evaluate the two average costs: one in terms of labor time lost in milling as a fraction of the total labor time devoted to cereal production for personal consumption, the other in terms of the fraction of the harvest paid to the lord for use of his mill.[132] A distinction must be made between this case and the case in which a nonnegligible fraction of the harvest is destined for sale on the market: did the peasant mill the grain intended for the market in order to sell flour? Certainly not. In consequence, the question of choosing whether to do the milling himself by hand or to take the grain to the banal mill did not arise for the fraction of his crop that he sold on the market.

A) Evaluating Labor and Transport Time

The two problems to be disposed of first are:

1. How to evaluate the labor time devoted to producing for personal consumption?

2. How to allow for the time (and risks) involved in transporting the grain from the farm to the banal mill?

The first question is the more important of the two. A sharp distinction must be made between two cases:

Case 1: The peasant family occupies 3 hectares of land. To obtain annual yields of 5–7 quintals per hectare from intensive cultivation[133] at a time when the use of animal traction was costly,[134] approximately 10 hours per day of adult male labor were needed,[135] which amounts to half-time employment for the entire family.[136] This would have yielded the 18 quintals needed (on average) for family consumption (after deducting what was due the landlord, one kilogram of bread per adult male per day would have been left).

Case 2: The peasant family occupies 10 hectares of land. Using a horse, the family is employed full-time. But how much time did it take to produce the 21 quintals needed, allowing for the landlord's dues, to provide 4 kilograms of bread per day for family consumption?[137]

Daily labor time of "rich" peasant for personal consumption, assuming yields (in quintals/hectare) of:		
3	5	7
14 hr.	8.24 hr.	6 hr.

It can be seen that on the average the same 10 hours are needed to produce enough grain for the family's consumption; in other words, half of the family's working time was devoted to meeting its own needs.

The second problem is to evaluate the time lost in travel. If a round trip with a loaded donkey required a full day, then with one donkey as many days would have been wasted as were needed to transport back and forth between 1100 and 1800 kilograms of grain per year.! This would mean between 150 and 200 hours for the poor or "average" peasant; the wealthier peasant, on the other hand, who would have had more efficient means of transportation at his disposal, could have made do with just a few trips (thirty-odd hours).

The time spent on the road may be deducted from the time spent in milling (or at least part of it can be, since the intensity of the two types of labor was not the same), because use of his own hand mill would have spared the peasant the time wasted in transport.[138] We then calculate the ratio of the time spent in milling at home minus the hours of transportation saved to the total labor time needed to produce the daily allotment of bread, and compare this to the ratio of milling dues to total grain crop.[139] Since even the dimension of the wasted time is problematic, however, let us begin by "ignoring" this factor.

B) Comparison of Average Costs (Home Milling versus Banal Milling), Neglecting Transport Time

1) The average fractional cost of home milling in labor terms:[140]

For ten hours per day labor devoted to cereal production for personal consumption	Daily milling time	
	51 min.	66 min.
	0.085	0.11

Hence the average fractional cost was in the vicinity of $\frac{1}{10}$, meaning that a peasant family that spent 10 hours per day growing the grain it needed added only one more hour in milling flour enough to meet its own consumption needs, whether the family was average or rich.

2) The average fractional cost of the banal mill, determined by the multure dues,[141] amounted, as we saw earlier, to between $\frac{1}{20}$ and $\frac{1}{10}$, in other words

$$0.05 < S_B/P_a < 0.10.$$

Thus the average fractional cost was $\frac{1}{15}$ or .066, i.e., $\frac{2}{3}$ of a sheaf in dues for every 10 sheaves grown.

It would seem, then, that the banal mill offered a slight advantage, because the peasant would have had to pay only $\frac{2}{3}$ of a sheaf out of every 10, while he would have had to devote an hour of labor to milling at home for every 10 hours devoted to growing grain. This result holds true for both "average" and "rich" peasants.[142]

C) Comparison of Average Costs, Allowing for Transport Time

Now the problem is to redo the above calculation but this time subtracting from the time required for hand milling the transport time to the banal mill, so as to arrive at a figure for the actual labor time saved by use of the banal mill. For the "average" peasant, we estimate the transportation and waiting time at 100 hours per year (or 16.5 minutes per day), and for the "rich" peasant at just 30 hours per year (or 5 minutes per day). Or for the "average" peasant, an average of 0.069, and for the "rich" peasant, an average of 0.087.

Average fractional labor cost, allowing for the cost of transportation to the banal mill[a]		
	Milling time	
	51 min.	66 min.
"Average" peasant	34.5/600 = 0.057	49.5/600 = 0.082
"Rich" peasant	45/600 = 0.075	60/600 = 0.1

[a]This is the ratio (cost of milling − cost of transport)/daily cereal consumption in labor terms. The daily cereal consumption embodies 10 hours of labor in the case of "rich" and "average" peasants. The time potentially saved by the banal mill (t) is, for the "average" peasant, between 34.5 and 49.5 minutes, and, for the "rich" peasant, between 45 minutes and 60 minutes.

In the case of the "average" peasant (case 1), we find that home milling involved a loss of time equal to the banal dues: less than 0.7 hours of labor/10 hours versus $\frac{2}{3}$ of a sheaf for every 10 sheaves on the average.

In the case of the "rich" peasant (case 2), the cost for home milling would have been 0.9 hours of labor/l0 hours on the average, versus the same $\frac{2}{3}$ of a sheaf per 10 sheaves in banal dues: thus the banal mill would have offered a slight advantage.

No allowance has been made, moreover, for fraud by the millers, which, as we mentioned earlier, raised the effective cost of the banal mill to one sheaf out of every 10. Granting this, it would have been in the interest not only of the average peasant, but even (to a lesser degree) of the rich peasant, to do his milling by hand.

D) Critique of the Foregoing Calculations

The above figures are practically meaningless! In fact the "average" peasant was not at all out to save time (bear in mind that the family was employed only half time). Rather, he had just one objective: to maximize his grain production. Two consequences follow from this: first, the need to travel to the banal mill and waste a hundred hours of his time was not in itself a problem; second, the time spent in milling by hand was not, in the eyes of the peasant, a cost comparable to that of handing over a portion of his crop to the lord in exchange for the use of his mill: in the one case, all that was being sacrificed was time otherwise wasted in underemployment, while in the other case the survival of the family was at stake!

By the same token, the problem for the rich peasant (whose family was occupied full time producing for its own needs as well as for the market) was to decide whether the time saved thanks to the banal mill could be put to productive use. In other words, could the net loss of 50 minutes per day entailed by hand milling be turned to other uses in such a way as to increase output by an amount greater than the cost of multure?

IV. A Calculation at the Margin

Could the time saved thanks to the banal mill be used to increase grain production by an amount greater than that which had to be handed over to the master of the ban in exchange for the use of his mill?

Case 1: The "average" peasant could not use the time saved by the banal mill in a productively efficient way. In other words, the marginal productivity of his labor was near zero, owing to the constraint imposed by lack of land.[143] Consequently, it was in his interest in every sense to mill by hand!

Case 2: If the family of the "rich" peasant was indeed employed full time, the time saved by using the landlord's mill would have been welcome, for it would have allowed an increase of production.[144] But the problem is to know how much of an increase? Everything depends on the marginal productivity of labor, the productivity of the last "hour" (the hour saved by the mill) applied to the land. There are two extreme cases: first, the case of very low marginal productivity, near zero (which is the situation of the "average" peasant), and, second, the case of marginal productivity equal to average productivity (i.e., the twentieth or twenty-first hour of labor on the same plot is just as efficient as the others).[145] The interesting cases are those that lie somewhere in between these two extremes, however.

To begin with we shall calculate the amount (in quintals of grain) to be paid out in banal dues in exchange for milling what the family needed for its own consumption. This figure will give us a minimum threshold that the production increase must exceed if use of the banal mill is to be worthwhile.

Once we have this figure in hand, we shall estimate the feasible increases in production on two assumptions: first, assuming a constant productivity of labor, and, second, assuming a marginal productivity equal to less than 40 percent of average productivity.

1. Amount of grain paid out as surplus product in the form of banal dues, or annual production increase needed to make use of the banal mill profitable for the peasant:[146]

If the milling dues are	The surplus product extracted (in quintals) will be[a]
1/20	1.05
1/15	1.40
1/10	2.10

[a]Daily family consumption of 4 kg. requires production of 21 quintals of grain per year, exclusive of production for market.

2. Additional product obtained thanks to labor time saved:

a. *Assuming constant labor productivity.*—This case is interesting only in that it allows us to check the results obtained via comparison of average costs.

Increase in output (constant productivity)			
Time saved by use of banal mill	Yield (quintal/hectare)		
	3	5	7
45 min./day, or 274 hr./yr.	1.12	1.87	2.62
60 min./day, or 365 hr./yr.	1.50	2.50	3.50

It may be seen that, except where yields per hectare are low and milling dues high, use of the banal mill offers the peasant a slight advantage. On the average, the banal mill will cost him a quintal and a half of grain, whereas the time saved would enable him to produce more than 2 quintals (2.18 q.).

b. *Assuming decreasing labor productivity.*—This is a more likely situation. There is no way of knowing, however, to what extent the twentieth hour is less productive than the average. Let us take an arbitrary figure of 40 percent. We then obtain the following results:

Increase in output (decreasing productivity: −40%)			
Time saved by use of banal mill:	Yield (quintals/hectare)		
	3	5	7
274 hr./year	0.67	1.12	1.57
365 hr./year	0.90	1.50	2.1

It may be seen that if the milling dues are average (1/15), productive use of the time saved by use of the banal mill will compensate the "rich" peasant only if yields are high (assuming the rich peasant has a good *moulinet*). If banal mill dues are high, he is always the loser! Thus, allowing for fraud by the miller, even the "rich" peasant must often have found it advantageous to do his own milling.

Perhaps we have arrived at this conclusion because we assumed too great a decrease in labor productivity. Suppose we change our figures and assume that the productivity of the twentieth hour is 20 percent lower than the average productivity, in the case where the "rich" peasant has a good *moulinet* (so that the banal mill enables him to save only 274 hours/year net) and yields are average (5 quintals per hectare). We find that multure costs are almost as much (1.4 quintals) as the peasant would gain by putting the time saved using the banal mill to productive use (1.49 quintals)!

Conclusion (to get away from economic computations)

1. First consider the case of the poor peasant (case 3), who has just 1.5 hectares and must try to hire out his labor power, glean what he can from the land, and eat honey and meat from what animals can be raised without land. Naturally if he failed to get himself hired full time (and, practically speaking, he always failed), it was wholly in his interest that he use his own *moulinet*, even if it was of the simplest and most old-fashioned kind imaginable (primitive grindstones, say). Nor did he make up his mind by calculating at the margin! It may well have been a question of survival. No doubt this was the most common case in the Middle Ages.[147]

2. For the "average" peasant (case 1), the banal mill was always catastrophic. Still, an "economic" argument is not enough to explain why the poor or "average" peasant repudiated the banal mill: only the long struggle waged against the mill stands as proof of its disadvantages for the overwhelming majority of the peasant population (probably between 90 percent and 97 percent).

3. Even in the case of the rich peasant (case 2), a "class" that accounted for no more than 3 to 5 per cent of the population in the eleventh and twelfth centuries, it has not been proved that the banal mill was advantageous! If crop yields were low, milling dues medium to high, fraud by the miller considerable, corn consumption relatively high, time saved by the banal mill low (whether because the *moulinet* was on the whole rather efficient or because too much time was wasted in traveling to the mill and waiting for the flour), and, finally, if labor productivity decreased at a "normal" rate, then—even for the "rich" peasant—the hand mill was "competitive."

Most important of all, for the rich peasant it was certainly within the realm of possibility to buy or build a donkey- or horse-driven mill. No doubt the cost of such an undertaking was not negligible (in contrast to the simple *moulinet*), but even allowing for depreciation of the apparatus, the rich peasant would almost always have found it advantageous to do his milling at home.

It becomes clear, then, that only force could have compelled most of these men to use the banal mill. Moreover, we know that all these small-scale mills—whether driven by hand, by donkey, or by horse—were remarkably tenacious. The landlords' battle to get rid of them lasted until the eighteenth century.

Through most of the twentieth century, poor and "average" peasants have done their woodcutting with handsaws. Why didn't they go to the sawmill? Nowadays they are all buying chain saws for the purpose. The high productivity of the industrial sawmill does not mean that it is advantageous for the peasant to use its services!

4. If horse-powered mills were within reach of the rich peasant, they were also within reach of a collective of poor or "average" peasants. Communal organizations and more limited forms of collective organization were, as we know, traditional[148] and consistent with an extensively organized rural social structure exhibiting strong "collective constraints" (as the liberals like to say).[149] These practices lasted until they were destroyed in the wake of the "feudal reaction" and the individualistic rural revolution of the eighteenth century.

As was mentioned earlier, these relatively small animal-powered mills could grind 35 kilograms per hour, or enough to feed ten families per day! Of course, unlike the *moulinet*, their cost of production was not negligible. It is clear, however, that such mills were socially the most efficient means of production. Even technically they must have been the best solution to the problem, since they would have reduced transport time.

Moreover, as we have seen, even small-scale water mills, perhaps of rather crude design, were within reach of peasant collectives. Had not such mills been built, after all, during the ninth and tenth centuries?

4

As for the cruelty visited upon the slaves, however, what we read is incredible: and what would we say if what we read were only the thousandth part of what actually occurred? For the authors keep their silence on this subject unless the occasion to speak presents itself. Slaves were made to work the earth in chains, as they still do in Barbary, and to sleep in ditches from which the ladders were withdrawn lest they run away, or set the house afire, or kill the masters.

Jean Bodin, *The Republic*

Class Struggles in Europe
(Third to Ninth Centuries)

 Struggle there was, and not only open, armed conflict, the great recorded uprisings of history, but also the silent, unending struggles that went on day in and day out. And these struggles involved not only slaves, but also free or subjugated peasants, landowners and tenants; on the other side there was the violence of the masters, who kept "two irons in the fire," playing one system of exploitation off against the other, making up for what the slaves won by subjugating the free peasants, to the point where all the peasantry came under the yoke, forming a class which, despite its infinite geographic variety, was relatively homogeneous. Though social conflict is the very substance of the history of class societies, only occasionally does the antagonism between exploiters and exploited take the form of open warfare. Class war is nothing other than the continuation of the running opposition between the classes by other means. But why does conflict flare into open warfare at a certain moment? What determines the balance of power between

the classes, and why does it evolve? Although the economy is crucial to the explanation of the bourgeoisie's new power at the time of the transition to capitalism, here its role is secondary. Instead, what must be studied is the crisis of the imperial state and the failure of the Carolingian attempt to restore it, for it was this decay of the state that tipped the balance of class power. However, the crisis and decay of the imperial state were determined by the developmental logic of a slave society. As slave relations of production developed and spread they produced their own negation in an inner dialectic of the class struggle, which necessarily involved the state (in its various phases: birth, consolidation, crisis, decay), since the state was the crucial determinant of the relative power of the classes.

I. Slaves and the Struggles of Others

Finley's argument[1] is interesting in that it gives prominence in its discussion of the end of slavery to a cause of quite another order than any thus far criticized.

Finley begins by distinguishing between chattel slaves (whether owned by private individuals or by the state, chattel slaves were those that could be bought, sold, and potentially set free) and other forms of dependent labor in some respects similar, such as the Spartan helots, for example. The helots were not free men, but they could not be bought or sold; they worked the land of the Spartans, and they replenished their own stock (unaided by razzias, war, and the like).[2] They stand as a clear instance of a subject people, of which antiquity knew several sorts, in many cases of vague legal status somewhere "between the free men and the slaves,"[3] particularly in the ancient Near East (Asia Minor, Syria, Egypt). Finley also shows that rural slavery, which soon became what we have been calling gang slavery, was quite different from urban slavery, for in the urban setting we find slaves with *peculium*, hence owners of property—and in some cases of slaves—and enjoying living conditions in actuality far superior to those of the dependent peasantry.

For present purposes this distinction between chattel slavery and other kinds of dependent labor is all the more necessary in that, according to Finley, slavery spread into the countryside wherever dependent labor proved insufficient to meet the needs of landowners: "a slave labour force was imported—for slaves are always in the first instance outsiders—only when the existing internal force became insufficient."[4] This was the case in Athens after the Solonic reforms, and it explains the absence of chattel slaves in Sparta, where the helots sufficed. Finally, it enables us to understand why "when Alexander and his successors, and later the Romans, conquered large portions of the old Near East," they did not establish a slave system in the countryside: the dependent peasantries were adequate.

On this view, in order to find the cause of the end of ancient slavery in the late empire, we should merely reverse the process by which slavery took hold.[5] The peasantry in Italy and, more generally, throughout the West was transformed to dependent status, so that slaves were no longer needed: the transformation of the small free peasant into a *colonus*, of free status but in fact a "slave of the soil," made the old slave gang useless: "Once upon a time the employers of labour in these regions imported slaves to meet their requirements. Now their own lower classes were available, as they had not been before, from compulsion, not from choice."[6]

How did this transformation take place? Finley attempts to argue that the evolution began as early as Augustus and became more pronounced in the second and especially in the third century: little by little the majority of citizens lost any place in public life, particularly in the army; two new categories emerged, the *honestiores* and the *humiliores*, with distinct legal status from the second century onward. In the countryside the costs that weighed upon small farmers ultimately became almost insupportable, as the growing needs of a bureaucratic state gave rise to higher—and very unjustly distributed—taxes. In addition, the peasants had to bear the consequences of a variety of troubles, particularly in the third century. Finally, "the combined effect of the various developments . . . —increasing taxation, depredations and devastations, depression in status as symbolized by the establishment in law of the category of *humiliores*—were to drive him [the peasant, whether an independent proprietor or a tenant] either into outlawry or into the arms of the nearest powerful landlord,"[7] hence at once into protection and oppression. Ultimately the law effectively tied to the land those peasants who had become strictly dependent on a master. The law did no more than legalize what was actually being practiced: the *coloni* supplanted the now useless slave gangs, thus explaining the radical transformation of the mode of exploitation in the third and fourth centuries (although, as Finley points out, there were still free peasants in Gaul in the fifth century and slaves in the sixth and seventh centuries, these he maintains were of secondary importance).

While this argument rightly gives prominence to relations between the classes, it does not succeed in explaining either the increasing dependence of the free peasants or the end of slavery. Class violence here gives way to a process in which the slaves are totally passive and the peasants unresponsive, and in which even the masters, the great landowners, seem to be bystanders rather than agents of the transition to dependence from which they were to profit. It is not enough to point to increased costs, chiefly in taxes, to explain how peasants were transformed into *coloni*. The great landlords and patrons became as we have seen protectors of all orders in the manner of *mafiosi*, offering protection against their own violence or against the violence of others of their ilk. In the end the peasant had no choice but to join the Bacaudae—but if he was recaptured he ran a serious risk of being burned alive—or to accept the protection of the magnates.

It is surprising to observe that Finley ultimately places the accent on the "iron law of absolutist bureaucracy that it grows both in numbers and in the expensiveness of its life-style."[8] Thus taxes increase and small peasants are subjugated (the comparison with another "absolutist bureaucracy" is more or less implicit). However, this account neglects the concentration of the *latifundia* (though Finley himself gives this point sharp prominence in his discussion) and the active role of the great landowners as expropriators and rulers. But the state and its increasing burden of ever more unjust taxes are but an instrument in the hands of this group.

What about the slaves? Were they completely passive? The landowners need slaves, and, lo, slavery is created; slaves are no longer needed, and, lo, slavery is done away with. On this view, by the third century masters no longer recruited slaves and no longer encouraged their slaves to reproduce, because now *coloni* were available.[9] The assumption is that the masters "preferred" this second system, preferred the *colonus* to the gang slave. One of two conclusions must follow: *either* one of the arguments examined in the preceding chapters is correct, *or* this "choice" was in one way or another forced on the masters by the slaves themselves!

Still more is this true in the case of domiciling. Finley's apparent belief to the contrary notwithstanding, slavery was still of considerable importance as late as the ninth century, and persisted in France until the eve of the tenth century and even later in Spain (though by then rural slavery was relatively unimportant). This fact is far from insignificant, for the slaves of the fourth through ninth centuries would become serfs by way of domiciling (a process that had already begun in the late empire, though no doubt domiciling was less common at that time than later). Granting this, it follows that it was not *because* the great landowner could call upon dependent peasants that he offered his former gang slaves tenements and dismantled the centralized apparatus for managing the work force. Rather, he must have been impelled or even compelled to do so either by interest or by fear. To invoke "interest" is to fall back into arguments of the sort rightly criticized by Finley, concerning the disadvantages of slavery in terms of productivity, profitability, demographic reproduction, and so on, while to invoke "fear" or "compulsion" can only lead us directly to the class struggles of the slave class, which go unmentioned in Finley's argument, at least as far as a cause of the end of slavery is concerned. And yet he does take note of slave uprisings, he mentions the Bacaudae, and he is aware that the peasant had no choice but to become an outlaw or a "protégé ." But it would seem that these struggles were without the slightest influence on the "end" of slavery.

In this perspective, finally, slaves are in some sense strangers to their own history, to the history of their living conditions; their struggles are "tempests in a teapot," said to be without consequence. The cause of the end of slavery lies "elsewhere," in relations among the "other classes." And conflict is even excluded when it comes to the study of those relations, replaced by a social (rather than an economic) mechanism, not to say a mechanism that is entirely superstructural ("the iron law of absolutist bureaucracies"). Still, it is important, we think, to hold on to one idea from Finley's argument: namely, that relations between masters and slaves cannot be studied independently of the relations between large landowners and free peasants. But this idea needs to be reformulated. The concentration of landholdings in the hands of a few and the emergence of the *colonate* are two aspects of a single problem, since in the late empire estates grew in size while the former (free) peasant remained on the land (rather than being sent as before into the city upon expropriation). This twofold process—pauperization and subjugation of the masses on one side, concentration of agricultural production on the other—was not accomplished by taxation alone; rather, violence by the magnates and their state underlay the trend toward consolidation of society into just two classes, with slaves and *humiliores* grouped together at the bottom.[10] On the one hand, this trend may have met with the favor of slaves whose real status rose nearer to that of the *humiliores;* on the other hand, even more important was the provision of a dependent work force to meet the needs of the masters, which can hardly be regarded as negligible. It is worth noting that Finley is mistaken in supposing that Roman society grew more diverse in the late empire, with *humiliores* coming to occupy a position in a "more extensive range of statuses" between free men and slaves. On the contrary, late republican and early imperial society was extremely differentiated (see above), and by this date the rural social structure actually had grown simpler: eventually there were just a few landed magnates and slave masters on one side[11] and the immense mass of the people on the other, a mass in reality enslaved, whether legally of free status with decentralized management (*coloni* on their tenements) or of servile status with centralized management (gang slavery). Domiciling, and later fusion of these two systems, ultimately gave rise to a kind of serfdom—let us call it a dependent peasantry—more or less everywhere.

Thus reformulated to give prominence to the role of conflict, the argument can be extended to the early Middle Ages. When (after a preliminary attempt at restoration of order) the trend toward "protection" of peasants resumes, the increasing number of protégés, tenants, and the like is inversely proportional to the decreasing number of slaves, even if the domiciling of slaves—the partial abandonment of gang slavery—cannot be explained in terms of peasant dependence.

No doubt the most interesting point about the Middle Ages, though, is that we may look upon the period as illustrating the reverse of the argument laid out above: we often find a strong free peasantry along with an enduring slave system. Thus after the peasant struggles and victories of the ninth to eleventh centuries, the reaction of the magnates took two forms: not only banal seigniory and monopoly, but also in some cases a return of sorts to patterns typical of the "slave system," with direct exploitation of a demesne if not increased in size then at least no smaller than before.

In this respect Spain offers a good illustration: slavery not only held its own there but was able later on to make a fresh start on solid new foundations. In the Christian part of Spain during the early Middle Ages, as Bloch points out, slavery remained a vital force and yet there was also a sturdy free peasantry and even a "peasant knighthood."[12] Then, too, Verlinden, observing the growth of slavery in Catalonia in the thirteenth century, has criticized Kovalevski's argument (explaining this growth as the result of a decrease in the size of the peasant work force, which Verlinden does not find) and points out, in passing as it were, that during this same period the peasant's rights in the soil were enhanced. Verlinden himself draws no conclusion from this, believing rather (in line with his general outlook) that the cause of this enhancement was connected with the Reconquista. Although unquestionably the analysis in terms of the labor supply (Verlinden's argument) should not be neglected, we believe that some attention must also be paid to the argument in terms of the need for a *dependent* work force (and not, as Kovalevski holds, in terms of demand for labor), which would associate the masters' reaction in reverting to the slave system with the victories won by the peasants.[13] Our belief is strengthened by the fact that Verlinden has also noted a decrease in the number of serfs in Provence during the same period,[14] forcing him to conclude that slavery in the region was on the rise.[15]

Similarly Georges Duby has noted the coexistence in Germany of active assemblies of free men and a vital slave system.[16] In Great Britain as early as the twelfth century the peasant saw his status lowered nearer to that of the slave; direct exploitation was on the rise, along with slave-type agriculture (particularly on ecclesiastical estates), while at the same time the social differentiation of the peasantry was heightened by a rise in the status of a well-off segment. In France itself after 1250 there was a growing tendency comparable to that noted in Great Britain in the twelfth century. Duby relates this "second serfdom" to the emancipation movement ("To set a few dirt farmers free was at the same time to point out that the rest were caught in the toils of servitude"), a movement associated with the differentiation of wealth: those who became wealthy could stand up more easily to the pressures of feudalism, while the new lower class was placed at a disadvantage, the poor being caught up "in ever tighter bonds of subordination." The notion of slavery itself was revived.[17]

Thus more or less everywhere in the West (though with noteworthy time lags and local variations), the peasant victories or, more precisely, the victories of the wealthier segment of the peasantry—culminated in and were stabilized by the emancipation movement, after which the feudal reaction led not only to a lowering of the poorest peasants to the status of slaves but also to centralized management of the quasi-servile work force and direct exploitation. This was a logical reaction, since the loss of seigniorial rights over the tenures—and the diminution of feudal rents and *corvées*—contributed to and even increased the importance of the demesne, which henceforth had to be exploited in a manner very similar to gang slavery. In the same period, moreover, the importance of another type of worker grew along with that of the slave—both working under centralized management, eating the master's food at his table, and sleeping in his barns: this was the hireling, the wage laborer, often a seasonal worker paid off with a "small coin" once the season was over (if everything had gone well). His pay was in part security for his labor, in part wages, in part severance benefit—once paid off he was free to die of hunger and cold somewhere down the road. In no sense was this rural wage labor progressive as compared with "serfdom." At the time the wage earner made his appearance, he was worse off than the slave of the *familia:* he was fed only when the master had need of his labor. The evolution from "serfdom" to wage labor was not a "positive" social development brought about by a victory of the exploited! What sort of struggle would have induced the tenant, or even the "serf," to accept the frightful lot of the hireling? But the victories of tenants, reflecting their advance toward property rights in their parcels of land, brought on the feudal reaction, which led to slavery and wage labor, to a return to one form or another of centralized management of the dependent work force, to gang labor.

Thus we find advances by the well-off peasants provoking a reaction by the lords, undermining the status of the poor, and giving rise either to a new slavery or to something like a wage labor system in the twelfth and thirteenth centuries; while in the late empire, as we saw earlier, subjugation of the masses of peasants in the West led to a downturn in slavery. What if Finley's causal account of these two social processes could be reversed? What if the *colonate* was made necessary by the struggles of slaves, casting that system now in the light of a reaction by the latifundists? And what if—following up this reversed argument—the landlords' violent triumph over the weakest segment of the peasantry and the subsequent opportunity to revert to the use of gang labor on the demesne made the emancipation movement possible by reducing to some degree the interest of the masters in their feudal rents?

As is evident from the foregoing, what remains interesting about Finley's argument, even after it has been reformulated, extended, and turned inside out, is its emphasis on tripolar relations. There is no proof, however, that the driving force lay in the relations between great landowners and free peasants: the slaves' own fight for freedom and domiciling, or for that matter the violent subjugation of the poor by the magnates, might just as well have caused the evolution of the relations between the free peasants and the great landowners.

II. Slave Struggles and the State

As we saw earlier, the overt struggle of the slave masses came to an end with the terrible repression that followed the defeat of Spartacus.[18] To be sure, the covert struggle continued, with rebellion breaking out in one *villa* or another, but until the uprisings in Gaul, Egypt, North Africa, and along the Danube during the late empire, it seemed that the slave question had been settled. What is more, the late imperial rebellions were of a new kind, whether, as in Gaul, the result of an alliance between peasants and slaves, or, as in places where gang slavery had not developed, the result of revolts by the *coloni*. Why, after such fierce struggles, this calm, this apparent apathy?

Some have explained the end of the slave wars by a change in the manner of reproducing the slave stock. The end of the wars of conquest and the decreasing importance of piracy are supposed to have made slave births the main source of slave labor,[19] and it is assumed that slaves who in most cases had never known freedom would be less likely to fight for it, unlike Eunus, Spartacus, and their allies, who had been born free and whose memories of freedom fed hope and spurred courage. This is a rather powerful argument, as well as a very old one.[20] Such a belief is the secret or avowed hope of the various "fascisms," and the constant, anguished fear of mankind. But the helots rebelled and they were not free by birth. In the Middle Ages as today we find serfs and dependent peasants unaware of any other station in life, and there are proletarians whose horizons are limited to those of their present circumstances and of their fathers before them. And yet they rebel. In the case in question here, moreover, razzias continued to a sufficient degree that there were always men of free birth to be found in the slave gangs, and memories of freedom, passed on from one generation to the next, were on the minds of all.

Some writers also make reference to the supposed solution of the agrarian problem: the abandonment of *latifundia* in favor of small and medium-sized farms, along with the associated changes in work methods. This argument is incorrect. Despite distributions of land to veterans, particularly at the time of the transition from the republic to the empire, property sizes were stabilized for only a short while, and we know that on the immense *latifundia* of Gaul, Brittany, Spain, and North Africa slave gangs continued to toil! It is sometimes said that the estate described by Columella was of relatively small size. In fact, as we have seen,[21] if we disregard the author's stated intentions, it becomes clear that he was describing a great estate. To be sure it was not one of the enormous *latifundia* typical of the late republic, with extensive husbandry using slaves chiefly in the capacity of shepherds (as was the case in Sicily at the time of the great revolts, between 140 and 100 B.C.). Rather, this was a coherent, centralized, and disciplined organization, which put to work large numbers of slave gangs. The masses of slaves were not split up among innumerable small farms.

In consequence, progress was made in the art of exploiting and controlling this manpower. These slave gangs were hardly allowed to work on their own. With a high degree of specialization, heightened surveillance, and, wherever reproduction of the work force was necessary, less brutal treatment of the slaves, this was a substantial system, built to last and clearly designed to extract surplus labor for the benefit of the masters; relegated to the past was that early form of slavery that might almost be called "improvised" or even "haphazard," which had come into being when large numbers of captives were "loosed" upon the Roman economy in the wake of the republican conquests.

The durability of the slave system, from this point on a genuine mode of production, was not secured merely by specialization of slave skills or by the surveillance carried out by the private police of the *villae*. Indeed, the slaves continued to fight in a less obvious but determined and steady way. To understand why this fighting did not flare into open warfare, we must take account of the existence of a strong centralized state, capable of coordinating repression throughout the empire.

A) The Constant, Covert Struggles

Overt rebellions by the slave masses, such as occurred in the early days of gang slavery (late republic) as well as in its final phases (late empire, early Middle Ages), were in the nature of momentary flare-ups, though as they became increasingly frequent and widespread they came more and more to typify fairly long periods of time. These open uprisings mark the emergence into the light of day, into "history," of day-to-day skirmishes in an endless war without decisive battles, a war waged by individuals and yet always ready to broaden into a common cause of multitudes, to become a mass struggle.

Of these silent struggles, especially in antiquity, we know nothing but what is reflected in the writings of the masters: the writings of agronomists like Columella, for example, who recommends that slaves not be mistreated in order to keep them from damaging tools, animals, or themselves, in order to prevent them from going crazy with despair and rising against their masters. He goes on to say that slaves should be watched closely to guard against sabotage and dawdling on the job. Even for his "well-treated" slaves, Columella recommends a prison discipline intended to forestall rebellion: as we have seen, he suggests keeping chained slaves at night in underground cells lighted by tiny windows so high off the ground that the slave cannot reach them with his hand. These prisons, the *ergastula*, were apparently found almost everywhere in the conquered regions (where slaves far outnumbered free men). All slaves in those areas were locked up at night, under the watchful eye of guards. Later on it was common to lock up only dangerous or rebellious slaves.

The *ergastula*, whether used as precautionary prisons for the entire slave gang or even more as punishment for "dangerous" individuals, are proof of the terrible fear of rebellion. As the slave system developed and spread over virtually the entire rural West (not to mention urban workshops), slave gangs began to be organized more efficiently, on a hierarchical basis, following the principle of "divide and rule," ultimately bringing into play all the paraphernalia of "voluntary" servitude,[22] which made it possible for the *villa* to function ordinarily in the absence of free men. But at the same time repression had to be made more severe. We know some of the methods used to torture rebels and *fugitivi:* shackled at the ankles, the slave had his left hand raised high above his head and clamped in an iron ring, and remained in that position for hours or days, sometimes being left there, "forgotten," until he died; others were placed in heavy iron collars that held their heads and both hands for long periods; still others were suspended over stakes topped with forks, so that the full weight of their bodies rested on the cervical vertebrae. Slaves might be thrown to moray eels, or mutilated in various ways: they were castrated, deprived of a hand or a foot, or crucified. Along with the other news Trimalchio received from his estate, news of such punishment was, it would seem, normal, commonplace.[23] And Juvenal depicts a great lady who had slaves crucified at pleasure.[24]

Then there is Apuleius' description of fugitive slaves working a mill: "All their skin was streaked by the purple lash of the whip, their battered backs shaded rather than covered by the shreds of their clothing! Some wore no more than a thin sash, but all could be seen naked through their rags—their foreheads were marked, their heads half-shaven, their feet clamped in iron rings; the pallor of their flesh was hideous to behold; the pupils of their eyes had been eaten away by the atmosphere of smoke and dark vapors, so that they were hardly able to see."[25] Generally, the slaves who worked in the worst conditions (like these in the scene described by Apuleius in the mines or quarries, or those who spent their lives on the *villae* in moving cages like squirrels or turning millstones) were being punished for escape, rebellion, or insolence. For example, Plautus describes one master who wanted to punish a slave: "Take him away, put him in strong and heavy chains. And after that you'll go to the stone quarry, and if the others have to cut eight stones a day, you'll do half again as many or they'll be calling you a man of a thousand lashes."[26]

We mention these tortures only to point out that it was not generally[27] out of sadism that the masters administered them. Especially during the late empire, when slaves were relatively expensive and reproduction was encouraged, the master had an interest in going easy on his work force: no one was worked to death as in the extermination camps. But the masters had constantly to fight against persistent covert rebellion. Otherwise, what would have been the point of all those *ergastula,* crosses, forks, quarries, and mines from which no slave presumed rebellious or dangerous emerged alive? What would have been the point of the common proverb, cited by Jean Bodin, that "a man has as many enemies as he has slaves"?[28]

The living conditions of slaves did not improve in the early Middle Ages.[29] The slave was in the first place a person who could be beaten or mutilated without the decision of a court, as his master willed. There were three types of punishment: whipping or beating, mutilation, and death. From barbarian laws we know that slaves could be beaten far more than stubborn animals would stand for. Facial mutilations had the advantage of being visible (excision of the nose, ears, or scalp) and thus exemplary. Punishment often took the form of castration. Were the masters thus willing to hamper the reproduction of the slave gang? Not at all—for reproduction was the business of the women, there obviously being more than enough males for the job in systems in which the conjugal family was not the primary setting for the production of children.

The supreme punishment, death, remained among the master's prerogatives and was almost always recognized as such by barbarian law.[30] Nor was death sharply distinguished from mutilation, as is proved by the following passage: "They may cut off their noses, ears, tongues, lips, feet, pluck out their eyes, or sever any part of their bodies whatsoever."[31]

Such savage measures were generally applied only in cases of escape, rebellion, or disobedience. If a slave had sexual relations with a free woman, the slave was immediately put to death (along with his partner). In the reverse situation, of course, this was not true: a free man could perfectly well have relations with his slaves (but only his female slaves!), thus combining pleasure with reproductive efficiency.

The very severity of the repression, even when we make all due allowance for the generalized brutality of the time, shows that in antiquity as in the Middle Ages there were always slave struggles, covert, persistent, and capable of flaring up into social conflagration only in exceptional instances.

In all periods, the ways in which slaves fought against their condition may be classified as follows:

1. Sabotage of tools: Roman masters, like slaveowners in the southern United States in the eighteenth century, had to choose tools made of particularly heavy and durable materials for their slaves.

2. Mistreatment of draft animals and livestock: Some speak of the "cruelty" of the slaves of the Roman *latifundia* (as well as the American plantations) in order to justify and account for that of the masters, whereas in reality this was one form of struggle.

3. Systematic work resistance: The slave tried to take as long as he could in doing his job, letting up or stopping work whenever the overseer's back was turned, which meant taking risks. Of course some

authors refer to this as proof of the "laziness" of slaves: the lazy Negro of the plantations is the counterpart of the slothful slave of the *villae* and the shiftless, flabby, indolent *corvée* laborer.[32]

4. Escape: From the abandoned *latifundia*, so commonplace, as we saw earlier, from the third century onward, to the Negro maroons of the Antilles, escape was the exact opposite of breaking off combat. In some cases the fugitive slave joined others in armed revolt against repression, as with the Bacaudae or the maroons. In others the slave managed to find work and enter into a new status, as with slaves who fled from a Roman or medieval *villa* and succeeded in obtaining a hut from another master, perhaps nearby, perhaps relatively far away from his old estate. Then, too, there were peasants subject to *corvée* who fled to the cities, and maroons who got themselves hired as free workers by employers not particularly attentive to their origins.

The *fugitivi* were the terror of legislators in the republic and empire alike. Always an outlaw who could be legally slain by anyone, subject to immediate return to his master (severe punishments were meted out to anyone who hid a fugitive and did not denounce him, such a person being known as an *occultator*, or concealer of men), the fugitive slave was generally put to death. Augustus, who restored a strict law and order, distinguished himself by inflicting particularly cruel punishment in 36 B.C. on *fugitivi* who had joined Pompey in Sicily or Sardinia.[33] In the late empire penalties for the *occultator* were stiffened, and the term *fugitivus* was broadened to apply to *coloni*, as was the law regarding fugitive slaves.[34] Similarly, attempted escapes were brutally punished in the early Middle Ages. An entire book of the Visigothic codes is devoted to this problem alone!

How significant were escapes? In ordinary times they were confined largely to efforts by individuals or small groups, but at other times, as in the crisis of the third century, during the period when the Bacaudae were active, in the collapse of the fifth century, or the widespread crisis at the end of the Carolingian reign around the turn of the tenth century, the problem of escape assumed considerable proportions, aggravated by wave after wave of invasions, and gave rise to the social phenomenon referred to as *agri deserti* (thus accounting for the appeal to the barbarians[35]).

5. Self-mutilation or self-destruction: Again, some authors speak of the slaves' "barbaric cruelty" or courage. In slave systems generally, these forms of protest are practiced chiefly by the "free-born."

6. Refusal to procreate, abortion, or infanticide: Rejection of reproduction seems to have been common among slaves in the early Middle Ages.[36]

7. Theft and pilferage: Finally, pillage of one sort or another, devastation and burning of harvests, was a weapon of slaves.

The term "sabotage" serves rather well as a general characterization of all these forms of protest (sabotage of constant capital, of the product, of the slave's own future yield, and of himself as an item of variable capital). Sabotage of this sort was common only among gang slaves (in the countryside and in slave-run mines and factories), not among urban slaves (craftsmen, members of what we call the liberal professions), whose actual situation could be quite different (as Finley points out, "the *terra sigillata* ware of Arezzo, made by slaves, was much finer than the products of the free potters of Lezoux," and "no one can distinguish, in the ruins of the Erechtheum, which mouldings were carved by Simias, which by his five slaves"[37]). When the time of the great uprisings came, moreover, these urban slaves not only did not as a rule rebel, but often fought alongside their masters[38] (showing how effective were the various divisions within the slave group). Covert struggles were not always serious in the same degree: it would seem that when it became necessary to do away with the "concentration camp" system and replace it with a system allowing for internal reproduction, the masters must have been forced to make changes in the nature of their oppression, and there is no way of telling how much this new "mildness"—coupled with the fact that now most slaves were not free-born—may have served to temper the covert class war.

Not all social conflict ended with the shift to domiciling and serfdom: the scene shifted now to the dependent peasantry of the western Middle Ages, and the nature of the combat adapted to the new situation. Le Goff points out that the typical form of peasant warfare was "covert guerrilla action in the nature of petty thievery on the landlord's property, poaching in his forests, burning of his harvests. It involved passive resistance through sabotage of the *corvées* and refusal to pay dues in kind and taxes. And it sometimes took the form of desertion, of escape."[39] These are methods used by oppressed peasants everywhere, in China for example, as Jean Chesnaux has pointed out, where peasants relied on slow but steady pressure (through insubordination and sporadic attacks), which "could all at once burst forth in a violent explosion: mass peasant uprisings and peasant wars on a national scale."[40] It is not surprising then that we find slaves on the plantations of the United States and the Antilles[41] engaging in almost the same kinds of combat as their "ancestors," the Roman and medieval slaves.

It is important to stress the fact that the economic struggle cannot be separated from the ideological struggle, to say nothing of the political struggle ("economic" and "political" are to be interpreted broadly, in a sense appropriate to the era in question).[42]

Consider Columella's recommendations (copied from Cato) concerning the religious practices of the steward and the other slaves. He points to the dangerous influence of astrologers, soothsayers, and the like, laying it down in book i that the *villicus* "shall make no sacrifices without orders from his master. He shall receive neither soothsayers nor magicians, who take advantage of men's superstitions to lead them into crime."[43] He takes this question up again in book xi: "He shall shun familiarity with haruspices and sorcerers, two sorts of people who infect ignorant souls with the poison of baseless superstition."[44] The meaning of this advice will become clearer if we can detect in it signs of the ideological warfare waged by slaves in the late republic, during the brief period when the rebellious slaves had the upper hand.

The Sicilian slave wars of the period between 140 and 100 B.C. are relatively well known thanks to books 34–36 of the *Historical Library* of Diodorus of Sicily, who, it seems, reproduced almost verbatim the nearly contemporary account of the Stoic Posidonius of Apamea.[45] Apparently, certain philosophies or religions encouraged slaves to fight either by inspiring in them a preference for rebellion and death over slavery or by holding out the hope of establishing a kingdom in this world.

This may have been the case with the heretical versions of Stoicism inspired in one degree or another by the teaching of Blossius of Cumae. An egalitarian Stoic, Blossius was banished from Rome in 133 because of the subversive aspects of his doctrine. He then went to Asia Minor, where preparations were under way for a slave insurrection, the goal of which was to establish the City of Sun, a city in which the strictly egalitarian preachings of the Stoic would be realized. Admittedly it is far from certain that the Sicilian rebels were familiar with this utopia. There is some reason to think that certain egalitarian Stoics used this rebellion as an example not to emulate but to meditate upon.

Far more clear-cut was the role of a number of oriental creeds or religions involving initiatory rites of a relatively simple sort. In studying them one cannot help making the comparison with voodoo, which would be practiced many centuries later by Haitian slaves (among others). The religion practiced by the Sicilian slaves of that period was quite different from the religion practiced in the cities; prayer had the opposite orientation! The principal divinity of the Sicilian slave religion was the Syrian goddess Atargatis. Rather than ask her to maintain the status quo, i.e., the social and political order (as did the official cults in the cities), the worshippers of Atargatis prayed to her to tip the balance of power in their favor and to give them the courage to rebel.

The slave cult was inspired and spread by a slave, Eunus. He may have brought the religion with him full-blown from his native Syria. Eunus began, it seems, by recounting his dreams to other slaves. Later he claimed to have been vouchsafed revelations, even while awake, and ultimately contrived by straightforward and effective means to perform miracles.[46] Obviously he was unable to create either priests or sanctuaries. His preaching was limited to the coming of a slave kingdom, of which he was to be king. This prophecy was apt to amuse the masters, from whom he did not conceal it, and doubtless this openness was an important factor in the hopes of the slaves and in their temporary victory.

Although in his account of the second insurrection Diodorus of Sicily tells us much less about the religious practices of the leaders of the rebellion, we do learn that they elected as their king one Salvius, an expert in the art of soothsaying and a flutist. With good reason J.-P. Brisson regards this as sufficient evidence to view Salvius, too, as a prophet, probably of a slave kingdom promised by the gods.[47] The beliefs of Eunus and his comrades had most likely not disappeared, perhaps being kept alive by the glorious memories of victory thirty years earlier that many slaves must have harbored. In a similar vein, Spartacus was aided by a woman, a sort of medium in the Dionysiac orgies, who was capable of interpreting his dreams and of engaging in divination,[48] skills which seem to have contributed to her authority over her comrades and emboldened their actions.

It is beyond doubt that such cults, philosophies, and adepts of sorcery and divination were always to be found in the *familiae* of the empire. Popular and particularly slave religions have been studied in great detail, especially by E. M. Schtajerman.[49] These studies have shown that the important traditional divinities were rather indifferent to slaves, who preferred the lares or Silvanus, the god of the forests and brushland. Oriental religions, in particular the cults of Hercules and Mithra, made deep inroads into the slave masses, and research has thrown light on their anti-Roman, emancipatory, and egalitarian ideology, as well as their hostility to the official cults, the cults of the masters. In particular, it should be noted that labor, which was held in contempt by the dominant classes, was respected by the popular cults when freely performed. Schtajerman has shown in detail how these cults and practices correspond to a class mentality: a clear-cut ideology of social combat and liberation emerges from them.

But there was battle over religion: the masters tried to integrate their slaves into the *collegia*, admitting them to the altar of the familial cults. In doing so they hoped and often managed—to bind the *familia* more tightly together, ward off subversion, and encourage an honest day's labor. Thus it would be quite wrong to conceive of two distinct ideological blocs: ideological conflict was itself responsible for interpenetration, whether by propagating oriental cults among the free population (chiefly of course among the poor because their actual condition fell nearer to that of slaves, but also among the masters) or by integrating slaves into the family religion. Upon transmission from one class to another, however, the content of the message was altered and even reversed. What we see is cooptation of slave religion and a reversal of its message.

Accordingly, we have rejected the idea that Christianity played an important role in the liberation of slaves. From the time of the conversion of the aristocracy and the later Roman emperors onward, Christianity was a religion of the masters, which preached passivity and the expectation of liberation in the hereafter; the more obedient the slave had been in this world, the more likely his liberation in the next. But the message that had earlier been current among slaves was possibly of a quite different sort, probably openly subversive. Of this we cannot hope to gain more than a faint impression from a few scattered passages or sentences, so thoroughly has it been expunged from the written record.

What was the place of covert struggle in the repeated "ends" of slavery? First and perhaps foremost, without this steadfast refusal to give in, without this day-to-day battle, violent uprisings would have been impossible (and conversely, hope of the great rebellion, of winning freedom in a mass uprising, kept the slave from "taking it lying down" and asking "what's the use?"). As Chesneaux has written, "the dialectical unity of the continuous and the discontinuous is a central thread of all history."[50]

Furthermore, once this struggle has been brought to the fore, we come once again face to face with the arguments put forward by the proponents of economic, technological, and demographic determinism.

Sabotage invariably decreases the intensity and productivity of labor, destroys constant and variable capital, and ultimately decreases the rate of exploitation.[51] The cost of surveillance, which is needed to guard against these losses to some extent, is likewise a hidden cost that decreases the surplus accruing to the master. Indeed, it is true that the slave system can become less profitable than other forms of exploitation, such as serfdom, but everything depends on the relative importance of class struggles. Moreover, as Marx noted long ago, the costs of surveillance associated with class conflict alone are highest in slavery because slavery exacerbates conflict between the classes to the full.[52] He also explained that slaves who engage in sabotage, mistreat animals, and so on are embattled workers; only an interpretation of this kind, as Marx points out, can shed light on why slavery is an inferior system from the masters' standpoint, once class conflict has made it "unprofitable."

Similarly, while it is true that birth rates are often low in slave systems, this is not so in virtue of some natural law according to which men, like animals, reproduce less well when caged. Rather, low birth rates are the result of such practices as infanticide (comparable to self-mutilation and self-destruction) and refusal to procreate, which are ways of fighting against the master. But the demographic question is bound up primarily with the question of slave hunting. As we have seen, razzias continued and even grew in importance (the captives of the barbarians, as the saying goes, replaced the captive barbarians), and this tends to limit the import of the explanation that slavery came to an end because the supply of slaves fell. But the wars of conquest and the raids of pirates and slave traders depopulated vast portions of the known world, particularly in regions along the borders (internal and external) of the empire. One has only to think of Caesar capturing perhaps a million slaves in Gaul or of those barbarians who were systematically starved by the Thracian authorities so that they would be forced to sell their children into slavery (in 376).[53] To take some more recent examples, consider the Franks of Charlemagne depopulating Bohemia and Saxony or the huge numbers of Slavs seized in northern and eastern Europe. Europe, North Africa, and the Near East were obliged to pay a terrible tribute in men, which left them drained of their life's blood. In all the history of slavery the only comparable genocide occurred between the sixteenth and late eighteenth centuries, when Africa was drained of its manhood by the slave trade. When, moreover, the violence of the masters and their suppliers was met by embattled slaves refusing to reproduce the work force, slaves became scarce, but scarcity was a result of struggle—of a battle to the death—between master and slave or potential slave, and similarly escape and rebellion made slaves scarce on the *villae*.

Reinterpreting arguments based on productivity, profitability, or demography in terms of social conflict does not eliminate the criticisms we gave of them in chapter 2. However, such a reinterpretation does enable us to make use of whatever explanatory value they do have.

Having said this, may we go on to say that slavery disappeared because it was no longer profitable and that it was no longer profitable because of the class struggle waged by the slaves? Not exactly, because the word "profitable" refers to an economic calculation of some sort. It is my belief that the masters could no longer keep hold of their slaves: they scarcely had a choice, in the proper sense, which is too bad for the economists!

Since one of the most common ways of fighting against the slave system was that adopted by the *servus fugitivus*,[54] individual or collective escape, or *marronage*, to use a term from the Antilles,[55] and since this form of struggle was responsible for the *agri deserti* of the late empire and gave rise to brigandage, the masters responded either by making increased use of *coloni*, i.e., of effectively subjugated peasants (particularly in the late empire), or by agreeing to domiciling (perhaps the most important response in the Middle Ages), for which the slaves were fighting. Indeed, allowing slaves to have a family attached them more firmly to the soil than any authoritarian legislation. The main point was not to make slaves procreate more efficiently in order to make up for the lack of manpower, or, in other words, to counter the high price of slaves. Rather, it was to attach slaves to the *villa* by incorporating them in families, which of necessity were far less tempted by flight, and by weakening their resolve with "responsibilities" accorded to the father and family head, which amounted to holding his wife and children hostage.

The tenement given to the slave by the master played the same role: it gave him something to lose. This made the slave weak. Nor was it the only cause of weakness, as we shall see: domiciling, won in struggle by slaves, was the basis of a certain "serialization" of the *servi casati* and before long of the serfs.

The method chosen by the masters was not altogether effective, of course, and large-scale escapes by *coloni* or serfs were not unknown in the late empire and early Middle Ages. The term *fugitivus* was even extended to "escaped" *coloni*, and severe penalties were meted out not only to the escapee but also to the *occultator*, or person who concealed or gave shelter to a fugitive.[56] Moreover, during the late empire escape was at its height,[57] involving not only *coloni* but also *corporati* of the urban guilds, soldiers, and even *curiales*. Similarly, serfs fled their manors throughout the Middle Ages. Where did they seek refuge? Jean Gagé lays stress on religious refuge during the late empire including the early forms of monasticism, anchoritism, and group asceticism[58]—thus the first "monks" of Lérins, the *monachi*, who disappeared into the forest. They were not alone: throughout the period that begins in third-century Gaul with the Bacaudae and continues until the feudal stabilization after the year 1000, the forests, brushland, and mountains were in the hands of armed bands of brigands."

Still, even though the shift to *coloni* and to domiciling was not enough to tie the subjugated work force to the soil, it should be borne in mind that the masters had no choice: this new technique for exploiting men and therefore land was their only hope of maintaining some control over the work force. Once the state collapsed, they had even less choice: centralized exploitation of workers became impossible. With this observation we come back to the question of the relations between the state and gang slavery.

B) From Slave Gangs to the State

The republican state, the city-state, lacking taxes and a standing army, small in size, and having virtually no bureaucracy, is an intermediate stage between clan society (which is not strictly classless; rather, the components that will ultimately develop into classes are associated with particular families) and the mature form of class society. This accounts for the fragility of this form of government, as well as for the civil conflicts (totally different from those that would rock the late empire) and slave wars that disrupted the city-state, standing at the crossroads between a declining clan system and a rising class system.

It was this republican system, along with the city-state, that produced Roman imperialism (most of the conquests were complete by the end of the republic) and its derivative slave system (although families had held slaves at an earlier date[59]). It was not the strength of the republic that drove Rome to rule the world (as the cliché would have it), but rather its internal contradictions that were the driving force behind Roman expansion, which was carried out by citizen-peasant smallholders who would soon find themselves landless for the sole profit of the great warrior families, whose power the citizenry would later challenge, in vain. Imperialism and the slave system ruined the smallholders and led to their expropriation and humiliation (turning them into that "vile mob," the idle Roman plebs, of which Marx speaks), and later to their loss of all political power and soon thereafter to their enslavement on a vast scale.

If the republican system gave rise to imperialism and the slave system, and hence permitted class society to mature, its state superstructure would seem to have been strictly incompatible with the social relations of the empire. To keep a rein on the provinces, a powerful repressive apparatus was needed at the center: many historians have pointed to the contradiction between the conquest of the world by a city-state and the impossibility of holding on to that conquest without transforming the city into the capital of an empire. Furthermore, in order to cope with slavery on a vast scale, coordinated repression by a "modern" centralized state was needed. The rebellious masses of slaves of the late republic were opposed only by the modest repressive apparatus held in private hands. If rebellion succeeded for local reasons in a particular *villa*, it spread immediately, winning certain victories everywhere (the master's guards could not do much once the masses had risen in open revolt and were helpless if the slaves had already taken control of some other *villa*). We see this situation occur in Sicily on two occasions and again with Spartacus, whose revolt began with just a few gladiators!

This incompatibility between the conquered empire and the new social relations, on the one hand, and the city-state, on the other hand, does not, in our view, signify that the state necessarily had to adapt itself to the new relations. The possibility of a central state had to exist. This raises the prior question of the social base of this future imperial state. Had relations among the other social strata or classes precluded the emergence of the imperial state, the slaves could have won their victory and eliminated slave relations sooner than they did.

Rebellion itself helped give concrete shape to the social foundations of the new type of state, not only by suppressing rivalries between the two dominant groups or classes (senators and equestrians), but also by unifying against the slaves the whole of the free citizenry, the masses of nonslaves that had been challenging (from the time of the Gracchi onward) the power of the great. Nowadays it should present no difficulty to imagine the fear the Romans felt when Spartacus marched on Rome, a fear skillfully orchestrated by clever propaganda designed to awaken terror in the populace. Around what theme? It is of course difficult today to plumb the minds of the rebel slaves. What did they want? The written record does not prove much: the slaves of that era were making history, not writing it! One thing is certain: as slaves, they wanted to win back their freedom, they wanted a city of their own (i.e., a community) and land to cultivate (but we must beware of projecting our own individualistic notions onto them: they wanted land, but they wanted to work it according to the then current collective structures of peasant communes). The basis of their community was to be the family farm (and once again, family is a slippery word for us: in this context it refers neither to the couple nor to the nuclear family in the narrow sense, but rather to a broad network of relations having to do once again with the clan). As foreigners, they would have wanted to establish their community in their own homeland and reestablish ties with their families and their religions: if, however, such a return proved impossible, Sicily (where they rose in rebellion and where Spartacus tried to head) could have served as home to their renaissance, to the attempt to establish social relations typical of the free peasantries of antiquity.

But what do the experts tell us? Not only that the slaves did not want to abolish slavery as an institution[60]—a point we are willing to concede, since such a level of analysis or consciousness is not easy to achieve in battle—but also that they merely wanted to reverse the position of master and slave, putting themselves on top and the Romans underfoot. That a spirit of revenge did exist (Spartacus organized a huge gladiatorial contest using soldiers taken prisoner[61]), that there was a need to use festivals and games to embody symbolically the "upside down world," and that many accepted the idea that a prisoner might be made a slave are to be expected; but to impute to the masses of slaves the design (I do not say the desire) to turn the tables in this way is merely to set oneself up as continuator of the propaganda of the master class. And it was an astute propaganda, evoking anxieties which were the inverted counterpart of the desires of the slaves. Not only was it astute, it was also effective: the slaves were unable to achieve the coalition they sought with the lower strata of free men.

If the propaganda of the ruling class was effective, however, it was only because the objective situation in which the lowest of the free men found themselves was utterly different from servitude. These men feared the rebel slaves because they stood to lose their civic rights, various benefits of imperialism and the slave system, and even in many cases their land. And they were made to believe that they were in danger of losing their liberty as well. The fact that there was no objective basis for an alliance between them and the rebel slaves is proof that there was a social basis for the imperial state then in embryo.

The new state—the imperial slave state forged by Caesar and Octavian, not, as we saw earlier, just the Roman state, but also the state of the dominant class (which was more than just Roman, and which became less and less Roman as time went by) born of the fusion of senators and equestrians, broadly based on a systematically organized hierarchy of social distinctions welded together by imperialist ideology and fear of slaves and barbarians—this state, with its standing armies stationed throughout the empire, its tax system, and its bureaucracy, symbolizes the impossibility of the slaves' achieving their aims through overt struggle. The inception of the imperial state marks the end of such tactics. Of necessity slaves were divided up into gangs, and an uprising in any one *villa* would be met very quickly not only by the private guards on the estate but also by the police and the army, agencies of the state in its role as the coordinator of repression. Under the state run by the masters, moreover, no large-scale uprising was even imaginable, for there was no central organization of slaves and all contact between one gang and another was forbidden. This being the case, trouble on a single *villa* amounted to no more than a common police matter, a "family" affair.

C) From the Decline of the State to the
End of the Slave Gangs

In the absence of a genuine central state, a master will not run the risk of maintaining a large gang of slaves, for to do so would leave him alone with his guards (a force necessarily limited and not necessarily reliable) to face the concentrated power of an adversary capable of being readily organized for rebellion. With this in mind, the weakness of a fragmented work force, as well as the advantage of concentration and centralization, appears in a new light.

Plato understood this quite well. In the *Republic*[62] he explains that a master who owns many slaves in the city runs no risk on that account, because in case of rebellion "the entire city is ready to defend each citizen," in other words, because the state of free men ("that is, of the masters"[63]) exists as an organ of repression. On the other hand, the *isolated* master runs an extreme risk if he does not follow the precept "divide and rule": "And would he not forthwith find it necessary to fawn upon some of the slaves and make them many promises and emancipate them, though nothing would be further from his wish? And so he would turn out to be the flatterer of his own servants."[64] Indeed, a master wafted away into the "desert," far from the aid of his fellows, from the support of the masters' state, "would certainly have to [flatter his servants], or else perish."[65]

The same Plato explains in the *Laws* that, owing to the threat of rebellion, the ownership of "human animals" is a "perplexing" problem, especially when the slaves are "all of one stock." Accordingly, "only two courses" are left open to the masters: either they must treat the slaves "properly," or they must take care to see that slaves "who are to submit to their condition quietly should neither be all of one stock, nor, as far as possible, of one speech."[66]

The crisis of the imperial state in the third century, followed by its disintegration in the fourth and fifth centuries, could not help but modify the relative power of center and periphery (both inside the empire and along its borders), as well as the relative power of masters and slaves. Indeed, we once again find overt mass risings (quite different, to be sure, from those of the first century B.C.), some of them successful.[67] A historian like Fossier does not understand this, as is evident when he writes, quite characteristically, that it is not clear why the collapse of Roman authority should have altered the situation with regard to slavery![68]

The slaves rose, then, and their rebellion met with some success, incomplete to be sure, sometimes impermanent, sometimes won back after temporary loss. Above all, their successes had the contradictory consequence of weakening their position, thereby allowing the masters to regroup and consolidate their power, to continue their exploitation by changing its form.

We have seen what the slaves who rebelled in the first century B.C. aimed to achieve. These aims had not much changed in the interim. What must be understood is that to obtain a tenement, even though one's status remained servile, to obtain the power to dispose of a portion of one's own labor time, even if part of what was produced had to be given to the master and even if the rest of one's time was given over to *corvées*, and thus to something very like slave labor—to win these concessions was a noteworthy victory in the social war. It was, as Duby has written, "one of the major events in the history of labor,"[69] and above all one of the greatest victories of the exploited. To be sure, the slaves did not become peasant proprietors or even free tenants, but who was free when everywhere (or nearly so) the majority of peasants were exploited in one way or another? The fact is that the slaves succeeded in raising themselves nearly to the level of the *coloni*.

The counterpart of the power of slaves concentrated in gangs was the weakness of peasant proprietors or individual tenants, a weakness not lessened by the persistence of the peasant "commune." Individual smallholders were often isolated, divided, and therefore weak in the face of the landlord's violence, owing to the very conditions in which they labored. Once slaves had won the right to huts of their own, they drew nearer in respect of their relative weakness too to other rural laborers. The slave family, domiciled on its own tenement, was "serialized," hence weak. The victory of the exploited, which was won thanks to the new balance of power, tipped that balance in favor of the masters.

There were those in the Middle Ages who sought intentionally to maintain this serialization of the serfs, one proof of which may be seen in the fight against *conjurations*, or sworn conspiracies. It should not be forgotten that the Church at this time took a very grave view of the oath and that Charlemagne had forbidden the swearing of oaths except in courts of law or to bind oneself to a superior: oaths sworn among equals were to be avoided at all cost. What frightened the emperor's counselors was the formation of associations of peasants through the swearing of mutual oaths.[70]

This does not mean that huts and tenements were readily granted to slaves by their masters. Would it be correct, however, to say that what we might nowadays call the "advanced" segment of the master class understood relatively quickly that the decrepit state could no longer effectively carry out its repressive functions and that therefore central-ized management of the work force had to be abandoned? Whatever the relative importance of class struggle as against recognition by the masters of their own interest given the new spectrum of possibilities, everything depends on a shift in the balance of power which was connected with the "end" of the imperial state, and all factors contributed to this shift. "Divide and rule" had always been an important precept in managing the slave system of the *villae*. Nevertheless, the masters had been willing to allow masses of slaves to eat together, sleep together, and work to-gether. The social, technical, and hierarchical division of labor was im-portant, but it did not split the slave class sufficiently to prevent rebellion except in "normal" times, when the state assured that any attempt to rebel would be suicidal. In effect, with domiciling the workers won their own serialization. Very quickly the peasant became king in is own cas-tle (with recognized rights over his own hut), and his neighbor ceased to be his comrade or companion (in the etymological sense of these words). Of course the technical division of labor did not bring about the desired results right away: peasant (pagan) conjurations seem to have been common in the ninth century, and the full weight of the Church would be needed to suppress them; the peasant commune survived, although there is reason to think that the integration of newly domiciled peasants was not always easy and that rivalries must have existed, re-sulting in some loss of power. Centuries more would be needed to get rid of these communes, beginning with the trend toward hedging (per-manent enclosure of farm land) together with evictions as early as the twelfth century and more especially in the thirteenth,[71] down to the Enclosure Acts and *Edits de clôt* of the eighteenth century, the progress of individualism in the French Revolution, the parcelling out of com-munal lands, and so forth. Banal seigniory and encastlement, it seems, were based on village communities regrouped around the lord.

The need to domicile some slaves, to which certain masters may have acceded rather quickly, while others gave in only after open warfare, was connected with the fear inspired by the slaves: masters were afraid of seeing their harvests and their *villae* burned, and they feared for their lives. Of course there was nothing new about that. As Finley points out, "the literature of the Roman Empire is filled with doubts and qualms about slavery; fear of slaves, of being murdered by them, of possible revolts, is a recurrent (and old) theme."[72] But he goes on to say that this fear was not responsible for the end of slavery, that "this literature can be matched, passage by passage, from the American South, and in neither society was the practical conclusion drawn that slavery should be replaced by other forms of labour, should be abolished, in short."[73] The observation itself is not incorrect, but the way Finley uses it is mistaken. Naturally, so long as the possibility of a central repressive apparatus exists, the masters will not draw the conclusion that slavery should be abolished. However, in the absence of such an apparatus, does not the fear of the slaves being held in chains begin to take its toll, particularly when prowling around the walls of the *villa* are bands of brigands, often made up of escaped rebels in arms? And the master has to be afraid not only of open mass risings, but also of more silent and frequently more individualized forms of rebellion, which could indeed go so far as murder.[74] We shall have more to say later on about the conflicts with which these fears were associated, as well as about the shift to overt rebellion, the victory of the slaves, and their domiciling, all viewed in relation to the state, when we come to lay out a periodization of the process. Wherever and whenever the state was weak or moribund, gang slavery gave way to domiciling. Whenever there was a resurgence of the state, the slave too returned, working in a gang on the demesne, eating his master's bread, and sleeping in his barns.

Accordingly, if, as we have seen, the slave system on a vast scale—and imperialism—made the state necessary (and thus effective, since the social basis for it existed), the end of the state caused the end of slavery—and the undoing of imperialism. This is the reverse of Max Weber's argument, according to which the end of gang slavery, the basis of urban life and of the monetary economy and thus of the central state, inevitably led to a subsistence economy (*oikos*) and the end of the Roman state. If, on the other hand, the end of the state caused the end of slavery, as we believe, this does not mean that once domiciling had been carried out to some degree and the master could and did live on his land, the urban money economy was not disrupted as a result, so that, with tax income in particular diminished, the state was weakened still further. The process was a cumulative one, like the barbarian invasions: the invasions did not cause the end of the Roman Empire, but they met with a virtual vacuum in central governmental authority (though not an absolute power vacuum, for the *villae* still existed) and could not but contribute to the further weakening of the state.

How, then, do we account for the disintegration of the imperial state?

D) Why Did the Imperial State Come to an End?

Here we shall merely try to give a systematic account of the process we saw at work in the first chapter.

A mode of production is not, as is sometimes supposed, a "pure type" abstracted rationally from a given economic and social formation. If it represents the essence of that formation, the reason is that the characteristic mode of exploitation contains certain dynamic internal contradictions, which drive the entire formation. Furthermore, this internal dynamic tends to reveal the nature of the mode of exploitation with increasing starkness; in other words, the tendency is for all social relations within the formation to be reduced to the class relations associated with the mode of production in question.

I do not know if it is possible to generalize the idea that every economic and social formation tends to reduce itself to the social relations characteristic of its determinant mode of production, thereby giving rise to its own negation and, accordingly, to the social relations characteristic of the subsequent mode of production (or at least dominant within that mode). What mode of production underlay the medieval formations of the eleventh to fifteenth centuries? Despite the "second serfdom," serfdom was certainly not the dominant social relation; the social relation of lord to serf was not the one that was spreading! It could not have been otherwise, unless we assume that in the early medieval feudal mode of production there was a tendency for serfdom or other forms of peasant dependency to develop (seventh and eighth centuries), leading (in the "liberated" ninth century) to their disintegration in favor of another formation of the same mode of production, now characterized not by the manorial system but rather by banal seigniory (in the tenth and eleventh centuries: the mode of production was the same, since surplus labor was still extracted chiefly from the peasant tenant or even proprietor, but in a different way, which has been dubbed the F.M.P.$_2$).

However, if we consider the capitalist mode of production and the slave mode of production, we find that they are sufficiently alike in certain respects[75] to make it impossible to look upon the idea of a kinship between slave and proletarian (so often expressed by socialists, and particularly by Marx and Engels) as a mere slogan or metaphor. Moreover, we have seen that the system of wage labor that grew up on the directly exploited demesnes in the thirteenth century was the successor of the slave system and that the two systems coexisted for a long while. In the one case labor power is sold, in the other the slave, both being commodities[76] (or chattels, as Finley says of the slave), although the master buys labor for the day and slaves for life, and the slave is generally sold by a third party (though in some cases he sold himself to redeem a debt, and it might be said that slaves exchange labor for life on a day-by-day basis), whereas the proletarian sells his own labor power (though the capitalist can resell it, not only in the form of a product, but directly, as in the case of firms selling temporary manpower, which accounts for their resemblance to slave suppliers, more striking here than is usual with wage earners). In both cases the master has the use of labor power for a longer period of time than is needed to reproduce it. There is no market for slaves or labor power in modes of production involving a dependent peasantry, nor in the "Asiatic" or feudal modes of production.

Furthermore, it is this commoditization of men or labor power that creates money capital, and in both cases the inevitable tendency is toward centrally managed "large-scale production units," or gang labor, even if with the wage system the chains are less visible, in many cases not even physical, and even if the proportions of "carrot to stick" tend to be different (though the "carrot" side is not to be underestimated in some slave systems, and not only in the southern United States).

Finally, as Chesneaux has observed,[77] the fact that both systems are dependent on the outside world also seems to be essential. As regards capitalism, this is not the place to examine the validity of Rosa Luxemburg's views. But both capitalism and the slave system are imperialist modes of production, and imperialism is fundamental to the origins of the slave system (which is by nature the fruit of war, conquest, razzia): this is especially true of the form of slavery we have been calling the "concentration-camp system" (which draws its labor from an outside supply of captives, whom it destroys). Furthermore, Rome eventually lived on the tribute in kind paid by the provinces (and this, too, was a form of imperialism, no longer linked directly to forcible provision of labor, but rather to pillage of what was produced). Can a slave system rely solely on internal reproduction to replenish the work force? Doubtless it can, but only if it is forced to do so (as, for example, in the southern United States after the English blockade of the slave trade).

Based in the one case on the slave as commodity and in the other on labor power as commodity, as well as on the money capital that commands the services of men or labor power, both the slave mode and the capitalist mode of production foster the development of a commerical money economy and a centrally managed work force. It bears repeating that before long the typical slaveholder ceases to be the peasant proprietor with a slave or two to his credit. By the same token, the typical capitalist before long ceases to be the owner of a small business, scarcely larger than a craft workshop, employing just a few men.

The slave system has its own internal dynamic, which promotes concentration of land and labor and ultimately leads to immense *latifundia* and extremely large slave gangs.[78] Or rather, it is more accurate to say that this is the tendency inherent in the developmental process, though in many cases this tendency is thwarted or even reversed by the economic and social crises it provokes (as, for example, at the time of the

Gracchi, or again with Caesar and his distribution of land to veterans). We have already seen that the size of estates grew throughout antiquity (chap 1). This process of concentration, which proceeds in a variety of ways, necessarily takes place at the expense of the independent small-holder. Thus it leads to proletarization (in the ancient sense) and pau-perization, processes which ultimately affect all of civil society until it is reduced to just two antagonistic groups: on the one side, a few large landowners, patrons, slave masters and on the other the subjugated masses of peasants, *coloni*, and slaves, deprived of citizenship. The large-scale slaves system drives out small slave owners, and the great landlord expropriates the smallholder by dint of a law inherent in the social relation between them, supported by the legal and political relations presupposed by such a social relation (namely, a centralized state and private property), to say nothing of naked violence.[79]

Once the free men had been reduced to just two classes, the *honestiores* and the *humiliores*, and the actual situation of the latter had fallen near to that of the slaves, the nature of class struggle changed radically from what it had been at the end of the republic. At that time the slaves had fought to forge a "class front" with the poor peasants. Now they actually succeeded in fashioning such an alliance. In third-century Gaul the Ba-caudae stirred up both slaves and peasants who were sinking further and further into subjugation. This union attests to the transformation of the social scale, to the "breakdown of such social equilibrium as the early Empire had achieved."[80] The new alliance spelled collapse for the foundations of the society that had made the centralized imperial state possible, just as the slave system had made it necessary.

Thus the adversaries were reduced to two: on one side the masters, few in number but prodigiously rich in land, men, and money, on the other side the subjugated masses.

At first, the masters, who had never before had so clear an interest in the existence of a strong central state, could not, as individuals, keep from thwarting its power, owing to their own strength (the state was helpless to act against them) and to their conflicts over control of the government (whereby they could add to their power and wealth). The contradiction could not have been more stark between their collective interest in a strong state to cope with social and national problems (which were closely related) and their individual interests as "feudal barons" in conflict with one another over control of the state: the state could no longer force them to comply with measures which in fact were in their own interest, but only in a collective sense, as an aggregate of conflicting individual interests.

The key question is here. Indeed, what must be understood is how the magnates could have fought against their own state and contributed to its destruction. The importance of the state's fight against the patrons at the end of the fourth and during the fifth century now becomes clear. The patrons, as we know, extended their protection to the *fugitivi*, to peasants in dire financial straits, and to merchants in debt for taxes. Even brigands found refuge with them. Not only did they appropriate the lands of those under their protection (in many cases entire villages), but also the state's land and before long also its attributes, its judicial powers in particular.[81]

It is beyond doubt that the state fought against the patronate, proscribing it in edict after edict and imposing ever stricter penalties on patrons and on their protected *coloni*.[82] But the colonate continued to spread, and peasants tied to the soil found themselves in a situation closer and closer to that of slaves. Before long their official status came to be modeled on that of the slave. And in the end the state was forced to recognize that land acquired under the patronate was validly possessed.[83] Acquiescence in the rise of the colonate, followed by its legalization, was the other side of the question of the patronate.

The great landowners, masters of slaves and *coloni*, patrons who reigned over vast territories, administered justice, and protected the peasants against the state and against other magnates in exchange for absolute obedience to their own rule, were inevitably above the law by virtue of their great power. Inevitably these "barons" thwarted the state, even if that state was their own, the root of their power. Moreover, as it was inevitable that they fight one another for control of the state, for a share in its offices as well as in lands and men, they contributed to the further weakening of its authority.

Later on, the disintegration of the imperial state, which as we have seen was made inevitable by imperialist conquest, led to the downfall of the imperial economy based on tribute and razzia, an "international" economy that had not only made the center wealthy but had also distributed a portion of the fruits of imperialism to a large number of Romans and Italians. The solidity of the broad social base of the early imperial state and the triumph of imperialism were inextricably intertwined. But the collapse of the state left the empire, that prodigious mechanism for ingesting the surplus product of the periphery, in disarray, and so undermined its own social base.

The barbarian invasions should be looked at from the same angle. On the outer periphery of the empire, Germany both benefitted and suffered from the invasions. There was a tendency in Germany to look to Rome for guidance, and when the imperial state there fell into crisis, the German tribes were forced to march—whether with peaceful intent or not—toward the city.

Finally, the state could no longer disguise from the masses its true nature: that of an apparatus of social repression. Thus it became impossible to recruit an army among the Roman populace. Think of the legend of the Roman citizen grown effeminate and incapable of fighting, no longer competent to defend "civilization" against the barbarians! That the luxury that went with great wealth, so evident among the master class, had made the great landlords "effeminate" we are willing to concede, but only in a certain sense, because the times were quite violent, as were the men who lived through them. Obviously that is not the real question. Later the subjugated masses would prove that they knew quite well how to wield a flail or a pike! But the arming of slaves was forbidden—this was only a natural precaution. Nor could the magnates arm the *humiliores*, the *coloni*, who were no longer willing to fight in behalf of their masters; indeed, before long they would be fighting on the other side. Earlier, the magnates had been able to mobilize citizens, smallholders, and even most of the systematically differentiated social groups that formed the social base of the imperial state, which was held together ideologically via the cult of the emperor and the fear of barbarians and slaves. But ideology could not long endure once the social conditions that had made it possible changed: the alliance between the small peasants and slaves at the time of the Bacaudae rising led ultimately to acceptance of the barbarians by the subjugated masses (until the new masters clearly entered into alliance with the old). Hence the masters in the late empire had to resort to foreign mercenaries to defend them. We know, of course, that ultimately these barbarian[84] troops played a key role in a military and political contest characterized by the decay of public authority. But we must be careful not to confuse cause with effect: the reason the masters were forced to entrust their defense to paid foreign soldiers was that there was no one else left to defend the empire, for it was no longer possible to mobilize the servile masses. This proves that the social base of the state had crumbled, and therefore that the state had fallen into decay (of course the mercenary armies contributed to this collapse!).

The collapse of the state's social base, the concentration of power and wealth in the hands of a few, and the crisis of imperialism inevitably caused the collapse of the fiscal system as well: the magnates were able to avoid paying taxes (here, once again, the contradiction between their individual and collective interests was aggravated), and since the burden of taxation now fell exclusively on the poorest elements of society, it contributed to their ruin (hastening the process of concentration-pauperization). Tax revenues fell in consequence (since the poor had nothing more to give), necessitating increased reliance on repressive means (such as tying men to the soil or to their trade), and this in the end killed off the urban economy (the connection between the fiscal and the urban crisis is central to every history of the late empire).

The senators, the great landowners, left the cities for tax reasons, taking with them their protégés and dependents, who relied for their livelihood on what their patrons spent (thus precipitating the end of the urban economy, and hence of the monetary economy, establishing the *oikos* everywhere); they went to live on their lands in the countryside. Another reason for their departure, perhaps even more important, was that they needed to manage their estates and maintain order in person, the land being the chief source of their income (and with their departure from the cities, the only source). Above all, and for our purposes the crucial point, the enfeebled and before long moribund central state no longer supported the gang slave system: the strength and therefore the stability of the "feudal" system established by the owners of the great *villae* depended on having as fragmented a work force as possible. The struggles of peasants and slaves succeeded in winning domiciling as a concession by the powerful; this victory of the masses put an end to the old mode of exploitation and stabilized the new.[85]

E) The Connection Between the State and the
Slave System: A Tentative Periodization

If it is true that the end of the centralized state caused the end of gang slavery via mass struggle, we should be able to find a correlation between the timing of episodes of class conflict, periods of weakness or reconstitution of the central repressive apparatus, and the "ends" of slavery; furthermore, in regions where the state remained strong, slavery should have continued to flourish.[86]

The course of the death throes of public authority in the empire is well known: in the third century there was a crisis, followed at the end of that century and the beginning of the next by a despotic reaffirmation of state power; then, in the second half of the fourth century came a crisis, which led to the final collapse. We also know the timing of the inroads made by the barbarians in the third century (250–80: thirty years of attacks by the Franks and Alemanni, until finally Probus accepted their gains). Then, beginning in the middle of the fourth century, there were invasions on a large scale, followed by even greater onslaughts in the fifth century: these would continue until probably the middle of the seventh century. Effects and symptoms of the weakening of the empire, these invasions were one cause of accelerated economic, social, and

231 Class Struggles in Europe

political decay. But they were not the primary cause of that decay: in all, over a period of four centuries there were perhaps a million invaders, who penetrated the empire in small groups, usually peacefully.

What connections are there between these events and the end of slavery? To begin with, there is the fact that their timing coincides with overt mass struggles by slaves and oppressed peasants. The Bacaudae led things off in Gaul at the beginning of the third century, by the end of which they seem to have been in control of the country. The resurgence of despotism under Diocletian (see chap. 1) had its consequences here, for it seems that the Bacaudae were temporarily defeated in a military campaign (which gives some indication of the importance of these so-called bands of brigands!). Historians agree, however, that they bounced back between the mid-fourth and fifth centuries and even beyond, if we are willing to accept that their activities were related to the later widespread unrest and brigandage in Merovingian times.

Let us take note of the severity of oppression and repression, which seems to have been particularly drastic in the fourth and fifth centuries. Since masters could no longer rely on the state, they had to resort to private means of violence to control their slave gangs and tighten their hold on the peasants in the face of widespread escapes and rebellions. But violent measures were contradictory in their effects, in that they incited rebellion and stiffened resistance (when such measures were used as a last resort and carried to extremes, they might tip the balance of power in favor of the rebels, thereby increasing the frequency of uprisings and the determination of the rebels). Remember the tortures inflicted on slaves, and the punishments meted out to captured fugitives, who were sometimes burned alive or crucified. Many fugitives are known to have joined the Bacaudae,[87] and some also tried to link up with the barbarians, in particular the Visigoths[88] and Ostrogoths (who, in 378, allied themselves with rebel miners in the Balkans[89]). In this respect the fate of the subjugated peasants differed little from that of slaves. If we believe what John Chrysostom has to say on the subject, they were forced to perform very painful tasks, being used "like donkeys and mules"; they were forced to pay usurious rates of interests and were beaten and tortured.[90] Similarly, Salvianus mentions *humiliores* who were "flayed alive, beaten, killed."[91] One man wonders "who can oppress more than the great landowner?" Another explains that the peasant has no choice but to hand his land over to a protector or flee to join the Bacaudae or the barbarians.

From the third century onward, and particularly after the middle of the fourth century, the decline of slavery was considerable. Vast estates lay uncultivated, the slaves who had worked them having fled, rebelled, or joined the Bacaudae or barbarians (in the time of Constantine, for example, and later in the time of Theodosius, 130,000 hectares are said to have lain uncultivated in Italy alone). What is sometimes euphemistically referred to as a shortage of slaves should rather be seen as a situation in which it was no longer possible to employ slave labor: the time of the slave gang was past because the slaves had risen in rebellion—a rebellion that could not have taken place, been sustained, or emerged victorious had centralized repression still been possible. The terrible private repression enforced by the great landowners did not make up for the absence of the state.

We also know that landowners called upon barbarians largely to make up for the shortage of slaves (a scarcity due not to natural but to social causes), from the third century onward and above all in the second half of the fourth century. The system used was based on the domiciling of barbarians (the *laeti* of the third century known as *tributarii*), soon generalized in the "hospitality" system. Here the barbarians played the role of "scabs": they took the place of slaves who had rebelled or fled. Bearing in mind that the barbarian chieftains were quick to throw in their lot with the great landowners, it becomes clear that it makes no sense to regard them as allies of the slaves or rebellious peasants: wherever they could, they preserved the oppressive *villa* system, content to share in the fruits of exploitation. But the invasions, made inevitable by the disintegration of the empire, naturally strengthened the hand of the embattled slaves and peasants, at least until the barbarian chieftains took a hand in restoring the order desired by the landed magnates.

During the crisis of the late empire the decline of slavery was not in any way the result of changes linked to economic criteria such as profitability, to technological factors, or to a slackening of the slave trade. Rather, it resulted from the refusal of slaves to tolerate the slave system (whether by armed rebellion or by flight). The substitute labor supplied by the barbarians was altogether inadequate, so that latifundists from the third century on, and particularly at the time Diocletian undertook his repressive measures, were forced to turn to *coloni*, to poor or landless peasants "serialized" by virtue of their working conditions (small plots, perhaps even fragmented into tiny parcels) and in spite of a vigorous tradition of collective practices; it had become necessary to finish the job of subjugating these peasants (Diocletian bound them legally to the soil), and this drove them into rebellion. Masters were forced to take this final step by the recalcitrance or rebelliousness of their slaves, who did not accept it without opposition! The Bacaudae enlisted those who broke the bonds of ancient slavery, as well as those who fought against the new medieval bonds.

It is also known that throughout the long period of unrest that followed the establishment of the barbarian kingdoms (and even earlier, in the late empire), latifundists were forced, in order to hold on to their slaves, to domicile some of them in huts of their own. Landowners did not suddenly discover that it was profitable to domicile their slaves, give them wives, and allow them to work their own plots, as Duby says.[92] Rather, they found that it was dangerous and even impossible to continue to rely on centralized management of slave labor except in periods when genuine and effective repression was enforced by the central state. On the other hand, the relative autonomy of the rural worker settled in his own home on his own tenement with his own family assured that continued exploitation would be possible for the foreseeable future. Not that peasant uprisings involving *coloni*, domiciled slaves, and serfs were no longer possible. On the contrary, the ranks of the Bacaudae included not only slaves but also peasants and *coloni*, and rebels of this sort were known throughout the Middle Ages. Domiciling did not halt the class struggle, but it did shift the balance of power: gang slavery of the sort practiced on the *latifundia* of the period between the first and third centuries was no longer possible. Although the possibility of exploiting domiciled slaves, *coloni*, and before long serfs still remained, it must not be supposed that such exploitation was submitted to passively!

A glance at two other periods will enable us to shed light on the social consequences first of the restoration and later of the fresh breakdown of the central state: the Carolingian period, with the year 800 at its center, during which an attempt was made to restore a central authority similar to that of imperial Rome, and later the period of breakdown of the Carolingian Empire.

Nowadays, as we have seen, all historians are agreed that the Carolingian *villae* were provided with abundant slave manpower, which was put to work on the demesne,[93] even if for obvious reasons it is very difficult to estimate the numbers of such slaves. It would seem, however, that in comparison with earlier periods the importance of slavery on the Carolingian *villa* was great, in other words, that there had been a resurgence of the slave system: the restoration of the state made possible the restoration of the slave system, and razzias on a large scale resumed in Bohemia and beyond the Elbe.[94]

What made this restoration of the state possible? Founded on military might, the state's power stemmed from the strong support it still received from the Franks, a people that could boast many free warriors among its number; it benefitted, too, from the revival of the traditional freedoms enjoyed collectively by the native tribes and from the large number of allodialists and freeholders common not only in the Merovingian period but also during the rise of the Carolingians, as well as the period during which their empire was at its height—the upshot of the social and tribal wars that marked the end of the Roman Empire. The intermediary strata of society had disappeared during the late empire, leaving only the two antagonistic classes associated with the slave mode of production (the *humiliores* having been assimilated to the slaves in actual fact), but now with the rise of the Carolingians these middle strata were once again flourishing.

However, the process of concentration of lands and subjugation of free men resumed (had it ever stopped? countervailing tendencies had temporarily taken the upper hand), thanks in particular to the state itself, the basis of the imperial aristocracy's power. Whoever could no longer wage war effectively—given that warfare now required a fairly substantial initial investment, having lately become the business of a new group of professionals—lost, along with his freedom, his land, or at least ownership of it. Similarly, the peasants, who had managed during the period of uprisings and invasions to work themselves free of slavery or the colonate, were now once again caught up in trammels which the masters were able to tighten by means of state repression. Far more than the economy,[95] it was the power of the magnates, backed up by their state apparatus, that caused the resumption of the process of expropriation and subjugation and thus the Carolingian attempt to restore the state.

Charlemagne, as we have seen, tried to maintain direct ties to the free peasants (through the oath campaigns), but the whole dynamic of society worked against this effort, as the imperial aristocracy snapped up the land, took men and sometimes entire peasant communities under its protection, and grabbed the offices of government. The *villae* grew larger, and the *villa* system itself gained ground. In many cases the families of these same lords of manors controlled the local or regional forces (and after the breakdown in the tenth century, this was to become the source of the new banal seigniory).

This restoration of social and political order, which was made possible by a state controlled by the aristocracy, strengthened the hand of that aristocracy against the poor peasants, eliminated the intermediate strata of society, and led to the subjugation of free men, but at the same time it pitted the barons against *their own* state as its most determined enemies. Once again we witness an aristocracy withdrawing its support from the state, even though the state was its own creature, and turning from legitimate force to outright robbery, "fratricidal" war, and forcible seizure of public office: behaving, in short, as its nature dictated.

Thus at the end of the Carolingian era, the fresh disintegration of the state (which could find no social base beyond the imperial aristocracy that it served) once again opened the way to invasions, anti-imperialist ethnic or "national" uprisings, and overt social conflict. We know that slavery disappeared from Gaul as a major form of exploitation in the tenth century (*mancipium* and *servus*, the two "conscious expressions of the ancient notion of servitude," vanished from Dauphiné in 957 and 1157, respectively[96]). Thus at the end of the reign of Louis the Pious, during a period of political disorganization marked by the last of the invasions, the ancient mode of exploitation disappeared as a result of a wave of domiciling and of failure to replenish the old slave gangs. Although Duby has explained the end of slavery in terms of economic, demographic, and technological factors, he also observes that "the disruptions consequent upon the last invasions rapidly loosened these bonds [of slavery] in Gaul,"[97] a remark we think worthy of emphasis. It is too bad he did not make it somewhat more explicit. If social unrest and invasions made it impossible to keep up the old slave gangs, this was because it was dangerous for the masters to sit atop veritable powder kegs of social tension and because those gangs fell apart owing to many escapes and uprisings.

Of course the periods of unrest during which the state tottered or collapsed were not the same from one region to the next. We should really couple our tentative periodization with a geographical description of slavery. Thus, to start with Provence, for example, there were two periods of crisis and unrest in the early Middle Ages: that of the reconquest by the Frankish kings in the second half of the eighth century and then the uprisings of the native tribes and their eventual suppression in the ninth century. In both cases J.-P. Poly[98] has found that the problem of slave escapes was so serious that the landed magnates had scarcely any choice but to employ varlets and hirelings.

In a similar vein, Poly has studied the epic of the Saracens of Freinet, who throughout the tenth century were the scourge of Provence and the Alps. It is in the Alps that their adventures become pertinent to our account, for there they entered into an alliance with "Christian robbers."[99] Contemporaries had of course little to say about this episode, but the few texts found by Poly show that these bands did not hesitate to commit murder, sometimes acted as guides, and even occupied territories of their own.

What is fascinating is the name by which they were known: *marrons*, an old word meaning "a domestic animal gone wild," the same given to the "Negro *marrons*" (fugitives) in the Antilles, slaves who had fled and "gone wild," meaning that they were out of control, *clandestins* (the

word meant "pirate" in the fourteenth and fifteenth centuries) who lived
by pillage. Thus Poly was led to hypothesize that these were fugitive
slaves, "*servi* escaped from the great estates in the turbulent last days
of the empire, or their descendants."[100] What we know of the extent of
escapes and of slave uprisings at the end of the empire and again during
the unrest of the late ninth and early tenth century seems to confirm
this hypothesis.

The most important point about these Saracens of Freinet is that their
strength, at first sight so extraordinary, like that of the earlier Bacaudae,
the barbarian invaders, and the brigands found all over Gaul, can be
explained by the internal contradictions of the society: "The Saracens
of Provence were merely the symptom of an internal crisis, and not the
cause. . . . The true destroyers of the Carolingian state, sometimes concealed from our eyes by the Moorish pirates, were none other than the
families of the imperial aristocracy. For them, once the great danger was
past, there was no further need of the state, if they so much as understood the meaning of the word, and consequently no reason for it to
exist."[101] The great families? Surely they played a part, as they had done
in the late empire, too. But there was also another factor: the impossibility of a state whose social base was limited to the exploiting class
alone.

From another angle, Pierre Toubert has described the social conflict
in Sabine at the end of the Carolingian Empire in the following terms,
placing the Saracen invasions in proper perspective: "The Saracen thrust,
in our region limited to the years 870-910, was not a cause but rather a
consequence of the dissolution of the administrative structures that followed the Carolingian collapse after the death of Louis II (875). It was
just one more episode in the social crisis of the time, made manifest by
a spate of brigandage in which the *latrunculi christiani* seem to have been
no less active than the pagan guerrillas."[102]

Toubert goes on to explain that in the same period, gang slavery
disappeared, thanks to domiciling and manumission (pious works), as
well as because the domiciled slave freed himself (by cash payment).[103]
Labor dues owed by tenants (*angariae*)—which were already relatively
low (no more than three weeks per year at the beginning of the ninth
century) disappeared almost entirely, along with the term *angariae* itself
(these dues had been distributed at regular intervals in eight- to twelve-
day periods falling at key points in the agricultural labor process). As
Toubert says, "the social landscape changed in the eighth decade of the
ninth century."[104]

How can we fail to see that the social combat waged by the guerrillas,
Christian and pagan alike, was in large measure successful in killing off

the old manorial system, so successful that when the masters came to forge a new coalition in the form of feudalism, the new mode of exploitation, encastlement, had nothing to do with the old?[105] How is it possible for Toubert to believe that *pro anima* emancipations of prebendal slaves always had moral motivations in the period 870-920 and that domiciling of these slaves was due to economic causes encouraged by the decline of direct exploitation, when the opposite was true? If, moreover, we find evidence of very few paid manumissions, perhaps the reason was that slavery was ended, and domiciled slaves were manumitted by force, at the same time free tenants were relieved of their *corvée* obligations?

Obviously it is not very easy to give further proof of slave struggles in the early Middle Ages. In *Les Six Livres de la République* of Jean Bodin, however, we do find this passage:

And in fact the might of the Alarbes [Arabs] grew only in this way [by giving or promising freedom to the slaves]. For as soon as captain Homar, one of Mehemet's lieutenants, promised freedom to the slaves who followed him, he attracted so many of them that within a few years they made themselves lords of all the East. Rumors of freedom and of the conquests made by the slaves inflamed the hearts of slaves in Europe, whereupon they took up arms, first in Spain in 781, and later in this kingdom in the time of Charlemagne and of Louis the Piteous [= Pious], as may be seen in the edicts issued at the time against sworn conspiracies among the slaves. And even Lothar, son of Louis, after losing two battles to his brothers, called upon slaves to aid him, who thereafter gave chase to their masters in 852. All at once this blaze broke out in Germany, where slaves, having taken up arms, shook the estate of princes and cities, and even Louis, king of the Germans, was forced to assemble all his forces to rout them. Little by little this forced the Christians to relax servitude and to free the slaves, excepting only certain *corvées* and the ancient right of succession of their freedmen who died childless.[106]

Based on this passage, it would seem that:[107]

1. The Saracen advance was preceded by "rumors of freedom," a fact which in Bodin's view accounts for their success; it probably also accounts for the strength of the Freinet bands throughout the southeastern part of France (in addition to which contemporary historians confirm that large numbers of slaves fled captivity in Spain at the time of the Arab conquest).

2. Apparently slave wars were a severe problem in Europe, particularly during the period of unrest associated with the wars of the sons of Louis the Pious and the collapse of the Carolingian Empire.

3. And, above all, this slave war "little by little forced the Christians to relax servitude and to free the slaves."

So the Arab armies, as Bodin maintains, were liberators, a fact we have evidently been quick to "forget"! For is it not true that only Christianity could have been a liberating force? But note that the Arabs offered freedom only to those who followed them. The rest, the enemy, might be reduced to slavery (just as both Christians and Jews were willing to accept enslavement of members of the other religion, as well as pagans). Bodin knows that Omar was not the first to promise freedom to these slaves: history, he tells us, is full of such offers, often quite effective. These should not be confused with the idea of doing away with slavery altogether.

For our purposes, the important thing is to note that Bodin saw the slave struggles of the ninth century as the cause of the end of slavery in Europe. It would seem difficult to tax him with being blinded by the ideology of a social revolutionary!

Finally, it is interesting to note that beyond moral strictures Bodin's basic criticism of slavery is that it is an unsuitable relation on which to base society, for slavery leaves society vulnerable to the incessant rebellions of its slaves.

While the social upheaval of the late ninth century rid western Europe of the last vestiges of the slave system (or, rather, of its early medieval survivals), slavery continued to exist elsewhere (chiefly in the cities of the Mediterranean, although rural slaves were still to be found). A glance at the geography of this latter-day slavery will enable us to make the connection between the state and slavery even more clear.

Surely the most typical case is that of Spain, where we know that even rural slavery continued to flourish in the tenth century; in the Christian portion of Spain, slavery became even more substantial as early as the eleventh century and above all in the twelfth. As was mentioned earlier, Verlinden explains these developments by pointing to the volume of the slave trade, and we have already indicated what role might have been played by a strong, free peasantry. It should also be noted, however, that according to Marc Bloch[108] Spanish feudalism was weak and the Spanish king remained strong and active: public authority there was not eclipsed by the private power of the lords.

Next consider England. From the work of Georges Duby in particular,[109] we know that slavery was flourishing there after the eleventh-century conquest and that it even gathered strength in the latter part of the twelfth and throughout the thirteenth century. Now, notice that from the eleventh century onward the English monarchy was very much more powerful than its Continental counterparts and, furthermore, that by the thirteenth century a portion of the English peasantry enjoyed freedom and relative wealth; these two phenomena were related, since the well-to-do peasantry provided the social base for a powerful monarchy.

Let us turn now to Germany in the twelfth century. Whereas in England first and later in France direct exploitation made headway along with types of exploitation relying on slaves, throughout northwestern Europe lease farming was on the rise. Duby has pointed to the interrelationship of the decline in central power, the conflict and devastation that left this part of Europe barren and desolate, and the development of a decentralized mode of exploitation.

In the fourteenth century, when social unrest finally led to a decline of centrally managed labor more or less everywhere in Europe, Duby tells us, "the regions in which direct exploitation continued to flourish most strongly, in the east and certain parts of the southwest of Germany, along with northern Italy, were precisely those in which the princes or urban authorities had taken rather strenuous measures to maintain conditions of employment favorable to the masters,"[110] in particular by preventing rural laborers from escaping to the cities and by tying them to the soil. Once again, only in areas where public authority continued to be strong was it possible to maintain slavery as a mode of exploitation of men, along with the complementary system of rural wage labor from the thirteenth century onward and the concomitant method of working the land, namely, direct exploitation of the demesne. The latter did not determine the former, but rather the reverse: whenever—and wherever—the public authorities were in a position to take violent measures to coordinate and supervise the violent measures being taken privately by the masters, we find slavery in one form or another, hence direct exploitation under the master's supervision, relying on stewards, overseers, and division of labor.

Throughout thirteenth-century Europe, however—a Europe of forest and brushland through which bands of brigands roamed, a Europe in which slaves always could and often did escape to the cities and woodlands, a feudal Europe of castles and abbeys and clashes among lords and princes, a Europe of cities and their bourgeois inhabitants—although the poor peasant, an object of fear and loathing,[111] was exploited quite heavily, and although his attempts to rebel were put down with frightful violence,[112] the hour of absolutism's rise had not yet struck. The state remained weak, even in Spain and England; the dislocation of the peasant masses had only just begun, and the bourgeoisie was still fragile (as witnessed by the political setbacks it suffered). The process of social differentiation that would later on make it possible to regroup the new strata of society around the masters' state had just gotten under way. Further development would be needed before systematic imprisonment of the expropriated poor, the vagabonds, could begin, before barracks-factories could be built,[113] before the proletariat could be concentrated in the first industrial plants. The origins of wage labor are inextricably intertwined with the use of force to impose discipline. In the same period the slave system was being reborn in America and the Antilles.

If the force of the state was necessary at the beginning of wage labor to enforce this new relation of production, still only a relatively modest use of force was needed, because enormous concentrations of workers did not yet exist. As these were gradually built up over the course of the nineteenth and twentieth centuries, the state became increasingly indispensable. Of course the principle of "divide and rule" and the hierarchical organization of labor, or, in other words, a system of voluntary servitude in which each man exerts power over his inferiors only by virtue of obeying the orders of a superior, have enabled this system to function smoothly (just like the *villae* of the Roman empire, which could operate in the absence of the master or any other free man). Still, repression, based on the police powers of the state, remains the last resort: in back of voluntary servitude there always lurks the possibility, held in abeyance in "normal" times, of recourse to force.

Once let the logic of capitalism deepen the gulf between the two classes, thereby shrinking the social base of the state, and we shall see whether wage labor will endure forever!

5

*Where did he get so many eyes to spy on you with,
if you didn't lend them to him? How did he come
by so many hands to beat you with, if he didn't
take them from you? The feet with which he
tramples on your cities—where did he get them
from, if they're not yours? How can he have any
power over you except by your own doing? What
could he do to you if you didn't protect the thief
who robs you, if you weren't the accomplice of the
murderer who kills you, if you weren't traitors to
your own cause?*

Etienne de La Boétie, *Discours de la servitude volontaire*

Epilogue: By Way of Conclusion

This essay has been concerned exclusively with the causes of the end of ancient slavery. In considering the question why slavery came to an end between the third and the tenth centuries, however, we could not avoid giving a partial answer to the question why the slave system—and not mere slavery—took hold in the two centuries centering on the beginning of the modern era. The wars of conquest and razzia and the sale of huge numbers of slaves on the Mediterranean markets, particularly those of the "center," preceded the formation of the imperial state. This state was necessary if the system based on imperialism and slavery was to endure. For all that it was necessary, the imperial state had to be possible before it could exist. And, as we have seen, it was possible in the time of Caesar and Augustus, precisely because this system, then just beginning, had not yet developed its internal contradictions, which ate away at the systematically differentiated and stratified social and ethnic foundations of the state and hence of the entire system.

But why did the republican wars of conquest and razzia take place? Why did they succeed? The question is too broad. Surely land and slaves constituted wealth before imperialism and the slave system—this is why undertakings designed to provide greater quantities of them could be viewed as normal activities. Moreover, the relations that obtained among the social groups that constituted the republic made these wars necessary, because the power of the dominant groups, even within Rome itself, depended on foreign wars. Of course there is no way to say exactly what the bases of Roman power were. We do not, however, believe that a satisfactory answer to this question can be based either on the efficiency of the economic system (power as a by-product of agrarian wealth) or on its inefficiency (power seen as the product of a "creative tension" arising out of poverty, which supposedly necessitates conquest and pillage). We would sooner accept the "classic" answer, which places the emphasis on the social system, on the strength of citizen armies and free independent peasants (which would also account for the later weakness of the Roman state, after the effects of the slave system had had time to make themselves felt).

All in all this analysis is the same as that given by Engels in *Anti-Dühring*, when he explains that the armies of republican France were strong because they were able to take advantage of a new form of organization, which only the Revolution could have allowed.[1] The material bases of military might also and in some cases primarily include social relations.

Note that the relations of power that made possible the military victories, conquests, razzias, and consequently imperialism and the slave system, were "international" relations directly productive of social relations, in that slaves were in the first place vanquished foreigners. At the same time the relations of production associated with the slave system gave rise to the complementary necessity of imperialist relations of power.

The same holds true for the case of slavery between the sixteenth and nineteenth centuries in the Antilles and America, which depended on the availability of Negro captives. Once again an imperialist power relation was transmuted into a relation of dominance between classes. This phenomenon should not be seen in isolation, however. At the same time in Europe the poor were wrested from their fields and shut up in factories, charity workshops, and hospitals, subjected to a regimen of forced labor and strict discipline. For the armed men in the service of the masters, these poor vagabonds were also foreigners. And is it not true that proletarians today are always viewed as foreigners by the capitalist state?

Ultimately, what we learn from the study of the development of slavery into the slave system at the beginning of the modern era is that imperialism and the slave system are inextricably intertwined. Not only does the rebirth of the slave system[2] in the West Indies in the sixteenth century confirm this lesson, it further teaches us that slavery (like forced labor in Europe in the same period) is one way for the dominant class to compel the workers to work (as the slave owners saw perfectly clearly) under a new system. Slavery is an apprenticeship in true obedience. Neither the Negro wrested from his village nor the poor peasant plucked from his land was "ripe" for wage labor. Used to working just as long as they pleased, they never would have accepted the new regime. We all know the familiar litany of capitalists and slave masters on this score: the Negro and the vagabond are lazy. Does this not merely serve to confirm that they were fighting against the conditions imposed on them? They had not (yet) been "molded" into free workers.

Today we see the proof of this contention in the zones of the underdeveloped periphery dominated by fascism, where prisons masquerade as factories and plantations. Ultimately these are signs of the weakness of a relatively newly established capitalism in these areas, where workers have not yet internalized capitalist discipline.

While it is true that slavery was a constant feature of antiquity and that it never altogether vanished in the Middle Ages, save for a few fortunate regions, it nevertheless developed into the slave system only during a period lasting no more than a few centuries, and chiefly in western Europe. Similarly, the slave system of modern times, as it existed in the Antilles and in the United States, was not capable of general application and remained subordinate to capitalism. Yet slavery has always been known, even down to the present day, not in its "classic" legal form (as private property in human beings) but as a social relation based on the power of life and death over other human beings is or more precisely on the power to spare the life of the captive, who was generally seen as one already dead, on the absolute prerogative of the master to cut short when he will the life of the slave, whose survival is tolerated only because it is controlled by the master.

This is why the lesson of this lengthy history, the history of the end of the slave mode of production and the slow transition to feudalism, seems to us all the more important: the slave system did not disappear because the latifundist slave masters found a new way to manage the work force which made possible an increase in its productivity, nor even because the new system allowed the masters to increase the amount of the surplus product they extracted for their own advantage. Nor did it come to an end because the old social relations impeded the development of the productive forces, or because domiciling had become the only way to reproduce the work force. The slave system was done in by clandestine struggle and social conflict. And these were effective because the state, the crucial element in the balance of power between the classes, collapsed when its foundations were undermined by a process of concentration of land coupled with pauperization, a process inherent in this mode of production.[3] The new system was born of the struggles of workers, but also of the reactions of the masters in attempting to hold on to their power over men, their power to exploit, and their customary surplus. The new mode of production that emerged from this conflict did indeed become more efficient economically and demographically than the slave system had been, in the first place because the slaves' struggles, as we have stressed, reduced the productivity of the servile work force, as well as its capacity to replenish itself, and later because the social classes that drew the bulk of the profit from the medieval evolution, namely, the rich peasants and above all the bourgeoisie, used the liberties they had won for the purpose of economic development.

"Slavery no longer paid, and therefore it ceased to exist." No, but the slaves' struggles ultimately made slavery impossible, as the slave system itself destroyed the social bases of the masters' state. As a relation of production, then, slavery produced its own negation: a *peasantry*, no doubt dominated and exploited, no doubt scorned, loathed, and feared by the masters, but in possession nonetheless of the means to acquire its own future freedom.

Notes

Acknowledgments

1. Rosier's note on work in progress, "Changements techniques et rapports sociaux dans l'histoire des sociétés rurales ouest-européennes: un réexamen de la 'révolution agricole,' " *Cahiers A.E.H.* 11 (1977), should be read as a complement to the present work.

Introduction

1. In the same vein, the rate of exploitation in the United States today may be as high, and perhaps even higher, than in the average underdeveloped country.

2. This does not mean that slavery was one of the original forms of production; we are speaking only of a primary and primordial relation of exploitation, and agree with Marx: "Slavery, bondage, etc. . . . is always secondary, derived, never original, although [it is] a necessary and logical result of property founded on the community and labor in the community" (Karl Marx, *Grundrisse*, trans. Martin Nicolaus [New York: Vintage, 1973], pp. 496–97). He goes on to criticize as "a piece of nonsense" the idea that slavery in one form arose out of individual relations between men, since slavery in fact arises in the community and from the relations between communities.

3. See below.

4. Friedrich Engels, *Anti-Dühring* (New York: International Publishers, 1939), p. 199: "But at the stage of the 'economic order' which had now been attained the prisoners acquired a value; their captors therefore let them live and made use of their labor." Furthermore, this was progress, for "up to that time they had not known what to do with prisoners of war, and had therefore simply killed them; at an even earlier period, eaten them." As Victor Hugo said, "slavery is a step forward from cannibalism." The idea is an old one: Rhodiginus, for example, in 1516 depicted slavery as a measure of clemency (*Lectiones antiquae*, book lxxv, chap. xvii) and gives the putative etymology of *servus: servare*. Jean Bodin made fun of this alleged "charity" of thieves and pirates (*La République*, book i, chap. v [1583 ed., p. 50]).

5. From the first draft of Marx's letter to Vera Zasulich (Marx and Engels, *Werke* 19:384–95, especially p. 386), where Marx discusses the sense of the word "revival" as used by the American writer L. H. Morgan.

6. See, for example, the memoirs of Albert Speer.

7. Bertolt Brecht, *Der Aufhaltsame Aufstieg des Arturo Ui,* epilogue.

8. See below, the definition of slavery and the slave system.

9. The slave is a commodity, in the sense that the labor power of the wage laborer today may be called a commodity. If slaves are not always produced for their exchange value (i.e., produced as slaves, whether physically or by razzia), this tends more and more clearly to be the case. J.-P. Vernant rightly believes that "in antiquity, labor power was not a commodity; there was no labor market, but there were slave markets—quite another thing" (see *Mythe et société en Grèce ancienne* [Paris: Maspero, 1974], p. 22). This is certainly correct, because, as Marx wrote, "the slave did not sell his labor power to the possessors of slaves. . . . The slave was sold." Thus it was the slave who was the commodity, not his labor power.

10. Hitler's concentration camps are interesting in this respect. The master (the state) and its representatives had effective power over the *usus, fructus,* and *abusus.* Exchange resulted from this only within the concentration camp system, (since the state was the only master), but it was nonetheless real. Every concentration camp system tends toward this absolute.

11. [The definition, taken by Dockès from Littré's *Dictionnaire,* was translated into English by me.—Trans.]

12. Cf. H. Lévy-Bruhl, "Théorie de l'esclavage," *Quelques problèmes du très ancien droit romain* (Paris: Domat Montchrétien, 1934). Reprinted in M. I. Finley, *Slavery in Classical Antiquity* (London: Heffer & Sons, 1959), p. 29, n. 2, a citation from Pomponius Sextus. This etymology is arguable to say the least.

13. D'Olive, *Oeuvres* (Lyon, 1657), 1:216; and Boutaric, *Les Instituts de Justinien conférées avec le droit fraçais* (Toulouse, 1738), p. 370, and see also p. 257. Italics added. Philippe Didier has called our attention to the case of the *servus fugitivus* whose situation was imprescriptible and who was therefore considered as possessing himself on behalf of his master: his *animus* was never his own, being alienated absolutely to the master in all circumstances; hence he could neither gain his freedom nor be claimed by a new master. Like death, servile status was definitive, unless the master chose to give back life.

14. See Michel Foucault, *La Volonté de savoir* (Paris: Gallimard, 1976), 1:177; English edition, *The History of Sexuality* (New York: Pantheon, 1979).

15. In the Nazi concentration camps, the prisoners were effectively slaves. Reprieved (briefly) from death, they are not really comparable to the subjects of the Third Reich, even though the latter, too, could be condemend arbitrarily to death. The difference is that the subjects of the Nazi state faced death only as a future possibility, whereas the slaves were, in some sense, already beyond death, hanging for a few precious moments over the void. As Solzhenitsyn has written on more than one occasion in *The Gulag Archipelago,* you were already dead when you entered the camp and those who went on fighting soon became aware of it.

16. G. W. F. Hegel, *The Phenomenology of Mind,* trans. J. B. Baillie (New York: Harper Torchbooks, 1967), pp. 239–40. [The translation has been modified to

conform more closely with the French translation by J. Hyppolite cited by Dockès.—Trans.]

17. Ibid. This first moment is essential to the Hegelian dialectic, whereby the master becomes dependent on his productive slave.

18. J. F. Steiner, *Treblinka, la révolte d'un camp d'extermination* (Paris: Fayard, 1966); A. Solzhenitsyn, *The Gulag Archipelago*, trans. P. T. Whitney (New York: Harper & Row, 1978).(Yes. I know, comparison is odious. But still!)

19. See G. Debien, *Les Esclaves aux Antilles françaises* (Basse-Terre, 1974), chap. 19.

20. This helps to clarify the connection between historical situations that appear to be different a priori, but still, in our view, are characterized by slavery. In the concentration camp, forced-labor camp, or factory, the power of life and death does not derive directly from the relations between the guard or manager and the forced laborers: they are not privately owned and appropriated; but it does derive from a delegation of the power of the state over the lives of these quasislaves. In the case of ancient slavery or slavery from the sixteenth to the eighteenth century, what happened was that in the end the power of life and death tended to be taken from private hands and placed in public hands, with the state taking exclusive charge. By contrast, in the case of forced labor by prisoners, this power tends to move out of the hands of the state and into the hands of its functionaries.

21. See J.-P. Vernant, *Mythe et société*, p. 28: "Because he stood outside the city, the slave stood outside society, outside humanity. His only being was that of a productive tool."

22. Emile Benveniste, *Le Vocabulaire des institutions indo-européennes* (Paris: Editions de Minuit, 1969), 1:355–61; it is observed that the designation of the slave is borrowed from another tongue.

23. My remarks have benefitted from conversations with J. M. Servet.

24. Aristotle adds: "Such goodness is possible in every type of personage, even in a woman or a slave, though the one is perhaps an inferior, and the other a wholly worthless being" (*Poetics*, 1454a20). See P. Vidal-Naquet, "Esclavage et gynécocratie dans la tradition, le mythe et l'utopie," *Recherches sur les structures sociales dans l'Antiquité classique*, Caen colloquium, 1969 (Paris: Centre Nationale de Recherche Scientifique, 1970).

25. The value of the slave relative to that of the horse seems rather higher than in America in the eighteenth century.

26. See P. Bonnassié, "De l'Esclavagisme au féodalisme," paper delivered to the Société d'études du féodalisme.

27. Aristotle, *Politics*, book i, chaps. 2, 5, 13, 15.

28. Situations in which services are destined for sale as commodities are rare.

29. In the *Wealth of Nations*, Adam Smith explained how a man impoverished himself by employing many domestic servants, but enriched himself by employing many workers in manufacture.

30. Nazi ideology amounted to a slave system: for example, it envisaged the subjection of the Slavs, who were to be made productive slaves.

31. Was this rebirth of slavery in the modern era a reemergence of a slave system? To be sure, slaves were used as productive laborers on plantations in America, in the Antilles, in the Southern states in the United States, and in Brazil. Slave relations of production were *predominant*, but only regionally. On the world level, this relation was subordinate to capitalist relations.

32. With the partial exception of the Mediterranean regions (see below, chap. 4), where the connection with slavery persisted.

33. See below, chap. 1.

34. Following the death of a *servus casatus* with no descendants, the lord could call upon a free peasant to "accept" the charges associated with the land.

35. It is easier to recognize the man who has become free, for emancipation, whether individual or collective, may leave traces.

36. C. Van de Kieft, "Les 'colliberti' et l'évolution du servage dans la France centrale et occidentale (X–XIIᵉ siècle)," *Revue d'histoire du droit* 32 (1964): 384.

37. Prisons or barracks in which slaves in labor gangs were sometimes lodged.

38. [Dockès includes here a brief discussion of the German term *ökonomische Gesellschaftsformation*, used by Marx. The problem, he says, is that Marx used this term in two senses. In the first, the word *formation* is taken to refer to a process in natural history (as in *Capital*, book i, for example), and particularly to the notion of a *geological formation*, "as is proven," says the author, "by the various drafts of his letter to Vera Zasulich." (See Marx and Engels, *Werke* 19:690, for Marx's remarks on this point.) The author then considers the problem of translating this term into French, where, he says, the literal translation, "la formation économique de la société," will do when one is thinking of the process, but not when one is thinking of the result of the process (i.e., in the sense in which, in English, one refers to a "rock formation" as the result of the geological process by which it was formed). He is unhappy with the translation of the term most often found in French versions of Marx, namely, "formation économique et sociale," which is inadequate because it affords an equal status to economic and social factors, whereas Marx, he feels, clearly intended with the German to give precedence to the economic. He finally decides to use "Formation économico-sociale," though this, he says, is "scarcely better." One might render this into English as "economico-social formation," or "economic social formation," as fairly literal translations of the German. However, the most recent and widely respected translation of *Capital*, by Ben Fowkes (New York: Random House, 1976), uses the term "economic formation of society," and I have decided to use this wherever the author has put, in French, "Formation économico-sociale." Since he often abbreviates this in French, I have abbreviated in English (EFS). In other places the author refers merely to "formation sociale" (just as Marx sometimes used simply *Gesellschaftsformation*), and this I have rendered as "social formation," a term probably more familiar to readers of English works in the Marxist tradition (such as those of Perry Anderson) than "economic formation of society." My apologies to the reader for this confused state of affairs.— Trans.]

39. Rome installed throughout the empire a network of cities, each of which was a replica of the capital. The phenomenon is rather similar to that of crystal formation, starting from a basic unit.

40. Louis Althusser, "Marxisme et lutte de classes," *Positions* (Paris: Editions Sociales, 1976), p. 63; Etienne Balibar, "Sur la dialectique historique," *Cinq études sur le matérialisme historique* (Paris: Maspero, 1974), p. 229 passim; Nicos Poulantzas, *Les Classes sociales dans le capitalisme aujourd'hui* (Paris: Seuil, 1974), p. 16.

41. Althusser, *Positions*, p. 16; Balibar, "K. Marx et le marxisme," *Cinq études*, p. 48 (Balibar has since abandoned this "Althusserian" position).

42. Karl Marx, *The Poverty of Philosophy* (New York: International Publishers, 1963), p. 173.

43. Georg Lukács, *History and Class Consciousness*, trans. Rodney Livingstone (Cambridge, Mass.: MIT Press, 1971).

44. See below, chaps. 1 and 4.

45. When the slaves, or later the serfs or peasants in the "jacqueries," shouted "Kill them all," referring to the masters and lords, were they not expressing in the only way they could the idea of eliminating the relation of domination itself?

46. Vernant, *Mythe et société*, p. 14.

47. See E. M. Schtajerman (Staerman), *Die Krise der Sklavenhalterordnung im Westen des römischen Reiches* (Berlin: 1964), translated from the 1957 Russian edition, pp. 112–31, 238–48.

48. Christianity itself, when it made its first inroads, may have been close to a servile cult.

49. See below, chaps. 1 and 4, and J. P. Brisson, *Spartacus* (Paris: Club du Livre, 1969), passim.

50. The distinction between the economic, political, and ideological levels may help us to understand the class struggle, but should not be regarded as a way of dissecting a social conflict into separate segments. See below our critique of Althusser's views.

51. Richard Lefebvre-des-Noëttes, *L'Attelage et le cheval de selle à travers les ages, contribution à l'histoire de l'esclavage* 2d ed. (Paris: Picard, 1931), 2 vols.; see also *De la Marine antique à la marine moderne* (Paris: Masson & Cie, 1934).

52. The slave relation and the slave struggle are but two aspects of the same thing from the first; the struggle even precedes the existence of the relation, which is born out of the original violence.

53. It might be said that the vulgar materialist tradition begins with Aristotle and his assertion that the slave system would persist until the advent of automation. But clearly this meant that "he regarded the slave economy as nontransitory"; Marx, *Marginal Notes on Adolph Wagner's "Lehrbuch der politischen Ökonomie."* (The French edition is cited: Marx, *Oeuvres* [Paris: Gallimard], p. 1530.)

54. In *The Poverty of Philosophy,* Marx says that what Proudhon "has not understood is that these definite social relations are just as much produced by men as linen, flax, etc. Social relations are closely bound up with productive forces. In acquiring new productive forces men change their mode of production; and in changing their mode of production, in changing the way of earning their

living, they change all their social relations. The handmill gives you society with the feudal lord; the steam-mill, society with the industrial capitalist" (chap. 2, Second Observation, p. 109 of the previously cited edition).

55. Joseph Stalin, *Problems of Leninism*. [I have rendered this passage from the French, cited from *Questions de Leninisme* (Paris: Editions Sociales, 1946), 2:199.—Trans.]

56. See *The German Ideology* (1845); *The Poverty of Philosophy* (1847); *Grundrisse* (1857–58).

57. Karl Marx, *A Contribution to the Critique of Political Economy* (New York: International Publishers, 1970), pp. 20–21.

58. [A problem arises here because of the existence of alternate translations into English of this key phrase in Engels's letter of 21–22 September 1890 to Joseph Bloch (see *Marx and Engels, Selected Correspondnece* [Moscow: Foreign Languages Publishing House, n.d., p. 498). In German Engels used the phrase *in letzter Instanz*, which in the English translation just cited became "ultimately": "According to the materialist conception of history, the *ultimately* determining element in history is the production and reproduction of real life." Althusser, with whom the author will argue later on, rendered the German into French as *en dernière instance*, and, largely through Althusser's work and its English translations (where the phrase becomes "in the last instance"), it has entered English usage. (See, for example, Louis Althusser, *For Marx*, trans. Ben Brewster [New York: Vintage, 1970], pp. 111, 203 n.) Here I shall use "in the last instance," to emphasize the allusion to both Engels and Althusser, which will be important in what follows; it may also be of interest that "instance" in English preserves, but rather more faintly than either the French or German, the echo of the judicial system, the court of appeals.—Trans.]

59. See below, Appendix to the Introduction.

60. See Appendix.

61. See Appendix. On the connections between banal seigniory and water mills, see below, chap. 3.

62. In anthropology the relation between productive forces and social relations has been studied by F. Pouillon, *L'Anthropologie économique*, Dossiers africains (Paris: Maspero, 1976), pp. 57ff.

63. Stephen A. Marglin, "What Do bosses Do?" (Mimeographed, Harvard University, August, 1971). [The passages cited here have been rendered from the French.—Trans.] See chap. 3, for further discussion of the conflict studied by Marc Bloch.

64. As noted by Jean Gimpel, *La Révolution industrielle au moyen âge* (Paris: Seuil, 1975), p. 20.

65. See chap. 3.

66. Marglin, "What Do bosses Do?"

67. In the Preface (see Appendix to Introduction). As we shall see, this is not the argument of *Capital*.

68. Marx, *Critique*, p. 20.

69. Balibar, *Cinq études*, p. 80.

70. Ibid., p. 80.

71. Ibid., p. 181.

72. See his analysis in *Capital*, book i, chap. 7.

73. Balibar, *Cinq études*, p. 182.

74. Marx, *Capital* (New York: International Publishers, 1967), vol. i, part 4, p. 371.

75. Ibid., p. 364. See P. Dockès, *L'Internationale du capital*, pp. 240ff.

76. Marx, *Capital*, vol. I, part 4, p. 367.

77. Ibid., p. 427.

78. Ibid., vol. I, part 8, p. 763. This phrase occurs again in Marx's letter to Mikhailovsky: Marx and Engels, *Selected Correspondence*, pp. 376–79.

79. Mikhailovsky letter, *Selected Correspondence*, p. 376. See P. Dockès, "Notes sur le matérialisme historique," *Cahiers A.E.H.* 9, (1977): 77ff.

80. In the letter to Mikhailovsky mentioned in n. 78, p. 377.

81. Letter to Vera Zasulich, Marx and Engels, *Selected Correspondence*, p. 412.

82. Letter to Mikhailovsky, *Selected Correspondence*, p. 378. Italics added.

83. Marx was not alone, moreover. Note how many doubts and questions are expressed in these two remarks of Engels: First, in comparing Tacitus's picture of the Germans with the "redskins" of the United States (in his letter to Marx of 8 December 1882, *Briefwechsel*, p. 690): "The resemblance is in fact all the more surprising in that the modes of production are so fundamentally different in the two cases. . . . This shows precisely how at this stage the mode of production is less decisive than the degree of dissolution of the old blood ties and of the old reciprocal community of the sexes in the tribe." And second, with reference to "medieval and feudal society" in his letter of December 22, 1882 to Marx (cited in *Pre-Capitalist Economic Formations*, p. 148): "It is certain that serfdom and bondage are not a peculiarly medieval-feudal form, we find them everywhere or nearly everywhere where conquerors have the land cultivated for them by the old inhabitants—e.g. very early in Thessaly." See also chap. 2 below.

84. Marx, *Capital*, vol. 3, part 6, p. 791.

85. Etienne Balibar, "Plus-value et classes sociales," *Cinq études*, p. 178, cites the following sentence from Marx, in a letter to Engels (dated 30 April 1863): "And, to conclude, the class struggle, which is the movement and resolution of all this shit" [rendered from the French—Trans.].

86. Althusser, "Soutenance d'Amiens," *Positions*, p. 40.

87. See Appendix to the Introduction.

88. Marx, *Capital*, vol. 3, part 6, chap. xlvii, p. 791.

89. Ibid., p. 791: "Under such conditions the surplus labor for the nominal owner of the land can only be extorted from them by other than economic means, whatever the form assumed may be." Also, on p. 792, he says that surplus labor "appears directly in the brutal form of enforced labor for a third person." As is well known, Althusser has made a distinction between the dominant political, ideological, economic, and regional structure and the determination in the last instance by the economic, or, as we should say, by the antagonistic class relations or relations of production.

90. Marx, *Capital*, vol. 3, part 6, chap. xlvii, p. 791. The entirety of chap. xlvii, section II, "Labor Rent," ought to be cited.

91. Engels, *Anti-Dühring*, p. 184.

92. Direct compulsion makes reproduction of the system possible, by making "labor rent" "a reality," but the basis of this compulsion is the relation of production. It is true, as Marx emphasizes, that "here as always it is in the interest of the ruling section of society to sanction the existing order as law and to legally establish its limits given through usage and tradition. Apart from all else, this, by the way, comes about of itself as soon as the constant reproduction of the basis of the existing order and its fundamental relations assumes a regulated and orderly form in the course of time" (*Capital*, vol. 3, part 6, chap. xlvii, p. 793). Thus straightforward extortion first becomes a custom and tradition, and is finally sanctified by the law, and in this orderly and almost necessary form becomes an indispensable factor of reproduction itself.

93. Jean-Paul Sartre, *Critique de la raison dialectique* (Paris: Gallimard, 1960). A social group is said to be "serialized" when it is decomposed into an "infinity" of competing individualities. It becomes a series.

94. In the context of the present study, we aim only to outline an interpretive scheme.

95. This does not mean that we view the state only as a repressive instrument, an organ in the class struggle. It is clearly also an "administrator of things." But these two aspects are inherently associated, since these "things" are the possessions of the ruling class and are nothing other than the materialization of the primordial social relation.

96. We are merely setting forth a simple hypothesis that may be useful for interpreting the data. Obviously, it was out of the question to envisage writing a history of slavery in antiquity and the early Middle Ages. Why not write another "Considérations sur les causes de la grandeur des Romains et de leur décadence"? Nor do we intend to elaborate a theory of one mode of production or another, or a theory of the transition from one to another. Rather, we hope to specify the ways in which two abstractions are interrelated: the history described by historians on the one hand, and a theory of history on the other.

97. Plato, *Republic*, 578d, e.

98. Marx, *Critique*, p. 20.

99. In *The German Ideology* (New York: International Publishers, 1970), Marx and Engels emphasize the division of labor above all else.

100. This causality is historical and must be differentiated from a logical determination, whether of the very short-term type (e.g., supply and demand determine price) or of the synchronic type, as in laws of physics or statistical regularities (.e.g, old age is the cause of suicide).

101. Marx, *Capital*, vol. 1, part 1. Was the objection raised by the German-American newspaper as limited as Marx pretends it was, however, or did it challenge determinism itself?

102. Marx, *Capital*, vol. 3, part 6, p. 791. See above.

103. Balibar, *Cinq études*, p. 115, observes that the accelerated development of labor productivity in certain capitalist countries is "inconceivable" theoretically if one accepts that the capitalist relations of production have become fetters.

104. Even if Marx and Engels did state unequivocally in *The German Ideology* that "each new productive force, insofar as it is not merely a quantitative extension of productive forces already known (for instance the bringing into cultivation of fresh land), causes a further development of the division of labor" (*The German Ideology*, p. 43).

105. See Mao Tse-Tung, *On Contradiction* (Peking: Foreign Languages Press, 1968), p. 26.

106. Is it the exploited class that triumphs, or in part thanks to the participation of this class in the class struggle, a new "parasitic" or exploitative class that had grown up within the old mode of production?

107. Marx and Engels, *Werke*, 39:205ff. (An English translation may be found in Marx and Engels, *Selected Letters* [Peking: Foreign Languages Press, 1977], p. 100.) Engels has just finished saying: "Political, legal, philosophical, religious, literary, artistic, etc., development is based on economic development. But all these react upon one another and also upon the economic basis. . . . Interaction takes place on the basis of economic necessity, which *ultimately* always asserts itself."

108. Marx and Engels, *Werke*, 37:462ff.; English trans. in *Selected Correspondence*, p. 498.

109. Borgius letter: "Die Menschen machen ihre Geschichte selbst" (see n. 107).

110. Ibid., "Aber in einem gegebenen, sie bedingenden Milieu."

111. "In letzter Instanz bestimmende Moment in der Geschichte."

112. See above.

113. B. Rosier, *Cours de systèmes et structures économiques* (mimeographed, Aix).

114. Engels, *Anti-Dühring*, pp. 184–85.

115. Ibid., p. 189.

116. Ibid., p. 190.

117. With respect to the materialism of the mechanism of the productive forces.

118. Althusser, *Positions*, p. 64.

119. Althusser, *Pour Marx* (Paris: Maspero, 1965), p. 215. [I have preferred to give my own translation. In the existing English translation, previously cited, the passage quoted appears on p. 209.—Trans.]

120. Althusser, *Positions*, p. 64.

121. Ibid., pp. 138 ff.

122. Ibid., p. 140.

123. Ibid., p. 145.

124. Ibid., p. 146.

125. Ibid., p. 63.

126. Ibid., p. 146.

127. Mao, *On Contradiction*, p. 26.

128. "There are many contradictions in the process of development of a complex thing, and one of them is necessarily the principal contradiction whose existence and development determine or influence the existence and development of the other contradictions. For instance, in capitalist society the two forces in contradiction, the proletariat and the bourgeoisie, form the principal contradiction. The other contradictions, such as [that] between the remnant feudal class and the bourgeoise . . . are all determined or influenced by this principal contradiction" (Mao, *On Contradiction*, p. 51).

129. Ibid., p. 54.

130. Ibid.

131. Ibid., p. 58.

Chapter 1

1. Marx, *Capital*, vol. 3, chap. xlvii, sec. 5, p. 804.

2. These initials are now commonly used to designate the feudal mode of production and the capitalist mode of production, respectively.

3. "Domiciled," i.e., installed in a hut (*casa*) and provided with a land tenure.

4. We distinguish between *villa* and *latifundium* only in that the latter may consist of more than one *villa* perhaps scattered geographically.

5. The small farm was just sufficient to provide a family with subsistence. Heavy indebtedness made it "unprofitable," all the more so as competition from the great estates increased.

6. Brisson, *Spartacus*, passim.

7. Finley, *The Ancient Economy*, pp. 99–106.

8. Ten *jugera* (or *iugera*) amount to slightly more than 2.4 hectares.

9. These 10 *jugera* may be compared with the 30-hectare farm need to turn a profit—just barely—in France today. It then becomes apparent that a 250-hectare estate was a far more significant piece of property than a farm of comparable size today.

10. Finley, *The Ancient Economy*, pp. 80–81. This was the gross salary, from which expenses for food and various other costs must be subtracted to arrive at a net figure. It is probable that a sesterce was worth between $.40 and $4.00 (in 1979 dollars). Such a calculation makes practically no sense, however, like any such attempt to compare two quite disparate social and economic systems: relative prices of commodities are necessarily quite different. In particular, an *urna* of wheat (13 liters) was worth 4 sesterces during the century of Augustus; in 1976, the world price for a U.S. bushel (36 liters) of wheat was $5.00, which would give an exchange rate of 1 sesterce = $.46 for the two dates. But wheat was then very cheap at Rome (see R. Etienne, *Le Siècle d'Auguste* [Paris: Coolin], p. 53), and fluctuations in the price of wheat on today's world market are enormous (factor of two, for example), so that the same calculation carried out in August 1978 would give 1 sesterce = $.25. In a note to his edition of the *Satiricon* (Paris: Folio), p. 237, no. 1, P. Grimal estimates that 50,000 sesterces amounted to 12,500 gold francs (in the era of Nero, there having been considerable inflation after Augustus), which is not very illuminating.

11. According to Finley, *The Ancient Economy*, p. 101.

12. M. Capozza, *Movimenti servile nel mondo romano in eta reppublicana* (Rome: L'Erma di Bretschneider, 1966); P. A. Brunt, *Social Conflicts in the Roman Republic* (New York: Norton, 1971).

13. It would be interesting to know why this "class front" was constituted then and there. We shall come across it again in the crises of the third century A.D. and later. See below and chap. 4.

14. Proletarius, the proletarian, was a poor citizen, a member of the lowest classes in society, who counted in the city only by virtue of the children—future citizens—he might produce.

15. To belong to the senatorial class, one had to be inscribed in the census rolls as possessing a million sesterces worth of property in land, since commercial activities were in theory forbidden to this nobility. In principle this was not the case for the equestrian order, which required inscription for 400,000 sesterces or a *call by the emperor* to serve him.

16. From *imperium*, in the sense of domination, hegemony: *imperium populi Romani* (hegemony of the Roman people); Cicero, *Verrine Orations*, 5, 8.

17. Ten to twelve cohorts of 700 men.

18. The great families brought up their children for the military and high administrative posts.

19. Naturally the fabulously wealthy Trimalchio, the freedman in Petronius' *Satyricon*, comes to mind for the era of Nero.

20. Etienne, *Le Siècle d'Auguste*, p. 9.

21. From an abundant literature, we may single out: P. R. C. Weaver, *Familia Caesaris* (Cambridge: Cambreidge University Press, 1972); R. H. Barrow, *Slavery in the Roman Empire* (New York: Barnes, 1928); M I. Finley, ed., *Slavery in Classical Antiquity* (Cambridge: Cambridge University Press, 1960), particularly the article by A. H. M. Jones, "Slavery in the Ancient World"; A. H. M. Jones, *The Later Roman Empire* (2 vols.; Oxford: Oxford University Press, 1964); P. A. Brunt, *Italian Manpower, 225 B.C.–A.D. 14* (Oxford: Oxford University Press, 1971); K. D. White, "Latifundia," *Bulletin of the Institute of Classical Studies* 14 (1967): 76 ff.; W. L. Westermann, *The Slave Systems of Greek and Roman Antiquity* (Philadelphia: American Philosophical Society, 1955); D. B. Davis, *The Problem of Slavery in Western Culture* (Ithaca: Cornell University Press, 1966); C. A. Forbes, "The Education and Training of Slaves in Antiquity," *Transactions of the American Philological Association* 86 (1955):321–60; F. Kiechle, *Sklavenarbeit und technischer Fortschritt im römischen Reich* (Wiesbaden, 1969); E. M. Schtajerman, *Die Krise;* "La Villa romana," *Giornata di Studi Russi*, 10 May 1970 (Faenza, 1971); particularly R. Chevallier, *Problématique de la villa gallo-romaine*, pp. 37 ff; *Actes du colloque sur l'esclavage*, Besançon, 1972, 1973 (Paris: Les Belles Lettres, 1974, 1976); G. Boulvert, *Domestique et fonctionnaire sous le Haut-Empire romain: la condition de l'affranchi et de l'esclave du Prince* (Paris: Les Belles Lettres, 1974); J. M. Manjarre, *Esclavos y libertos en la Espana Romana* (Salamanca: University of Salamanca, 1971); J. Vogt, *Skalverei und Humanität, Studien zur antiken Sklaverei und ihrer Erforschung* (Wiesbaden: Steiner, 1965); P. P.

Spranger, *Historische Untersuchungen zu den sklavenfiguren des Plautus und Terrenz* (Wiesbaden: Steiner).

22. See, for example, "Détection aérienne," *Bulletin de la Société de préhistoire du Nord*, special issue, no. 7 (1970); and "La Villa gallo-romaine dans les grandes plaines du nord de la France," *Archeologia* 55 (February 1973). See also *Dossiers de l'archéologie* 22 (May–June 1977).

23. Marcel Le Glay, *Histoire de la France rurale* (Paris: Seuil, 1975), vol. 1, *La Gaule romanisée.* This work is essential for an understanding of the relative importance of the *villae* and their estates, as revealed by recent research. For an idea of the regional diversity we can only refer to reader to this book.

24. See what Columella says, below.

25. See S. Applebaum, *The Agrarian History of England and Wales*, 1:240–44, 266–67.

26. In Italy even the collective rules remained intact, because the state was able to take advantage of them in imposing the *consortium* (collective fiscal responsibility of the villagers) in the fourth century.

27. Le Glay, "La Gaule romanisée," *Histoire de la France rurale*, 1:241 ff.

28. Ibid., p. 242.

29. G. Fouet, "The Gallo-Roman Villa of Montmaurin," *Gallia*, suppl. 20 (1969) (the villa is located near Toulouse).

30. Le Glay, *Histoire*, 1:241.

31. Ibid., "Les Villae," p. 209.

32. See, for example, R. Agache, "La Villa gallo-romaine"; and *Dossiers de l'archéologie* 22 (1977).

33. Columella, *De re rustica.*

34. Le Glay, *Histoire*, p. 247.

35. See above and chap. 4.

36. Musée du Bardo, Tunis.

37. Also to be consulted are Cato, *De agricultura;* Vitruvius, *De architectura*, vi, 6–8; Varro, *De re rustica;* Palladius, *De re rustica*, 1. It is clear that there was much borrowing among them (in particular, Columella repeats what Cato had laid out).

38. Contemporary with the reigns of Claudius and Nero.

39. See book i, 3.

40. See above, pp. 00 ff.

41. *De re rustica*, i, 6.

42. In the case where the chief activities were grouped together ini a single building.

43. See A. Grenier, *Habitations gauloises et villas latines* (Paris, 1906). See also Vitruvius, vi, 6–8; Columella, i; Varro, i, 13.

44. See O. Wormser-Migot, *Le Système concentrationnaire nazi* (thesis; Paris: Presses Universitaires de France, 1968); J. F. Steiner, *Treblinka*, concerning the self-organization of a camp in accordance with the principle, "divide and conquer."

45. See book i, 8, and book xi for what precedes and what follows.

259   Notes to Pages 72–76

46. Book i, 8.

47. Book xi, 1.

48. The time wasted by the slaves in going to borrow a tool was worth more than the tool itself; book i, 8.

49. Book ii, 21.

50. Book xii, 3. On the frequency of injuries, see book xi, 1.

51. Book i, 8.

52. Ibid.

53. Ibid.

54. Ibid. 7.

55. Ibid. 8.

56. "I am averse to allowing our political adversaries, in their forlorn state, to be visited like animals. They are men, and I wish them to be treated as men" (Wormser, Le Système, p. 63). Right down to the final verdict, Goering claimed responsibility for the camps, assuring his judges that he only wanted to limit the "abuses."

57. De re rustica, book i, 8: "these unfortunates," he wrote.

58. Book i, 8.

59. Cato (De agricultura) had earlier laid down principles of conduct for the paterfamilias and his villicus (in the case of a smaller estate). The master was to begin his visit by first paying his respects to the household god, then taking a tour of the property on the same day. The next day he would summon the villicus to render his accounts and supply information. The master must verify the account given by the villicus if he claimed that work was not done because of escape or illness (note the importance of escapes), bad weather, or the need to participate in public works (bad weather did not prevent certain kinds of work, and illness among the slaves should cut down on the quantity of food consumed). After the accounts were checked by amount of labor (numbers of workers and days) expended on each job, accounts of purchases and sales, stores, and advances had to be examined. Everything had to be recorded. Then the master examined the livestock (book ii). The duties of the villicus included maintaining high moral standards and observing religious holidays; he was enjoined "not to lay hands on another man's property" (the fear of a dishonest villicus was always rampant), to refrain from fraud (in regard to seeding, purchases, and sales), "to encourage the others to do good," to keep them in a good sweat, to know what was on their minds, and to avert disputes between slaves. Obviously he was to leave the villa as little as possible, maintain its security, buy nothing without the master's knowledge, make no sacrifice without consulting the master, and consult "neither haruspex, nor augur, nor soothsayer, nor Chaldaean." He must be the first to rise in the morning and the last to retire in the evening and must oversee the condition of men, animals, and tools, and organize work in the fields and workshops. (book vii).

60. See Finley, The Ancient Economy, pp. 98 ff.; and P. Petit, La Paix romaine (Paris: Nouvelle Clio, 1971), pp. 162 ff.

61. C. Lachmann, ed., *Gromatici veteres* (Berlin, 1848), p. 53, cited in Finley, *The Ancient Economy,* p. 148.

62. *Very roughly,* 1 sesterce was worth between $.40 and $4.00 (see n. 10 above). On the fortune of Herodes Atticus, see P. Graindor, *Un Milliardaire antique* (Cairo, 1930), and Finley, *The Ancient Economy,* p. 101. On that of Trimalchio, see Petronius, *Satyricon.* During Nero's reign Trimalchio lost 30 million sesterces relatively easily, regretted not having married a "dowry" of 10 million sesterces, and on one ordinary day put 100 million sesterces back into his coffers because they could not be invested.

63. Finley, *The Ancient Economy,* p. 102.

64. Ibid., p. 102. Concerning the imperial estates, see Petit, *La Paix romaine,* p. 164.

65. See R. Rémondon, *La Crise de l'Empire romain* (Paris: Presses Universitaires de France, 1964), as well as E. M. Schtajerman, *Die Krise;* A. H. M. Jones, *The Latter Roman Empire, 282–602;* M. Rostovtzeff, *The Social and Economic History of the Roman Empire* (Oxford: Oxford University Press, 1926) and *La Crise politique et sociale de l'Empire romain au III* siècle (Musée Belge, 1923); Proceedings of the Eleventh International Congress of the Historical Sciences, Uppsala, 1960; S. Mazzarino, *La Democratizzazione della cultura nel Basso Imperio,* pp. 78 ff.; D. Stojcevic, *De l'Esclave romain au colon,* pp. 93 ff; P. Collinet, *Le Colonat sous l'Empire romain,* Recueil de la Société Jean Bodin (Brussels, 1937), 2, "Le Servage"; Stevens, "Agricultural and Rural Life in the Later Roman Empire," *Cambridge Economic History,* vol. 1 (1942); M. Palasse, *Orient et Occident à propos du colonat romain au Bas-Empire* (Lyon, 1950); idem, *Notes complémentaires sur le colonat,* Recueil de la Société Jean Bodin (Bussels, 1959); W. Seyfarth, *Soziale Fragen der Spätrömischen Kaiserzeit im Spiegel des Theodosianus* (Berlin: Akademie Verlag); M. Bloch, "Comment et pourquoi finit l'esclavage antique," *Annales E. S. C.,* 1947, pp. 30–44, 161–70; J. Gagé, *Les Classes sociales dans l'Empire romain* (Paris: Payot, 1964).

66. Rémondon, *La Crise,* pp. 98–99.

67. He possessed the gold ring.

68. Rémondon, *La Crise,* p. 147.

69. Ibid. See also F. Lot, *La Fin du monde antique et le début du Moyen âge* (Paris: Collection "Evolution de l'humanité," 1927–68); Rostovtzeff, *The Social and Economic History;* Finley, *The Ancient Economy.*

70. We shall see that, on the contrary, it was the slaves who "abandoned" the *villae!*

71. "From the last few centuries of the empire onward, this second method (domiciling) became more and more widespread. . . . great landowners took large chunks from their estates and chopped them up into a myriad of small farms. . . among the beneficiaries of this parcelling out of land were a good many slaves" (Marc Bloch, "Comment et Pourquoi").

72. Finley, *The Ancient Economy.*

73. See below, chap. 4.

74. See Rémondon, *La Crise,* pp. 221 ff.

75. See below, chap. 4.

76. *Paganus*, 'inhabitant of the *pagus*, countrydweller.'

77. Or *dominus*, 'master'; the vocabulary, imagery, and so forth are frequently associated with slavery or serfdom. For example, "no man can be the slave (or serf) of two masters" (the translation "no man can serve two masters" obscures the force of the verb *servire*).

78. Gregory of Tours, *History of the Franks*.

79. See below.

80. See the letter from Marx to Vera Zasulich, third draft, cited in Karl Marx, *Pre-Capitalist Economic Formations*, ed. Eric Hobsbawm (New York: International Publishers), pp. 144–45.

81. The "new community," according to Marx, was the descendant of the "agricultural community," "not yet in existence . . . in the time of Julius Caesar," and vanished by the time of the invasions; it was described by Tacitus (ibid., p. 144).

82. "Evolution du système féodal européen," *Sur la féodalité* (Paris: Editions Sociales [Comité d'Etude et de Recherches Marxistes], 1974), p. 19.

83. According to Marc Bloch, *Les Caractères orginaux de l'histoire rurale française* (Paris: Colin, 1968), 2:97ff. (translated into English by Janet Sondheimer as *French Rural History* [Berkeley: University of California Press, 1966]), the importance of the village chieftainships was far greater than he himself had judged earlier. A form of political lordship would ultimately result from their tendency toward reduced community control, greater power for the chief, hereditary transmission, and transformation of gifts into regularly obligatory prestations.

84. In a certain sense, moreover, the German tribes constituted a "reserve army" of slaves "outside the walls" of the empire. There, slave merchants replenished their supplies, and the tribes themselves at first came to work in the empire. See below, chap. 4.

85. See E. A. Thompson, "Peasant Revolts in Late Roman Empire, Gaul and Spain," *Past and Present* 2 (1952), reprinted in *Studies in Ancient Society* (London: Furleyed, 1974); Schtajerman, *Die Krise*, pp. 5, 147, 243, 270, 405–30, 441, 453–61; Gagé, *Les Classes sociales*, p. 405; M. Mazza, *Lotte sociale e Restaurazione Autoritaria nel Terzo Secolo D.C.* (Catane, 1970), pp. 326–27; V. Sirago, *Gallia Placidia e la transformazione dell'Occidente* (Louvain, 1961), pp. 376 ff.

86. As Rémondon has written (*La Crise*, p. 221).

87. Slavianus, *De gubernatione dei*, v, 5, 21.

88. Querolus (Hermann edition, 1937).

89. Perry Anderson, *Passages from Antiquity to Feudalism* (London: New Left Books, 1974), p. 103.

90. See e.g., Le Glay, *Histoire*, 1:281.

91. See Duby, in ibid., p. 31.

92. Finley, *The Ancient Economy*, p. 89; Thompson, "Peasant Revolts."

93. I say "primarily" because peasants might work their own parcel and still be subject to *corvée* labor on the directly exploited portion of the demesne.

94. E. A. Thompson, "Peasant Revolts," is very clear in this respect: "Our sources seem to suggest that these revolts were above all the work of rural slaves, or at least that such slaves played a leading role in them" (p. 11). Nevertheless, he does not neglect the role of the *coloni*. See Anderson, *Passages*, pp. 102–3.

95. This is the view of Gagé, *Classs sociales*, p. 407.

96. Ibid., p. 409.

97. Ibid., p. 407.

98. See below, chap. 4, on the use of this term in the tenth century.

99. *Eucharisticos*, v, 377–96, cited by Gagé, *Classes sociales*, p. 408.

100. *Epigramma* (Schenkel ed., in Corp. Script. Eccl. Latin., XVI, pp. 503–5, cited by Gagé, *Classes sociales*, p. 408.

101. "Alliance" means neither that the two aristocracies fused nor that the process unfolded without conflict! As is well known, there is no dearth of instances of "Roman" landowners being massacred or reduced to slavery. In the midst of all this violence, however, the new aristocracy was forged from these various antagonistic elements.

102. For example, Pierre Toubert, "L'Italie rurale aux VIIIᵉ–IXᵉ siècles, Essai de typologie domaniale," Settimane di Spoleto, 1972, published as *I problemi dell'Occidente nel secolo 8*, vol. 20 (1973).

103. What is needed is either to revise the concept of the feudal mode as composed of two successive forms within a single mode of production, or to regard the Middle Ages as a prolonged transitional period between the slave mode and the capitalist mode of production.

104. The fact that nondomiciled slaves were regarded as movable property, generally not included as part of a man's fortune, has led to their numbers being underestimated. See, for example, Bloch, "Comment et pourquoi."

105. See Pierre Toubert, *Les Structures du Latium médiéval* (Rome, 1973), 1:474 ff.

106. Charles Verlinden, *L'Esclavage en Europe médiévale* (Bruges, 1955), vol. 1: *Péninsule Iberique, France.*

107. P. Bonnassié, *La Catalogne du milieu du Xᵉ à la fin du XIᵉ siècle, Croissance et mutation d'une société* (2 vols.; Toulouse, 1975); see also "De l'Esclavage au féodalisme," paper delivered to La Société d'étude du féodalisme, 1977. The Visigothic codes were promulgated by the kings of Toledo between 642 and 700.

108. See below, chap. 2 for a discussion of mortality and emancipation and chap. 4 for a discussion of escapes. Were emancipations due to the Church important—more important in the early Middle Ages than in the third century, for example?

109. These sales were authorized by the penitentials as long as the child was not yet fourteen years of age. Countless examples are known from such accounts as that of Gregory of Tours and from the barbarian laws, as well as the formularies (that of Marculf, for example). See Bonnassié, "De l'Esclavage."

110. As Bonnassié says.

111. See chap. 4.

112. See below, D and chap. 4.

113. See Marc Bloch, *La Société Féodale* (Paris: Albin Michel, 1968), p. 358; trans. as *Feudal Society*, by L. A. Manyon (Chicago: University of Chicago Press, 1961).

114. Toubert, *Les Structures*, 1:481.

115. Ibid., p. 476: the *portiuncula* was a 'tiny plot' allotted to a gang slave.

116. Georges Duby, *Guerriers et paysans* (Paris: Gallimard, 1973), translated by Howard B. Clarke as *The Early Growth of the European Economy* (Ithaca: Cornell University Press, 1974).

117. Ibid., p. 53. (English ed., p. 42).

118. Bloch, *Feudal Society*, p. 259, and "Comment et pourquoi."

119. Let us say that they were heavier at the beginning of the ninth century than in the seventh century. See Duby, *Guerriers et paysans*, p. 106; for the aggravation during the Carolingian era, see R. Doehaerd, *Le Haut moyen âge* (Paris: Nouvelle Clio, 1971), pp. 194–95.

120. Toubert, *Les Structures*, 1:480.

121. On encastlement and banal seigniory, see below and ibid., pp. 303 ff.

122. On Latium, see Toubert, *Les Structures;* on Provence, see J.-P. Poly, *La Provence et la société féodale, 879–1166* (Paris: Bordas, 1976); on the Loire region, see P. Gasnault and J. Vezin, *Documents comptables de Saint-Martin-de-Tours à l'époque mérovingienne* (Paris, 1975); on Catalonia, Bonnassié, *La Catalogne;* on the hypothesis of the chiefly local importance of the "classical" estate in the seventh century, see F. L. Ganshof, "Quelques aspects principaux de la vie économique dans la monarchie francaise du VII⁰ siècle," Settimane di Spoleto, 1957 (Spoleto, 1958), pp. 73 ff.

123. See Duby, *Guerriers et paysans*, p. 110; Bloch, *La Société féodale*, pp. 339–41.

124. We shall make use of Toubert's article "L'Italie rurale aux VIII⁰–IX⁰ siècles, Essai de typologie domaniale," in *I problemi dell'Occidente nel secolo 8*, 20: for the south of France, see also Poly, *La Provence*, pp. 76 ff., and "Régime domanial et rapports de production 'féodalistes' dans le Midi (VIII⁰–X⁰ siècles)," Colloque de Rome, 1978 (Paris: Centre National de Recherche Scientifique, in preparation).

125. Bonnassié, "De l'esclavagisme," stresses the example of Christian Spain, particularly the Asturoleon kingdom in Catalonia, where allodial property was by a large margin in the majority, in certain locales accounting for up to 85 percent of the parcels; he also points to Anglo-Saxon England in the seventh and eighth centuries, where originally the *ceorl* emerged as a free peasant, and to Picardy, where he says small property was similarly predominant.

126. See Bloch, *Les Caractères originaux*, vol. 1.

127. Concerning the development of the productive forces and mills, see below, chap. 3. Bonnassié assiduously develops the argument that technological progress is attributable to peasant communities.

128. The campaigns to obtain oaths from people throughout the empire presupposed a highly developed centralized organization, surely, but it also shows the importance attached to the oaths by the state, given the enormous administrative effort required.

129. See Duby in Le Glay, *Histoire*, p. 31.

130. Bloch, *La Société féodale*, p. 359.

131. See especially the article by Marc Bloch, "Les *colliberti*, étude sur la formation de la classe servile," *Revue historique* 157 (1929): 1–48 and 225–63. An excellent synthesis of the debates may be found in C. Van de Kieft, "Les Colliberti, évolution du servage dans la France centrale et occidentale," *Revue d'histoire du droit* 32 (1964): 362 ff. See also Duby, *La Société aux XIe–XIe siècles dans la région mâconnaise* (1953).

132. Doehaerd, *Le Haut moyen âge*, p. 197.

133. Duby, *Guerriers et paysans*, p. 110.

134. Doehaerd, *Le Haut moyen âge*, p. 203.

135. Bonnassié, "De l'Esclavagisme."

136. Georges Duby, *Les Trois ordres ou l'imaginaire du féodalisme* (Paris: Gallimard, 1978), p. 199 (*The Three Orders: Feudal Society Imagined*, trans. A. Goldhammer [Chicago: University of Chicago Press, 1980]).

137. Toubert, *Les Structures*, 1:330.

138. *Incastellamento*, that is, occupation of the soil by means of the *castrum*, or "permanent assemblage of dwellings, grouped together and fortified" (Toubert, *Les Structurtes*, 1:314, n. 1.

139. See Lynn White, Jr., "Stirrup, Mounted Shock Combat, Feudalism, and Chivalry," *Medieval Technology and Social Change* (New York: Oxford University Press, 1966).

140. The stirrup is supposed to have made the use of heavy armament possible, and this in turn is supposed to have been more effective in combat, whence the necessity for this new type of cavalry and hence the creation of fiefs, for the upkeep of the knight and his "lance." See White, "Stirrup." Would it not be possible to suppose, conversely, that feudalism "made" the stirrup (which had been known in the west for several centuries, having been introduced by the Vandals in the seventh century—why did it not become widespread before the tenth and eleventh centuries?).

141. See above, Introduction: as Engels asked Dühring, Where did Robinson get his sword?

142. To simplify matters, it was doubtless true that in some regions—in Provence, for example—certain specific institutions continued to function. See Poly, *La Provence*, p. 39.

143. Duby, *Guerriers et paysans*, p. 199. See especially, Duby, "La Seigneurie banale," in *L'Economie rurale et la vie des campagnes dans l'occident médiéval* (Paris: Aubier, 1962). Marc Bloch had already explained the nature of the "ban," in *Les Caractères orginaux*, 1:82 ff. (English ed., pp. 79 ff.)

144. Poly, *La Provence*, pp. 127–28.

145. Bonnassié, *De l'Esclavagisme*. When he says "wholly novel," he is thinking of the south of France.

146. Toubert, *Les Structures*, 1:325.

147. E. de La Boétie, *Discours de la servitude volontaire* (Paris: Payot, 1976), p. 111.

148. Bloch, "Comment et pourquoi," and "L'Esclavage dans l'Europe médiévale," *Annales d'histoire sociale*, 1939.

149. See Bloch, "Comment et pourquoi"; Charles Verlinden, *L'Esclavage*, 1:53.

150. For example, Verlinden, *L'esclavage*, 1:53.

151. Finley, *The Ancient Economy*.

152. H. Wallon, *Histoire de l'esclavage dans l'Antiquité* (Paris, 1847–79), 3 vols.; E. Meyer, *Die Sklaverei im Altertum* (Dresden, 1898).

158. Max Weber, "Die sozialen Gründe des Untergangs der antiken Kultur," 1896; s.v. "Agrargeschichte," in Lexis, *Handwörterbuch der Staatwissenschaften*, 1 (2d ed.): 81. *Die römische Agrargeschichte* (Stuttgart, 1891); "Agrarverhältnisse im Altertum," *Gesammelte Aufsätze zur Sozial und Wirtschaftsgeschichte* (Tubingen, 1924), pp. 4 ff.

154. Fustel de Coulanges, *Recehrches sur quelques problèmes d'histoire* (Paris, 1885), with a lengthy treatment of the colonate, pp. 15–24.

155. Rostovtzeff, *The Social and Economic History*.

156. Lot, *La Fin du monde antique*.

157. R. Fogel and S. Engerman, *Time on the Cross* (New York: Little, Brown, 1974); P. David and P. Temin, "Slavery, the Progressive Institution," *Journal of Economic History*, (September 1974; J. Kahn, whose article in *Nouvelle Critique* (1970) has been reprinted in *Aujourd'hui l'histoire* (Paris: Editions Sociales, 1974), p. 159; A. Conrad and J. R. Meyer, "The Economics of Slavery," *Journal of Political Economy*, April 1958, reprinted in *The Economics of Slavery* (Chicago: Aldine, 1964); H. G. Gutman, *Slavery and the Numbers Game: A Critique of "Time on the Cross"* (Urbana: University of Illinois Press, 1975); P. A. David, et al., *Reckoning with Slavery: Critical Essays in Quantitative History of American Negro Slavery* (Oxford: Oxford University Press, 1975); E. S. Morgan, *American Slavery, American Freedom* (New York: Norton, 1975); E. D. Genovese, *The Political Economy of Slavery* (New York: Random House, 1967); idem, *Roll, Jordan, Roll* (New York: Pantheon, 1974). On the Antilles, see G. Debien, *Les Esclaves aux Antilles françaises* (Fort de France, 1974); on Canada, M. Trudel, *L'Esclavage au Canada français* (Montreal: Presses Universitaires Laval, 1960); on Brazil, G. Freyre, *The Masters and the Slaves* (New York: Knopf, 1946).

158. J. Chesneaux, *Du Passé faisons table rase?* (Paris, Maspero, 1976), shows that to write for a master, in the academic sense of the term, often comes down to writing for the masters.

Chapter 2

1. Friedrich Engels, *The Origin of the Family, Private Property, and the State* (New York: International Publishers, 1970), p. 137.

2. Duby, *Guerriers et Paysans*, p. 50 (italics added); English ed., p. 40.

3. Bloch, "Comment et Pourquoi," p. 34.

4. Conrad and Meyer, "The Economics of Slavery."

5. *De re rustica*, iii, 3.

6. Finley, *The Ancient Economy*, p. 117.

7. See above, chap. 1.

8. Pliny the Younger, *Letters* 3, 19.

9. Duby, *The Early Growth,* pp. 92–93.

10. S. Mazzarino, *La Fin du monde antique* (Paris: Gallimard, 1973), pp. 147–48 (originally published in 1959).

11. Ibid., p. 148 (italics added).

12. Lot, *La Fin du monde antique,* pp. 118 ff.

13. Fogel and Engerman attempted to measure the relative efficiency of slavery in the southern U.S. in *Time on the Cross,* and even for this relatively recent period encountered enormous difficulties.

14. Are we to suppose that these *corvées* resembled the old system but for a reduction in space (from the entire *villa* to the demesne) and in time (limited to certain days only)? Surely the answer is no, for the new system associated with domiciling inevitably altered the efficiency of work on the demesne—the question is whether that efficiency was increased or decreased. See below, my critique of Marc Bloch in this connection.

15. Lot, *La Fin du monde antique,* pp. 118 ff.

16. Marx, *Oeuvres* (Paris: Gallimard), 2:375.

17. The qualification "relatively rapid" is added because *all* social relations evolve!

18. A phenomenon still in evidence today. As an epigraph to chap. 1, we chose a remark made by Aimé Césaire, about Haiti, pitying the country that knew the "anarchy of millet and sweet potatoes in those tiny plots."

19. See Pierre Dockès, "La Critique de la division du travail," *L'Internationale du capital* (Paris: Presses Universitaires de France, 1975), pp. 229 ff.

20. Marx and Engels, *The German Ideology,* p. 45.

21. Marx, *Capital,* vol. 3, chap. xlvii, part 5, p. 807.

22. Finley, *The Ancient Economy,* p. 83, based on the work of Slicher van Bath (see Finley, chap. 3, n. 67).

23. See chap. 1, n. 157 above for recent works on this question.

24. W. Fogel and S. Engerman, "Explaining the Relative Efficiency of Slave Agriculture in the Antebelum South," *American Economic Review,* June 1977. The authors write that "large slave plantations were 48% more productive than the small free farms of the South" (p. 290).

25. Ibid., p. 291.

26. Paul A. Samuelson, *Economics,* 10th ed. (New York: McGraw-Hill, 1976), p. 783.

27. Georges Duby, *L'Economie rurale et la vie des campagnes dans l'Occident médiéval* (Paris: Aubier, 1962), 2:435.

28. Ibid.

29. Ibid., p. 514. In the fourteenth century the *corvée* labor laborer may have eaten two to three times as much as the domestic slave.

30. See Duby, *L'Economie rurale.*

31. See above, and Duby, *Guerriers et paysans,* p. 5 (Eng. trans., p.40).

32. See, for example, Finley, *The Ancient Economy,* pp. 109–10.

33. The "rate of consumption" is defined as the volume of goods consumed by a family in a given period of time.

34. Marx, *Capital*, vol. 3, chap. xxiii, p. 385.

35. Ibid., p. 386.

36. Ibid., p. 386.

37. Ibid., p. 384.

38. See Dockès, *L'Internationale du capital*, pp. 241 ff., and B. Rosier, *Croissance et crises capitalistes* (Paris: Presses Universitaires Françaises, 1975), pp. 203 ff.

39. Marx, *Capital*, vol. 1, chap. xiii, p. 332, n. 2.

40. Max Weber, *Die sozialen Gründe des Untergangs der antiken Kultur*; G. Salvioli, *Le Capitalisme dans le monde antique* (Paris, 1906); Lot, *La Fin du monde antique*; Schtajerman (Staerman), *Die Krise der Sklavenhalterordnung im Westen des römischen Reiches*.

41. Finley, *The Ancient Economy*, p. 83.

42. E. Meyer, *Die Sklaverei im Altertum* (Dresden, 1898).

43. Werner Sombart, *Der Moderne Kapitalismus*, 2d ed. (Munich, 1916–17).

44. P. Dommergues, *Le Monde diplomatique* 2 (1976): 19, although the cause he cites—high demand for cotton—is incorrect.

45. Lot, *La Fin du monde antique*, p. 118.

46. Marx, *Capital*, vol. 2, chap. xx, part 12, p. 478.

47. W. L. Westermann, *The Slave Systems of Greek and Roman Antiquity* (Philadelphia: American Philosophical Society, 1955); I. Beizunska-Malowist, "Les Esclaves nés dans la maison du maître en Egypte romaine," *Studii Classici* 3 (1962): 147–62; "La Procréation des esclaves comme source de l'esclavage," *Mélanges K. Michalowski* (Warsaw, 1966), pp. 275–80.

48. Westermann, *The Slave Systems*, pp. 32–33.

49. Petronius, *Satyricon*, 53: 30 boys and 40 girls.

50. *De re rustica*, i, 8. "The hope of liberty that the masters held out to those who brought the largest number of children into the world" (Jean Bodin, *La République*, p. 53).

51. See above, pp. 133–35.

52. Weber, *Die sozialen Gründe; Agrarverhältnisse im Altertum*, p. 19.

53. See above, pp. 133–35.

54. Anderson, *Passages*, p. 78, and for Anderson's critique of Finley's contrary opinion, see p. 77, n. 36.

55. Such arrangements were already found in the sixteenth century: Bodin writes that "the king of Portugal maintained stud farms for slaves just as for animals" (*La République*, p. 64).

56. See above, pp. 133–35.

57. See the work of C. Deglas and E. Edinval on living conditions in Guadeloupe (mimeographed, Centre Universitaire des Antilles-Guyane, Pointe-à-Pitre).

58. See below, chap. 5.

59. Anderson, *Passages*, pp. 76–77, 99–100, acknowledges the delay between the time the borders were closed and the time that the relative importance of

slavery began to decline, which he explains by way of the possibility of resorting to such expedients as breeding. He also observes that slaves became not only less numerous but also more burdensome, though he does not expand on this point.

60. Finley, *The Ancient Economy*, p. 86. See G. Fouet, "The Gallo-Roman Villa of Montmaurin," *Gallia*, suppl. 20 (1969), pp. 43–46.

61. In 406, for example, the victory of Radagaisus threw enormous numbers of Ostrogothic slaves onto the market. Mazzarino, *La Fin du monde antique*, p. 150.

62. The *expositio totius mundi* (a geo-economic portrait of the Roman world in the late empire) informs us that Pannonia and Mauritania owed their wealth to export of slaves, according to Mazzarino, *La Fin du monde antique*, p. 151 .

63. R. Fossier, *Histoire sociale de l'Occident médiéval* (Paris: Armand Colin, 1970), p. 64.

64. Anderson, *Passages*, p. 99; see Jones, *Slavery in the Ancient World*, p. 197.

65. Duby, *The Early Growth*, p. 40.

66. Fossier, *Histoire sociale*, p. 65.

67. Verlinden, *L'Esclavage*, pp. 717–18.

68. See chap. 1 and ibid., pp. 705–6.

69. Whence the link between the slave system and the slave trade; but was it not the slave system that gave rise to razzias, and not the slave trade that gave rise to slavery?

70. Verlinden, *L'Esclavage*, p. 706, and Fossier, *L'Histoire sociale*, p. 65.

71. Verlinden, *L'Esclavage*, pp. 717–18.

72. See Duby's explanation (p. 135, above) for the increase in the price of slaves on the heels of rising demand in the east and south, which Duby believes made it necessary for the masters to practice breeding and hence to domicile their slaves; Duby, *Guerriers et Paysans*, p. 50 (English ed., p. 40).

73. Bloch, *La Société féodale*.

74. Ibid., p. 349 (English ed., p. 251).

75. Ibid., p. 360 (English ed., p. 258).

76. Ibid., pp. 109–10 (English ed., p. 68).

77. Marc Bloch, "De la grande exploitation domaniale à la rente du sol," *Bulletin of the International Committee of Historical Sciences*, February 1933, pp. 122–26. In 1931 Bloch, in his *Les Caractères originaux*, 1:102, explained the impossibility (or rather the great inconvenience) of selling the surplus by pointing to the absence of any exact method of accounting in the tenth and eleventh centuries, the absence of administrators on whom the lords could rely (as Suger observed, these administrators, the sergeants, almost inevitably transformed themselves into hereditary feudatories and seized power and land from those they served), and the lack of transportation facilities, as well as the dearth of markets in the towns or elsewhere. But at this time his argument was intended to show why *corvée* labor and the size of the demesne were reduced; we shall have more to say on this point.

78. This is also Engels's argument in *The Origin of the Family*, p. 136: "The country estates and their owners had been ruined through the impoverishment of their owners and the decay of the towns. The system of *latifundia* run by slave labor no longer paid. . . . Small productions had again become the only profitable form. One country estate after another was cut up into small lots . . . for the most part . . . given out to *coloni*. . . . The slavery of classical times had outlived itself. Whether employed on the land in large-scale agriculture or in manufacture in the towns, it no longer yielded any satisfactory return—the market for its products was no longer there. But the small-scale agriculture and the small handicraft production to which the enormous production of the empire in its prosperous days was now shrunk had no room for numbers of slaves."

79. The great slave estate tended to become autarchic only in regard to its own needs. By contrast, it sold commodities to the cities and armies. Furthermore, the great landowner lived in town with his dependents on the surplus taken from the slave system, again made urban life possible thanks to his payment of taxes, and even contributed to the building of the city by his public benefactions. See P. Dockès, ed., *Production d'espace et formes d'urbanisation* (Paris: Centre National de Recherche Scientifique, n.d.), espeically A. Gravejat, "La Rome antique républicaine et impériale."

80. No doubt this was a temporary state of affairs: it would have tended to reproduce an urban, mercantile economy.

81. Bloch, *Les caractères originaux*, 1:103 ff.

82. Bloch, "De la grande exploitation," pp. 122–26.

83. See Charles Parain, "La Lutte des classes dans l'Antiquité classique," *La Pensée* 108 (1963): 15. It is clear that Christianity first spread successfully either among oriental merchants or in the slave class or among the most heavily exploited of freemen. Celsus (in his *True Word against the Christians*, following the 1965 French edition edited by J.-P. Pauvert) explains that the Christian "fable" succeeded in part because it gained converts among the credulous and infantile masses of people over whom no *paterfamilias* kept a close watch. Other beliefs, frequently oriental, had already spread among these masses, thereby becoming components of the slaves' ideological struggles. The same was true of Christianity originally, which may account for the harshness of state repression of the religion. This did not prevent the subsequent "rehabilitation" of Christianity and its transformation into a ruling class religion in opposition to the pagan masses.

84. Bloch, "Comment et Pourquoi." The same argument is used by M. K. Trofima in a supplementary chapter to the Italian edition of E. M. Staerman's work, *La Schiavitù nell'Italia Imperiale* (Rome: Riuniti, 1975): behind the apparent resignation in Christian teaching there lay a subversive ideology that restored the slave to life by radically repudiating existing social relations.

85. Bloch, "Comment et Pourquoi."

86. Finley, *The Ancient Economy*, p. 89.

87. See Verlinden, *L'Esclavage*, pp. 34 ff. and 99.

88. "Although remission of the original sin is granted to all the faithful by the grace of baptism, the just God has instituted discrimination in human life, making some slaves, others masters, so that the freedom to do wrong may be checked by the power of those who dominate. For if all were without fear, how could evil be prohibited?" Isidore of Seville, *Sentences* iii, 47, cited by Duby, *Les Trois ordres*, p. 90. Duby adds that "according to this, not merely inequality was necessary, but also repression. . . . We find 'slaves,' who are afraid, and 'masters,' whose yoke weighs upon the necks of other men. Membership in one class or the other is dependent upon God's arbitrary choice."

89. Duby, *Les Trois ordres*, p. 52: "Sin makes one subordinate to the other according to the variable order of merit."

90. Toubert, *Les Structures*, 1:474 ff.

91. Ibid., p. 477.

92. Ibid., p. 475.

93. Ibid., p. 312, concerning the social crisis following the death of Louis II in 875.

94. See below, chap. 4. Concerning the role of the Church, see Bonnassié, *De l'Esclavagisme*. A fantastic argument, yet one that cannot but remind us of the prohibition of strikes and grievances by workers in "socialist" regimes, said to be justified because the factories belong to the people.

95. Verlinden, *L'Esclavage*.

96. Ibid., pp. 675 ff., 704.

97. See above, beginning of this chapter.

98. See IV B above.

99. R. Livi, *La Schiavitù domestica nei tempi di mezzo e moderni* (Cedam, 1928), pp. 61 ff.

100. Engels, *The Origin of the Family*, p. 136, criticized the "moral" argument: "Christianity is completely innocent of the gradual dying out of ancient slavery. It was itself actively involved in the system for centuries under the Roman Empire, and never interfered later with slave-trading by Christians . . . or with the later trade in Negroes."

101. Finley, *The Ancient Economy*, p. 88. Certain Stoic ideas, however, did spread among slaves and, in helping to mold their ideology, were a weapon of liberation. Such a Stoic as Blossius of Cumae (second century B.C.) preached radical egalitarianism during the republic, and his ideas may have influenced the slave revolts (see below, chap. 4). We wish merely to assert that the Stoic theories current among the master class did not lead to an elimination of slavery.

102. See above, chap. 1.

Chapter 3

1. See Rosier, *Changement technique*.

2. Simplifying somewhat by neglecting regions in which "second serfdom" developed. See Fourquin, *Histoire de la France rurale*, 1:476 ff.

3. Details concerning this debate can be found in *Sur le mode de production asiatique* (2d ed.; Paris: Editions Sociales, 1974; 1st ed. 1969).

4. Ibid., pp. 257 ff.

5. Ibid., p. 267.

6. Ibid., Ibid., pp. 273–74 (italics added).

7. Ibid., p. 280.

8. Marx and Engels, *The German Ideology*, p. 48. See above, Introduction.

9. Which may be found in *Quel avenir attend l'homme?* Entretiens de Royaumont (Paris: Presses Universitaires de France, 1961), in the article entitled "De l'Antiquité esclavagiste au féodalisme," p. 39. See also the December 1977 issue of *La Pensée* (no. 196), "Le Développement des forces productives dans l'ouest du Bas-Empire," where the same comparison is made.

10. Finley, *The Ancient Economy*, p. 83; and "Technical Innovation," *Economic History Review*, 2d series, no. 18 (1965), p. 43.

11. See E. D. Genovese, *The Political Economy of Slavery* (New York: Random House, 1967), p. 59.

12. Ibid., pp. 49–50.

13.. D. Dufourt has rightly pointed out to me that the southern farmer was a capitalist whose slaves represented a portion of his capital. He should therefore have compared the profitability of this investment with that of other possible uses of his capital: here calculation made sense, while in antiquity it did not. To assume that the great Roman landowner behaved in an economically rational way is, as was mentioned earlier, debatable to say the least (see above, chap. 2, sec. 1). Nevertheless, Columella does indicate that he faces a choice between slaves and *coloni* (even if this choice was not solely or even chiefly economic). By way of contrast, however, as we shall see, the slave system died out because the slave owners had no choice.

14. See V. de Magalhaes-Vilhena, "Essor scientifique et technique et obstacles sociaux à la fin de l'Antiquité," internal document of the Berlin Academy of Sciences on "Problem der Spätantike," December 1963, reprinted in *Cahiers du Centre d'Etudes et de Recherches Marxistes*, no. 42; and "Progrès technique et blocage mental dans la pensée antique," *La Pensée* 102 (1962). See also A. Aymard in the epilogue to volume 1 of *L'Histoire générale du travail*, under the direction of L. H. Parias, Nouvelle librairie française, Paris, 1959–61.

15. Parain, "Développement des forces productives."

16. Ibid., pp. 29 ff.

17. In *Quel avenir attend l'homme?* p. 36, Parain returns to almost the same formulation as that found in his 1977 article, "Le développement des forces productives." He expressly rejects Marx's ready-made formula: "No social order is ever destroyed before all the productive forces for which it is sufficient have been developed," which may be found in *The Critique of Political Economy*, p. 21.

18. Piganiol, *L'Empire chrétien*, p. 422; Parain, *Quel avenir attend l'homme*, p. 36. Similarly, Perry Anderson defends the thesis that the fall of the Roman Empire in the west was utterly catastrophic, the barbarian invasions touching off the collapse of an empire torn by internal crisis as a result of the impossibility of maintaining the slave system after the closure of the borders (in the early second century) and the seizure of land by the western aristocracy, which led to a

polarization of society into just two groups. In his view, feudalism was a synthesis of the Germanic organization and the Roman organization, both first disintegrating and then recombining in a new amalgam: "The catastrophic collision of two dissolving anterior modes of production—primitive and ancient—eventually produced the feudal order which spread through mediaeval Europe" (*Passages from Antiquity to Feudalism*, p. 128, and passim). For an analysis of feudalism in Gaul as a "balanced" synthesis (northern Gaul, southeastern Europe) of feudal elements stemming from the slave society and from the barbarian tribal communities, see Z. V. Oudaltsova and E.-V. Goutnova, "La Genèse du féodalism et ses voies en Europe," *La Pensée*, no. 196 (December 1977), pp. 45 ff. The idea is an old one, going back to Marx and Engels in *The German Ideology*, p. 90, and see also pp. 45–46, as well as our own remarks on the subject below.

19. Parain, *Quel avenir*, p. 36.

20. See his 1963 and 1977 analyses, summarized below.

21. In *La Pensée*, no. 108 (April 1963).

22. Ibid., p. 3.

23. See above, chap. 1.

24. We should prefer to say between slaves and their masters, the owners of the *villae*.

25. Parain, "La Lutte des classes dans l'Antiquité," p. 15.

26. Ibid., p. 14.

27. Ibid., Ibid., p. 20.

28. Parain, "Le Développement."

29. Ibid., p. 29.

30. Ibid., p. 30.

31. Ibid., p. 30.

32. Columella, as Parain himself observes, mentions these innovations and does not, it would seem, regard them as at all difficult to apply. Not all of them demanded increased amounts of labor or greater labor intensity, and, what is more, a complex system of rewards made it possible to improve the condition of slaves who did more and better work (see above, chap. 1, p. 72 ff.), in particular in the case of the method adopted for the care of vineyards. As for the weeding of cereal crops, the practice seems to have been common. See *De agricultura*, ii, 11.

33. This was the case with the heavy wheeled plow. It is known to have owed more to barbarian than to Roman origins and to have spread throughout the plains of northern Gaul only in the early Middle Ages; furthermore, it was well adapted to the type of soil found there, and far less well to Mediterranean agriculture. The *servi* of the Carolingian gangs used it. Moreover, in what respect was this plow, which was drawn by teams of oxen, a "labor using" innovation in comparison with the swing-plow (particularly on hard soil)?

34. See above, chap. 2.

35. See above, chap. 2.

36. An analysis similar to Parain's is found in J.-P. Vernant, *Mythe et société en Grèce ancienne* (Paris: Maspero, 1974), p. 29: the resistance of the slaves was seen

on the level of the productive forces, since, for one thing, by impeding technological progress slavery made it impossible to develop the productive forces in any way other than by extending the slave system itself, and, for another, slave resistance "established increasingly stringent limitations on yields," while growth in the number of slaves tended to threaten the equilibrium of the social system.

37. See above, chap. 2, sec. VI.

38. See "Matérialisme dialectique et matérialisme historique," in part of chap. 4 of the *Histoire du Parti communiste (bolchevik) de l'U.R.S.S.* See also the article by M. E. Sergueenko, "Iz istorii sielskovo khziaistva drevniei Italii," *Vestnik drevnei istorii*, 1953, no. 3, pp. 65–76, whose argument Parain in 1977 called "brilliant."

39. As is stressed by A. Deman, *Latomus*, 1960, pp. 991–92. See above the analysis of Melekechvili, for example.

40. See Vittinghoff, *Die Theorie des historischen Materialismus über den antiken Sklavenhalterstaat der alten Geschichte bei den Klassiker des marxismus und in der modernen sowjetischen Forschung* (Saeculum, 1960); and *Die Sklavenfrage in der Forschung der Sowjetunion* (Gymnasium, 1962).

41. Schtajerman, *Die Krise*.

42. See above, chap. 2.

43. Schtajerman, *Die Krise*, pp. 34–35, 69.

44. Ibid., pp. 48–74.

45. Less by dint of Constantine's 331 edict than by actual deeds, the edict serving merely to confirm the social situation in attempting to generalize it.

46. Schtajerman, *Die Krise*, pp. 56–60, 232–33, 258–68.

47. For this criticism, see Paul Petit, *La Paix romaine*, pp. 373 ff.

48. Thus, for example, J. Gagé, *Les Classes sociales dans l'Empire romain* (Paris: Payot, 1964), writes: "The journals of ancient history published in the Soviet countries usually highlight slave conditions in the Roman Empire in their research, and a number of studies have appeared in these journals that cannot be neglected." He explains that, since his point of view is not that of an economic historian, he intends to study chiefly "the spectrum of social positions of free men," which in fact he does very ably. But he almost forgets about slaves, though he does mention that "the slave was ubiquitous in Roman imperial society" (p. 43). What troubles the bourgeois historian in the Soviet analyses is the place afforded the servile class struggle, while what troubles us is the subordination of that struggle to economics.

49. Petit, *La Paix romain*, p. 377.

50. To illustrate the subordination of social struggles, we cannot resist giving in to the pleasure of citing this passage from Oudaltsova and Gournova: "Aware though we are of the importance of the social struggle and the evolution of culture and ideology in this process [the genesis of feudalism], we have had to exclude them from our analysis on account of the brevity of our report"! ("Genèse du féodalisme et ses voies en Europe," *La Pensée*, no. 196 [December 1977], p. 44).

51. In *Quel avenir*, p. 39; the same comparison is also made in "Le Développement des forces productives dans l'ouest du Bas-Empire," *La Pensée*, no. 196 (December 1977).

52. The expression is Parain's, in "Comment caractériser un mode de production," *Sur le mode de production antique*, p. 279.

53. Parain, "De l'Antiquité esclavagiste," p. 37. The following citations are from the same source.

54. On French feudalism and the feudal mode of production, see the preliminary report by Charles Parain, "Caractères généraux du féodalisme," *Sur le féodalisme* (Paris: Editions Sociales, 1974), p. 16. The quotation is from Marx, *Capital*, book ii, section vi, chap. ii.

55. Doehaerd, *Le Haut moyen âge*, pp. 66 ff.; Duby, *The Early Growth*, pp. 21 ff.

56. See Bloch, *Les Caractères originaux*; and *Annales d'histoire sociale* 1934, pp. 485 ff.

57. On the plow, see A. G. Haudricourt and M. Jean-Brunhes-Delamarre, *L'Homme et la charrue à travers le monde* (Paris: Gallimard, 1955).

58. See Doehaerd, *Le Haut moyen âge*, p. 69; M. Renard, *Technique et agriculture en pays trevire et remois* (Brussels: Latomus, 1959); D. Furia and P. C. Serre, *Techniques et sociétés* (Paris: Colin, 1970), pp. 34 ff.

59. Furia and Serre, *Techniques et sociétés*, pp. 34 ff.

60. From what is known, it would seem that quite often the lord had more than enough *corvée* labor at his disposal.

61. Doehaerd, *Le Haut moyen âge*, p. 77. She mentions only demographic pressure.

62. Parain, "Rapports de production et développement des forces productives: l'exemple du moulin à eau," *La Pensée*, no. 119 (1965), pp. 59, 61.

63. Ibid., p. 64. On the mill, see B. Gille, "Le Moulin à eau, une revolution technique médiévale," *Technique et civilisation*, vol. 3 (1954).

64. Duby, *Guerriers et paysans*, p. 22 (English ed., p. 13).

65. Ibid., p. 25 (English ed., p. 16).

66. Doehaerd, *Le Haut moyen âge*, pp. 90 ff., on depopulation.

67. Productivity *per man*. Obviously 100 men will get a given plot of land to "yield" more than 10 men will, but each will eat less, producing less per head. If there is only one man, however, the product (per head) may well be less than if there are ten.

68. Parain, "De l'antiquité esclavagiste au féodalisme," p. 37.

69. *Voprossy Istorii* 5 (1964).

70. In *Sur le mode de production antique*, p. 273.

71. Marx and Engels, *The German Ideology*, p. 90.

72. Ibid., p. 90.

73. Ibid., p. 90.

74. Ibid., p. 45.

75. See appendix to chap. 1 above.

76. Marx and Engels, *The German Ideology*, p. 45.

77. See B. Rosier, "Changements techniques et rapports sociaux dans l'histoire des sociétés rurales ouest-européennes," in "Questions aux historiens" (in collaboration with Pierre Dockès), *Cahiers A.E.H.* (University of Lyons II), no. 11 (1977), p. 98.

78. Bonassié, *La Catalogne; De l'Esclavagisme au féodalisme.*

79. See E. Magnou-Nortier, *La Société laïque et l'église dans la province ecclésiastique de Narbonne* (Toulouse, 1974), pp. 212–13.

80. Toubert, *Les Structures du Latium,* 330, 455.

81. "Avènement et conquête du moulin à eau," *Annales,* 1935, pp. 538–63.

82. "Rapport de production et développement des forces productives," *La Pensée* (1965). See also Parain, "Développement des forces productives."

83. See Duby, *Le'Economie rurale,* 1:73 ff.; Fourquin, *Histoire de la France rurale,* vol. 1, 3, and 4, particularly pp. 403 ff.

84. R. J. Forbes, *Man the Maker,* ed. Schumann, 2d ed. (New York, 1959).

85. Parain, *La Pensée* (1965).

86. It is interesting to note that the war of the mills drags on interminably. Thus A. Maurizio, *Histoire de l'alimentation végétale* (Paris: Payot, 1932), tells us that in Galicia in 1914–18 peasants, because of flour rationing, stopped taking their grain to the factory and used their hand mills instead, and that the police tried to destroy these. And what about the grain harvest crisis in the USSR in the twenties?

87. In *La Pensée,* no. (1965), p. 66 (italics added).

88. Ibid.; see also "Développement des forces productives," p. 40: "This also satisfied the peasants, who were able to use their strength and their labor time in a more rational way."

89. In *Quel avenir,* pp. 36–38.

90. That is, post-Vitruvian, geared mills with vertical wheels, cf. appendix to chap. 3.

91. Along with the water mill, horse-driven mills are often found (in the event the water mill is unable to function because of flood, drought, or freezing weather. See R. Bennet and J. Elton, *History of Corn Milling* [1898], pp. 196–97).

92. Bloch, *Les caractères originaux,* pp. 82 ff.

93. Dues for use of the press were high, however: ⅛ or ⅑, and the almost universal use of individual presses (and also of ovens) after the ban was eliminated proves that this *banalité* was exploitation pure and simple.

94. Communal mills may have been common before being driven out by the mills of the great estates. See R. Latouche, *Les Origines de l'économie occidentale* (Paris: Albin Michel, 1956), reissued in 1970 in the Evolution de l'humanité collection, p. 102. These collective means of production were consistent with the survivals of collective peasant organization, with what remained of the village "communes." See chap. 1 above, as well as Bloch, *Les Caractères originaux;* and Rosier, "Questions aux historiens."

95. These apparatus of large scale were the only ones to be constructed, whence the fascination they exert: their productivity is evident, but not that of possible alternatives, which they killed off.

96. Fossier, *Histoire sociale*, p. 200.

97. As Fourquin correctly observes, *Histoire de la France rurale*, vol. 1, 4, p. 391.

98. For example, Duby has written: "The old hand mills, driven out and destroyed by the landlords' sergeants wherever obligation reigned" (*L'Economie rurale*, 1:195); see also *Guerriers et paysans*, p. 213; see Fourquin, *Histoire de la France rurale*, 1:404.

99. In 1331, cited by Jacques Le Fogg, *La Civilisation de l'Occident médiéval* (Paris: Arthaud, 1972), p. 373.

100. See above, chap. 1.

101. Fourquin, *Histoire de la France rurale*, 1:203.

102. Obviously it is impossible to distinguish between a "reaction" by the masters to a reduction in the surplus won by the exploited or even to the destruction of a mode of exploitation, and an "action" intended to increase the surplus, or even to give rise to a surplus of a new type.

103. The water mill increased the labor productivity of milling and in the end increased the labor productivity of the whole production process of flour from grain. It was not introduced *for* that purpose. It had a further effect, of considerable importance, of largely freeing women from the demanding work that had been their "specialty." This consequence of the water mill is worthy of systematic study in the context of a history of social relations within the family. Of course, it was not introduced *for* that purpose either!

104. See Dockès and Rosier, "Questions aux historiens."

105. Duby, *L'Economie rurale*, 2:437, and see 1:73 ff.

106. Poly, *La Provence et la société féodale*, gives the figure $\frac{1}{16}$ (which a misprint made $\frac{1}{6}$!), p. 218, n. 34; for Salon, see the twelfth-century municipal statutes, published by R. Brun, *La Ville de Salon au moyen âge* (Aix, 1924), p. 287; for Toulouse, the municipal statutes of 1152, published by Devic and Vaissette, *Histoire générale du Languedoc* (Toulouse, 1875). Oven dues mentioned in the work of Brun cited are: Salon = $\frac{1}{20}$, Aubagne = $\frac{1}{20}$, Cuers = $\frac{1}{30}$.

107. *Histoire de la France rurale*, 1:509–10. Were dues relatively lower in grape-growing regions, with landlords making up the difference on the press?

108. *Histoire sociale de l'Occident médiéval* (Paris: Colin, 1970), p. 200.

109. Ellul, *Histoire des institutions*, 4:208.

110. As late as the seventeenth and eighteenth centuries, according to J. Bastier, *La Féodalité au siècle des Lumières dans la région de Toulouse* (1975), pp. 158 ff., oven dues varied between $\frac{1}{16}$ and $\frac{1}{24}$, and multure could run as high as $\frac{1}{6}$ and as low as $\frac{1}{18}$; and M. Broquerau, "Des Banalités en Poitou aux XVIIe et XVIIIe siècles," *Bulletin de la Société des Antiquaires de l'Ouest*, 1960, p. 408, mentions a figure of $\frac{1}{16}$ and in some cases much higher, up to $\frac{1}{10}$.

111. See J. Mainsard, *Les Banalités* (Paris, 1912): a miller who wished to be honest could not pay his rent; extortion was the norm. See Claude Gindin, "Aperçu sur les conditions de la mouture des grains en France, fin du XVIIIe siècle," *Contributions à l'histoire paysanne de la Révolution française*, ed. A. Soboul (Paris: Editions Sociales, 1977), p. 184.

112. Jean Gimpel, *The Medieval Machine* (New York: Penguin, 1976), p. 8.

113. R. J. Forbes, *Studies in Ancient Technology,* (New York: Heinman, 1955): 90.

114. Se L. A. Moritz, *Grain-Mills and Flour in Classical Antiquity* (Oxford: Oxford University Press, 1958); A. P. Usher, *A History of Mechanical Inventions* (Cambridge, Mass.: Harvard University Press, 1929).

115. Moritz, *Grain-Mills,* p. 126. See also Lynn White, Jr., *Medieval Technology and Social Change* (Oxford: Oxford University Press, 1962), reprinted 1978, pp. 105–6, for the use of the crank in particular. Geared mills could be operated with horizontal cranks. This may have been the case with these "large" geared mills operated by slaves or soldiers (the so-called Saalburg mills).

116. M. Benoit and M. Julien de Fontenelle, *Manuel de boulangerie* (Paris, 1829), p. 374. Ten kilograms of grain gave approximately 7.5 kilograms of flour.

117. Ibid.

118. Forbes, *Studies in Ancient Technology,* p. 83.

119. In the article on mills in the eighteenth-century *Encyclopedia* we learn that the price of the *moulinet* was quite low.

120. Of course bread was not made every day, and frequently grain was milled only once a month.

121. At that time the flour for a "black" bread represented between 60 percent and 70 percent of the grain, but it took on a third as much water (⅛ of which would be lost in cooking). "Black" bread represented between 75 percent and 80 percent of the grain. See A. Maurizio, *Histoire de l'alimentation végétale* (Paris: Payot, 1932), p. 551: in millings about 65 percent flour.

122. Fernand Braudel, *Civilisatin matérielle et capitalisme* (Paris: Colin, 1967), pp. 97, 101; English ed. by Miriam Kochan, *Capitalism and Material Life* (New York: Harper & Row, 1973), pp. 89–91.

123. M. Rouche, "La Faim à l'époque carolingienne, Essai de quelques types de rations alimentaires," *Revue historique,* 1973, pp. 275 ff.; carters at Corbie in 717: 1.308 kg.; churchwardens at Corbie: 1.7 kg.; monks at Corbie in 822: 1.7 kg. But these figures must be approached with extreme caution, since this was a period when weights and measures varied (see Rouche, pp. 303–4), and, as Rouche tells us, bread rations (for canons) seem to have gone from one *livre* to four *livres* between the seventh century and the 816 Council of Aix, while in the same period the livre itself went from 327 grams to 430 grams, which makes 1.72 kg. of bread in 816, but there is a chance that the daily ration of 327 grams is incorrect (unless they ate something else!). Moreover, I confess to be in the dark whether a carter who received 1.3 or 1.7 kg. of bread ate it all himself or had a family to feed. So large are the rations for certain foodstuffs that Rouche even supposes that they must have resold a portion, since the amounts received by far exceeded what one man required; similarly, the pig (nearly whole) given a prebendary seems to me a yearly ration for a family (p. 306).

124. Counting four children as 2.7 adult males and one woman as 0.8 adult males, or 3.5 adults at 1.5 kg. ("short rations"!), for 5.25 kg.

125. Suggestive calculations made by R. Delatouche, "L'Agriculture aux temps carolingiens," *Journal des Savants,* April–June 1977, p. 86.

278 Notes to Page 187

126. See *Histoire de la France rurale*, 1:347, for the Carolingian era. At Saint-Germain-des-Prés, to judge from the Irminion polyptych, around 7.43 ha. for the servile manses, 10.59 ha. for the ingenuous manses. For 4 *villae* south of Paris, according to Charles E. Perrin, 0.25 ha. for the servile, and between 1.5 and 15 ha. for the "free." Measured in *bonniers* (1.5 ha.[?] of arable land?) based on the Saint-Bertin polyptych, between 9 and 12 *bonniers*. But these large manses were overpopulated. Thus, R. Delatouche, taking a manse (at random) from the Irminion polyptych, found it inhabited by five adults and thirteen children ("L'Agriculture aux temps carolingiens"). As we know, moreover, Caesar's veterans with three children received 10 jugera, or 2.4 ha., lots, but smaller lots (of 1.2 ha.) were also distributed in the second century B.C. (Finley, *The Ancient Economy*, pp. 105, 120).

In the late eighteenth century, the peasant population of Cambresis is said to have consisted of 12 percent marginal peasants (living in poverty in small huts without land, hiring out their labor to any taker), 33 percent on microfundia, obliged to hire themselves out in order to survive, 36 percent without plow gear, but able to enjoy a certain security, and 19 percent "rich," among whom 16 percent were "comfortably off," with 3 ha., and 3 percent in plenty (*Histoire de la France rurale*, 1:569). At Garges, two-thirds of the families had less than one acre in 1311, hence much less than a hectare (an acre being 0.4 to 0.5 ha.; ibid., p. 571). In Ile-de-France, however, 50 percent of the peasants had perhaps 2 or 3 ha., while few had more than 20 acres (between 7 and 8 ha.), with many having 2 to 3 acres (ibid., p. 571). The average peasant family (2 adults, 4 children?) may have been protected with 4 or 5 ha. (ibid., p. 573, based on work of G. Sivery). Thus there may have been an increase in the area undercultivation between the Roman Empire and the Carolingian Empire, but at the same time an increase in the size of the family (the conjugal family probably declined between the fifth and ninth centuries), followed by a reduction in the size of the tenement but along with it a reduction in the size of the family.

127. Yields in the vicinity of Annapes (near Lille) have been the subject of a controversy. Georges Duby found harvest/seed rations of 2.7 (after correction, since his calculations were made after subtracting grain destined for future sowing, and hence gave a net harvest/seed ratio; see *L'Economie rurale*, p. 85). R. Delatouche redid these calculations and arrived at a figure of 4/1 (*L'Agriculture aux temps carolingiens*, p. 76), which is what survival of the population of the manses required. It is clear that for Duby the Carolingian peasant was constantly "racked by hunger" (*L'Economie rurale*, p. 87), while for Delatouche, the peasant in this period suffered only from a psychological hunger (the fear of falling short of the 1.7 kg. daily allowance of bread, as in the case of the monks and laymen of Corbie studied by M. Rouche, whose results he cites; see above). One is free to choose between Delatouche's "fat lumps" and Duby's "scarecrows"!

128. Slicher van Bath, *Yield Ratios (810–1820)*, A.A.G. Bijdragen, 10 (Wageningen, 1963).

129. Which is what Marc Bloch gave in *Les Caractères originaux*, p. 26 (English ed., p. 26), and which covers precisely the "normal" range given by Slicher van

Bath! See B. Rosier, *Structures agricoles et développement économique* (Paris: Mouton, 1968): in the eighteenth century, still only three to four times seed, p. 57.

130. Fourquin, *Histoire de la France rurale*, 1:452. Furthermore, the 5 quintals/hectare figure is standard for ancient two-field agriculture. B. Rosier, *Sturctures agricoles*, p. 67, cites 6 quintals on the average as late as the eighteenth century. Moreover, the same figure is given for grain-growing on the ancient system in Algeria at the end of the nineteenth century (J. A. Battaudier and L. Trabut [Paris, 1898], p. 72).

131. The 15 percent figure is no doubt low, more appropriate to banal than to landed seigniory. *Cens, champart, taille,* tithe—the variety of exactions was extreme from one region or period to the next, and even from one peasant to the next. Remembering, howeever, that everyone paid the tithe, which already amounted to 10 percent, the bracket must have been between 10 percent and 35 percent in the eleventh and twelfth centuries (see, e.g., Fourquin, *Histoire de la France rurale*, 502 ff., for the twelfth and thirteenth centuries).

132. C_{lm}/P_{la} (C_{lm} = cost of milling dues in labor terms, P_{la} = amount of labor embodied in the product for personal consumption), or S_B/P_a (S_B = surplus amount of grain paid to lord for milling, P_a = production in terms of amount of grain taken to be milled).

133. Thus eliminating yields of 3 quintals per hectare.

134. If an ox was unavailable on a yearly basis, the peasant could rent one or hire a pair of oxen and a plow from a plowman, which would mean cutting back on family consumption or else assuming higher yields.

135. This approximation is altogether too arbitrary. We know, however, that in the so-called rural "peasant" economies that preceded mechanization (France in the eighteenth and nineteenth centuries), cultivation of ten hectares occupied a peasant family full time. Furthermore, an "old-fashioned" peasant in an underdeveloped country today can be occupied half-time by a single hectare of maize, for example.

136. We assume that the woman and 4 children do the work of 1 adult male worker (which is not much). This means assuming that yields of 3 quintals per hectare are ruled out by the intensity of labor provided by the family, which has time on its hands and a small amount of land. With yields of 5–7 quintals per hectare, it produces the 18 quintals consumed by the family (more precisely, between 15 and 21 quintals).

137. With 20 hours per day (full-time family labor), it produces 30–70 quintals, depending on the yield.

138. This transport *time* must be added to the milling dues expressed in quantity of grain. This raises a number of problems.

139. The ratio $(C_{lm} - C_{lt})/P_{la}$ with C_{lm}: milling time, C_{lt}: transport time), compared with the ratio S_B/P_a, which is only approximate.

140. C_{lm}/P_{la}, or quantity of labor for milling/quantity of labor for producing the grain.

141. S_B/P_a, or surplus product paid in grain/product for personal consumption taken to be milled, in grain.

142. Perhaps the rich peasant had a better *moulinet,* so that his average cost in labor terms of milling at home was nearer 0.085; he would then have been less interested in using the banal mill.

143. $dP/dL \approx 0$, with dP = total increase in production and $dL = C_{lm} - C_{lt}$ = time saved.

144. $dP/dL > 0$.

145. We are considering the case in which the means of production are assumed given, along with the surface area of the tenement: the productivity of labor is then decreasing. This case differs from that in which the means of production available to the peasant may change. The rich peasant, for example, can, with the help of his horse and of various improved implements, produce as much for family consumption in 8 hours per day as the average peasant can produce in 10 hours.

146. $S_B = dP^*$.

147. Theoretically, of course, the poor peasant could hire out his labor and so be fully occupied. But the question only crops up again in a new guise: we would have to compare the hourly wage he received (and lost if he did his own milling) with the grain he had to hand over if he chose to use the banal mill. What we know of the large banal mil profits and the low wages of the time makes it clear that it would have been advantageous to use the hand mill. Above all, the notion of "full-time" employment makes no sense when it is a question of earning the few kilograms of bread needed for survival, and the chance of there being such a full-time occupation is nil.

148. Latouche, *Les Origines de l'économie occidentale,* p. 102.

149. Bloch, *Les Caractères originaux.* Chiefly, as we know, in regions where the open-field system was practiced.

Chapter 4

1. Finley, *The Ancient Economy,* especially pp. 63–93.

2. A detailed study of the relations between the Spartans and the helots is needed, which would look into the class struggles connected with the conflict between two different ethnic groups (unlike the Athens' slaves up to the time of the Roman conquest, the helots rebelled; was this because they were *also* a people?). The precept "divide and conquer" played no part here. However, large numbers of helots were incorporated into the Spartan army in wartime. Were their arrows used against their own generals?

3. Pollux, *Onomasticon* 3:83 (quoted in Finley, *The Ancient Economy,* p. 64) gives this definition of the helots.

4. Finley, *The Ancient Economy,* p. 70.

5. Ibid., p. 93.

6. Ibid.

7. Ibid., p. 91. See G. Gardascia, "L'Apparition dans le droit des classes *d'honestiores* and *d'humiliores,*" *Revue Historique du droit,* 1950.

8. Ibid., p. 90.

9. Notice, furthermore, that recruitment continued and breeding became more important.

10. Who were liable to punishments "worthy of a slave, such as being burned alive" (Calistratus, *Digest*, 48.19.18.11). In an inversion characteristic of the rule, Aemilius Macer informs us that "as for the slaves, the rule is that they should be punished as the *humiliores* are" (ibid., 48.19.10).

11. Along with speculators in real estate, financiers,, and the like.

12. Bloch, *La Société féodale*, p. 266 (English ed., p. 187).

13. Verlinden, *L'Esclavage*, pp. 287, 289.

14. Ibid., p. 745.

15. Ibid., p. 733.

16. Duby, *L'Economie rurale*, pp. 407–8.

17. Ibid., pp. 207, 413, 485–90, 501–4; in *Guerriers et paysans*, Duby tells us that in England in 1180 the great Benedictine abbeys ceased to put their lands to farm and resumed direct exploitation. The lords sought increasingly to bring the status of villeins closer to that of former slaves (p. 299, English ed., p. 269).

18. See above, chap. 1.

19. Brisson, *Spartacus*, pp. 244–45. Notice in passing that this contradicts the idea that it was impossible to breed slaves under gang conditions (see our criticism of this idea in chap. 3 above).

20. At least as old as the *Discours de la servitude volontaire* by Etienne de La Boétie (Paris: Payot, 1976), pp. 125 ff.

21. See above, chap. 1.

22. See above, chap. 1.

23. Petronius, *Satyricon*, 53.

24. " 'Prepare the cross for that slave.' 'What crime has earned him this death sentence? Who has testified against him? Who accused him?' 'Fool! He has done nothing. Never mind, I want him dead. I order it. My good pleasure is reason enough' " (Juvenal, *Satire*, vi).

25. Apuleius, *The Golden Ass*, ix, 198.

26. Plautus, *The Captives*, v.

27. See n. 2 above.

28. See below.

29. See P. Bonnassié, "De l'Esclavagisme au féodalisme," paper delivered to the Société d'étude du féodalisme, 1977.

30. In 650 or so a Visigothic law attempted to impose limits on this right. See Bonassié, ibid.

31. As stated in a Visigothic law of 670, in explaining how the prohibition on the killing of slaves was circumvented. Cited by Bonnassié, ibid.

32. According to Duby, *L'Economie rurale*, p. 429. Bernard Rosier interprets this as clear proof that peasants subject to *corvée* fought back (working paper, "Un réexamen de la révolution agricole"). This resistance was so strong that Walter of Henley, in his mid-thirteenth-century treatise *Housebonderie*, intended for the guidance of modern estate owners using direct exploitation under a quasi slave system, finally reaches the conclusion that a horse was worth no more than an

ox, since "the malice of the plowmen prevents the horse-drawn plow from getting the job done any more quickly than the ox-drawn plow" (cited in Le Goff, *La Civilisation*, p. 374; the word "malice" should be interpreted in the strongest possible sense).

33. Gagé, *Les Classes sociales*, p. 68.

34. Ibid., p. 415.

35. See Bonnassié, "De l'Esclavagisme au féodalisme." Thus, at the time of the Arab conquest of Spain, many slaves escaped, and this confirms Jean Bodin's remarks on the subject.

36. See E. R. Coleman, "Infanticide dans le Haut Moyen Age," *Annales E.S.C.*, March–April 1974, p. 315.

37. Finley, *The Ancient Economy*, p. 82.

38. Finley, *Ancient Sicily* (New York and London, 1968), chap. 9.

39. Le Goff, *La Civilisation*, p. 373.

40. Chesneaux, *Du Passé faisons table rase*, p. 132.

41. See G. Dabien, *Les Esclaves aux Antilles françaises* (Basse-Terre et Fort-de-France, 1974), chaps. 13 and 14.

42. See above, Introduction, p. 00.

43. *De re rustica*, i, 8. Similarly, see Cato, *De agricultura* vii.

44. Columella, *De re rustica*, xi, 1; Cato, *De agricultura*, vii: "neither haruspex, nor augur, nor soothsayer, nor Chaldean."

45. See Brisson, *Spartacus*, pp. 60 ff.

46. Apparently by spitting out sparks, which Diodorus tells us he contrived to do by a crude method: he placed in his mouth a small ball of sulfur, in back of a nutshell with a hole pierced through it! See Georges Dumézil, *La Religion romaine archaïque* (Paris: Payot, 1966), p. 508.

47. Brisson, *Spartacus*, p. 165.

48. Ibid., p. 207. Dumézil, *La Religion romaine*, pp. 496–97.

49. Schtajerman, *Die Krise*. Concerning the lares, see p. 65; on Hercules, Mithra, and eastern religions, pp. 129–31; on the class ideology of slaves, chaps. 2 and 4; on the ideology of slaves and free workers, pp. 112–36; on the ideology of the masters, chap. 6, pp. 232 ff.; integration into the familial cult, pp. 65, 126. Also see F. Bömer, *Untersuchungen über die Religion der Sklaven in Griechenland und Rom* (4 vols.; Wiesbaden: F. Steiner, 1957–68).

50. Chesneaux, *Du Passé*, p. 132.

51. See Parain, "La Lutte des classes dans l'Antiquité."

52. See above, and *Capital*, vol. 1.

53. Rémondon, *La Crise*, p. 192.

54. As Gagé writes, "*Fugitivus:* under the republic and during the early empire this term was used specifically and excusively to denote slaves who had fled their masters, who thereby became liable if caught to being returned to the *dominus* or subjected to brutal punishment—generally execution. Without rights of his own in his servile status, the slave automatically became an 'outlaw' once he escaped from his private master, through whom 'the state recognized his existence' " (see *Les Classes sociales dans l'Empire romain*, chap. 4).

55. As we shall see shortly, the term "marron" (maroon in English) by which fugitives in the Antilles were known may just be an echo of the tenth century.

56. See Gagé, *Les Classes sociales*, p. 414. For instance, burning at the stake for a steward of an estate who had hidden a fugitive in 379.

57. Ibid., chap. 4.

58. Ibid., p. 429.

59. Marx, *Formen*.

60. Finley, *The Ancient Economy*, p. 67.

61. Brisson, *Spartacus*, p. 214. Finley argues that the Bacaudae only wanted to alter social relations to their own advantage.

62. See above, Introduction, and Plato, *Republic*, 578d,e.

63. Plato, *Laws*, book vi, 776–77.

64. *Republic*, 578d,e.

65. *Laws*, vi, 776–77. In referring to the danger of having slaves drawn "all of one stock." Plato has the Helots in mind.

67. Concerning these conflicts and brigandage, see E. A. Thompson, *Peasant Revolts*; Schtajerman, *Die Krise*, p. 294; P. Olivia, *Pannonia and the Onset of Crisis in the Roman Empire* (Prague, 1962); D. Tudor, "Interfecti a latronibus," *Ac. Rep. Rom., Stud. Cerch. Ist. veche*, 1953; Gagé, *Les Classes sociales*, pp. 143–48; L. Falm-Zuckermann, *Etude du phénomène du brigandage dans l'Empire romain* (Brussels: Latomus, 1970). On the uprisings in Gaul, see above, chap. 1, and, more generally, see below.

68. Fossier, *L'Histoire sociale*, p. 65.

69. Duby, *Guerriers et paysans*, p. 51.

70. Duby, *Les Trois ordres*, pp. 43–44.

71. Duby, *L'Economie rurale*, 162 ff., but the interpretation should be more in terms of the lord's war against the peasant community than of a "new attitude of man with regard to nature" (p. 165).

72. Finley, *The Ancient Economy*, p. 84. See the selection of texts in Schtajerman, *Vestnik drevnei istorii*, 1965, 1, pp. 62–81. "As many enemies as slaves," as Jean Bodin points out in *Les Six Livres de la République* (1583 ed., p. 65. Bodin observes that no one dared fit slaves out for war or enlist them (p. 56), and in some cases there was fear even of enlisting them as galley slaves (p. 57). See especially p. 53 for mention of the fear that slaves would kill their master by burning his house down.

73. Finley, *The Ancient Economy*, p. 84.

74. Bodin, *La République*, writes: "The estate (*estat*) of families and republics is always shaky, always on the verge of ruin, whenever the slaves league together; all the histories are replete with tales of slave wars and rebellions" (p. 53). Moreover, when the master was murdered "in his house, no matter who did it, all the slaves were killed" (ibid., p. 53), merely as a precaution.

75. As noted by Chesneaux, *Du Passé*, though we do not agree on which features are similar. He mentions only that the slave system, like capitalism, can only exist at the expense of its environment (barbarian, Asiatic, or underdeveloped Third World). From this he concludes (along with many others) that the

empire fell because of the barbarian penetration. He neglects the internal causes of the collapse.

76. The slave is a commodity because he is produced for sale (produced, i.e., either bred or captured); thus he represents an exchange value, as well as a use value for the master.

77. See above.

78. In *The German Ideology*, Marx and Engels observe that "in Italy, on the other hand, the concentration of landed property was accomplished by inheritance, and also by purchase and indebtedness. . . . Under the ensuing conditions the free population disappeared almost completely."

79. In *The Origin of the Family*, Engels says that slavery brought about the end of the Athenian state by impoverishing the masses: "It was not democracy that ruined Athens . . . but slavery." Similarly, for the end of Rome, he places the accent on the fact that the "great landowners and the wealthy . . . little by little absorbed the land of peasants ruined by military service and set slaves to cultivating the enormous estates formed in this way, depopulated Italy, and thereby opened the way not only to the empire but also to its successors, the German barbarians." Here, the impoverishment and expropriation of the masses are related directly to the crisis of the state.

80. In the words of Finley, *The Ancient Economy*, p. 89; we do not agree with his formulation, however.

81. Rémondon, *La Crise*, pp. 202 ff.

82. Ibid., p. 202.

83. Ibid., p. 204.

84. By the end of the fourth century not a single Roman was in the army. The emperor, clad in animal skins, was lifted on a shield to receive the acclamation of the troops. This Germanization of the army had begun as early as the third century.

85. By contrast, in the eastern provinces, the peasantry was dominated, "subjugated," but not enslaved, prior to the Roman conquest; the slave system scarcely made inroads there (as Finley noticed, see above). There was not the same process of concentration of lands in the hands of a smaller and smaller class, opposed to the masses of *humiliores* and slaves. The state continued to possess a somewhat broader social base, because of the persistence of a middle-level aristocracy, a certain social continuum, and was therefore more solid. Conflicts within the aristocracy over control of the state were accordingly limited, and consequently another source of weakness in the state was eliminated. The masses of peasants in the east remained "serialized"—each peasant on his own parcel of land—and never achieved the strength of the masses of slaves concentrated in the *villae* of the west.

86. Of course this does not prove that the key determination was that the disintegration of the state caused the end of the slave system, rather than the reverse (Weber's argument), but it is at least necessary. If the argument that ultimately yields this schematization, arguing from the slave system to the "law"

of concentration-"proletarization" to the disappearance of the state's social base to the disintegration of the imperial state to the end of the slave system, is incorrect, the correlation proves nothing but merely suggests the possibility of some sort of link between the state and slavery, whether direct or indirect.

87. Verlinden, L'Esclavage, p. 637; Thompson, "Peasant Revolts," pp. 11–23.
88. Rémondon, La Crise, p. 173; Verlinden, L'Esclavage, p. 637.
89. Fossier, L'Histoire sociale, p. 64.
90. According to Finley, The Ancient Economy.
91. Salvianus, De gubernatione dei, 5.25, 38–45.
92. See the long quotation in chap. 2 above.
93. See above, chap. 1.
94. See above, chap. 1. The direction of causality should not be reversed by making this revival of the slave trade a cause of the revival of the slave system (see chap. 2), for the slave trade continued to pass through Gaul in the tenth century, when the slave system had already vanished.
95. See Engels, The Origin of the Family: "We must now inquire how, on the basis of this allod, there grew up a social and political organization which—with history's customary irony—ultimately led to the dissolution of the state and, in its classic form, destroyed all allodial property." He is mistaken here in taking the allod of that period for a commodity and using this to explain how land came to be concentrated in a few hands. Force played the determining role. However, he does see clearly that the dissolution of the state was the necessary consequence of the system that produced it. Hence this was not exactly the same process that occurred during the late empire: then landed property accumulated in the hands of the magnates via the medium of money, through the sale of these lands. In the early Middle Ages, force, whether veiled or not, had no need of following this monetary detour.
96. Duby, Guerriers et paysans, p. 209 (English ed., p. 184).
97. Ibid.
98. Poly, La Provence, p. 109.
99. The quotation marks are needed for both terms.
100. Poly, La Provence, p. 109.
101. Ibid.
102. Toubert, Les structures du Latium, 1:312. He gives a counterexample: when the Hungarians arrived between 927 and 942, their "raids had no profound effect on the situation . . . society had already been taken back in hand." In any case, these Hungarian raids were in no way responsible for the movement of the population to hilltop sites (encastlement) which in fact came after these attacks and attests to a restoration of control and reestablishment of order, as well as a "leap forward" in the economic and demographic sense.
103. Ibid., p. 474: "the elimination of rural slavery."
104. Ibid., p. 472.
105. See above, chap. 1.
106. Bodin, La République, pp. 57–58.

107. The qualification "it would seem" is necessary because Bodin is not a reliable source. Notice, however, that Bodin did not confound the slave and the serf, since he is studying the transformation of one into the other.

108. Bloch, *La Société féodale*, p. 266.

109. Duby, *L'Economie rurale*, pp. 207, 410–13, 502.

110. Ibid., pp. 573–83, 585.

111. Foul-smelling, ugly, hideous, greedy, ferocious. This hatred, this fear, was the child of the Romans' hatred of rural slaves. See Fossier, *L'Histoire sociale*, p. 244; Le Goff, *La Civilisation*.

112. The revolts in Normandy in 997 and in the eleventh century were crushed with extremely violent means. It is unfortunate that so little is known of these uprisings in the eleventh and twelfth centuries. Similar repression would follow the jacqueries in France and England in the fourteenth century.

113. I have in mind those barracks-factories in which Colbert recommended incarcerating *les filles*, who were not to be allowed out and who were fed very little to keep them alive. See Dockès, *L'Espace dans la pensée économique*, p. 76, 197.

Chapter 5

1. See the Introduction above.

2. Though of course the social relations of capitalism were dominant on the world scale.

3. It bears repeating that this process was not a continuous one. There were restorations of public order, through tyrannical states (Diocletian), through military governments (German kingdoms), and above all through empire under the Carolingians. Each time, however, the "same" process was set in motion, as we have seen.

Index

Agache, Roger, 63, 66
Agrarian reform movements, 53–54, 227
Agricultural communism, 219; Germanic, 86–87; medieval, 172–74; Roman, 64, 223; and the banal mill, 179–80, 195–96
Althusser, Louis, 22, 30, 43–44
Anderson, Perry, 137–39
Antilles, 137, 244–45
Apuleius, 209
Aristotle, 7–8
Army, Roman, 58–59, 78–79, 229; landholding and, 51, 53, 57–58
Augustine, Saint, 89
Augustus, 57, 211

Bacaudae insurrection, 101, 211; and class struggle, 87–88, 163–64, 227, 229, 233; and the end of slavery, 231, 232. *See also* Rebellion
Balibar, Etienne, 26–27
Barbarians, 79, 138; alliances of, 84–85, 229, 231; and the fall of Rome, 158–59, 170–72, 230–31; Germanic, 85–87, 170–72, 228–29; invasions by, 78, 93, 140
Bloch, Marc, 63, 94, 111, 204, 238; and Christianity, 145–46; and domiciling, 83; and the end of slavery, 3, 19, 118–19, 141–44; and mechanistic materialism, 23–24; and perishable capital, 134; and productivity of serfdom, 124–25, 128; and the profitability of slavery, 133, 137; and the water mill, 174–76, 181; works: *Les Caractères originaux du monde rural français*, 144; "Comment et pourquoi finit l'esclavage?" 141–43, 145; *Feudal Society*, 141–43
Blossius of Cumae, 213
Bodin, Jean, 209, 237–38; *Les Six Livres de la République*, 237
Bonnassié, Pierre, 8, 92–93, 108, 173
Bourgeoisie, 28–29, 246
Boutaric, E., 5
Brisson, J.-P., 53, 214
Bureaucracy, Roman, 59–60, 79–80

Caesar, Julius, 56–57
Capitalism, 3, 225–26, 239–40, 245
Carolingian Empire, 100–102, 233–38; demise of, 102–4, 235–36; and a free peasantry, 173, 234; and a razzias, 140
Castellan. See Encastlement
Charlemagne. *See* Carolingian Empire
Chesnaux, Jean, 212, 215, 226
Chrysostom, John, 231
Church, 215, 222–23; medieval, 145–49; Roman, 85–86, 88, 100. *See also* Religion
Circumcelliones, 88–89
Class consciousness, 16–17, 163–64
Class struggle, 16–30, 199–240; in Althusser, 43–44; and the end of slavery, 158–64; and the exploiting class, 27, 55; and the fall of the Carolingian Empire, 103–5, 236–37; and the fall of the Roman Empire, 87; historical role of, 21–22, 24–25, 114; and the mode of production, 27–30, 38–39, 42, 153–54, 159–61; nature of, 18–20, 27–39, 44; in Parain, 153, 159–62; and religion, 30–31; in Roman society, 159–60;